A Walk in Jerusalem

Also by Samuel Heilman

The Gate Behind the Wall
The People of the Book
Synagogue Life

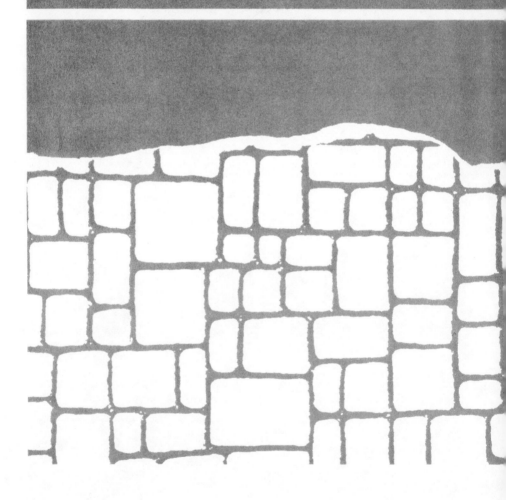

A WALKER IN

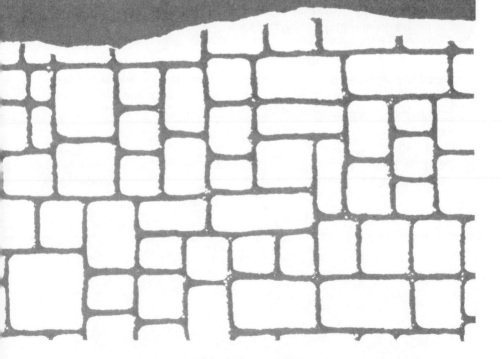

JERUSALEM

Samuel Heilman

THE JEWISH PUBLICATION SOCIETY
PHILADELPHIA and JERUSALEM

837.14
—436w
99 59
1/23/96

Published by The Jewish Publication Society, 1995

Manufactured in the United States of America

First published by Summit Books, 1986

Library of Congress Cataloging-in-Publication Data

Heilman, Samuel C.
    A walker in Jerusalem / Samuel Heilman.
    p. cm.
    Previously published: New York : Summit Books, c1986.
    Includes bibliographical references.
    ISBN 0-8276-0556-0
    1. Jerusalem — Social life and customs. 2. Jews — Jerusalem — Social life and customs. 3. Christians — Jerusalem — Social life and customs. 4. Palestinian Arabs — Jerusalem — Social life and customs. 5. Muslims — Jerusalem — Social life and customs. 6. Heilman, Samuel
C. I. Title.
IN PROCESS
956.94'4—dc20   95-31540
                                                                              CIP

In memory of my grandparents
Frania and Samuel Heilman
and
Frayda and Chiel Kirschenbaum
who dreamed of Jerusalem but never got there

CONTENTS

9959

2

3

Epilogue

*Walk about Zion, and go round about her;
count her towers. Pay heed to her bulwarks;
traverse her palaces, so that you may tell it to
the generation following.*

PSALMS 48:13–14

*My task which I am trying to achieve is, by the
power of the written word, to make you hear, to
make you feel—it is, before all, to make you
see. That—and no more, and it is everything.*

JOSEPH CONRAD

FOREWORD

In my original conception, *A Walker in Jerusalem* was to be an interpretive excursion, an effort to penetrate forms of existence and reveal the inner life of this timeless city and its very real inhabitants. It was not to be a hiking book or another walking tour, as some merchandisers expected from the title. This walk with a social anthropologist was to be a journey into the invisible but nevertheless real Jerusalem, which I hoped would make visible and palpable the perspectives of a discipline that I had absorbed and would now enlist.

To accomplish this, I blurred the genres of ethnography — the systematic anthropological quest to describe an insider's life in terms an outsider can comprehend and share — with narrative nonfiction, whose imperatives are to remain engaging and vivid. I did this because, like writer Mary Louise Pratt, I was struck by the fact that all too often, "ethnographic writings leave out or hopelessly impoverish some of the most important knowledge they have achieved," and that this too frequently results in interesting people who have done interesting things, been in extraordinary places, or encountered profoundly interesting people, nevertheless producing dull or unreadable books. [1] Accordingly, following the counsel of anthropologist Bronislaw Malinowski, the father of the modern fieldwork method, I believed that "it is good for the ethnographer to put aside the camera, notebook, and pencil, and join in himself in what is going on. ..." [2]

I went further. I not only put myself into the world of the Jerusalem I walked, sharing the sometimes conflicting visions of its various neighborhoods and inhabitants; I also put myself into the text, an actor in the narrative rather than an out-of-sight narrator, the latter having been the preferred and normative position for most of my ethnographer predecessors. Moreover, in my writing, I eschewed the academic style, with its footnotes and scholarly references or explicit theoretical articulation. Instead, I kept the theory implicit and allowed the voice of the people I met and the character of the places I visited to emerge by using the tools and language of narrative nonfiction. Through this I hoped to avoid the common accusation leveled at ethnography — that it reduces experiences intensely lived to affectively neutral descriptions.

Crossing boundaries carries risks. Most readers have viewed this book totally within the realm of narrative nonfiction; some have seen this as a travel book; few have been willing to see the anthropological and ethnographic aims that are the deep structure of this effort. In fact, however, my walker in Jerusalem is not simply any ambler; he is always a social anthropologist and ethnographer interested in the culture of Jerusalem that he discovers in people and places. He is one who seeks to take those who walk with him not only to the physical Jerusalem but to the Jerusalem of people's dreams, of their attachments, and of their beliefs. He is one who, in words borrowed from Clifford Geertz, sees that "the past is not only not dead, it is not even past," and that the Other is not completely beyond comprehension, that one can experience "being there" and "being here" simultaneously. [3] Thus, the Jerusalem he leads us through cannot be found on any map, nor can it be fully captured in photos (which is why this book has neither). It is a Jerusalem of the human imagination and the spirit of faith and reasons.

Although in these days I still return to the city of Jerusalem, where I have left my heart and deposited my inmost hopes, the walk about Zion that these pages detail is often beyond recovery, part of my memory. Some of the people I encountered are dead; others have changed — like the city in which they dwell. Although many of the journeys I took can still be retaken today, the walk is different. The boundaries whose outlines I could see as I traversed space and time in Jerusalem have in many ways become more pronounced than they were in 1985, the year of these writings. In 1995, walking about the city is not quite as easy. Jerusalem is, these days — even more than it was ten years ago — an intensely contested city. The freedom with which I could move back and forth across the many boundaries is now more restricted. The remedies of memory don't work quite as they did even a decade earlier.

In present days, as the Jews prepare to celebrate three thousand years of Jerusalem's history, with a special emphasis on their attachments to it, there remain questions as to what the nature of those Jewish attachments should be, whether shaped by religion or culture, yesterday or tomorrow, realpolitik or eschatology. In the meantime, Arabs press their claims to a part of Jerusalem's history and its territory even more than they did when these pages were written. And there is no easy way to untangle all these attachments. Messiahs are still eagerly awaited in this town.

Still, one senses that at such a time, perhaps even more than before, there is a need to walk this city, to understand that the past is not dead nor past, that the Other is not beyond comprehension and touch, and being there and being here can still be experienced simultaneously. The reader who walks with me will, I hope, understand these things and, like me, join in praying for at least a piece of Jerusalem.

[1] Mary Louise Pratt, "Fieldwork in Common Places," in James Clifford and George E. Marcus, eds. *Writing Culture: The Poetics and Politics of Ethnography* (Berkeley: University of California Press, 1986), p. 33.

[2] Bronislaw Malinowski, *Argonauts of the Western Pacific,* (London: Routledge, 1922), introduction.

[3] Clifford Geertz, *Works and Lives: The Anthropologist as Author* (Stanford: Stanford University Press, 1988), p. 135.

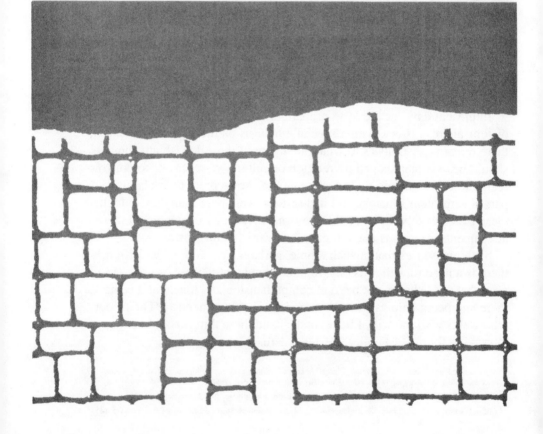

PROLOGUE

JERUSALEM: A TAPESTRY IN TIME

I will rise now and go about the city, in the streets and in the squares....

SONG OF SONGS 3:2

*J*erusalem: it is not one, but many. It is a place in which people actually live; it is a place that lives in them. It is a figment of the imagination, an idea. It is visible, open to discovery; it is unseen, hidden to all but insiders. It is constructed of mortar and stone and inhabited by flesh and bone; it is formed of spirit and faith and filled by belief and memory. It is the Omphalos Mundi—Navel of the World; it is a centuries-old but recently rebuilt city in the Judean Hills, situated on the western edge of an arid wilderness.

Jerusalem is also called the city of peace; but throughout all memory, it has been a focal point of conflict. And so what is significant to some may be irrelevant to others. One people's shrine becomes another's ruin. The center for one group is the periphery for another. What one inhabitant wishes to save, another would destroy. What one would uncover, another would bury. One's dream and hope is another's nightmare and curse.

There are those who look upon the city as layers of history, a site to be archeologically uncovered, a place where one epoch is built upon another: the ancient Jebusite city lies beneath the City of David, which in turn merges into houses from the Second Temple and Hasmonean periods, built hundreds of years later. Then, with the Roman conquest of the city and the final exile of the Judeans, Jerusalem—or Aelia Capitolina, as the conquerors now called the place—went through two millennia of incarnations: Byzantine, Persian, Moslem, Umayyad or Syrian, Abbasid or Baghdadi, Fatimid, Crusader, Mameluke or Egyptian, Ottoman and British. After 1948, the city—a vulnerable border town—was divided for nineteen years by an armistice between the Israelis and the Jordanians. And in 1967, after the armistice was broken, it became at last the united capital of the modern state of Israel.

To those who dig, tracing the lines of history in the dirt and reconstructing it from the shards thus uncovered is what gives this city its ultimate meaning. Only in the journey toward the deepest layers, through other people's memories, down to the bedrock, does Jerusalem reveal itself and its attachments.

But everyone digs to the level of his interest and concern. For the Jews, only relics from the ancient period—a short spell in the days of the Patriarchs and then from David in 1200 B.C.E. to the destruction of the Second Temple in the year 70 C.E.—and the period of the Return to Zion, beginning under the Ottomans, growing under the British and blooming after the Israeli War of Independence, are important. All else remains a rime of exile.

Yet despite that long exile, to many Jews the memories and attachments of Jerusalem are visible, comprehensible and undeniable. This is our land, say many of them, the land of our forebears. Here is our history and here is our future. We have never forgotten thee, O Jerusalem, and now that we are returned, we shall never leave.

And why? Because over the course of nearly two and a half millennia, Jerusalem remained the spiritual center of the universe, the crown of Jewish glory and apex of all hope. Distance from it was measured not in space but by the intensity of yearning to be there. Six hundred and fifty-six times the city is mentioned in Scripture, and scores more in liturgy. On the summit of Mount Moriah, atop the *Even Sh'tiyyah,* or Foundation Stone, the Patriarch Abraham bound his son Isaac to be offered up to God, and upon that same stone, many believe, Jacob—the father of the children of Israel—rested his head during his prophetic dream. In

Jerusalem, King David set up his capital, Zion, and on Moriah his son Solomon built the Holy Temple—God's resting place and, for the children of Israel, the holiest spot on earth. From Jerusalem and Zion, many have come to believe, began the Jewish exile, and here, the faithful say, upon arrival of the Messiah, bringing with him the resurrected dead, the final redemption will come. "The Lord loves the gates of Zion more than all the dwellings of Jacob," sang the Psalmist. "And the people blessed all those who were willing to dwell in Jerusalem," proclaimed the prophet Nehemiah.

Even in the face of that prophecy, some Jews ironically prefer a Jerusalem whose image is formed by the patterns of life that emerged in Eastern Europe, in the ghettoes of Sanz or Mattersdorf, Ger or Belz. If God happened to have placed His Holy Temple atop Moriah, they have only to close their eyes when they pray at its remaining stones, and thus be transported back to the Jerusalem of their Eastern European dreams, awaiting the days of the Messiah when those dreams will come true.

But Jerusalem is not important only to the faithful Jew. Others, for whom religion is but a relic or at best a part of national consciousness and folk life, hear more clearly the distant voice of Nehemiah and look upon the city as the soul of their homeland, the starting point of national history, the ground in which are planted the seeds of a growing national consciousness.

Many Jews who live the Zionist dream—call them Israelis—see Jerusalem in this way. For these people, beneath what *their* prophet Theodor Herzl called in his diaries "the musty deposits of two thousand years of inhumanity, intolerance and uncleanliness" lie the nuggets of collective memory in which are embedded all the hopes of an exiled people for national revival in the land of its origins, the Promised Land. To retrieve and re-collect them and thereby overcome the estrangement of exile, Jerusalem must— these Jews believe—be penetrated, explored, plumbed and protected. As the Bible would have a man know a woman, so must the people of Israel know this Jerusalem : in body and spirit.

Since the days of its conquest by King David, no other nation has made Jerusalem its capital, the heart of its nation. To Jerusalem Nehemiah and Ezra returned to renew the days of old. Here Solomon's Temple which the Babylonians had destroyed was rebuilt. In Jerusalem began the short-lived revolt of Bar Kochba against the occupying Roman legions. From here, some believe, began the Diaspora, that most unnatural condition of the Jews ; and here, some trust, the Return to Zion, the naturalization of the Jews, will at last be completed.

Although overlooked during the Zionist settlement process, in the days when Tel Aviv grew miraculously out of sand dunes and the swamps of the Hula Valley were drained while the fields of Degania were plowed, the return to Jerusalem remained the ends of hope. The last word of "Ha-Tik'vah," the song that would become the national anthem of the new Jewish State of Israel, was and remains "Jerusalem."

For Moslems, here since six hundred years after the Jewish exile, Jerusalem is al-Quds—the Holy. In this place, according to some, Mohammed, the first prophet of Islam, came riding from Mecca atop his magical steed, el-Burak. And here, from atop Moriah, on which he began his *isrā'* or night journey, he left the outline of his heel as he ascended slowly through the seven heavens, there to learn the great secrets of creation and commune with prophets from the past. Inside the dome built over the stone, *al-Shakhra,* on which he left his mark, the faithful guard the memory of that visit. Some say that in the end of days, the Ka'aba stone, in holy Mecca, will come to the *Shakhra* Stone, in al-Quds, joining together once and for all these sacred places—the *qibla*—of Islam.

To the Arabs who live here—Moslem and non-Moslem alike—Jerusalem is also not simply a religious shrine; it is their home, the place where they have raised a family and make a living, and the place of their fathers for generations. This is where their memory begins. Part of the Arab Middle East, this land, which they now call Palestine but once called Greater Syria, belongs to them—or more precisely, they belong to it. They too are the children of Abraham. And slowly but surely, as their memory ripens into national consciousness, Jerusalem is becoming for some the symbol of their national aspirations. The Zionist dream has its Arabic translation.

For the Moslems, the ancient has meaning, but the true story begins in the seventh century with the decline of the Byzantines—and yet it is a past with which the people are not obsessed. For them the layers of history are buried in timeless tradition. What counts most is the closest yesterday and nearest tomorrow, Mandate Palestine and a new Arab Palestine whose capital is al-Quds. Title comes not from digging; it comes from residence. Never, say those Arabs who live in this place, must the sites upon which they dwell be removed to reach some earlier layer upon which others may have a claim. Their claims are surface claims, resting on deeply rooted beliefs.

For Christians, Jerusalem is the entrance into the everlasting, the site of restoration, the place of Gethsemane, Calvary, Golgotha and the Holy Sepulcher. Here their Saviour, the dreamer from Nazareth, spent His final days. Here He was judged and sentenced, scourged, crucified and buried. Here, believers say, He rose to eternal life, opening the future to a new faith; and to here, these same believers affirm, He will someday return. For a time, with the ascendance of Christianity in the days of Emperor Constantine and Queen Helena and later during the reign of the Crusaders, Jerusalem became the center of Christian concerns, the heartland of the faith, off limits to all infidels. And although, since those early days, Christianity has spread its canopy over other fields, many Christians still return today to walk the streets that Jesus walked, to bear His cross upon their shoulders and to worship in the place from which He rose, awaiting the millennium and all it promises.

With the conquests of the Moslems—first in the seventh century and then again at the end of Crusader rule—Christians for the most part left their Jerusalem in the safekeeping of trustees— monks, nuns or priests, who, like the shrines they inhabit, patiently await the Second Coming and in the meantime, between prayers, host pilgrims when they visit. To many Christians—excepting those Arabs whom the missionaries converted but whose home remained the Middle East—the holy places, although sacred in themselves, became in time more attached to an idea than bonded to a place. The message of the Saviour was, after all, universal, even if it came out of Jerusalem. And so, while they still follow in the footsteps of their Christ, still carry out their pilgrimages, pray at the shrines and bear the cross through the Via Dolorosa to the Holy Sepulcher, these Christians often leave the Holy City. When they have finished their visits, they put the cross away near the door, gather up their memories and go home—and home is always somewhere else. These days no one seems to expect any more Crusades to gain the lost Jerusalem.

The Catholics go now to Rome and Lourdes, Czestochowa and Guadalupe, while the Eastern Orthodox remove Christ to their capitals and put Him in the hands of their patriarchs. As for the Protestants, reformers of the faith—for them Jerusalem, although still a sacred site of fundamental faith, became symbolic, a state of mind, a memento of the past and a model for the "New Jerusalem," a temple of the spirit to be reconstructed and inhabited anywhere. And while there are those Protestant fundamentalists who have come to the city to prepare the way for the Second Coming, most of the others have, as William Blake once put it, "built Jerusalem in England's green and pleasant land."

"The heavenly sanctuary," Saint Jerome declared in an epistle to the faithful, "is open from Britain no less than from Jerusalem, for the Kingdom of God is within you." For many Christians, Jerusalem is the eternal life of Christ, the countenance divine that shines forth upon all earth. They need no excavations to find what they are seeking. It is beyond the terrestrial; it is in the heart. And if it happens that some Christians are here in the earthly city, it is because their hearts are here.

Around these various memories and attachments to Jerusalem there is also a modern city, a mix of the East and West, largely formed in the crucible of the nineteenth century. Emerging at the end of a four-hundred-year period of often indifferent Ottoman rule, this Jerusalem became the product of political capitulations to Europe. It was a city into which pilgrims, spurred by the imperialist appetites of the European powers and by reawakened dreams of a Jewish return to Zion, began to flow. Joining the fellahin who had made their lives in the surrounding villages, these pilgrims— except for some monks, priests and missionaries—were mostly Jews.

While the Western powers thought how to divide the spoils, the Jews began their long-awaited return. Starting in the last third of the nineteenth century, as the city slowly awoke from generations of neglect, European Jews became the single largest group of citizens in the city. In 1840, Jerusalem was a small walled city containing about fifteen thousand souls. In 1870, as people began to move beyond the walls, the number grew to twenty-two thousand; by 1913 it had reached nearly seventy-five thousand. During those years of rapid expansion, the Moslem population grew from five to ten thousand, the Christians from three and a half to sixteen thousand and the Jews from seven to forty-eight thousand. Forebear of contemporary Jerusalem and heir of the ancients, this became a city of monasteries and hospices, of courtyards and yeshivas, *kolelim* and ethnic enclaves. From the perspective of today's Jerusalem, this city—reborn during the last one hundred and fifty years—is the place of freshest memories and often the most compelling attachments.

And then there is today. Jerusalem, the capital of Israel, is a metropolis of about half a million people, a city in which Jews make up nearly three-quarters of the population. But it is also a city containing a conquered population. And while the Jews claim sovereignty, the Arabs contest it and the Christians await the action of Heaven. It is through this city that one in search of all the others must pass.

Nearly twenty years ago when, in the aftermath of the 1967 war, I made my first trip to Jerusalem, I came as a tourist, a Jew suddenly beckoned by time-honored religious memories and national attachments. Since that first visit, I have made half a dozen others; and during the last six years, my family and I have lived almost two and half in Jerusalem. In the past, some of my visits were motivated by a spiritual search and took on the character of a pilgrimage, but because I am also a student of human behavior, a social anthropologist by training, other visits were generated by the needs of academic research and took on the character of social-anthropological field trips. About these I have written elsewhere.

And yet, while my time in and knowledge of Jerusalem grew, the city itself remained always outside the focus of my attention, part of the background against which life played itself out. I felt increasingly close to it; I came to love Jerusalem—but that was all. I understood little about it.

A city, sociologist Robert Park once explained, represents "man's most consistent and, on the whole, his most successful attempt to remake the world he lives in more after his heart's desire." To understand Jerusalem, it would be necessary to comprehend those desires in all quarters of the city, to meet with a variety of people—the religious and the secular, the cleric and the lay person. To explore these various Jerusalems, both imagined and real, I would have to share a variety of perspectives. And these in turn would require, as the great student of collective memory Maurice Halbwachs once suggested, joining with those anchored to those perspectives. Empathy is crucial here; "I momentarily . . . re-enter [a] group in order to better remember." After all, he concludes, "remembrances reappear because other persons recall them to us." I have come to Jerusalem to find such persons, their attachments and memories. And through them, I have come to find Jerusalem.

• • •

When I began my wandering throughout the city, I supposed that with the proper discipline and openness, I would be able to gain access to all quarters; I would expose all memories and discern all attachments. I would decipher the city. So I went to every corner of it, tried to find persons who came from each of its worlds and share the view from there. If my Jewishness informed my understanding and colored my emotion, I would try to prevent it from blinding my perception and restricting my motion. Analysis, explanation and interpretations would come forth, wherever possible, not from me but from the mouths of the people with whom I spent time.

But perhaps because this is a contested city and because I am a Jew, I found barriers to my understanding that I could not easily cross. I have heard it said that everything in Jerusalem becomes a symbol—even the people who live there. My being a Jew was undeniable. My sociological pretensions notwithstanding, in a city where Jews are sovereigns and conquerors, I symbolized the ruler and subjugator. Often that was too much to overcome. for me and for the people with whom I came into contact.

Still, I have walked about and seen a great deal. The journey was complex, for it ran through imagination and culture, the here and now as well as the there and then, rising and declining hopes and dreams. For generations, as populations entered into or were exiled from the city, the here and now and there and then exchanged places. Those exiled gave up the real city for its recollection, while those entering into it had to transform their idea of Jerusalem in light of the reality. And with each exchange, the one Jerusalem became intertwined with the other, until today, as I discovered, it seems to many that the real and the recollected, the here and now and the there and then, are indistinguishable from each other.

And so in the end, Jerusalem must be understood as a tapestry in time. Woven into its present is an unforgettable past, and intertwined with both is an idealized future. Normally, the sequence of time imposed by everyday life cannot be reversed or reordered; but in Jerusalem normal time can be rearranged. It is therefore not surprising that people who wander within its borders often find the present least accessible or engaging, while they make their ways easily into the past or gain sudden access to some messianic timescape yet to come. Sometimes they can even grab hold of the ephemeral moment outside the flow of time as we know it—an interval which, although hardly more than a promise or hope, is clung to with the greatest fervor by those who are touched by it. So those who spend time in the city sooner or later find themselves somehow leaping back and forth from ancient days to distant prophecies, occasionally getting caught up in the spaces in between.

All of this, however, is prologue; and as the text in Maccabees— the account of those early conquerors and protectors of Jerusalem —has declared: "It is a foolish thing to make a long prologue, and to be short in the story itself." The story of Jerusalem is in the people who inhabit it. Through them the city ultimately reveals itself, and from them some of the insights at which I have hinted here emerge. And so, on to Jerusalem and its people.

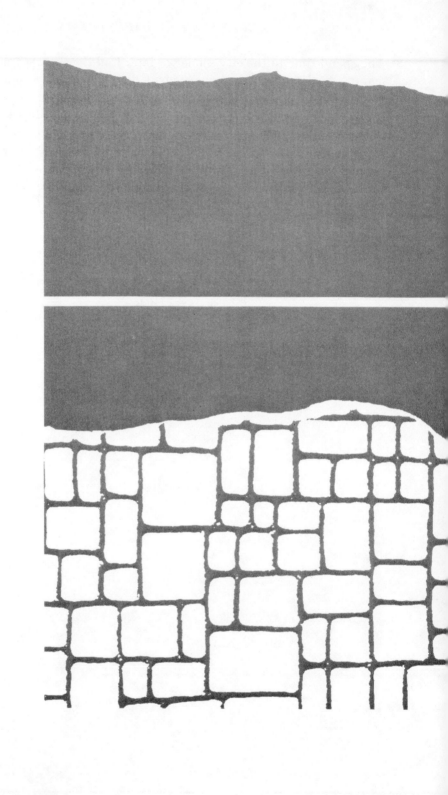

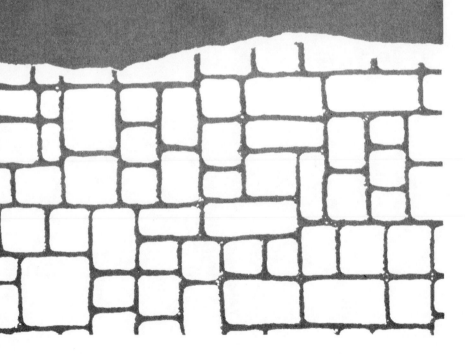

PART

•I•

CHAPTER
·I·

INSCRIBER OF THE BOOKS OF LIFE

*We will never remember anything by sitting in
one place waiting for memories to come back to
us of their own accord!*

MILAN KUNDERA,
*The Book of Laughter
and Forgetting*

*B*y 8:30, the late-summer sun shining on Jerusalem's Talbieh
quarter was beginning to radiate the day's heat as well as
the morning's light. Not only sunglasses, but also short sleeves were
in order; and I observed both during a walk through the neighborhood in which I now lived. At this hour, there were few noises to
disturb the quiet. Most of the people who live here had already
begun the routines of their day. Except for the presence of a lingering. pensioner who stayed behind in one or another *besmedresh* to
review a page or two of some holy book or to exchange a few stories
with a friend, the synagogues were empty. Even the latest morning
services had long since been completed. Children, their book bags
on their backs, and gathered in the little groups in which they
travel, had already left for school. There was room again at the bus
stops. The early shoppers—those who come to the neighborhood
groceries to snap up fresh bread and sweet rolls for their breakfast

before these have been pawed over by others or the flies have had a chance to meander across their sticky crust, and those who like to get the milk first thing in the morning—were already cleaning up the breakfast dishes.

At the stand on Marcus Street, the two young fruiterers were setting out their most polished plums and apples and uncovering their bananas, avocados and tomatoes, while around the corner, Mahmoud, the dry cleaner, was hard at work pressing trousers and folding shirts. Every now and then, he prepared a *talit*, a Jewish prayer shawl, someone brought him for cleaning before the onset of Rosh Ha-Shanah and the Days of Awe in three weeks.

In the *m'tivtah*, the academy where the next generation were being schooled in the ancient texts venerated by their forebears, the young boys, down from their dormitories, could once again be heard in the singsong of Talmudic review. Even the cats which linger at the black garbage baskets in front of every apartment block had finished their morning rummaging and now were lazily stretched out in the late-summer sun.

At the center of Sokolov Street, in the little island of a park there, the meticulous municipal gardener was already on his second round of watering. Since the early hours of this day, he had been moistening every square centimeter of grass. Carefully, he watched to see that most of the precious water (the last rains had fallen in March, around the Jewish holiday of Purim) from his sprinklers fell on the grass rather than on the asphalt paths which crisscross it. The greener the grass at the end of the summer, the more impressive his accomplishment and the greater his pride. He needed to complete his work before the young mothers and nannies brought their babies to sun in the park or, at the very latest, by the time the schools let out and the older children began their soccer games on the little patches of lawn they imaginatively transformed into an Olympic-size stadium. On the other side of the park, at the Mitchell Workers College, bells rang marking the beginning of classes.

On Balfour Street, in front of the Prime Minister's residence, the security men who since early in the morning had been sitting in their twin Chevrolets and waiting to drive the head of the government to his office across from the Knesset were gone. Not far away, the Interior Minister's driver, who had finished wiping clean the windows and mirrors on his car while waiting for his boss to come downstairs for the short ride to the ministry, was finally starting up the engine as he saw him come walking down the steps from his apartment.

From the Rubin Academy for Music (once the home of publisher Zalman Schocken) on Smolenskin Street, the sounds of a Mozart string quartet floated out the windows. Passing the long building, a stout gray-haired woman in her fifties, walking arm in arm with what looked at first glance like her twin but was not, crossed toward the bus stop on the corner. Here she could catch the ubiquitous Bus Number 4 to the center of town.

At the Collegio San Antonio, opposite the President's residence, the nuns—having already offered their Matins—were taking care of the few children in their day nursery. They spoke softly to their wards in Arabic. In the other part of the building, researchers of the Hebrew University were beginning their workday. And at the Mo'adon Ha-Oleh, the immigrants' club on Alkalai Street, *ulpanim* —intensive classes in Hebrew—subtly shaped the newcomers' future with new meanings.

From a veranda on Ahad Ha-Am Street a stream of water splattered noisily on the ground below, a sure sign that someone was cleaning, doing what Israelis call a "spongea." Farther down the block, the thud of carpets having the dust beaten out of them echoed through the quiet street; an *ozeret*—cleaning lady—had begun her work. And I was out walking, in search of a Jerusalem I could comprehend.

To this moment, I do not know what made me go to the Hansen Hospital. Many times I had passed it by; never yet had I dared enter the grounds. Located at Talbieh's southern edge, not far from where I lived, it was a small sanatorium which once housed most of Jerusalem's lepers. Today it was mostly empty, a silent reminder of a previous century. It had been built with money donated by a Prussian baron who, during his visit in 1866, was moved by the forlorn condition of the lepers he discovered huddled against the walls of the Old City. Together with Lazarist monks, German Templars and the Anglican Bishop Ghobat, the baron found a first site for his hospital opposite the old Moslem cemetery in the nearby Mamilla district. Here those afflicted with the "accursed disease" —who since biblical times had been "sent out of the camp," and who in the nineteenth century were living in a corner of the Old City near the Zion Gate—would at last find the succor and care they merited.

But as poor as the conditions of their lives were, the lepers of Jerusalem were reluctant to give up what little freedom they had and enclose themselves in an institution, and among them the Moslems in particular feared the pressures of the missionaries, whose motives they suspected. They were unwilling to heal their bodies at the expense of their souls. So in 1869, only eight patients had found their way into the new hospital. But by 1880, the institution, which had managed to win a degree of acceptability, was filled to the walls, and new quarters were needed. These were built in 1887 on the southern edge of what was then the sparsely populated Christian Arab village of Talbieh.

Conrad Schick, the self-taught Swiss architect who had already left his mark on many of the buildings put up outside the Old City walls, was called upon to design the hospital. Along its front he had carved in colossal letters "JESUS HILFE," a promise of healing which once confronted the sixty patients—most of whom at first were Arabs—who filled the hospital rooms. As they walked the grounds, pondering their condition among the eight cedars of Lebanon planted there, they needed only look up at the facade to remember who it was that truly healed them—that, at least, was the premise. Then they would perhaps be moved to go inside and pray in the hospital's little chapel.

Once, the hospital and its surrounding property were closed to the public; iron gates separated those inside from those who passed by on the surrounding streets. Biblical and traditional anxieties about leprosy were deeply embedded in local beliefs. Today, when many such beliefs have been uprooted and the dangers of contact with lepers have been relegated to myth, and when—what is perhaps most important—but a few patients remain, the paths leading inside are open. The main entrance, no longer used, and the stone wall surrounding the hospital are now largely meaningless, and as I would soon discover, the lawn has become tangled and overgrown with weeds and untended vines. In the evening only a few lights fill the lonely windows, and a kind of gentle silence hovers over the place.

Reading through the reminiscences of Ya'akov Yehoshua, an old-time resident of the neighborhood, whose book on Talbieh had become a kind of guide for me, I was struck with a desire to visit the hospital's garden, which, echoing with memories, now lay, as Yehoshua put it, "solitary and deserted." Perhaps, I thought, I might hear echoes of the past, meet a patient, an aged nurse or physician who recalled the early days or at least knew some stories about them. And then, with such help, I might be able to catch a hitch into the past. At the very least, I wanted to sit in the garden.

For about half an hour I had wandered the neighborhood, trying

to feel its pulse. Now I wanted to go to the hospital. The most direct route seemed along a road once named Street of the Military Police. Today it was named after Benjamin Disraeli. My wandering had disoriented me slightly, and for a moment I was unsure whether I was indeed on the right block. The municipal authorities often hid street signs on the corners of buildings, and if you were at the wrong corner or a sign had fallen off or somehow become covered, only the help of a local could help you find your way.

"Can you tell me where Disraeli is?" I asked a white-haired woman who walked nearby.

"Buried in England," she said with a laugh, and then added, "It's on the next block. Come—if you carry this package for me, I'll show you the way. I'm going there myself."

She handed me her groceries.

"Do you live here?" I asked.

"Almost thirty-eight years. And you—where are you from?"

The American accent in my Hebrew must have given me away.

"New York."

"Ah, there you only have to know numbers to find your way around. Fifty-sixth Street is after Fifty-fifth and before Fifty-seventh. Here in Jerusalem, you have to know history," she said, still smiling.

Like other neighborhoods of the city, Talbieh was ·oriented around themes which determined the names of streets.

"A walk through Talbieh," my guide continued, "is a review of the literary history of Zionism. Nahum Sokolov, Yosef Hayim Brenner, Leon Pinsker, Simon Dubnov—these are the great writers of our people."

Others, she explained, were memorialized by their *noms-de-plume*: Shalom Aleichem, Mendele Mocher Seforim, Ahad Ha-Am. And still others were remembered by the books they wrote: Ha-Lev Ha-ivri (*The Hebrew Heart* by the Zionist writer Akiva Schlesinger), Dor Dor V'Dorshov (*Each Generation and Its Seekers* by Rabbi Isaac Weiss).

"And Disraeli?"

"Ah, he and Marcus are great Jewish foreigners."

"You see," she added, "here in Jerusalem, asking for directions is no simple matter."

She was right. Inquiries like "Can you tell me the way to The Hebrew Heart?" or "How far am I from Mendele?" have the unexpected effect of subtly exciting the collective consciousness of the Jews who ask and answer them. Can those speakers, who understand the meaning of what they say, be totally oblivious to the *double-entendres* in their conversation?

"Turn here," the old woman said as we walked into Hovevei Zion (the Lovers of Zion) Street. "Are you a tourist?"

"Yes, more or less."

"More or less?"

"Well, I have come for the time being to write a book about Jerusalem."

"What sort of book?"

"One that will explain what it means to live here."

"That's quite ambitious. How much time do you give yourself?"

"As long as it takes."

"Ah, good," she said, a teasing smile crossing her face. "You have come on *aliyah* [to immigrate], then." Both of us laughed.

"If you are interested in this neighborhood, you should look on this block. I can recall," she continued, "when Martin Buber moved into Number 3." She pointed toward a large stone house, now nearly covered by creeping ivy and wreathed in sweet-smelling jasmine.

"In 1948, during the heaviest battles, Buber ran away from his home in the eastern sector, in Abu Tor. This house had been vacated, and so he moved in here. He was not very happy in those days. Of course, the street was not like it is today. Then it was hardly more than a dirt path. But the house, abandoned by its former inhabitants, was fine. Still, Buber was inconsolable because he had fled without his books, which were still in the east."

"What happened?" I asked.

"What happened? He said that he could not go on living without his books."

"Was there anything to be done about it?"

"What do you think? A great philosopher without his books. Would we Jews allow that?" A tinge of sarcasm colored her voice. "A group of graduate students from the university took time out from defending the city and dragged cartons of his books over to here.

"But I suppose it was worth it, because later, after the war, on Friday evenings, Buber gave wonderful Bible classes in that building." She pointed to the Mo'adon Ha-Oleh.

"Do you know who lived in the house before that?" I asked.

"The Mo'adon? That was, if I am not mistaken, the Romanian Consulate."

"No, I meant Buber's house. Do you know who the Arabs were who lived there?"

"As it happens, I do. They were the Habash family. A son, George, became a doctor and then a terrorist. I'm sure you've heard of him."

"Didn't Wingate live a few houses down?" I asked, recalling something I had read in Yeoshua's book.

"You have been doing your homework." She looked up at me and then turned into Alkalai Street.

"Yes, a bit farther down, in the house with the green metal shutters."

Orde Wingate, a son of missionaries, was a British Army officer who served in Palestine at the end of the 1930s and who came to be a supporter of the Jewish struggle for a homeland, teaching the Jews how to fight night battles—a then-unorthodox but extraordinarilly successful tactic in countering Arab attack.

"He was a precious friend," she went on. "When we thought all was lost, he changed our minds, showing us that we could overcome the numbers against us by bold tactics and new strategies.

"Just before he died, he wrote a letter to my uncle's friend which he began in Hebrew with the words 'If I forget thee, O Jerusalem . . .' "

We walked on in silence, the recitation of Wingate's echo of the psalmist's lines hanging in the air like some endless refrain that had moved from a humanly crafted text into the natural reality of the place.

"This is my house . . . if you will be kind enough to give me my package. Disraeli is at the next corner."

She walked into the path leading to her door and then turned and added, almost as an afterthought: "Good luck with your tour. May you recover many lost memories."

Turning right onto Disraeli, I walked to the corner and then headed south toward the hospital, which was near the bottom of the hill. As I descended, my sandals slipping forward, I felt myself starting to hold back. Part of my braking came from my not wanting to slip, but there was another, deep-seated reluctance holding me back as well. For all that I had learned about the popular misconceptions associated with leprosy, my heart, like many others, still beat with the ancient warnings I grew up reading in the Bible: "And the leper in whom the plague is shall have his clothes torn, and the hair of his head shall go loose, and he shall cover his upper lip, and shall cry: 'Unclean, unclean!' "

Biting my lip and sliding my hand over my scalp, I stopped for a moment at the edge of the enclosure. Nothing struck me so much as the stillness of the place. I tiptoed in, feeling as if any noise would desecrate the quiet. I wanted to find someone there, but I had no idea whom. And at the same time, I half-expected and probably wanted to be thrown out for trespassing. But there was no one about except for a little yellow-bellied bird which had perched itself atop a wide stone wall that separated one part of the lawn from another. Where, I wondered, were the cedars of Lebanon? Yehoshua had written of eight such trees brought specially to be planted in the garden here. One still stood here somewhere; but I could not tell a cedar from the cypress trees that had since been planted.

Weeds had forced their way through the cracks in the path that led toward the now unused front gate. From my entrance at the back, I walked down toward the locked and rusty gate, turned and trod back up the path again, trying to imagine the feelings of those entering these grounds. As they raised their eyes and gazed at the huge letters spelling out the message of Jesus' healing powers, which they probably could not read, what could have gone through the minds of these new patients? Did they expect a cure or simply hope for sanctuary? Behind them the gate was locked by one of the Sisters of Mercy. Inside the mission, they must have felt the anxieties of the unknown, wondering whether, just as they had already lost control over their bodies pussing with lesions, they were now about to lose control over their souls. But then, perhaps not; this hospital was built after the first one, in Mamilla, in which the missionaries had already established a good reputation for the medical care they offered.

Roaming thus in my imagination, I had stopped halfway up the slightly rising path when I suddenly heard footsteps which jogged me out of my reverie. Instinctively, I edged backward, wary of approaching a leper too closely.

From around the corner through one of the open side gates came a tall but stocky man. He had a strange waddling way of walking, with his toes pointing sideways from his body, as if trying to walk in two directions at once. Besides his odd gait, which seemed to accentuate his weight, the other distinguishing feature about him was a large, rather tired-looking panama that he wore on the back of his head. In his hand he held a plastic bag containing what I later discovered to be bread crumbs. As he ambled toward one of the flat stone walls inside the enclosure, the bird perched upon it flew to a nearby tree.

I kept my eyes on the man. His girth and lumbering gait were matched with a ruddy complexion, a broad but somehow angular face crisscrossed by lines of time, high cheekbones which looked as if they were about to burst through the skin stretched over them and folds in his neck which made him seem to have several chins. As he moved closer, I could hear his wheezing breath; he methodically inhaled through his mouth and let the air hiss slowly through his nose, whose nostrils pulsed like those of tired horses I had seen. He was obviously a man in his late sixties or early seventies, yet there was something about him—in spite of his appearance—that exuded vitality and a stubborn refusal to bow to age. Maybe it was the provocative obviousness of the dye in his hair which puffed out from under his hat. It seemed to flaunt his refusal to be counted among the gray heads of the world. Or maybe the way he wore his hat, a once-fancy panama whose brim had been folded to make it look a little like a cowboy hat, was what made him look younger than his years.

Collapsing onto the wall where before him the little bird had perched, he quickly emptied the contents of the plastic bag in his hand. The bird swooped down from somewhere inside the tree and began nibbling at the crumbs.

"*Shalom! Boker tov!*" the man said, turning toward me and offering his morning greetings with a strong, sure voice that seemed totally unaffected by his continuing wheezing.

I was startled. I must have believed that while I could see him, I nevertheless remained invisible. It was one of those mistaken assumptions of my profession; we students of human behavior often believed we had ways of watching without being seen.

"*Boker tov,*" I answered, my voice much weaker than his.

"I like to come here sometimes in the morning," he continued, less—it seemed to me—in the way of explanation and more as a way to identify himself. "The birds keep me company, and I like the quiet that surrounds us here."

He paused and watched the birds that were now flocking to his feet. "And you? You like the birds too?"

"Very nice," I said, still a little afraid of being struck down by leprosy and therefore not eager to engage in a long interaction. All my plans about encountering the past here were evaporating in the heat of my anxiety.

"I live not far from here, on Smolenskin. But there is far too much traffic there to bear. When I first came here only a few people had cars. The neighborhood was far more peaceful, still a bit like the village it once was. Now everyone drives a car, or else people use buses, which make even more noise. And then, of course, since the Prime Minister took the house on the corner the traffic is even worse. I escape whenever I can." He paused and nodded toward the birds. "They really brought me here; they prefer the place."

The birds were practically at the toes of his shoes by now.

"You want to sit down? Come sit. Plenty of room." He patted the top of the wall next to him. If he lives on Smolenskin, I thought while walking toward him, he is probably not a leper.

Although his Hebrew was fluent and his vocabulary rich, his accent betrayed his immigrant origins. From the way he rolled his *r*'s, I was pretty certain he was a Spanish speaker. Since the horrors of the Inquisition had largely succeeded in chasing the Jews from Spain, the chances were greater that he was from my hemisphere.

"You are from South America?" I asked.

"Argentina; really, Patagonia."

"How long ago?"

"Probably when you were still pissing in your pants," he answered, laughing. He pursed his lips and whistled, as if exchanging a word or two with the birds that were quietly jumping around at our feet, still eating the bread crumbs.

"These are my dear friends," he said, swinging a thick arm and pointing an overstuffed finger at them. "We meet in various places throughout Jerusalem."

"And since coming from Argentina, have you always lived in Jerusalem?" I asked.

"No, in the beginning, I was on a kibbutz in the Galilee. I came there from Patagonia, where I had been what you might call a gaucho. We worked in the fields, lived outdoors, under the sky. It was a good life."

"So why did you leave it?"

"I left Patagonia because of Perón. There were many who loved him, but I was not one of them. When he came to power, I saw that for me there would only be more troubles. Even the wide spaces and big sky of Patagonia would not protect the likes of me."

"Why?"

"I was a Jew."

"So you came to the Jewish homeland," I concluded.

"No, I came to a place where there was the possibility of living my life on horseback, living outdoors, to a place where I knew no Peróns would ever rise up and make me think of myself as only a Jew. You know, here, for the first time, I could forget that I was a Jew, because no one ever talked about it. Here we were all Jews.''

''Except for the Arabs,'' I added.

''But the Arabs were not on the kibbutz.'' He looked at me. Then his focus seemed to blur and he sucked in and smacked his lips. ''In those days,'' he continued after a moment, ''the kibbutzim did not import their labor from among the Arabs. We did for ourselves—*avodah ivrit* [Hebrew labor]. We took pride in even the lowliest job.''

''And was the kibbutz as good as Patagonia?''

''I never thought about it. Patagonia quickly became a memory, and I had put away its notebooks.''

''Notebooks?''

''Yes, like this one.'' With some effort, he reached back into his pants pocket and pulled out a little pad, no larger than a small address book. Its corners were dog-eared, and the edges were frayed in parts.

''For almost my whole life, I have kept notebooks like this one in my pockets. And each day, I write down in them things that happened to me on that day, something that made the day different from the others, something that will remind me where my life took me that day. A day would sometimes take up several pages, sometimes even a whole notebook, and I would have to write in very small letters so that I would have enough space to put down the whole story. Other days, a few words were all that I needed for everything.

''It is a very good practice, this—something I think everyone should do. Life, after all, moves very quickly. There is no present, only a succession of pasts, and we forget most of them. But how can we dare forget them? What else do we have to review that really matters as much to us? Imagine, because of my notebooks, I can return to my apartment and look up the memories of any day of the last sixty years. So you see, these notebooks have made my life a two-way street—unlike the case with most people, who fail to record their memories and the experiences of their lives and who have therefore become ruled over by time and can go one way and one way only.'' He smiled broadly.

''These notebooks are my most precious possessions.'' He patted his pocket. ''I have inscribed my life in them. At home, in one room of the apartment, I have stacks of shoe boxes on each of which are marked the dates of the notebooks inside. This is my archive, my memory room, where I can relive everything. Maybe someday I shall assemble it into a book—a most marvelous book, which I alone shall read and savor.'' He laughed.

While he was speaking, I found myself wondering why he was telling all this to me, a stranger. But as I continued listening and watched his eyes, which, except for that momentary look at me when I had asked about Arabs on the kibbutz, continued to stare off into some middle distance toward a point I could not see, I realized that, really, he was not talking to me at all. Like the record in his little notebooks, his words were for him alone to savor. At best, I could eavesdrop.

''Why did you leave the kibbutz?''

''The kibbutz? I did not leave the kibbutz; events pulled me away. You want to hear?''

He looked at me with what I tried to convince myself was a clearer eye.

''Yes.''

''Come, then; I think the birds have had their fill. We can walk.''

He stood up and began his laborious walk, the awkwardness of his body seeming such a contrast to the gracefulness of his prose. In his conversation, he was able to move swiftly and easily from one topic to another. There was an economy in his language—perhaps honed by his years of squeezing his memories into his little notebooks—that made it possible for him to impart a great deal with few words.

His body was something else—quite the opposite. His getting up from his place here in the garden of the hospital was labored. But he moved with a purposefulness which belied the physical difficulties. There was something about it that stopped me from offering to help him. I sensed that what he did was a challenge to his body, and any help I might offer would make him lose far more than he could gain from me.

Shoving his hat down on his head so that the bumping which his odd walk caused wouldn't shake it off, he turned up the path and began climbing the steps toward the back exit. The steps were narrow at first and then wider, allowing at last for a more relaxed pace and less climbing. He paused a moment when we had reached the wider steps and threw the empty bread-crumb bag into a nearby rusty barrel. Just beyond my toes a lizard scampered across the steps and disappeared into the weeds. We turned and walked out through the archway, past the open green metal door through which, before, we both had separately entered.

Now that I knew he had spent years atop horses, his gait appeared less curious. He was severely bowlegged and, I guessed, arthritic as well. His legs and feet seemed simply to have frozen into a position such as would have been fine for sitting on horseback but was decidedly out of order for walking. His heels were poised to give a gentle nudge to his mount, but that mount was no longer there. He was an equestrian damned to end his days as a pedestrian.

To anyone passing by on Marcus Street, we must have looked an odd pair as we left the grounds of the leper hospital: he about a foot taller and wider, taking his clumsy steps while I, with my far less distinctive gait, tagged along at his side.

We turned southward on Marcus and then around the corner past the closed gate of the hospital along Gedalyahu Alon, a street named for the twentieth-century scholar of the Jewish history of the Second Temple Period. Most of Alon Street ran along open fields. Huge limestone boulders strewn atop the gentle slopes amid the cypresses, pines, olive trees, pistachio oaks and bushes seemed dropped from Heaven, relics of some monumental battle of the gods. To the south we could see the Hebron Hills and the peak of Mount Gilo. Somewhere a donkey brayed, perhaps fed up with carrying its load of bricks or branches. A gentle breeze blew from the south, and the sun moved close to the center of the sky. The birds which had stuffed themselves on my companion's bread crumbs had returned to their perches in the trees, and they seemed to be greeting us with chirps as we passed into what was surely their territory. Here along this path, it was possible to imagine Talbieh as it must have looked for centuries—a rocky hill to the west of the Old City. For a moment, it was possible to forget we were in contemporary Jerusalem.

My companion—whose name I later learned had at birth been Oscar, and then in Argentina changed to Octavio, but now was simply Tavio to most of those who knew him—was silent for a long time while we made our way past the boundaries of the hospital. But when he began to speak, nothing seemed to hold him back; he appeared perfectly willing to review his life, even if it meant he was revealing himself before a stranger.

For a few moments more as we made our way along Alon Street, he remained silent. Behind us we could hear children's voices from a nearby school, but soon the shifting breeze carried the sound in another direction and once again only the chirping of birds accompanied us.

"I came to the kibbutz," Tavio began at last, "and immediately realized that I would never see Patagonia again. That was just fine. Now that I was here, I could see that in Argentina only I had considered myself a gaucho. To all those who rode with me, I was a Jew. But here, I was 'the Gaucho'!"

He laughed. "You see, only in this country could I be seen as a gaucho, because the Jew in me disappeared among all the Jews around me. On the kibbutz there were Germans and Russians and Romanians; they too had been nothing but Jews until they came here.

"I liked being a gaucho. For the first time in my life, I could speak and act with an authority that had always been denied me in Argentina. And soon I was leading the riders. Never before had I been such a gaucho! I worked hard. We pulled stones out of mountains—bigger stones than these." He pointed to one of the enormous boulders that appeared inseparable from the hill.

"We plowed the ground, again and again. I rode about patrolling the borders of the kibbutz on horseback. My notebooks from those days are blotted with sweat, and inside the bindings I am sure you will find pieces of soil that rolled from my fingers when I sat down to write."

He scratched his head and adjusted his panama.

"And then I met Miriam." He puffed heavily.

"Your wife?"

"In a way and for a time. She was from Poland, but her parents had managed to get her out before the horrors. They themselves did not survive. She lost everyone and she belonged to no one.

"I think her blond hair, blue eyes and fair skin had made it possible for her to escape. She looked absolutely Aryan. The Argentines would have loved her. This Argentine did.

"We met while pulling out stones. She liked the way I rode my horse, she said. She claimed I was the only one on the kibbutz who looked as if he belonged on a horse. 'The others look like shopkeepers visiting a farm,' she often told me. She wanted to learn how to ride like me.

"Soon we were riding together. Galloping around the fields, we were a sight. She held on tightly to my waist, her blond hair flying behind her, like the tail on the horse. And soon we were sleeping together."

He looked at the *kippah* (skullcap) on my head. "Maybe this bothers a religious person like you, that we were living together and not actually married, but I was never religious, and at the kibbutz we felt an attachment to nature and not to tired old moralities, if you will pardon me.

"Sometimes we slept under the stars, planting seeds in the dark earth we had tilled in the daylight. In those days, I had little time to fill my notebooks, and when I did, what I wrote was usually fragments of descriptions which today make me smile. But I do not really have to read them very much. I have only to close my eyes and I can see her golden hair against the ground and smell the moist soil mingling with the odor of her." He sucked in on his lips, pursed them and wheezed. "I am sorry if this embarrasses you," he said, but I don't think he meant it.

We had come to the end of Alon Street. A man with a heavy gray mustache came out of his house carrying a little brown hose with which he watered the bushes and trees in front. He looked up at us, and Tavio waved at him. "Moshe!" Moshe smiled back.

We turned slightly to the north up Mohliver Street, already beyond the borders of Talbieh and along the ridge of a neighborhood that some called Emek Refaim (the Valley of Refaim) and others called "the German Colony," after the German Templars, Protestants who several generations before had come here and settled the neighborhood, awaiting the Day of Judgment and Salvation. In the end, they had left too early.

There were a number of large houses here. Some had been built by and for the Arabs who had lived here before and were in more or less their original state, with large entrances and different sorts of stones marking off the stories from each other. Others were hostels the pilgrims had built, many of which were inscribed with devotional tablets and cornerstones. Still others were modern and restored versions of these same structures. The Americans and English who were of late moving into the neighborhood and who were accustomed to living in detached houses with little yards around them were quickly snapping up these houses and transforming them into Jerusalem versions of the English Tudor or Cape Cod Colonial.

We turned onto Dor Dor V'Dorshov Street and then entered Gan Ha-Shoshanim, a lovely little park festooned with wild roses. Tavio led us toward one of the benches snuggled in the half-dozen flowery alcoves inside the park. He took out a handkerchief and wiped his forehead and also the band inside his hat. I could see now that he was balding on top. His chest heaved in and out slowly. As if to parallel our return to this built-up area of the neighborhood after our brief passage through the open fields of Talbieh, Tavio changed the venue of his narrative.

"And then one day Miriam decided we needed to leave the kibbutz. She wanted to change the course of her life. For her, the future was just too definite where we were: we would clear away all the stones, till all the soil, plant all our seeds and then watch everything grow until we too were grown. Her gaucho would turn into a farmer, maybe a father, and she would be trapped in a life without any turns or complications."

"*Sivuvim v'sibuchim*"—the Hebrew phrase for "turns and complications"—had a kind of poetry to it, and he repeated it several times, almost wistfully. And then he concluded: "To her life was meaningful only if it was filled with turns and complications."

"Did you leave the kibbutz then?"

"Yes, but not exactly as she supposed we would. That was in 1956, just before the war in Sinai broke out. Before we made any move, most of the men—including me—left the camp in the general mobilization."

He was silent.

"Not good. We gained nothing from that war except the knowledge that we could fight better than we had imagined. And we also learned that we could win wars much more easily than we could win peace.

"We are still winning wars and losing peace. You see Lebanon. We have won there a new enemy, and who knows what we have done to those among the Arabs who were, or at least thought about being, our friends?

"But what do I know about politics? And where shall I go with my dissatisfaction—back to Argentina? Even Raul Alfonsín does not need an old Jewish gaucho from Patagonia.

"Time to write," he concluded abruptly.

He took out the little pad, pulled a chewed little pencil from his breast pocket and with knotted hands, which I could now see trembled slightly, jotted down a few lines. I sat still, absorbing the sounds and sights of the rose garden. Then, just as I felt myself getting caught up in the quiet, Tavio turned toward me, told me what he was called and asked for my name. It was as if he suddenly realized that to complete his notes there was a need to identify me.

I turned the conversation back to him again. "When did you come to the city?" I asked.

He continued his story. "When I came back from the war to the kibbutz, I learned that Miriam had gone to Jerusalem. For a few months I tried to forget about her and to get back to the routines of life on the kibbutz. After the war, I wanted some normality in my life. But without Miriam at the kibbutz, nothing seemed normal. I found no routines that I could retrieve. When I rode the horse, I missed her behind me. When I went to my rooms, they were too empty. Even when I dug my fingers into the black earth, I thought of her hair in it and the smell of her body. It was impossible, impossible. After the war, it was impossible to go back to the way things had been before.

"So I followed her to Jerusalem, where I found a flat near Mahne Yehuda."

This was a neighborhood off Jaffa Road near the main Jewish market. By the fifties it had become a small series of alleys in the growing downtown of the Jewish side of town.

"The rooms were very small, but they were cheap, and when I left the kibbutz I had nearly no money of my own. I had never realized how poor I was until I came to the city."

"Did you find her right away?"

"Jerusalem was a small town in those days, so I found out *about* her right away. She had taken up with an American painter, a bohemian type. For a time, she and the painter managed to move into a *ma'abarah* in the asbestonim."

A *ma'abarah* was a transit camp. Forced to absorb twice its population during the fifties when the Jews expelled from Moslem countries immigrated, the fledgling state had simply set up huts or large apartment blocks to provide shelter for the thousands who came. One of the largest and longest-lasting of those camps had been set up in a valley in the southwest corner of the city. The camp came to be known as the "asbestonim" because many of the shacks in which the immigrants were housed were made of something that looked like asbestos. On the slopes surrounding but in a sense oblivious to the asbestonim, another neighborhood, Kiryat Ha-Yovel— "Jubilee City," in honor of the fiftieth anniversary of the Jewish National Fund, which was being celebrated that year—had been built. This was housing for the city's emerging middle class, most of them Jews of Ashkenazic (European) background

For years the asbestonim housed mostly Moroccan Jews, the largest single immigrant group from an Arab country. Looking up at their Ashkenazic counterparts on the hill, some of the Moroccans over time improved their property, and many of the onetime huts became sprawling Rube Goldberg–style houses. Each one had its own unique series of additions. The camp became one of the most colorful neighborhoods in the city. But to government planners, it was an eyesore and an uncomfortable reminder of the state's inability to complete the absorption of all its citizens. A plan was launched to build a large apartment complex on the hill above, in Kiryat Ha-Yovel.

But the plan which looked fine on paper turned into a nightmare. In time a row of apartment blocks would be built on Stern Street, housing approximately six thousand people. There would be no room in these blocks, which looked like huge freight cars, for a person to improve his living situation, to enlarge his space according to his needs and his abilities as had been the case in the asbestonim. The curve of the street, built on a huge rock, made a sense of neighborhood such as there had been in the little shack village physically impossible. There was one grocery and no school to service the thousands squeezed into the massive six-story apartment blocks. The rest of Kiryat Ha-Yovel wanted nothing to do with Stern Street, and the neighborhood gradually spawned hopelessness and crime.

"In time, Miriam and her man moved out of the asbestonim. The painter had sold some drawings in America, and that gave them enough money for a start. They found an apartment on the upper part of the hill above the asbestonim, on Stern Street. That was before the blocks went up; they lived on the other side of the street —the good side."

"Did you go to see her?"

"I wanted to, but for a long time I found I could not. I did not want my memories of her on the kibbutz to be blotted out by what I would see here. I heard that she had gotten a job as some sort of assistant in the Bikur Cholim Hospital, but I was afraid to come near her.

"In the meantime, I found a new life in Jerusalem. I walked about the city again and again. And each day I found some new corner that I had never seen before. For a time I worked for the post office, delivering mail, and then as a gardener. There was no need for gauchos in the city.

"The more I learned about Jerusalem, the more I began to pine for the Old City, even though I had never in my life been there. Before '67 we could see the Old City only from afar. I would climb Mount Zion, which was always in our hands, and stand near what we then thought was King David's tomb—now the archeologists tell us they are still searching for it—and we could peek at the walls of the ancient city which the Jordanians kept us from visiting.

"You know, in those days even taking a look was dangerous. I remember going to Kibbutz Ramat Rachel, which was then on the southern edge of the city—for a time I thought I would join it. From there you could look past the Jordanian border and see the cupola over Rachel's Tomb. I was not then nor am I now a religious man, but I always felt something for Rachel, dying like that on the road to Bethlehem and then being left alone." He paused for a moment and kicked a pebble near his feet.

"But you know, when we stood at the lookout on the kibbutz, we were often shot at by Jordanian snipers. Once there was a conference of archeologists at the kibbutz guesthouse, and as they stood on the hill they were shot at, and several were wounded and killed.

"But the more risk there was in looking at the Jerusalem on the other side, the greater was my yearning for it. And in '67, when at last we made our way past the shells and reached the heart of our longing, I was among the first to go. I cannot tell you the pleasure of that moment, the sweetness of that penetration. I shall never forget it—how we pressed our bodies against and held on to the round stones of the Temple Wall and kissed them. Never did I love Jerusalem more than at that moment. Never did I love anything more than at that moment."

He stopped talking; only his wheezing broke the silence.

"And you forgot about Miriam?"

"No, but I began to think more about myself. And then, one day, as if awakened from a dream, I decided I would go look for her. It was a cloudy day in March, the kind when you are not yet certain the winter rains have passed and expect a downpour any minute.

"For some reason, I chose to go first to speak to the painter. I had heard that he was sketching views of Talbieh, and so I went one day to find him. I thought for some reason that it would be easier for me to talk to him than to her. But when I found him, I discovered that he was not much of a talker. He was not even a listener.

"At first I just came up to him—he was not difficult to find; how many painters were there on these streets? I stood watching him work; his canvas was a dark-looking horizon, filled with browns and bronzes where other people might have seen white and gold. While I watched, he hunched his shoulders, as if to keep me from looking over them. And when that did not work, he began again and again to stare at me with a fierce look that told me to move away. But I disregarded his glances and instead began to ask him what he was trying to capture in his painting.''

Tavio stopped, clumsily removed a handkerchief from his pants pocket and noisily coughed some phlegm into it. Listening to his story, I had slowly found myself ignoring his puffs and wheezes, and then, caught up in his narrative, had forgotten that I was not sitting next to a young Patagonian gaucho turned gardener. Now these involuntary movements and noises woke me from my dream of him and colored his tale with the pathos of old age. He put away his handkerchief, looked at me and, as if aware that he had reminded me of his age, said, ''Maybe you find it hard to believe that after all these years I can recall that moment so clearly. But you must know that I wrote it all down afterward in my little notebooks, and have since reread my recollections many times.''

He looked intently past my eyes.

''But I'll tell you,'' he said after a moment's pause, ''I am not certain any longer whether I can remember the event itself or whether I have simply sharpened the memory so much that it has gained a life of its own.

''I have retold myself this story so many times,'' Tavio continued, ''that I tell it exactly the same way each and every time I repeat it.'' He laughed.

''As I talked to the painter—his name was Zysk, Arthur Zysk—he finally turned to me and asked in a rough, smoker's voice what I wanted.

'' 'Miriam,' I said.

''He wanted to know why, and who I was.

'' 'I am Tavio,' I told him. 'Has she ever mentioned me?'

'' 'Maybe,' he said. 'She has mentioned lots of names. How could I remember all of them?'

''I asked him did my name not mean anything special to him, and he said it did not.

'' 'I have come here to paint and not to palavèr,' he said, and turned back to his canvas. Then, maybe to get rid of me, he said, 'Look, Miriam has never mentioned you. Anyway, if you want to see her, why have you come to bother me? Go over to the hospital.' ''

Tavio stopped.

''And what did you say?'' I asked at last.

Tavio laughed again, and then he began coughing. Again he took out his handkerchief and spat into it.

''Nothing. Zysk must have known there was nothing I would say.

He well knew how to stop even such a one as me from talking. I left him. It was clear he was not at all interested in me or my story."

"And did you then go to Miriam?"

"Why? If Zysk was telling me the truth, she had already put me out of her memory. There was nothing for me to do but put her out of mine."

"But you obviously did not."

"I would have. More and more I fell in love with another woman: Jerusalem. I spent days losing myself in her, and my longings turned toward the parts of her that were beyond my reach, the Old City, on the Jordanian side. I thought I had put Miriam out of my mind forever.

"And then one day I saw her on the street, not far from the hospital. It was odd how I had managed not to see her for so long in this small town, this little *shtetl* we call Jerusalem. She still had her wonderful blond hair, but now she had tied it in a knot on top of her head, and a little gray, I think, was creeping into it. I have always hated gray hair, but on her it looked good; it gave the blond a kind of silvery shine.

"She did not see me, but I followed her at a distance. I did not know what I would say to her if we met, but I felt compelled to follow.

"She walked into a café on Jaffa Road near Zion Square. I stood outside for a few moments, trying to collect my thoughts, to decide if I should go in too, and if so what I would say to her. Suddenly, there was a blast—one of those terrorist bombs.

"There was a lot of screaming and confusion, and of course smoke and flying glass. As far as explosions go, I think it was a small one; the bomb was inside a bicycle pump. Only one person was killed."

"Miriam?"

"Miriam. When they took her out, I could see her lovely hair covered with blood and hanging loosely off the side of the stretcher on which she lay. A piece of glass had torn open her throat. That was the last time I saw her."

"What happened to Zysk?" I asked.

"He had been inside the café waiting for her. The blast blinded him."

"Is he still alive?"

"Yes, if you can call it living. He still lives in Kiryat Ha-Yovel. I went once to see him, after I retired. He is sick, older than his years and bitter. The apartment is dirty, and smells from his urine. There are ashes and cigarettes all over the floor, and his dark pictures—which he cannot see and no one else comes to look at—cover the walls. I don't think he ever sold very many. He lives off a small allowance the government gives to victims of terrorist attacks. A social worker comes in a few times a week. He needs help to get his groceries and to clean up the place. But I have since heard that he refuses help, and they are threatening to stop the visits entirely. When I visited him, he claimed he did not know who I was.

"I asked him for a picture of Miriam, but he said he did not know where he had one. Pictures were of no use to him now. And then he said nothing else. I never went back."

We were quiet for a while.

"Where are you from?" Tavio asked me at last.

"America."

"Your Hebrew is excellent. And why have you come?" It was the first real interest he had shown in me, besides using me as an audience for the story he wanted to tell.

"I want to learn what Jerusalem means to the people who live here, to collect memories."

"And has my story helped you?"

I didn't know, and so I said nothing.

"You don't have to answer," Tavio said, and began to cough his heavy, phlegm-filled cough. He spat into his handkerchief.

"Well, maybe it tells you that there are people who value memories here, that there are love and death here, that Jerusalem is not just a Holy City but also a place where simple people play out the little dramas of their lives."

He reached for the flowers nearby. "They bloom and die like these flowers." We were quiet, and then, after a few moments, he spoke again.

"But if you are really interested in memories of Jerusalem, I have many others that are far more to the point. I have filled my notebooks with them. I told you that I have come to love this city more than any person; she is my greatest love; she is my own."

"What about the Patagonian gaucho?"

"A man has to know when to get off his horse, no?"

The alarm on my watch went off. It was past noon. "I have to go pick up my boys from school, but I would very much like to hear more about your Jerusalem. Could we talk again?" I asked.

"Why not?" he said. "Are you in the Mish'mar Ez'rachi?"

The Mish'mar Ez'rachi was the civilian defense, the local re-minder that Israel was a country surrounded by those who would see her destroyed. Each night, from late evening through early morning, volunteers, in pairs and equipped with rifles, flashlights and walkie-talkies, would walk the streets of the neighborhood checking for "suspicious objects"—the national euphemism for bombs—and dubious characters. In some quarters, especially those closest to the old borders, the guards served an important defensive purpose, and they often managed to find terrorist bombs or home-made mines before they went off. But in wealthy Talbieh, the job was more one of checking for break-ins and car thieves. So here the lame, the halt and the aged—like Tavio—could be part of the force.

"No," I replied, "I'm not a member."

"I am a regular," he said, seeming to puff out with pride. "Vol-unteer. They need young fellows like you who aren't yet in the army. And if you join, you will be able to walk with me a few times a month. We'll talk, and I'll tell you all you want to know. It's a great service. The evenings in Jerusalem are even nicer than the mornings; you'll see."

"And where do I go to join?" I was standing already, imagining the tears in my son's eyes when he looked out of his kindergarten and didn't see me there, among the other mothers and fathers, waiting to take him home.

"The base here is at the Mo'adon Ha-Oleh, on the ground floor at the side." He pointed over his shoulder in the direction from which we had come. "Go in the early evening and someone will be there to sign you up."

"I know nothing about guns or bombs."

"Don't worry—what you need to know they can teach you. You're not going to be a sapper, and I assure you that you will chase no one with the bullets flying. They need your eyes." He coughed. "And I wouldn't mind your company."

"You're sure they won't turn me away? I am not yet an immi-grant."

"You are a Jew. You are working here. You want to help. They will take you. So go."

"I must."

I left Tavio on the bench among the flowers. The sun was high in the sky now, having melted all the morning shadows. Inside the grocery at the corner, all the rolls were gone. Only a few cracked loaves of bread were left, the ones nobody wanted. Carrying a plas-tic bag filled with her morning's cleaning, which she threw into a garbage receptacle, an *ozeret* trudged exhaustedly out of a nearby doorway. At the fruit stand on Marcus Street, the best of the tomatoes were already gone, while the green ones hurried to ripen in the noonday sun.

CHAPTER
·2·

THE REMEDY OF MEMORY

Memory is a remedy for solitude and exile.

FATHER MARCEL DUBOIS,
speaking at the award ceremony for
the Jerusalem Prize, May 1985

A few days after my morning with Tavio I walked over to the Mo'adon Ha-Oleh to sign up in the Mish'mar Ez'rachi. The little room in which the local headquarters was set up was sparsely furnished—just a desk, a steel cabinet and some maps on the wall.

"*Shalom*," the woman, a stocky gray-haired matron filling a chair behind the plain desk, said.

"I am interested in volunteering for Mish'mar Ez'rachi," I explained.

There followed some questions about my status in Israel, my passport number and all the other details that make up the normal exchange involved in entering an organization like the civil guard. And then, as we got to the matter of when I would volunteer, I added, "There's a complication: I know nothing about how to use a rifle."

"No problem," the woman answered simply; "we'll teach you."

And then she told me where I was to go to get lessons. ''When you learn, come back and we'll sign you up.'' She gave me a note to get me into the shooting range.

Thursday afternoon I turned up at the assigned spot for my lessons. There were a variety of others there—all people who had volunteered for civil-guard duty but who either wanted a refresher in rifle use or else, like me, knew nothing about it. The group was made up of those people who did not at present serve in the army. Since every healthy male up to the age of forty-nine is a member of the reserves, that meant that any men in the group were either temporary residents like me, new immigrants who had not yet been called but who already felt a responsibility to ''do their share for defense'' or those who were too old or who had some disability that let them out of the army. And there were women—those with no small children to care for and not too old to walk the long route.

While we waited for our contact, a few of us shared our fantasies about what we would do while on duty if we found a terrorist planting a bomb. In the end, everyone seemed to agree that in fact what we would do if it ever happened would be use the walkie-talkie to call a professional to handle the matter.

''You can put a gun in someone's hand, but it requires much more to make a gunman out of him,'' said one of the older men, a portly gentleman with fingers that looked too chubby for grasping a trigger.

A van pulled up abruptly and a young boy got out, checked our identification and then loaded us into the truck for the short ride to a shooting range at an army base in the Judean Hills. And there we were taught how to hold and fire a rifle.

In several hours, I learned where the safety catch was, how to put a clip into a rifle, how to take it out, how to shoot at a target and handle the recoil of a rifle. Most important, I learned that I did not like shooting. But for someone who was going to be in the civil guard, that was probably enough.

The next day I returned to the headquarters and signed up for duty during the first evening shift on the following Tuesday. My route would take me around the neighborhood and into nearby Yemin Moshe for about three hours. Anything out of the ordinary was to be reported over the walkie-talkie. That was it.

When I arrived on Tuesday, I saw Tavio and reintroduced myself.

''So come, walk with me,'' he said simply—the guards patrolled in pairs. Taking a carbine and handing it to me while the clerk signed me in and registered the weapon, Tavio also handed me a flashlight, while he took the walkie-talkie. With that, we walked off into the night.

We walked slowly—ostensibly to be on the lookout for marauders and suspicious objects, but in fact our slow pace allowed Tavio to luxuriate in his discourse and catch his breath.

Life in Talbieh, he explained, flowed in two directions: while local residents strove to build up the walls of their private lives, others—temporary residents and interlopers—threw open windows through which the outside world rushed in.

"The hotels bring in the tourists, and the government ministers attract everyone else.

"But believe me," Tavio added, "Talbieh was not always what it is today."

In the early years of the previous century, it was an isolated Bedouin settlement on a slope west of what was then all there was to Jerusalem and is today called the Old City. In time, much of the land around the hill was acquired by the Greek Orthodox Patriarchate, who wanted to own the lands that connected their convent in the city with the Valley of the Cross in the west, where they believed the tree stood from which the True Cross had been hewn. Here they built a monastery, to which they would journey regularly on foot. To secure the connection, the Patriarchate bought every dunam (about a quarter-acre) it could from the villagers, who claimed that their families, generations before, had received the lands out of the beneficence of Salach-e-Din, the Ottoman ruler who had redeemed Jerusalem from the Crusaders. Since then, these villagers asserted, they had been the guardians of the walls.

"They had a special method to their guarding: half of them were thieves and the other half sold protection. If you didn't want them to guard you, they were just as happy to rob or murder you. Only the stone walls of the Old City or one's own courtyard provided any real protection.

"You know, in the beginning no one wanted to live in Talbieh." Its windy hills, Tavio explained, were too distant from the protection of the walls. For the Jews there was nothing to draw them outside and away from houses that hugged the Temple Mount, where they believed the remnants of God's mercy and spirit still hovered over them. As for the Moslems, their elders believed that those who lived too far from the city were dangerously close to the provinces in which Satan no longer bowed to the demands of Allah's will. Only the Christians (and not many of them) would stay here—and of course, the Bedouin, who lived everywhere their flocks went.

After a few turns, Tavio and I had arrived at Gan Ha-Shoshanim, the park at which we had ended our last conversation.

"Maybe we had better sit here awhile," he said, pointing to a bench in the corner. "To check for terrorists hiding in the bushes," he added as he plopped onto a bench with a chuckle.

A soft breeze, with just a hint of the cold that would come in a few more weeks, rustled the bushes. In the dark there was a mystery about this place that made it feel very different from the last time. The bright roses and leafy arbors were now only shadows; the children who normally played here, ghosts. For me, coming from an America where only the foolhardy wandered into city parks after dark, to be here, even with a rifle in my hand, evoked feelings of apprehension. Oblivious to my anxieties, Tavio continued his history of the neighborhood.

"The British and the Franciscans," he told me, "really brought life here more than anyone else." Between 1853 and 1856, when British consul James Finn—who chose this place for his summer residence—tried to find fifty Jews who would at least work the surrounding fields, he could find only those who, starving from poverty, felt they had nothing more to lose and thus were willing to leave the security of the city for this distant village on the hill. But after the First World War, when the Europeans came into the Middle East in the wake of the Ottoman Empire's collapse, and specifically after the opening of nearby Terra Sancta College by the Franciscans in 1924, the neighborhood began to grow. By the time the British had come into full control of the city and quite a number had come to Talbieh, they had begun to mold the neighborhood in their image, marking it with several wide avenues and stately homes built in their English style. Now Talbieh began to attract even more new residents. From being a small outpost on the outskirts of Jerusalem in which, among the grape arbors and mulberry trees, a number of the larger houses were turned into little silk workshops ("At first people were willing to come out for day work but remained unwilling to stay overnight," Tavio explained), the neighborhood gradually acquired over the years a kind of urban charisma, becoming one of the choicest addresses in the new city.

"So, I see the park is safe," Tavio concluded with a snort. "We can move on."

We turned along what is today called Dubnov Street, walking past some of the most expensive homes in all Jerusalem, their carved stone facades looking south and toward the Hebron Hills. But Tavio looked beyond what was new here. And as he described the scene, it became apparent to me that I needed to alter my attention only slightly to see outcroppings of the past below the surface of the present.

"You know, there were once houses here built by Haj Ali Namer, who was the Turkish superintendent of lands. Now the Turks have removed even their consulate from the neighborhood. The red flag that we used to see waving from every high building and flagpole in the city is nowhere to be seen these days."

Tavio crossed to the other sidewalk.

"Come this way." Turning south, he led me up Marcus Street. He puffed heavily as we climbed the steep hill.

"Look carefully at the houses here," he said between puffs. "I shall tell you about them when we reach the top."

Later he explained that what were once old Arab houses and silk factories—the few mulberry trees planted to nurture the worms and create a cottage industry here are long gone—had been converted to Jewish dwellings.

"But the greedy contractors have made changes."

"What do you mean?"

"Did you look carefully? See here." Tavio pointed to a building near the top of the hill at the corner. "During the 1930s that building was the Mont Srara or Munsara [Montserrat, I later learned] Institute for Biblical Research, founded by Spanish priests who were translating the Bible into Castilian. Later, like most of these other old houses, it was turned into apartments. But then, twenty years ago, a rapacious builder decided that two floors were not enough, so he added two more. And now look."

Even in the dim light of the streetlamps I could see that buried within the frame of the newer building was the distinctive outline of the earlier structure, a mix of the local Arab style, with its convex strip of roughly dressed stone—*tubzeh*—between stories, and the Italian Renaissance style of columns and arched windows. For all its ugliness, the addition did have a kind of poetic legitimation. To me it showed how the present tries to swallow up the past here, but how, to the careful observer, that past is still visible. I shared my insight with Tavio.

"Very good," he said, "but how many people are careful observers? Shall Jerusalem be only for them?"

"Well," I answered, "maybe it would be easier to make more people into careful observers than to change the nature of greed."

"There are others like that all over the neighborhood," Tavio added. "In their greed they have forgotten how much we need to protect what already exists." He began coughing heavily.

"Let's stop here," he said, collapsing onto one of the benches at the top of the street. Here the broad avenues paved by the British during the 1930s met around a circle that was once called Salameh, after the Palestinian family (the brothers, Dimitri and Constantine, had been travel agents for Thomas Cook & Sons) that owned several of the large houses which still dominated the hilltop. Later, the square was renamed for Orde Wingate, who billeted in the vicinity.

"In 1948," Tavio was saying as he regained his breath, "the fields in this neighborhood made up one of the front lines of battle."

Near what is today the Jerusalem Theater, at the corner of Marcus and Dubnov streets, a unit of the Iraqi Army camped. From here they hoped to make the final push that would drive the Jews into the sea. In what was once the Jasmine Hotel, a few blocks away on what is today Hovevei Zion Street, the Arab forces gathered arms, while across the street, "in Gross's basement," the Haganah —the Jewish Defense Army—did the same.

"In the beginning, the local Arabs paid their relatives to turn their guns in other directions. They wanted to protect their homes, because they planned to return to their normal lives after what they thought would be a short war."

The war, however, dragged on, and with it came a rising Arab anxiety about its outcome. Then, during the fighting near the edge of the neighborhood, an Arab bullet struck a Jew. Fearing a wave of revenge—a fear which some of the Jews were happy to stoke with threatening announcements made over a bullhorn set up in front of the Jasmine Hotel—almost overnight nearly all of the local Arabs disappeared. Many of those fleeing and those remaining behind were certain they would again be neighbors when peace came. But that kind of peace never came, only more wars.

"We were sorry that things ended this way. For years, Jews and Arabs had lived together peacefully on these streets."

Even after the war had torn the fabric of coexistence here, "we kept a room in our homes in which we gathered the furniture and possessions that some of our Arab neighbors had left behind, expecting to return them to their owners in a short time."

Throughout the evening, as we wandered the streets of the neighborhood and Tavio shared memories of it with me, I had been struck by something vaguely odd which at this moment became startlingly clear. Few if any of his recollections of events came out of experiences he had witnessed personally—some had come from books, and others from locals he had come to know. Yet from the way he spoke, it was plain that the seeds of others' memories had been planted in his own and had grown into a solid mass of remembrances that were as personal and real to Tavio as if he had beheld the events he detailed on his own. Even when we spoke about events that took place before he was born, Tavio spoke about the period as if he had been part of it, as if the memories were jotted in his little notebooks.

"What do you mean 'we'?" I asked at last. "You speak as if you were here then."

"I was."

"But you told me before that you were on the kibbutz until after the '56 war."

"I was."

"So how could you be here too?"

Tavio looked quizzically into my eyes. "What is the problem?"

"Well, you tell me these stories about Talbieh and what happened here, and you say 'we' and 'our' as if you witnessed everything, but you were really living elsewhere at the time. And you have already told me how careful you are about jotting down details in your notebooks. So what—"

"I see you have a lot to learn about Jerusalem," Tavio remarked, breaking into my words and squinting at me.

"I don't understand."

"I see that. Don't you know that Jerusalem is part of every Jew? What happens here happens to all of us."

"That's very nice, but there is a difference between sharing destiny and sharing experiences or memories."

"Let me ask you something. You live here in Jerusalem now, in Talbieh?"

"Yes."

"And what do you think that means—that you simply have a new address, and that is all? When you live here, you have a direct contact with the past. You return to your cradle. You start again. You restore what history has tried to rupture. If you do not acquire memories here and add them to your own remembrances, if you cannot share in the life that was here yesterday, you cannot share in the life that is here today; you have no right to call this place your own and you have no right to remain here. That is Tavio's 'first law of return.' When you return to Jerusalem—for as Jews, we all 'return' to it—you have to search out the past and plant yourself in it. I have learned that lesson, and you must learn it too, believe me."

He leaned toward me, pressing his face into mine until I felt his warm breath against my cheek. I dared not look away. Without taking his eyes off mine, he continued : "Do you really believe that to be a guard in the Mish'mar Ez'rachi, all you need is a rifle, a walkie-talkie and a flashlight?"

He quoted a line from Isaiah which, slightly changed, had become part of a popular folk song : " 'Upon your ramparts, City of David, I have set guards.' What do you think that is all about? Guards have a responsibility to know what it is they are guarding. You must protect the memory of the past as if it were your own—because it is your own. If you don't do that, you disqualify yourself as a guard."

"But doesn't that confuse the truth?"

"Confuse the truth! What, my young friend, do you think the truth is—just what *you* have lived in your few years of life? In my notebooks I have added all the recollections I have accumulated. I see no difference between those and what you might call my own. That is how Jerusalem has become my own, a part of my life. That is how to love her."

He coughed a bit, and then spat out some phlegm. "Why do you think I like to tell these stories again and again?"

He gave me no chance to answer.

"I'll tell you. It is because with each telling, I see the past more clearly. You must do the same. Say 'we' and 'ours' whenever you speak about this city and what happened here. Never call another place home. Never. That is the only truth. That is how you shall return to Jerusalem and to Zion."

It was not enough simply to hear stories ; one had to enter into the tale, to dip into the stream of another consciousness. Anything less was a surface vision, a staring without seeing. That was how the narrative became assimilated into memory and was possessed. And at least for the Jews, life was in words ; reality was the chronicles and narratives which we could inhabit and which could live in us. The challenge, as Tavio made clear by his example, was to reach a point where there was no useful difference between what was actually witnessed and what had been learned.

Over the course of the year, I saw Tavio quite a few times, but never again would his contribution to my sense of Jerusalem be so vital as it was that evening on the hilltop in the golden lamplight when he included first himself and then me in the past that in fact neither of us had actually experienced but which forever after would be part of the collective memory in which I had a share.

CHAPTER
·3·

HERITAGE

Each memory is a viewpoint on the collective memory.

MAURICE HALBWACHS,
Les Cadres Sociaux de la Mémoire

*F*or the next weeks, as I continued to travel about Jerusalem, Tavio's ''first law of return'' grew roots in the back of my mind. I began to look for signs of the kind of assimilation of memory, shifts of consciousness and assertive attachments he evoked. These were memories that served to support the ancient Jewish dream of a return to Zion.

One night, as we walked our beat, I asked Tavio if he thought tourists shared this kind of memory, if they operated according to his law of return. ''I tell you,'' he began, ''they could, and I suppose that some do. But most of them take lots of pictures yet see nothing. Then they claim they will look at everything when they get home. And you know, when they get home, they remember nothing. They recognize nothing. They have attached themselves to an image, but they have completely missed the reality. The Jews are the ones that bother me the most. The others—I'm not talking about the pilgrims who walk the Via Dolorosa with their crosses; I know nothing about them; but the other tourists, the Germans, the Japanese, some of the American Christians—maybe they come here and see a Jerusalem that is so Jewish that they cannot ever relate to the reality. Maybe they cannot bear to look at it directly; so they take a picture that they can look at when they are back in the safety of their own homes. Maybe they put it on the wall, a Jerusalem they can look at somewhere in California or wherever they live. It's just a memento of another holiday for them in a foreign place. No harm in them or in that.''

How odd, I thought, this otherwise sensitive man cannot see any of the attachments or imagine the memories of the non-Jews.

''The Jews who act like foreigners, who think 'over there' is home and this is a vacation, who cannot look at the reality—they are too much for me to bear sometimes. And you know, where we live we see them all from all the hotels.''

To Tavio these Jewish foreigners were so deeply immersed in their exile and the habits of its life, so blinded by their wealth and possessions, that they could no longer attach themselves to this place. Of course they spoke no Hebrew, knew nothing about our history.

''I tell you,'' he said, concluding his diatribe, ''many of them, as far as I'm concerned, have stopped being Jews.''

As the summer ended, most of the tourists began to disappear. They would of course be back, but for a while the city would be filled mostly with locals. Now, perhaps, I would more easily find people who operated according to Tavio's law. Two days before the eve of Rosh Ha-shanah, the Jewish New Year, quite by accident, I did.

The day before, Jonah, our two-year-old, gave a glancing blow to a mirror in the furnished apartment we were renting. When the glass finished swinging, a sliver along its side had broken off.

''If you cut it just along the edge,'' my wife advised coolly, ''it will look almost exactly the way it used to.''

''I can't cut glass,'' I said in an exasperated voice.

''I heard that there's a very good glazier in Nahalat Shivah, but I'm not quite sure where that is,'' she continued calmly.

Ellin had a different perspective from mine about the importance of objects in life; she knew they could be fixed or replaced, while I always acted as if the thing in question were the last of its kind, in need of tender care and special attention because somehow the future of my existence hinged on its being in good repair.

"Where?" I asked, coming out of my fluster. My wife's great memory for the craftsmen all over Jerusalem who could help us get through the unsettling rapids of the flow of Middle Eastern life was unfortunately not matched by an equally strong sense of geography.

"Nahalat Shivah. Do you know where that is?"

Having wandered through and studied maps of the city for months, I already knew where Nahalat Shivah was; and although I was not certain exactly where the glazier could be found, I had an idea where his workshop might be. Along Yoel Moshe Salomon Street there was a variety of such places: one-room establishments in which tinsmiths, upholsterers and glaziers were housed side by side with chic little boutiques and shops. I did not recollect seeing a glazier there, but if there was one, surely he was down at the lower end of the street, where the smart set had not yet begun its gentrification of the old block.

My morning was tied up, and so not until late afternoon, when the shops opened after the 12:30-to-4 siesta—or *sha'ot menuchah* (hours of rest), as it was called here—would I be able to get the mirror fixed. At about half-past four and carrying the broken mirror under my arm, I walked down Yoel Moshe Salomon Street, the western boundary of Nahalat Shivah.

One of the oldest Jewish quarters outside the Old City walls, Nahalat Shivah is a neighborhood coated with the past, to which the contemporary world is trying to adhere. Inside one door is Kahal Hasidim, a tiny synagogue—one of the oldest in the city— in which the walls drip with plaques memorializing lives long since turned to dust. Here, where the carbon from generations of candles lit for prayers darkens niches in the corners, Jews still direct their devotions eastward toward the mountain where once King Solomon's Temple stood and recall the promises of their God to Abraham, Isaac and Jacob. Next door stands Salomon's Saloon, a bar where those who dwell in the East can down a shot of Southern Comfort, watch *Dallas* on television and turn their attention toward attractions of the West.

Yoel Moshe Salomon is a narrow passage, hardly more than an alley. Along its margins are sidewalks that seem more a symbol of pedestrian traffic than a walkway designed to enhance it. To make their way along it, people have to walk single file, one foot stepping almost exactly in front of the other. At the same time, the narrow

road requires drivers to navigate carefully so that the wheels of
their cars do not jam into the curb. Like many of the other small
streets in the older neighborhoods of Jerusalem, this thoroughfare
was never meant to pulse with both cars and people. At best it had
been built to accommodate a camel, a donkey, a small herd of goats
or sheep and a few pedestrians. Paving began slowly in the middle
of the last century, and only in the 1890s were some streets closed
to camels. But life has changed around these old neighborhoods;
the new world and modern times now course swiftly through the
old arteries and push against their sides so that at times the old
streets seem ready to burst.

Some modern boosters looking at neighborhoods like Nahalat
Shivah have seen a need to raze them and begin anew with wide
malls and sleek overpasses. Others, oppressed by the demands of
modern city life and all it stands for, try to lock out the present by
fiat or religious decree, their ideal a Sabbath neighborhood protected by police barricades put up on Friday afternoons behind
which timeless patterns of life can go on undisturbed and traffic
barred from entry.

Although urban renewal is creeping over Nahalat Shivah, for the
time being change has been rather hugger-mugger. The little alleys
and old streets and their narrow sidewalks and roadbeds have
found a way to deal with new realities: pedestrians walk along the
road, jumping to the side whenever a car passes by, and cars often
hop up onto the sidewalk to avoid hitting a pedestrian in the road.
And while some afternoon shoppers stop for a drink at the saloon,
others walk in next door to the synagogue for prayers, and outside
in the street in front, the sounds of prayer in the synagogue mingle
easily with the beat of the rock music that bounces out of the bar's
jukebox.

Improvised and absurd as the arrangement might seem, it nevertheless works. For one thing, it appears to encourage all those along
the street to enter spontaneously into the doorways along the route
—and that has improved business for some of the shops on the other
side of those doorways. In fact, the boundary between the inside
and the outside has come to be so elastic that at times it seems to
move, allowing one domain to intrude upon the other. On Yoel
Moshe Salomon, interiors make their claim on the street and sometimes move out into it. So, for example, at prayer times the little
synagogue in the middle of the block pulls in its quorum from
passersby, while a furniture-repair shop often uses the street for
drying the lacquer on its new tables and chairs.

Gingerly holding my broken mirror, I had to walk even more carefully than many of the others who threaded their way between street and sidewalk. And although I felt drawn toward several of the shops along the way, and was even called into the synagogue—a call I would answer on other days when I returned to this neighborhood—I continued for the present in my single-minded search for the glazier. The sun was already moving lower in the sky, its shine partially hidden by the surrounding tall city buildings in whose shadow this tiny neighborhood lay. From around the corners of a few houses, an occasional ray of light struck the mirror and bounced back along a wall, momentarily rekindling the day where it was already on the way out.

Past the saloon and the synagogue, after the sign advertising "NEW YORK BAGELS" and just beyond the tinsmith, was the glazier's workshop, into which I bent my path. The door—a relatively new addition to the archway in which it stands—was open. Some broken pieces of glass leaned against it. In front of them stood a small, ageless stool. It was hard to tell whether the stool was meant to allow those inside to sit outside or as a stopping place for persons passing by. Crossing under the arch, I found myself in a room dark with age. Along the curved walls were nooks where once candles gave light, but in their place electric wires now led to bare bulbs. Over the desk against the outer wall and above the work areas, the light was brighter. Still, although outside the sunlight had already begun draining from the sky, the visual contrast was so sharp that my eyes took a few moments to become accustomed to the overall dimness. There were no windows along the front—unless the tiny decorative circular window over the door was counted—and only a small one in the back, facing a small, dilapidated courtyard. Near the entrance, a broken piece of mirror caught a sunbeam, flashing it to another silvery glass and around the room. But these were isolated spikes of light which barely sliced through the darkness. And even they were filled with a gray dust that pervaded the air inside the shop.

Cutting my mirror, the glazier—who in his drab work coat, grizzled beard and woolen cap looked as gray as the air in the shop—informed me, would require some time.

"Happy is he that waits," said the prophet Daniel. In this city where waiting for the Messiah has been a way of life for millennia, I had already learned there is no point to being in a hurry. Setting my broken mirror down gently, I leaned it against the rounded and bumpy plaster wall.

Turning his back to me, the glazier resumed cutting the glass in his hand and said nothing else. In the little space among the shelves of glass, I could almost feel the concentration of his efforts: a wrong move and the entire piece he was working on would have to be recut.

There was not much to look at in the room, but still I allowed myself a few steps around the workshop while waiting for him to take my order and give me a price for his labors. Recalling Tavio's law of return, my imagination tried to begin working; I wondered what had gone on in this room a hundred years earlier, when the original settlers built and moved into the place. But imagination cannot work in a vacuum, and I simply did not know very much about that past. All I had was a desire, suddenly generated by the walls, archways and old stones of this place, to get into that past— if only in my mind. Since Tavio, it was an experience I was increasingly having in Jerusalem when some sight or sound, some vista or place name would call forth in me some historical consciousness I hardly ever knew I had. Walks in the Old City aroused these feelings most easily, but they were not uncommon in some of the older Jewish neighborhoods in the newer, western side of town.

The edge of the cut glass had to be beveled on a different machine in the back, and so, following the glazier, I walked around the shelves that separated the two parts of the room. Perhaps my eyes looked around a bit too much, or maybe it was not common for customers to go into the back. Whatever the reason, the glazier seemed suddenly more aware of me. I could feel him glance at me out of the corner of his eye. As he finished the edge, he looked up and said—as if reading my thoughts—"It doesn't look like much now, but once this place was the fulfillment of dreams."

The remark was all I needed to free me from my silent curiosity; time had come to act according to Tavio's law of return. "What was in this building before?" I asked.

For a few more moments, he concentrated silently on his hands, polishing off the edge of the glass with a file of some sort. And when the edge was beveled to his satisfaction, he blew on it and then looked up past my eyes and into the space around us. Gazing into the middle distance, beyond the dark walls that enclosed us, he began his answer, seeming able to dissolve the present into a past he brought back into force. He sat down on the stool in the doorway.

"This building? Why do you ask?"

"It seems to me to be more than just a workshop, I can almost hear the echoes of another kind of life here and thought you might be able to hear them too,'' I answered, hoping that my slightly offbeat reply would stimulate the kind of story that could illuminate a place. Some people collected photos of those places which lit their imagination; the anthropologist in me preferred collecting narratives.

''What are you, a tourist?'' he asked.

''More of a newcomer,'' I answered, thinking of what Tavio had said about tourists.

''With a broken mirror,'' he added, smiling. And then he paused for a long moment—as if he were settling in to tell a long story or as if he were somehow being propelled elsewhere and were waiting until he had fully arrived at that destination before commencing his tale.

''There is a long history here. First they had to find a field no one else would buy—the one here, in which we stand, at the beginning of the Valley of Ben Hinnom. For a hundred and seventy Turkish pounds, they got themselves the Gateway to Gehenna—the mouth of hell, as some called it.'' He chuckled, a kind of bittersweet expression on his face.

Later, in the city archives, I would read the story of this place which would put his stray remarks into some kind of context. I would read how the Jews who decided to buy this place came upon a field which they persuaded the Arab seller they would use for growing wheat for the *matzot* they used on Passover but in fact planned to use as the site of a new settlement, what would turn out to be one of the first successful Jewish developments beyond the borders of the Old City. Now, however, all I could see was darkened walls in a little vaulted room, while he could already look out past me upon a valley and a field that had been buried over the last hundred years by the buildings around us.

Without reflection, I tried to follow the line of his sight, assuming that I too would be able to see into the past and visualize the field in the valley if only I turned in the proper direction.

''Some people said they should go no farther than five hundred steps from the Old City's gates; others said five hundred steps from the corner of the walls would be acceptable. No one wanted to go because they were all afraid of losing the security of the Old City walls and the community in the courtyard where they lived. You can't imagine the desolation that was out here.''

''I thought Mish'kenot Shannanim had already been settled,'' I broke in. Mish'kenot Shannanim—''Tranquil Tabernacles''—was the name of the row of houses that Moses Montefiore had built with the money of the American Jew Judah Touro on a hill west of Mount Zion. Begun in 1860, it was to be the first Jewish settlement outside the Old City walls, meant to break through the barriers of fear and superstition which kept Jews locked into the overcrowded Old City. But it never really succeeded in attracting settlers until other neighborhoods, like Nahalat Shivah, that were organized by the settlers themselves became established.

"It was not really a neighborhood," he answered. "Montefiore built them a windmill to make a grain station there, so that people would be able to support themselves. But it was not enough. Later it failed again as a textile factory and then as a tile factory. They even had a plan to build a hospital there, but people said that a cemetery—that's what they thought it was—cannot become a place of healing."

"And there was no one else?"

"Sure, there were robbers, Bedouin, a few missionaries and consulates. But for the Jews, neither the robbers nor the *goyim* provided any security. For the Jews there was nobody.

"But these seven settlers—really Yoshe Rivlin; he was the *shtetl-macher* [village builder]—the seven were ready to take a chance. They had been looking for a place to move Jews out of the cramped quarters inside the Old City, especially when people began getting cholera, which the Arabs who were running away from the epidemic across the Jordan were bringing. They saw that the few people who lived outside the walls were not getting the disease. So that helped a few decide that they had had enough of the dirt and unsanitary conditions inside. Many of them were students of the Vilna Gaon or his disciples in Vilna, 'the Jerusalem of Lithuania.' A lot of the money they collected for buying the land came from the richer Jews of Shklov, the next town over. And like their teachers and supporters,·they believed they were living at the beginning of the Redemption, the coming of the Messiah, whose arrival depended on their making more room for more Jews in Jerusalem."

"Who were the seven settlers?" I asked.

He looked at me incredulously, as if the question were unimaginable, or rather as if it were unimaginable that I did know the answer.

"Is this not Nahalat Shivah [the Heritage of the Seven]? The seven Jews who organized a corporation to buy and settle the land were men of vision and of hope."

In a single breath, he rattled off their names. Later, sitting at a long table in the archives, I read more about them: Michl Hacohen, a writer and editor of the Jewish newspaper *Ha-Ariel*, secretary of the Vilna Kolel, the Jewish support association whose origins were in Lithuania and whose funds served as the financial lifeline for its sons and daughters who had migrated here to the Holy City; Chaim Halevy, a businessman from Kovno; Beinish Salant, son of the famous rabbi and spiritual leader of Jerusalem; Yehoshua Yellin, who would never actually move in here; Leib Horowitz, an orphan who was taken in by the Yellins and whose wife would play a key role in acquiring the plot; Yoel Moshe Salomon, born in Jerusalem, a poet, writer and publisher, and later to become a man of substance, one of the founders of Petach Tik'vah (Gateway of Hope), the city on the coastal plain—he alone of the seven would end his days here in the neighborhood; and Yosef (Yoshe) Rivlin, the moving spirit behind it all.

"They came," he continued, "from among the Ashkenazim who lived in the courtyard of the Hurva Synagogue, inside the Old City." He went on to explain that although the Sephardim—most of them Jews who had lived for generations under Moslem rule, who were part of the Middle East—had lived in Jerusalem far longer, they seemed far less capable of or interested in altering the conditions of their lives. The Sephardim, after all, were the Jews who benefited most from the status quo, and so they were in no great hurry to change it. But the European "newcomers" were far readier to make changes, to work out new patterns of life. Yet for all the improvements they tried to make inside, "they realized at last that there would never be enough room there for all of us."

"Us." It was not a slip of the tongue. Easily he made the transition from past to present. It was the same "we" I had heard from Tavio. All of us here in the new city were beneficiaries of the courage and the foresight of the seven. We of today, he seemed to imply, had a share in the events of yesterday.

As he spoke, the glazier seemed to be living in a kind of split time, somewhere within the folds of collective memory and historical consciousness. Yet it was not, I think, that this glazier was a remarkable man—no more remarkable than Tavio. More and more I would see other simple people accomplish much the same kind of leap through time and consciousness. Rather, it seemed, Jerusalem had the power to provide those who attached themselves to it with a kind of vision that other people did not or could not have.

"Under Ottoman law," he continued, "which then governed almost everything here, only those with Turkish citizenship could buy land. But the seven felt that it was God's wish that they buy the land. After all, hadn't the prophet Jeremiah promised: 'Houses and fields and vineyards shall yet again be bought in this land'?

"So they found a Jewish woman—Leib Horowitz' wife—who qualified. Altushe was her name; by birth she was a Rivlin. Altushe was officially a Turkish subject. So as not to call attention to herself or the plan, she got dressed up like an Arab when she went down to make the purchase. The Ottoman authorities approved the sale without anyone's discovering that the field was going to Jews who wanted to find a place to settle outside the Old City walls."

Saying these last words, he waved over his shoulder toward that place of New Jerusalem's origins.

"Why was it a secret deal?" I asked.

"Well, there were lots of reasons to keep it quiet." Hearing the story from somewhere outside on the street, another man had joined us. Without my noticing him, he had entered from behind me and was, it seemed, taking over the narrative.

But first, he had a more immediate concern. Handing the glazier a thousand-shekel note, he asked him, "Give me some change." While the other went off to the corner to pull out a few notes from a drawer, the newcomer took a few more steps and faced me now. In his fifties, with a sun-burnished bald head ringed by a band of silver-gray hair, the speaker had a face that appeared a cascade of wrinkles. One of these—his mouth, from which most of the teeth appeared to be missing—continued:

"At first, they were probably afraid the sellers might change their minds, especially if talk began about their letting Jews—Europeans—buy the land."

"Maybe even more than that they were afraid of what their own Jews would say," the glazier added from back in the corner.

"That's true. Many of them had decided that moving outside the city walls was prohibited by the Torah."

"Did the rabbis actually declare it out of bounds?" I asked.

"I'm not sure."

"They were afraid of change—any change," the glazier broke in, as he came back from the corner and handed the other man the notes.

"They're always afraid of change," said the other man as he left.

"And the seven cared what the rabbis thought. They were, after all, pious themselves. For them, the move out of the Old City was bringing the *Ge'ulah* [the long-awaited Redemption]. Wait—I'll show you," he added.

From a drawer he pulled a small gray pamphlet. Written by a

Rivlin, a descendant of Yoshe, it had been published in honor of the seventieth anniversary of the settlement of Nahalat Shivah. Thumbing through the pages, he came upon a photo of a document. He read from the photo:

"Here is what they wrote in their articles of organization: '... the inner desire that burns within us to build several houses increases mightily in our spirits, hearts and souls. And we have agreed among ourselves to remain courageous; each man shall help his fellow to make this place glorious, and the Lord God will help us to finish'—as He did in the beginning of time—'seeing that it "is good." '

"Look here." He turned a few more pages. "Rivlin's own explanation for his actions: 'to banish little by little the shame of being strangers from our heads and to make a place for the nation of Israel.' "

"He was following in the steps taken by Joshua, by Ezra and Nehemiah." The man with the wrinkled face, attracted by the narrative which he wanted to continue, had come back and was speaking in what seemed to me a wistful tone.

"But," he added, sounding a bit more matter-of-fact, "there was also a very simple reason for keeping things quiet. The Ashkenazim who lived in the Old City were renting space from Arabs. The more crowded it became, the higher would be the rent those Arabs could charge them. If the Arabs were to find out that there were moves to find housing over which they would have no control, they would put on pressure to discourage these sales. And all would be lost."

"Listen, my friend," the other broke in, "there were Jews too who were profiting from the crowding." He turned to me and explained. "There was a system they called *chazakah* whereby one Jew would get possession of an apartment, and he would rent it out to others. Whoever lived there would have to pay the Jew who had the *chazakah* on the place. So the few Jews who had it were making good money. If Rivlin and the others succeeded, the *chazakah* would not be worth as much.

"And then there was another good reason for being quiet. They were afraid too that the Russians who had already bought up tens of dunams across the road and up the hill for their colony would try to buy this field too. They were always looking for land to buy up to house their pilgrims. And this plot of land was right nearby. If they tried to buy it, that would raise the price at best and at worst make the seven lose everything. Already in other places they had failed to buy land they had set out to get."

"Yes," the other broke in, smiling, "but in the end the Russians are gone and we Jews are sitting in their colony." After the war and the Bolshevik Revolution, when the flow of pilgrims dried up, the British and then later the Jews took over the quarters that the Russians abandoned—although some maintained that the Russians still held legal ownership and declared that if they decided to come back, they would receive compensation.

"And the consulates were out here too," the glazier commented.

"Well, not really. Most of them were out in the western hills, in the Nikoferia, in Talbieh," the other man corrected him.

"In any case, the seven moved quickly. Two houses—the first was Rivlin's—were built within seven weeks."

"Rivlin's is gone now, blown up to make room for that large office building on the corner—Bet Yosef, they call it."

"The city had outgrown Nahalat Shivah," I added, trying to echo the sarcasm in the glazier's voice when he said "large office building." But more than that, I felt a desire to enter the narrative process and the collective memory beneath it. I too now felt the beat of another time more powerfully than the drone of the present.

"The future struggles with the past, even in Jerusalem," he said.

Listening to my hosts recall the past with a freshness that made it seem as if they had seen it firsthand, I looked out at the walls of another office building. Its bland exterior, its faceless windows and the hum of its many air conditioners made it seem quite dead, while this little room was alive with the past.

"I'm not really convinced that the future is anywhere close to overcoming the past in this place," I heard myself say, perhaps a bit too emphatically. And then, embarrassed by my outburst of enthusiasm and not knowing what to do with my eyes, I looked up at the vaulted ceiling. In the center was a circle, put there by the Jewish builders to prevent the formation of a cross where the arches meet.

My chroniclers seemed to ignore my comment, but perhaps not its sentiments, for they continued their journey through memory, each augmenting the other's version of the history.

"Yoshe Rivlin was really the one most associated with this place. Although Salomon and Michl Hacohen drew the first lots and were supposed to build the first two houses . . ."

"According to the agreement they made, there were to be two houses built a year," the glazier added.

"Michl Hacohen gave his lot to Rivlin, and he moved in first."

"There are many stories about the years he spent here. At first, he slept here—outside the city walls—only during the week, to show everyone else inside that it was possible to survive outside."

"They would wait for him in the morning at the Jaffa Gate, after it had been unlocked—in those days, the gates were still locked every night—to see if he was still alive." The man with the wrinkles laughed as he spoke.

"People opposed the idea of this sort of move from the start. Once—I read this in this booklet—" He held up the pamphlet he had shown me before. "Once, Rivlin, who used to keep maps of the area on his table in order to make plans for new settlements, left the map room for a few moments. When he came back, he found that someone had written 'dreams, insanity, *meshuggeh*,' all over them. And then had added: 'You start with one and in the end all the Arabs will kill you—all of us—if you don't buy each one's field.' They were afraid of his speculations."

"They were afraid of his vision," the other man added. "They called the neighborhood *Chalom Yosef* [Joseph's Dream].

"Once on an Arab holy day—I think it was at the end of Ramadan, Id el-Fitr—Rivlin's relatives begged him to skip that night in his new house. He was still traveling back and forth from the Old City to sleep here on weeknights. So they invited Yoshe to his brother Zalman Hayim's house, and after he was inside one of his friends closed the door and told him they wouldn't let him leave that night. But he stood up and answered that if he stopped going for even one night, the entire settlement would, Heaven forbid, end. So he burst through the door. And as he walked away toward the gates of the Old City, he was heard to say: 'God dwells in Zion.' Such was his fearlessness."

Outside, the street was growing darker, and in the twilight clouds of birds were settling into the trees. They filled the air with their screeching and whistles as they descended on what remained of the field in the valley. Their droppings were gradually encrusting the ground underneath with the soiled cover of neglect.

I tried to imagine what it must have been like to see Yoshe Rivlin walking alone over a dirt path, across the Valley of Ben Hinnom to a solitary stone house sitting here at its northern edge. At his house, along the road that was then known as Derekh Ha-Melekh—"The King's Highway"—but which had not seen kings pass on it for centuries, he sat alone, able perhaps to see a few lights from the Russian Compound on the rise to the north. In the rest of the world it was late summer of 1869, but in Yoshe Rivlin's Jerusalem it was at once a much earlier time and the dawn of a new age of hope and renewal.

"At the beginning he was all alone. Later, his brother Moshe moved in with him. In those first months, Rivlin began to write a Sefer Torah to keep with him in the house."

The Sefer Torah, the Scriptural scroll whose laws and legends surrounded the traditional Jews' every movement from Sinai onward into history, was for Rivlin his first companion.

"And they say that when he got to the fifth chapter of Genesis and the verse 'And he begot sons and daughters,' he learned that his wife, who had been barren for fifteen years, was expecting a child. The child, a girl—Nechamah [Comfort], they called her—eventually died here.

"But for his wife, this pregnancy was a sign from God, and so she decided to join her husband in the new house."

"I heard another story," the wrinkled face said.

"Heard? You probably read it in Rivlin's book like me," the glazier suggested.

They might have read these stories, but by virtue of their being here in Nahalat Shivah, and in the way they retold the events, they seemed to me to have legitimately made the stories their own. Among Jews, after all, the line between an oral and a written tradition is easily blurred. What Jews call the *Torah sheh b'al peh*—the oral law—is in fact thousands of pages of Talmud, and what they refer to as the *Torah sheh bichtav*—the Scriptures—amounts to far fewer lines of written verse.

The wrinkled face ignored his neighbor's gloss. "Once in the early days, Rivlin invited one of the others who had been in the Society of the Seven to sleep over with him, so that his partner might get used to the idea of living outside the walls. In the middle of the night, so I heard it"—he looked at the glazier for a moment—"the visitor took his blanket and pillow and lay down under Rivlin's bed out of sheer dread."

"I read somewhere," the glazier began, "I think in an article in *Kol Ha-Ir* ..." *Kol Ha-Ir* (The Whole City), the local supplement to the weekend paper, often ran feature pieces on neighborhoods in Jerusalem. These were more than column fillers; they were rather echoes of a local oral tradition of sharing information about life here. Some people would save these pieces, and a good many columns made their way into the files of the city archives. Later in the year, I would sit in those archives reading them, catching up on a tradition I tried to make my own.

The glazier continued: "After he had been living here for a while, Rivlin would invite guests to spend time with him. Being outside in an open field, he managed to have a beautiful garden. To people who had come out from the cramped quarters inside the Old City, this was no small luxury, and they would enjoy sitting in the garden, where the fresh breezes of the Judean Hills were not covered by the stench of sewage and human waste, as they often were inside.

"Rivlin took advantage of this, and he often kept people at his house far into the twilight. By the time they reached the Old City gates, they discovered that the authorities had closed them until the morning, and so they were forced to return to Rivlin's and spend the night. Rivlin had counted on this. From their experience of passing a night outside the walls unharmed, he hoped, they would overcome their fears of moving here.

"Once he invited two friends whom he planned to keep late in this fashion. One, Mendele Melamed—who later moved here, I think—and another. Like the others before them, they returned in the dark from the Jaffa Gate trembling with fear. Mendele Melamed accepted his mischance in good spirit, but the other visitor refused to talk with Rivlin the rest of the night. He even turned down Rivlin's offer of hot coffee. And when he returned the next morning to the Old City, he recited the *Birchat Ha-Gomel* [the blessing recited upon experiencing a miraculous escape from likely death]."

The speaker recounted each detail as if he had been there. And even if the facts were not exactly true—which was likely—they resonated with a kind of metahistorical truth. That is, if Rivlin or any of the others to whom these events occurred had been asked if this was how they wished the story to be told, they might have replied affirmatively. So there was a different truth for which the sensitive ear had to listen—one that spoke not only to the facts but to the dreams they engendered and traditions to which they gave birth.

Much had happened since those days. Rivlin moved on to other places. Yoel Moshe Salomon returned from the coastal plain and ended his days here in Nahalat Shivah. The seven rows of houses that he and the other six put up here in an unwanted field had grown by 1875 to 50, and by 1890 there were 120.

By Salomon's death in 1912, ancient Jerusalem, which had grown within the walled boundaries of a fortress, gave way before the modern city which had begun to grow up around a market and trade routes. The courtyards of Nahalat Shivah were no longer in a desolate valley outside the city's center of gravity but found themselves along what would become Jaffa Road, the main route of commerce linking Jerusalem to the cities and growing population along the coastal plain. So what once were residences in a field at the mouth of a valley became over time shops at the entrance to a downtown. Surrounded by traffic to which they catered, the little houses were at last overwhelmed by the growth around them and again were in a valley, this one created by the towering office and commercial buildings on either side. A few little workshops moved into the relatively cheap but small space of Nahalat Shivah, which was by now hardly more than a series of alleys behind the main streets of downtown Jerusalem. Of late, some chic little restaurants and the saloon were also working their way inside.

"And now a glazier scratches out his living in a room where once a Jewish family made their lives." The wrinkled face wagged his finger as he spoke.

"It's a long story," the glazier concluded, as he lifted my mirror and placed it on a shelf, "and we are still living inside it."

I wondered if I had by accident fallen into a nook where memories were ripe. Perhaps I was making too much out of the fact that two old-timers were telling me stories at twilight. Tavio and these men, were they representative?

I walked up a few stores and into one selling art supplies. A dark-skinned boy with a small knit *kippah* on his head helped me find a piece of green celluloid I needed. Probably too young, I thought, to be able to superimpose the past on the present as easily as his older neighbors. And then, to make sure, as he wrapped up the plastic, I asked him my question: "What was in this building before?"

He handed me my package and then touched the wall, his fingers lingering upon it just a moment longer than a casual touch would allow. It seemed more a gesture of affection, like the pat of a rider on his favorite horse.

"Do you know that we took three truckfuls of dirt out of here when we opened the shop? This place is buried in stories." And then, again a name, a person out of the past: "Yoel Moshe Salomon was here, and Rivlin." The names rolled off his tongue as if he were talking about our common acquaintances or members of our common family. He told me how during the 1960s the city had begun to tear down the buildings, to build a mall between here and Independence Park, a thoroughfare to directly connect the hotels to the south and the other side of the park with the business district.

"The old had to give way to the new." He shrugged his shoulders. "For the time being they've stopped, but who knows how long we can hold on to the heritage of the past?" It was a question I would hear echoed repeatedly throughout my days in Jewish Jerusalem.

CHAPTER
·4·

PROTECTIVE
SOCIETY

*Collective sentiments can become conscious of
themselves only by fixing themselves upon
external objects.*

EMILE DURKHEIM,
*The Elementary Forms
of the Religious Life*

*P*erhaps no other group so resolutely tried to hold on to the
heritage of the past as Haganat Ha-Teva—the Society for
the Protection of Nature. More than simply an environmental
group, Haganat Ha-Teva was an institutional reflection of Israel's
search for and exploration of its natural habitat. In Jerusalem as
in other parts of the country, this society included in its definition
of ''nature'' not only the raw stuff of creation but also that which
people attached to the land have added to it. And so it worked to
preserve in as close to their original condition as possible old buildings and neighborhoods as well as rivers and forests. In effect, the
Society did not just protect nature; it also protected history and
enlarged collective memory. And in a sense, it thereby reflected the
Israeli ideal of a new nation in touch with its ancient heritage in
the land of its forebears.

Wherever some natural or historic site was endangered, Haganat

Ha-Teva tried to hold back the destructive tides of change with public advocacy and political action. But the Society had yet another method to protect and hold on to the past: it sponsored tours over hills and through fields, to springs and deserts as well as old neighborhoods and historic sites.

The excursions the Society offered were not just photo-taking opportunities or voyeuresque peeks. They were instead imaginative surveys into the past and sometimes even into the imagined landscapes of the future which enabled the visitor to see beyond the two-dimensional surface of reality into other times and places. With the Society, as I would discover, one could stand at a wall and imaginatively see beyond it through an invisible door behind which appeared a life once lived. Or, on other occasions, a tour—such as one that traced "The Jerusalem of the End of Days"—would focus upon promises made but not yet fulfilled. And once having seen these pasts and futures, whether in nature or in the creations of human nature, the tour participant felt somehow connected to them and as such became a partner in their protection and preservation.

As if to celebrate its reverence for the past, the Society's Jerusalem branch offices were housed in a restored portion of one of the first buildings put up outside the Old City walls. Completed in 1862, the structure stood next to an imposing Russian Orthodox cathedral and had once served as a hospice for Russian pilgrims who began coming to the Holy City in large numbers following the Crimean War.

But the building itself was not all there was to the Haganat Ha-Teva headquarters. In the protective shelter of the hospice courtyard, there stood restored olive presses and other agricultural tools of the sorts used during biblical times, Israelite millstones, an ornate nineteenth-century fountain and the opening to a huge cistern from which the pilgrims once got their water. These visible elements of the preserved past, like the building itself, were unmistakable symbols of the Society's *raison d'être*.

Besides running tours—some by foot, some by bicycle, some by car—Haganat Ha-Teva was in the business of education. During school vacations, it organized courses and camps for children, and sometimes even for entire families, that took them through wilderness areas and old neighborhoods, "attaching them to the country and laying down their roots in the Land of Israel," as one member put it.

If I wanted to comprehend the Israeli attachment to Jerusalem, I had to go with them. And so I became a member of the Society and for days that turned into weeks and months joined tours through the city and surrounding countryside. Led in most cases by specially selected women soldiers—girls barely out of high school—who served the army by teaching civilians about the land and the city they were defending, the excursions went everywhere. On Sunday, we examined the ancient Israelite terraces that covered the Judean Hills, learning about the mountain agriculture with which our biblical ancestors sustained themselves. On Monday, we hiked to the Kastel, a fortress that marked the western edge of Jerusalem, and relived decisive battles fought in defense of the city during the 1948 war. On Wednesday, we explored the excavations below the Temple Mount, imagining what it was like to ascend the steps to the Temple, recalling the night that the city was sacked and its houses burned by the Roman invaders. On Thursday, we followed the line of the ancient aqueduct that brought water to Jerusalem from the Aroub spring in the Hebron Hills, and then with candle in hand flowed with the water through the nearly three-thousand-year-old hand-cut tunnel in the rock beneath the City of David, trying to feel the exhilaration the Judean carvers must have felt when, having begun at opposite ends of the tunnel, they met miraculously at its center. On Friday, we entered a newly excavated Hasmonean tower, trying to imagine the life of the Zealots. Then, with the new week, it all began again: the Russian Compound, the Hinnom Valley, the Old City's ramparts and each of its gates, the ancient Roman road—the Cardo—an Israelite tower, the medieval synagogues of the Old City's Jewish quarter, the tombs of the kings and the tombs of the Sanhedrin, the Citadel, the early houses in the Moslem quarter, the Mount of Olives and A-Tur. The list of tours was endless.

And then came Sabbath, the day on which the Society, following in the footsteps of the psalmist, urged its people to "Walk about Zion, and go round about her; count her towers. Set your hearts toward her ramparts; traverse her palaces, so that you may tell it to the very last generation."

On Sabbaths, while some Jews gathered in synagogues or homes to review portions of the Holy Scriptures and revered texts, others would meet to take a walk through and visit—or in many cases, revisit—streets, neighborhoods and particular points of interest throughout the city. A kind of unity exists between those who recite cherished texts and those who revisit cherished sites; while the one group goes over the ancient, sacred words, the other passes through the ancient, sacred places. Each has found its own way to enter into and review the past; each has found its own way to venerate the tradition.

Yet another similarity links these two activities. As those who reread and recited the words of the masters entered into a virtual communion and reaffirmed their ties with those who first wrote or spoke those words—especially when the texts were known by heart —so too those who walked along familiar streets and into quarters whose histories they knew and remembered well could likewise make contact with previous generations. For each group, the return to favorite old passages elicited a mood and offered a chance to enter into another kind of consciousness, to make contact with a time that others might think had long ago passed into oblivion but which those who still reviewed the ancient ways knew still lives. And thus they could find a way to make their own world and that of another time one and the same, and thus give life to memory.

When I first began taking the Haganat Ha-Teva tours of the city, I did not realize the full significance of these walks. I did not realize that through them I too could be transported not only to other places but also to other times, from which I would return with memories of experiences I had never had but could somehow share with those whose once they were. In time, however, as I returned again and again to search the present for the past and acquired new memories, the deeper meaning of what I was about revealed itself to me. And when at last this realization ripened into consciousness, it engulfed my entire experience of Jerusalem—as it no doubt did for the other faithful members of the Society.

But if the dawn of my comprehension came slowly, I nevertheless can still recall the moment—the walk—when its first rays reached my eyes, an afternoon when for the first time I briefly glimpsed it all—past, present and future—in ways I'd never experienced before.

The walk began in much the same way as many others I had taken in the past. The day before, Friday, while leafing through *Kol Ha-Ir*, the local supplement to the Friday editions of the newspaper, I turned to the page listing all the goings-on in town for the coming week. For Jews in Israel, Friday afternoon—the Eve of Sabbath, the tradition calls it—is a bit like an American Sunday, a day when time slows down, when people, having come home from work early, relax at home, go for a swim, tinker with the car, take a long bath or read the paper. Not published on Saturdays, the national day of rest, the paper is bigger on Friday than on any of the others. It sums up the past week and tries in some way to prepare its readers for the one to come. This is the edition with all the classified ads and public notices. As I glanced through it, I found amid the usual announcements of concerts, movies, lectures and exhibitions a list of all the tours—some free and others not—available during the coming week. My eyes moved down the page until I came to those offered on Sabbath.

Many of the tours were led by volunteers whose only compensation appeared to be the pleasure they derived from guiding others through places they knew well and which in many cases were filled with memories—both theirs and those of others whom they knew or knew of. Some of the tours were being given in the morning, during the time I would be repeating my prayers in the synagogue, but others met in the early hours of the afternoon, after lunch. One in particular caught my interest: "The Southern Neighborhoods of Jerusalem."

These quarters outside the Old City walls were all products of the expansion that began following the Crimean War in 1856 and that really developed in earnest at the end of the century. Since then, a kind of informal division of the compass had taken place among the various religions and ethnic groups who populated the city. The lines of settlement were not strictly drawn—nor, for that matter, were the quarters inside the city walls—but their general outlines remained fairly stable. From their crowded and increasingly unsanitary neighborhoods inside the walls, Jews moved out toward the west, along what would ultimately come to be called Jaffa Road. Moslems had turned toward the north, distributing themselves along the road to Nablus and Damascus, while the Christians had moved southward in the direction of Bethlehem. As for the east, between Jerusalem and Jericho on the Jordan lay the barren Wilderness of Judea and the Dead Sea; only those who had sought to flee the city—Jeremiah to the hills beyond Anatot, the Essenes to Qumran, the Jewish Zealots to Masada and later the Greek monks to their monasteries in the mountains and deserts—went to the east.

As advertised, the Sabbath afternoon tour was to include the neighborhoods of Shevet Zedek, Djoura el-Anav, Yemin Moshe, Sha'arey Zion, or Shamma, and Batei Yosef Navon. Of these I knew only Yemin Moshe, the row of houses along the side of the windmill built near Mish'kenot Shannanim, the first Jewish settlement in Jerusalem outside the Old City walls. But the Yemin Moshe I knew was one which, while retaining the body of the past—stone houses lining narrow stone alleys—had, since 1967 and the reunification of the city, taken on a new incarnation as a neighborhood housing art galleries and a population of rich Jews, many of whom either came from the English-speaking world or else still lived there and had simply purchased what they believed to be a breathtaking piece of property looking out upon the magnificent Valley of Ben-Hinnom and the majestic Old City walls above it to the east. This was a neighborhood Tavio and I would walk through on many a night of guard duty. But I knew little if anything of the Yemin Moshe that had begun as an effort by intrepid squatters to improve their living conditions by moving beyond the safety of the walled city into the unknown—the Yemin Moshe that would be explored in this afternoon's walk. And so I decided to join the tour.

According to the paper, the meeting point was to be the Jaffa Gate. In the late nineteenth century, when Jerusalem was rediscovered by the Occidental world and the port of Jaffa became an important entry point, Jerusalem had begun turning westward. With an interruption from 1948 to 1967, when the armistice line between Jordan and Israel cut right across its face, the Jaffa Gate had become the major opening into the Old City from the west. Indeed, both Kaiser Wilhelm and later the British conqueror General Allenby had triumphally marched into Old Jerusalem through it. After 1967 it regained its glory and once again became a major portal; these days people flooded the area around it.

Approaching the massive archway at about a quarter to two in the afternoon, I discovered a cluster of people gathered around a sidewalk portrait artist who had set up shop along the grass in front of the walls. A Bedouin leading a tired-looking animal drew near and, in heavily accented English, offered them an opportunity for "a genuine camel ride." The hair on the beast's knees was worn away from its years of bending and rising. Near the road leading out of the Old City some Italian tourists were being shepherded into groups of seven by their guide. They had a kind of dazed look in their eyes, as if coming out of the dark mysteries of the Old City and into the daylight of the modern city just beyond the gate had suddenly blinded and confused them. A few clutched their cameras tightly, as if by letting them go, they would become hopelessly lost. Dangling thus between past and present, they were quickly hustled into cabs which cruised about on the road outside and whisked back to their hotels.

Just outside the gate and standing next to a cart filled with fresh oval sesame rolls an Arab made change for a young man who had just bought three. Taking the rolls, his customer asked for *zatar* and was handed three tiny packets of folded newspaper inside which was the salty brown spice that the initiated sprinkled atop their rolls.

Along Jaffa Road, where during the early part of the century there stood a line of buildings of which the most famous was the Fast Hotel, the last stop before reaching what was then the center of Jerusalem, there was now a flowery mall, around which was a small stone partition. On it sat a row of old men and women who fingered ebony-colored worry beads. From their appearance, they seemed to be Middle East natives, and even when they muttered a few words to one another, the cadence of their speech was such that it was hard to tell whether they were Arabs or Jews who had come from Arab lands. In the mouths of these people Hebrew and Arabic sounded almost identical. Beside them sat two young blond girls who chatted in Swedish. On their other side sat a young man in a faded blue sweat shirt on which in letters that looked vaguely Hebraic were words that, if read upside down, spelled out an English obscenity. The souks on David Street inside the Old City had done a brisk business in this item several seasons earlier.

Along the path that ran near the Old City ramparts, a few people nibbled on what at first glance looked like walking sticks but on closer observation turned out to be freshly cut stalks of sugar cane. An enterprising young Arab boy of nine or ten had piled them on a donkey and was quickly selling them. In a few minutes, when his supply was gone, he climbed atop the animal and easily melted into the constant crowd flowing into the Old City.

The swift currents of the modern outer city and the languorous flow of the inner one swirled past each other and allowed those at the gate to float around and around in an eddy of time. Here, amid this meeting of places, people and time, Jerusalem gathered about itself.

Had this been my first time meeting one of the Haganat Ha-Teva tours, I'd have worried about finding my group in this swirl of humanity. After all, it seemed that everyone was either waiting for someone or something or on his way to or from somewhere. But my previous trips had taught me how to distinguish between those who came for these walks and those who had other trips in mind. There was something unmistakable about the type of people who chose the Haganat Ha-Teva way to spend their Sabbath afternoon. Not that they were all the same ; on the contrary, the group was really a mix.

First there were the "Old Israelis," people whose weather-beaten faces and wrinkled skin bespoke a lifetime of exposure to the elements. These were the men and women who, one imagined, had watched and guided—sometimes grudgingly and with a nostalgia for the past, which, while physically harder, seemed somehow simpler—Jerusalem's transformation from a sleepy backwater into the capital of a new Zionist State, the product of hard work and political machination. For them the walks through town were trips through personal recollections. But perhaps even more importantly, they were expressions of national memory, a chance to relive and to carry forward the Jewish people's reestablishment in the land of its origins. I had often found Tavio in this group.

Next came the young, the ones with knapsacks on their backs—the Israeli environmentalists, who, like the Old Israelis, saw these tours as affirmations of a tie to land, nature and people. What point was there in trying to preserve and protect the ancient and historical sites, in keeping things in the original, if one didn't return again and again to view them? If they did not have the personal recollections of the older Israelis, the pioneers, they could through these walks with the old-timers at the very least become touched by the memories of others and thus in some way share them. And so these young people, along with their older mentors, tripped through mountain and valley, aging and crumbling buildings as well as ancient, restored archeological relics—all the while enlarging their personal experience by depositing into it the living memory of their forebears.

There was a certain sense of kinship that these young people seemed to feel for the Old Israelis. They even seemed to emulate something of their appearance, wearing the same heavy sweaters or hiking boots and always munching on some fruit, vegetation of the land of Israel. They were the young protectors of the Zionist dream.

Then too, there were the new immigrants—often Americans and British, called by the locals "Anglo-Saxons" (only in a Jewish state could Jews ever be referred to as Anglo-Saxons). Searching for a reality behind their nascent historical consciousness, they had come to Jerusalem out of a mix of often vague Zionist aspirations and mild to extreme feelings of alienation from their Diaspora existence. On these walks, many came hoping to explore and discover the real estate they had yearned for and finally reached.

"After two thousand years of waiting and praying for Jerusalem, promising myself that next year I would be here, I want to see it all," a woman fresh off the plane once explained.

Many, if not most, of these newcomers were modern Orthodox, as was obvious from the *kippot* on the men and the kerchiefs on the women. But their Orthodoxy was not like the one that enclosed itself in the insulated precincts of the *charedim,* zealots of Me'ah She'arim and its associated neighborhoods, which preferred a Jerusalem that hovered primarily in the realm of the spiritual and behind the fence of exclusive tradition. Theirs was an Orthodoxy— embedded in modernity and laced with a Western rationalist tradition—which sought after visible reminders of the sources of faith. They wanted to see the Jerusalem for which they prayed, the city of the psalmists, the ancient home of their people. Their faith drew them to the tours; their rationalism made them want to see the reality beneath their beliefs.

During the temporal escape which Sabbath offered, they chose to travel to the past, perhaps hoping to visit a time and place they had missed but which, as new immigrants, wished they had not.

"What better way to observe Sabbath," one such man had once asked, "than to circle the ramparts of Jerusalem, to follow the urging of the Psalms, to walk in the footsteps of the ancients?"

They were not alone. Among them, too, were others with knit *kippot,* local modern Orthodox Jews who, although natives of Israel, felt the same need to see the real Jerusalem atop which had been built the superstructure of their religion. For them, to climb the stones of earthly Jerusalem was a way to scale the ramparts of faith. For some, these walks were necessary prerequisites to the expression of Jewish sovereignty over Jerusalem. To find that one's ancestors had been here gave credence to the claim that we, their heirs, had rights to our settlement. "Was this Jewish?" they asked again and again. "When?" "Why did we leave?" "Is it still ours?"

Among some of these Orthodox there were those inclined to see in the return to Zion hints of the millennium at hand. For this flock of the faithful, these Sabbath excursions sometimes seemed exercises in reconnaissance, preparations for the inevitable rebuilding of Kingdom Come.

There were also students. For Jews, "student" has always been an identity not tied to a particular time in life but rather linked to a kind of consciousness, a desire to absorb knowledge, a willingness to wander along the beaten paths of wisdom and reflect upon old truths. For the students, learning about Jerusalem was their expression of heritage. Lessons were learned not only from lingering inside pages of books; one could also study with his feet. These "students" were people of all ages. Often they came with notebook or tape recorder. But what especially distinguished them was an exquisite interest in getting the most accurate picture; collectors of information, they hungered after every detail, which had to be put straight in their minds. Theirs was a *Torah l'shmah*—what the rabbis had called learning for its own sake.

Sometimes when the guide was Orthodox—as was often the case on Sabbath afternoons—and he noticed someone recording his words, he would ask, in line with the Jewish prohibition against writing on the day of rest and worship: "Please do not desecrate the sanctity of this day." Then some of the note takers would put away pad and pencil or turn off recorder, and seem to open their eyes wider and ask more questions, as if turning themselves into the recording instrument. And those who refused to be bound by strictures they believed irrelevant to their lives moved quietly toward the back of the crowd and surreptitiously continued taking notes. Usually, the guide knew enough not to look too closely at what went on behind his back.

Finally there were those who, being on holiday, had decided to take advantage of the free tour. Often they brought along children who complained that the guide was talking too long or that they were tired of all the walking. They pushed hard to be in the front lines of the crowd, hoping to get the clearest look at the sites passed. And yet, though they tried to see, these outsiders—for that is what they seemed to be—were most often those who had the hardest time making out what exactly it was the guide was pointing at or what they were supposed to be observing. "Where is it?" they would often ask. In the end, they were frequently the first to drop out of the tour somewhere along the route.

Much later, I would realize that these people suffered from a blindness that came from their being completely caught up in the present moment. They looked only at the surface of reality, at what their eyes could see, while the guide invited his followers to behold less what was there than what had once been there. The guide was largely interested in preserving culture and the ties to it and less so in showing people sites. Trying to catch a quick tour, these tourists —interested in only what a hurried glance would reveal—remained unprepared to look past the present into another Jerusalem only hinted at by the sites the eye could see.

No single one of these groups would have stood out in the crowd at the Jaffa Gate. But their combination was unmistakable. As the appointed meeting time drew near and these people who in many ways seemed to have little if anything in common wandered around looking for one another and the guide, there would be no trouble finding the Haganat Ha-Teva crowd.

Walking over toward what remained of the wall of a moat that had once surrounded the Citadel of David near the gate, I then sat down. During the visit of the German Kaiser Wilhelm in 1898, the pit had been filled in so that the mighty ruler could ride his horse into the Holy City. Today, cars zipped over the road that had been paved atop the fill.

From my vantage point on the wall, I looked around some more. On my right sat some porters who made their living by wheeling or carrying heavy loads through the narrow passages of the Old City. Most wore woolen caps, having slung their flowing kaffiyehs around their shoulders; the heavy cord with which they strapped loads on their backs and around their heads did not allow for loose headgear. While I watched, a Jew who was not observant of Sabbath haggled with one of them; he wanted a piano taken into his home and obviously hoped for a better price than the porter was asking. In the end, the two seemed to strike a bargain. They shook hands, and the Arab followed the Jew to a flatbed truck parked nearby. He hopped into the back, beside the lashed-down piano, and the Jew started the engine and drove off in the direction of the Jewish Quarter.

To my left sat two girls whom I took to be environmentalists waiting for my tour. I recognized one of them from a previous walk. Looking a bit like a young Golda Meir, she wore her auburn hair loosely tied up in a crinkly bun and munched on an orange, while her friend, wearing a pair of granny glasses, stowed binoculars into her knapsack. Both wore scuffed hiking boots. At one time I might have had to ask if they were waiting for the Haganat Ha-Tevah tour. But now, after my months of participation, I was so certain of my being with the right people that I didn't bother. Sitting there with their feet dangling off the wall, they exuded an unmistakable calm confidence in their young bodies. No need for them to rush around looking for where to go. They would wait for precisely the right moment to wander forward and join the tour.

After several minutes of sitting on the wall of the moat, I decided to wander about a bit to see how the other components of the group were shaping up. They were all there. The Old Israelis, a few peeling oranges, stood near the entrance to the government tourist office just inside the gate. One of them chatted with a shoeshine man who was spit-polishing his brass stand. A couple of the modern Orthodox, still wearing their Sabbath finery, circled around outside but every few minutes returned inside to make certain they had not missed the start of the tour. One young man had a Bible in his hand. Three students, two holding notebooks and one with a pencil behind her ear, sat along the steps leading up to the walk atop the city ramparts. Outside, near the sidewalk artist and the camel ride, the people on holiday tried to control their children, who all seemed to want to either have their picture drawn or ride atop the Bedouin's camel.

"Not now; we'll be leaving any minute," one mother explained to her impatient little boy. She had to pull him by the arm to keep him from clambering onto the long-suffering animal which now rested on its knees. The Bedouin watched them expectantly.

A few minutes before two, when the guide, Ze'ev Bar-Tov, was to appear, the various groups began to converge. On the far side of the square inside the gate, the environmentalists walked toward the Old Israelis. They were joined by the Orthodox couple and students, who were now nibbling on broken stalks of sugar cane. Seeing the movement, the tourists corralled their children and moved toward the growing party of perhaps forty or fifty people.

"Is this the Haganat Ha-Teva tour?" the mother with her child in tow asked one of the Old Israelis.

"Apparently." The speaker, whose voice conveyed a kind of quiet assurance, was a short, trim-looking man with Ben-Gurion–style gray hair that made a halo around his tanned bald head. He wore khaki hiking boots that looked as if they had covered the hills and valleys surrounding Jerusalem quite a number of times. He stared off into the middle distance.

"Where is the guide?" someone asked. "Shouldn't he be here by now?"

"He'll be here; he's always on time," said one of the young environmentalists, undoing her bun and shaking it into a heavy braid that fell down to her waist. She took a handful of hairpins and put them into her backpack. Her friend sipped some juice—a herbal concoction of her own making, I later learned—from her canteen.

"Is this the tour of the southern neighborhoods? Does anyone know what we'll be covering?" A newcomer to the group was speaking.

"You'll see; we'll follow in the footsteps of our people." An old man wearing a *kippah* had answered. I had seen him on these tours before. The guides would often turn to him for some gloss on this or that site, and he could always oblige.

There was a kind of group process going on here as everyone waited for the formal proceedings to begin. Those in the know found subtle ways to identify themselves and set themselves apart from the new and uninitiated. I moved toward those who I knew would have contributions to make during the coming walk.

Seemingly out of nowhere, Ze'ev Bar-Tov appeared. A tall, plain-looking, dark-skinned man with a drooping mustache, he entered with a long stride from the back of the crowd. On his head he wore a knit *kippah* that might once have been white but had by now begun to darken under the soot of the city. He held nothing in his hands. Today, as on all occasions when I would later walk behind him, his recollections came not from notes but from events inscribed on his consciousness and preserved in his memory.

''And so, ladies and gentlemen ...'' He seemed to begin in mid-sentence, as if there were no real need for lengthy introductions because we were simply continuing a walk we had left off sometime in the not-too-distant past. Offering a *"Shabbat shalom,"* the traditional Sabbath greeting of peace, he continued without further social niceties to tell us where we would go this afternoon. He spoke in measured cadences—laconically, not in a monotone but also without particular animation, as if he struggled to sound ordinary in order to control the inherent drama of a narrative that would tell of extraordinary people and events.

''We are going to go out from the city walls today, as did our predecessors. But for them the trip was not as easy as it will be for us. Little of substance awaited them outside the walls. A few consulates, a monastery or two and Bedouin and marauders. Yet nonetheless, they went out.'' He paused, as if to let this act of courage sink in, and then he cleared his throat.

''We shall walk toward the impressive neighborhoods they built. We shall see what awesome souls they were. We shall feel again something of what they felt and look out upon vistas that greeted their eyes.''

Only later, as I reflected upon my experience and when I returned on my own to the places to which he had led us and realized that there were few actual sites to look at, would I realize that he had not promised us that we would actually *see* the neighborhoods but only perceive the ''awesome souls'' of those who had dwelt within them. This would be a tour not into what the outer eye could see but rather into the provinces of memory, a kind of mythic Jerusalem, visible only to the inner eye.

He turned toward the new city and walked a few steps before suddenly stopping and turning around. It was as if someone behind him had called to catch his attention. But no one I could see or hear had.

"Perhaps before we leave this place, we ought to recall some of the people and buildings that were here," he said.

"Here where you see the line of taxis today once stood the carriages and coachmen that took people back and forth from the new settlements outside the wall to their shops in the business center that was here. In his book about the Jerusalem of days gone by, Ya'akov Yehoshua tells us that the drivers Nachmias, Albalek and Abu Bukhar sat side by side—a Jew, a Christian and a Moslem—in easy cooperation. But all that has become a part of the past."

He turned his head toward David Street and drew our attention to a ragged-looking building now called the Petra Hotel and owned by Arabs but which, he reminded us, had once been the Amdorsky Hotel, owned by Jews. Again he quoted from Yehoshua's memory.

"Not only the Jews held their affairs at Yerach'miel Amdorsky's hotel. Businessmen from the Arab community came here too. They liked the service and appreciated his kosher food. Here they had no need to worry that there might be forbidden food on his table, for religious Moslems, like Jews, must shun pork.

"The sound of festivities, of weddings and other celebrations, often flooded out of the windows of the hotel and filled the ears of the coachmen who waited here below. On those special occasions, the horses of the carriages were decorated with paper chains, flowers or greens."

"Like the cars at today's weddings," someone offered.

Bar-Tov kept on talking. "And when the couple came out and entered the carriage, the people passing by in the square would smile or applaud. And the sound of Hebrew songs filled the air as the Amdorsky Hotel spread its life out into the streets."

Later, when I went into the hotel, I tried to see beyond the faded walls and flaking paint. I found myself listening to the silence in the deserted upstairs rooms, as if by an act of concentrated will I could hear the Hebrew that had once echoed in these rooms. Then I climbed past the large dining room, now an empty hallway with a few tables shoved up against the walls, to the roof, from where one could see the ancient pool of Hezekiah and the dividing lines between the four quarters—Moslem, Jewish, Christian and Armenian. But without help I could neither hear the past nor see past what had become a cesspool below, filled with refuse thrown from the windows of the surrounding buildings.

Bar-Tov stretched his arm in the direction of the Kishleh, alongside the Citadel of David. Today it was an Israeli police station, but once, he reminded us, it had served as a Turkish army base and later as a prison during the period of the British Mandate. In one of the continuing ironies of history, Jews who once had been imprisoned there for political activities later became the jailers and officers in charge.

Looking back the other way, he continued his selective scan of the Jewish panorama.

"Here stood the tailor shops of Moshe Casuto, Menashe Meshullam and Abraham Gabbai. Many of the stores you see today, especially those along the road leading to the Armenian Quarter"—he pointed southward—"were once owned by Jews who lived in the neighborhoods we shall visit today."

He pointed in another direction : "There was the Anglo-Palestine Bank."

"What about Valero's Bank?" someone asked.

"Farther down," Bar-Tov answered. One of the Old Israelis pointed toward David Street, and a few people stared off in that direction. From where we stood we could not really see the building, which was beyond the first row of souks. Bar-Tov could not resist the opportunity to say something about Valero.

"Hayim Aharon, the son of Ya'akov Valero, as is well known by those who know Jerusalem, was the most famous Jewish banker in the city. In Jerusalem, the name Valero was like Rothschild; it meant money. Buildings put up with his money still stand along Jaffa Road, and those who know where to look can still find remnants of his golden coins. From Valero's Bank came some of the moneys with which the Jews redeemed the lands of their forefathers. He was highly respected among the native Sephardic community—there were those who called him 'Lord,' 'Master' and 'Rav.' Later, like many others, he moved outside the city walls, even though the bank remained within. He was a small, bleary-eyed man who normally dressed simply and modestly in spite of his wealth. As was customary in the days of the Turkish rule, he wore a fez, and so he looked much like the other Jews of Jerusalem—citizens of the Ottoman Empire."

"That's what some people resented—his stinginess," one of the old men near me said. "He was, after all, not like the other Jews of Jerusalem."

"Only on holy days and Sabbaths," Bar-Tov continued, "did he put on his fine suit with its brocade and medals. Then he truly looked like a Turkish gentleman, a lord.

"Even among the local authorities—the consuls, and even some of the Turks—he was highly respected because he managed their financial affairs with great tact and fairness. When Franz Josef the First, Kaiser of Austria, visited Jerusalem, Valero's Bank handled some of his finances. Hayim Aharon kept up close ties with the ruling powers, and on their holidays he would hire a special carriage and visit the consulates and government ministries. On those occasions, with his neatly cropped beard, fez, fine coat, medals across his chest and gold watch and chain, he looked like a true pasha."

Behind me I heard the man with the Ben-Gurion–style hairdo talking to the woman beside him: "The father started the bank."

"But the son developed it and really gave it a name," she answered, and then added, "I think he began as a manager in the branch in Jaffa."

"When his first wife died, he married his niece."

"They said it was to make sure that all the money stayed in the family."

"And then they had that blind daughter who eventually married a cardplayer, an alcoholic who squandered all the money and ended up in a little booth on the street selling lottery tickets."

The two gossiped about Valero as if he were still very much a part of the present, as if this reference to him in places where he used to walk had brought him back into their lives.

I looked around at some of the others in the group. As Bar-Tov spoke, many of them did not look at him but continued to stare at the buildings toward which he had pointed, as if by their looking they could make out Valero in his carriage. It was not what the eyes could actually see that demanded attention but rather a way of life and personalities that once had inhabited this place.

"Still," Bar-Tov continued, "on weekdays, after he had moved out of the city, he stood here at the gate along with all the other plain people waiting their turns to board the carriages that took them from their work here to their new homes outside the walls."

"I heard," one of the Old Israelis added, "that sometimes, if he was slightly late, the drivers would pretend not to notice and leave without him, because when he got into the carriage, he would never agree to pay for more than his one seat. The coachmen thought that because of his wealth, he ought to have taken a separate cab and paid more than the rest of the passengers.''

''And why should it have been any different then than it is now?'' someone asked. It was a question which, in one way or another, I had heard and would continue to hear as I wandered the streets and neighborhoods of this city. These people who toured their own version of Jerusalem had a need to see a continuity between present and past; perhaps only thus could they be secure about their future in a city that had for generations been built, occupied, sacked and rebuilt.

''Valero was highly respected all his life by the businessmen of the Sephardic community,'' Bar-Tov continued, ''and served for years as one of its most revered leaders. As Ya'akov Yehoshua writes: 'He was the glory and magnificence of the Sephardim of Jerusalem.' Such was Hayim Aharon Valero, Jewish mukhtar of Jerusalem.''

''And the bank—what happened to it?'' one of the immigrants asked.

''By 1915, when the Ottoman Bank opened a branch here in Jerusalem, Valero's Bank found itself without the resources to continue. A Jewish-owned bank could not compete with the protégés of the ruling powers. But by then, anyway, the era of its great glory had passed.'' He paused, blinked his eyes a few times quickly and cleared his throat.

''Yes, my friends, much of what you see before your eyes was once owned by Jews. But let us not enter into that matter now; that is for another walk and another time.''

He turned again and began walking out through the gate. Although his pace was not unusually swift, he easily moved to the front of the group, and soon those in the back of the crowd found themselves half-running to keep up with him and his running commentary about everything we passed. The experienced knew that by staying close to the leader they would absorb far more than if they simply waited for the stops during which he gave his brief talks.

The Old Israelis didn't need to run. Reminiscing, they walked at an even pace near the back and exchanged their own accounts of the sites we passed. Near them walked some of the environmentalists, themselves occasionally sharing a ''reminiscence'' or two.

We walked down into the Valley of Ben-Hinnom toward the Vale of Tears. These places, whose names echoed with the poetry of Scripture, were becoming eroded at their edges by the litter of the late twentieth century : a large parking lot, jammed with city buses and mounds of rubble. I wondered if the garbage I was looking at would one day in the future be the stuff of important archeological discoveries. Jerusalem had made me begin looking at even the most mundane things of the present as if they were in some way already a part of the distant past. Sometimes I even thought of myself as a part of some existence long since gone.

Bar-Tov stopped in front of a half-destroyed building, pock-marked by nineteen years of shelling. The facade, now stained brown, was smooth limestone with what must once have been impressive carvings. It made me think of a photo of an unwrapped Egyptian mummy I had once seen : disintegrated but still dignified. The broken stones underfoot made a few people stumble.

"Here is the Tannous building," he began. "It was once an important landmark of the new business center here outside the walls."

"The Tannous brothers are at present in Beirut, I believe," one of the Old Israelis called out.

"Yes, I've heard that too," Bar-Tov answered, and then continued, "This was the industrial district for many years."

"But since the Carta project, it's been deserted," the environmentalist with the braid broke in. There was a hard edge to her voice.

Most of Jerusalem knew about the Carta project, which at least officially was meant to rebuild or at least upgrade the area. Over the last few years, the city had emptied all these buildings of their inhabitants. What was once a district with only a past, a dark corner at the blocked crossroads of a divided city, acquired almost overnight after 1967 a bright new future, with streets built during the first years of its development that after the war were again opened in all directions. In the heady days after the war, plans were made for malls, wide avenues and a glamorous shopping and housing district here facing the Old City walls. A new beginning was wanted. But in the last five years things had become caught up in red tape and budget cuts. A consciousness of the value of restoring the past had grown as well, and so people talked more and more about preserving the houses rather than razing them and starting anew.

Still, there were residues of the point of view that looked upon the area as a neighborhood simply waiting for its inevitable col-

lapse. Only a few weeks earlier, the civil defense had staged a mock drill here and in its zeal to bring reality to the exercise had burned down one of the crumbling buildings. The ashes and soot of the fire were clearly visible from where we stood; environmentalists and many of those who felt an attachment to the past still fumed over what they saw as wanton destruction.

"Yes," Bar-Tov responded, "what was once a living and vigorous place is now an empty shell."

He pointed toward the back of one building which looked out now on a garbage depository where the tractors that collected refuse from the narrow alleys of the Old City came to dump their waste.

"Theodor Herzl stayed in that building outside the walls during his visit to Jerusalem. Here, on Jaffa Road, were the best hotels, the places people stopped before visiting the inside. The Fast Hotel —you all remember."

Several of the Old Israelis nodded. Just two days before, I had read in Herzl's diary his reaction to the city on that occasion. Now I thought of what he had written:

> When I remember thee in days to come, O Jerusalem, it will not be with pleasure. The musty deposits of two thousand years of inhumanity, intolerance and uncleanliness lie in the foul-smelling alleys. The one man who has been present all this time, the amiable dreamer of Nazareth, has only contributed to increasing the hatred.
>
> If we ever get Jerusalem, and if I am still able to do anything actively at that time, I would begin by cleaning it up.
>
> I would clear out everything that is not sacred, set up workers' homes outside the city, empty the nests of filth and tear them down, burn the secular ruins and transfer the bazaars elsewhere. Then, retaining the old architectural style as much as possible, I would build around the holy places a comfortable new city with proper sanitation.

That had been done. And now even that new city was being torn down to be replaced with a newer one.

"You know, there is a beautiful synagogue upstairs in the Tannous building," I heard one man tell another. "The Persian Jews who lived in this neighborhood after '48 have kept up the *minyan* [quorum] there, even though hardly more than a handful live here anymore. They come back every morning and evening as a protest against the emptying of the neighborhood and see to it that the prayers are recited without interruption." An empty synagogue was the sign of a dead community, but one in which prayers were still recited symbolized life.

Later I would visit that synagogue several times. It was indeed a remarkable place. Inside a neglected and unlit building, up three flights of stairs reeking of urine, was a palace of prayer. Were it not for the fact that I had seen a man enter the stairwell before me, I would most certainly have turned back after the first ten steps, so foul was the smell and depressing the sight. At last I reached the top floor and entered through a pale green door on the side.

The space inside was immense, taking up the entire length of the building. What made it seem even larger, perhaps, was the few men who had assembled for prayers. Some stood at the windows, which on one side overlooked the valley and on the other the city walls. Benches topped with soft pillows surrounded the room. On some there were Persian rugs. Carpets also covered the walls and floor. There was a kind of faded, even stale, quality to the splendor here; the beauty was less visible than it was imaginable.

"Min'chah, min'chah!" they called, trying to find a ninth and tenth for the *minyan*.

Inscriptions large and small, composed of sacred verses which the devout often recited before prayers, hung on almost every conceivable spot along the walls. There were more than twenty. They were red and black, generously embellished with gold leaf. And near the bottom of each one were the name and dates of the person memorialized through the donation of the plaque. Painted by hand on paper or parchment, now buckling from age, they, like everything else about the room, reflected a kind of antiquated charm.

While I sat near the window, my eyes wandering back and forth between the amulets on the wall and the view both inside and out, a few old men entered. They touched hands with the others present and then kissed their fingers, a kind of greeting I had seen in the Arab side of town as well. A few of these rather impoverished-looking old men dropped some coins into the charity box on a table near the door. The heavy sound of metal hitting the bottom of the tin box echoed loudly in the silence of the twilight.

"When I was growing up outside Baghdad," one of these men once explained, "I always thought of myself as an Arab. There were Christian Arabs, Moslem Arabs and, like me, Jewish Arabs. It was only when we came here that we were suddenly 'whitened' and told that we were not Arabs. Here we were told that we were 'Sephardim,' Jews who came from Spain.'' He had laughed over this strange twist to his own history.

But this would all come much later. For now, I stood with Ze'ev Bar-Tov on a little rise above the Tannous Brothers building.

''We shall not talk about the Tannous building now,'' our guide announced, and began to walk farther down into the valley. Suddenly he turned sharply into a narrow path toward a dint in the valley. As we came closer, I could see that what from higher up on the hill had looked like a dense grove of trees was really just a few trees amid a thick growth of sumac weeds and wild grains. At the entrance to the narrow path that led toward the grove someone had left piles of cut branches and a few sacks of gravel. Bar-Tov clambered over the sacks and stopped several paces down the hill. The rest of us crowded into the brush behind him.

''There's room to move farther down,'' he explained. ''I've just stopped here so as to be in the middle of the group.''

But although he encouraged us to spread out a bit more, no one appeared willing to move farther into the valley. The group all wanted to stay as close as possible to the precise spot on which their guide stood. It was as if they believed that only in this way could they share his perspective, see what he could see, hear what he would say and share his view of Jerusalem.

Standing thus huddled together was not easy. The grade was rather steep and the path exceedingly narrow. People balanced precariously on the pebbles under their feet. A few tried to stand atop the bags of gravel. One or two even tried to perch themselves on the branches, which collapsed under their weight.

''Below you is the neighborhood of Djoura el-Anav,'' Bar-Tov began, while around him his followers were still trying to position themselves for the right view. ''When it stood, it was just a small cluster of buildings—two alleys—with no more than twenty-five families living in forty-seven houses. It began in 1892 when some North African Jews [''Mugrabim,'' I heard someone whisper behind me] individually bought small plots of land on which they built their very modest houses.''

Because they did not buy the plots together as a community, Bar-Tov explained, the neighborhood never managed to acquire a Jewish name. And then, in time, some of them sold their houses to Christians and Moslems who moved into the neighborhood.

''What does the name mean?'' someone called out.

"We're not certain, but probably it means 'the grape pit'—perhaps because people say that the waste from the grape harvest was thrown down here."

"But most of the wine growing is done farther south in the hills near Hebron, not here in Jerusalem," one of the students in the back broke in.

"Yes," one of the environmentalists near her answered, sounding unimpressed with this too-obvious demonstration of learning, "but a few tried it here on these hills. Why not?"

Bar-Tov continued speaking: "There are others who say that grapes were never thrown down here. If anything, carcasses were dropped into a pit here."

"Carcasses?" one of the Americans repeated.

"For generations the people of Jerusalem threw waste of all sorts over the walls. What was outside the city didn't matter. There was a tannery nearby, some say. And according to law, the dead could not remain inside the city limits. So people were buried in caves in the surrounding mountains, and animals were deposited in pits. And then, quite a number of people lived here who worked in the slaughterhouse," Bar-Tov explained.

"Of course." One of the Old Israelis who wore a crumpled khaki hat had begun to speak. With a wry smile on his face, he continued: "Our word *anav* [grape] has quite another meaning in Arabic." He paused. "It means 'plum,' and if you had looked into the valley when the houses were first put up, you would undoubtedly have discovered such trees growing there."

We looked toward the grove of trees below, but there were no plums to be seen today. The student who had spoken up earlier was writing all this down.

Bar-Tov once again continued: "And here above me was Shevet Zedek, a poor neighborhood of Aleppo Jews. They had been displaced from the houses they had built farther up the hill in what is now Yemin Moshe—I'll talk about that in a moment—and here they built little tin huts. I can see the huddled houses now. There was a café here where the hashish dealers gathered and where the merchants from Hebron and Jerusalem met to strike their deals. There was even a small hotel here until after the First World War. And surrounding the whole place was a protective wall.

"From the beginning, the neighborhood remained poor. Some of the houses that succeeded the little huts were not even built of stone but were made of a kind of thin wood which someone from London donated. There were none of the large, filtered public cisterns for collecting water that marked the bigger neighborhoods, only small private holes connected to each house's gutter. I recall reading that when bejeweled ladies—the Sephardim—of Yemin Moshe walked past this poor neighborhood, some of the people here used to throw stones at them. But if it was so, it was only in the later years when the people above in Yemin Moshe began to prosper a bit and the ones in the few houses here lapsed into even greater poverty."

"Yes, but"—the old man in the khaki hat was speaking again— "there was a kind of solidarity about the community here. Perhaps its smallness and the common poverty aroused a feeling of closeness that other places could not experience. I remember hearing that in the evenings families would get together and tell stories which sometimes stretched out for weeks at a time."

"Yes," the woman next to him added, "Ya'akov Yehoshua writes about them in one of his books. The women would knead and cut and prepare spaghetti which the visitors would eat after or during the storytelling."

"And they would sip arak, too," Bar-Tov added.

Around me, everyone was pushing and shoving to get a better view. But there were no houses to be seen, not even a broken wall. Much as we had done in the square near the Jaffa Gate and at all the stops since then, we all stared at the trees down below as if by some collective effort we could somehow see into the past and re-create the scene he described to us. If at our previous stop we could at least look upon the shell of the Tannous building and imagine what had been there before, here imagination was all there was— imagination and a story of a memory. To those who could not partake of this, both Shevet Zedek and Djoura el-Anav remained invisible. A few leaves on the trees and sumacs fluttered slightly. "How pleasant were the breezes here," Bar-Tov concluded. To him and to those who shared in his visions, the buildings we could not see were visible, while the breezes that now ruffled our hair was a memory.

The same thing would happen later as we looked down into the other, southern end of the valley to where the neighborhood called Shamma or Sha'arey Zion once stood. Looking at what was now an open field where some Arab boys from the nearby village of Silwan played soccer (much as their Jewish counterparts were doing farther north in the same valley), Bar-Tov would tell us there had once been a garden through which he would wander as a boy on Sabbath afternoons like this one.

''Often I would linger in this garden and look out on the city walls beyond, wondering how it was that I was so fortunate as to dwell in this place which I imagined would never change.''

''You know, I have been here dozens of times,'' one of the people behind me whispered to another, ''but I don't think I ever saw it just this way.''

But of course, here again there was nothing to ''see.'' The doors of his perception had simply been opened in this company and on this occasion to another dimension.

We walked back up the hill from Shevet Zedek and Djoura el-Anav, or what had once been Shevet Zedek and Djoura el-Anav, along the western ridge of the valley toward the neighborhood of Yemin Moshe and the older Mish'kenot Shannanim.

''Look, a funeral!'' someone called out.

On the other side of the valley, on Mount Zion, a long line of mourners walked behind a large wooden cross and coffin into what had once been the Bishop Gobat School and was now a Protestant institution for Bible studies. The Protestant cemetery was there, filled with pilgrims, nuns, priests, German and British officials and their family members and others whose connection to Jerusalem was made eternal.

Bar-Tov said nothing; this was not a past to which he was ready to connect. His tour aimed us in another direction.

''These are the houses of Judah Touro, called Mish'kenot Shannanim,'' he continued, ''and next to them stand the houses called Yemin Moshe [to the right of Moshe] after the lord, Sir Moses Montefiore of Great Britain, who collected the money for the houses of Mish'kenot Shannanim. The document of the sale reads...'' Bar-Tov looked off into the distance as if he were reading from the actual bill of sale.

'' 'This goodly mountain was purchased out of a love for its sanctity, for religion and the folk'—that was on the seventeenth of Av in the year that they [the Christians] count as 1894—'in honor of Sir Moses Montefiore and his wife, Judith, who joined him in all his good deeds and most of his journeys. May their memory be a blessing.

'' 'The aforesaid property is a plot of land which measures 47,429 square cubits in Turkish measurements, standing outside the gates of Jerusalem on the road which goes up to Hebron.' ''

He waved his hand expansively over the houses as he spoke.

''And where does Touro come in?'' one of the Americans asked in a heavily accented Hebrew.

"Touro was a rich American Jew."

"Is that the same Judah Touro of Newport, Rhode Island?" he asked someone next to him. The other shrugged his shoulders.

"Yes," whispered someone else, who had obviously heard this story before.

"This man Touro," Bar-Tov was explaining, "had made a lot of money, and when he died he felt for one reason or another that he owed something to his own people."

"Maybe he was trying to atone for his life," someone suggested without specifying what it was Touro had done that warranted atonement.

"Could be, because he left fifty thousand dollars to the Jews of Jerusalem. My friends, fifty thousand dollars was a considerable sum in those days."

"So he was atoning for the fact that he had stayed in America, that he hadn't returned to his homeland," said one of the immigrants.

"No one really knew what to do with the bequest, and so it was put aside and was not used until the time of Montefiore, who learned about it and had recently been on one of his many visits to Jerusalem—he came the last time, my friends, when he was into his nineties. Seeing the need for more space for Jewish settlement, he purchased this plot on the edge of which we now stand."

Bar-Tov moved a few steps onto a path that ran along the ridge. Again we crowded in behind him. Below us, he explained, was what had been called Birket Ha-Sultan—the pool of the Ottoman Sultan Suleiman the Magnificent. At its southern edge were the remains of an old fountain for the pilgrims and travelers coming to Jerusalem from the south. When we looked down into the "pool" itself we could see no water: only a wooden stage the municipality had set up for concerts, and seats carved out of the outcroppings of stone. Bar-Tov made a passing reference to this new open-air esplanade, but he was more interested in the view from the past and described the winter rains that once, before the creation of a network of streets and alleys which now crisscrossed the opening to the valley, would collect into a stream and flow down from the heights in the north to form a pool below. "El Rio de Montefiore," the Spanish-speaking Jews who lived above in Yemin Moshe had called it.

He began to tell us how Yemin Moshe had really been two communities: the Sephardim to the south and the Ashkenazim on the other side. It was a repetition of the divisions that existed within the Old City walls. But here, since neither had any kind of significant seniority over the other, they appeared to live in closer harmony.

"In the beginning, the field here lay empty. Next to it were the houses of Mish'kenot Shannanim, but this land too belonged to the Montefiore trust. Poor Jews from inside the Old City walls finally could not stand to live in their crowded conditions and so they overcame their misgivings about leaving the protection of the walls, came out here and grabbed the land."

"That's why some people called this place *'khap,'* " one of the Old Israelis called out.

"That is true," Bar-Tov replied. " *'Khap,'* as some of you know, is Yiddish for 'grab.' The neighborhood was grabbed, and overnight the squatters built twenty-six houses. Houses of wood and tin —shacks—but houses. And at last the heirs of Montefiore took them to court and moved them from here to Shevet Zedek.

"But what they had done, my friends, was arouse the conscience of the Montefiore trust. And soon a community was built on this land. The houses you see before you now are the products of that labor.

"At first there were no gates to the neighborhood," he explained. "But in the days of British rule, when the Arab uprisings against Jews began, iron gates were put up."

The British had begun by permitting, if not encouraging, Jewish settlement in and around Jerusalem, as they had throughout what was then called Palestine. But soon the British decided they needed Arab allies at least as much as, if not more than, they needed the goodwill of Jews, which they believed was assured anyway. To whom else could the Jews turn? But the Arabs could in fact turn elsewhere, and they were far greater in number; and in most lands, Arabs sat on oil. Nationalism was on the rise among them; in Egypt, Syria and Iraq the locals were chafing under the chains of colonialism. This feeling would undoubtedly arise among Palestinian Arabs too. And so the British, dominating two peoples in one land, encouraged both, though more and more they tilted toward the Arabs. And thus Arab uprisings against Jewish settlements were, if not tolerated, only lethargically controlled.

"The Jews of Yemin Moshe realized," Bar-Tov said simply, "that they would have to protect themselves. The old promises, like those the Dejanis who lived near Mount Zion once made to Montefiore that they would keep an eye on their Jewish neighbors across the valley, evaporated in the mist.

"On Friday, the twenty-third of August, 1929, came the beginning of the end for the original families of the neighborhood. The Arabs from Hebron broke in, and all the people here had to defend themselves with was piles of stones, a few metal bars and ancient guns and rifles. They could see before their eyes along the road from Bethlehem the wounded being brought from Hebron. And that too struck them with fear.

"And so what had been an open neighborhood, open to the influences of the surrounding world, became increasingly closed. Beginning then, many of the original families began to leave, some to other neighborhoods and others to other lands. And even today, those who have returned are not from the original families."

We walked the narrow cobbled streets of the neighborhood, and as we passed one or another house, near covered cisterns or aging trees, Bar-Tov led us through a series of reminiscences and narratives which all seemed aimed toward one realization: however distant and different the lives of those who once inhabited this place might be, they were somehow connectable to the way we live now. Again and again our walk took us into realms where the past became visible and a culture palpable. And all the time, we seemed to try to make, as anthropologist Clifford Geertz in another context put it, "the enormously distant enormously close without becoming any less far away."

Standing in front of a house that had once belonged to the Chacham Bochur Nissim, Bar-Tov called our attention to a large eucalyptus tree that bulged out into the alley. Its smooth shaft reached high into the sky, while its sparse leaves rustled in the breeze. The street and the surrounding steps worked their ways around it.

"There were very few trees in the neighborhood, even in the beginning. Two eucalyptus trees were planted, one by Sir Moses Montefiore and the other by Moshe Nissim. My friends, this was on Tu B'Sh'vat." We all knew that Tu B'Sh'vat was the Jewish arbor day—the New Year for trees, the rabbis had called it.

"Moshe Nissim, the brother of the Chacham, was from Constantinople, where he had been ordained a rabbi. The Chacham was also among the best-known cantors in the community. Here in the synagogue of the Sephardim, which stands not far from his home, his voice filled the worshipers with awe and aroused their devotion to their Maker."

"I remember reading in Yehoshua's book," a man standing next to our guide added, "that one Sabbath he made three mistakes in his reading of the Torah and it so angered the rabbi that he stood up and publicly announced that if the Chacham made one more error, he would have him removed from the pulpit.''

These personalities of the past were apparently not beyond the reach of the debunking criticism of their fellow Jews. But that kind of comment, it occurred to me, was yet another way of making contact with them, of humanizing them so that they were not simply characters in some myth but a part of the ongoing flow of life.

Bar-Tov, who in a way saw himself as guardian of the past, could not let the remark pass without comment.

''But it was Chacham Nissim who during the hard days of the War of Independence, when the bullets rained down from the city walls to the east, and even from the British side on the west, refused to abandon the neighborhood. He had to be carried away to save his life. Such was his attachment to this place.''

Bar-Tov paused; we looked silently at the eucalyptus tree.

Up a few steps, we came to another of the row of streets of Yemin Moshe. Two Bedouin women in long black dresses, one carrying a basket atop her head, crossed in front of us and headed down into the valley in the direction of Bethlehem.

''They tell a story,'' I heard Bar-Tov say to one of the men who walked near him, ''that once a pregnant Bedouin woman passed by here. Suddenly she felt the first pains of her labor. This was here, near the house where some Jews from Bosnia lived.'' He waved toward one of the houses on the level above us. ''So she put down the basket of figs she was carrying on her head, went into the Jew's yard, spread out a shawl and crouched down to give birth. And after she had delivered, she wrapped up the newborn in the folds of her dress and continued on her way to her village. Yehoshua repeats the story in his book.''

One good story deserved another. His partner turned now to Bar-Tov and repeated one about Ya'akov Kimchi, another of the people who lived in these houses. Kimchi was a tailor who specialized in making kaftans and robes, the kind that some of the rabbis of Jerusalem had taken as their uniform. ''He had no children, and it troubled him deeply.''

Every traditional Jew knew the biblical injunction to be fruitful and multiply. So sacred was this obligation that the rabbis had urged those who found they could not fulfill it with their present spouse to divorce and try with another. And so the elderly Kimchi and his aging wife approached the rabbinical court for a special dispensation. He wanted permission to take a second wife. Had not Abraham done this with Hagar?

The two people stood before the court as the old gentleman made his request. And then, as the court listened to their deliberations, the old woman spoke up: *"Señores,"* she asked, her Hebrew heavily freighted with the Spanish that was the language of her everyday speech, "rabbis, I am prepared to accept any judgment that you deem fit. And if my husband wishes a second wife, I shall serve them both. But I pray, allow me to ask, what is this haste, this rush to judgment that my husband has made? Is it not true that our mother Sarah bore a child when she was ninety?"

And so the rabbis sighed and turned toward Ya'akov Kimchi, and they say that a teardrop was slowly rolling down his cheek. And he turned to her and said, "Come, let us go home and you will make me some good lunch the way you always do."

"Exactly so does Ya'akov Yehoshua repeat this tale in his wonderful book," Bar-Tov said.

"Yes," said his partner, "I read it there, and I cannot but think of it here."

We had reached the far side of the neighborhood. Bar-Tov turned and began to speak.

"We have come now to the houses called Mish'kenot Shannanim. Today you see twenty-eight doorways on this, the longer of the two buildings."

"But the original building consisted of sixteen apartments of a room and a half each, with synagogues at both edges," someone broke in from the back.

Bar-Tov went on: "Yes, a Sephardic and an Ashkenazic one. The shorter building, higher up, had eight units, one of which was meant to house Montefiore on his visits to the Holy City, the last of which he made at the age of ninety-one in 1875. Each dwelling had a bit of ground in front where the residents could plant a few vegetables. This was far more space than they had in the crowded conditions inside the walled city." He pointed toward the slotted roof of the long building.

"Notice how an effort was made to make the place look like the walls of the Old City. These people, who were first to take the risk of coming out, needed to be reminded of the security they were used to inside the walls. Look carefully and you will see the inscription at the top of the building." He pointed to a place near the gable, and read aloud:

" 'Mish'kenot Shannanim, founded with the bequest of the lord Judah Touro from the holy community of New Orleans in America at the initiative of Sir Moses Montefiore.' "

"Not Newport?" one of the Americans whispered.

"New Orleans, Newport—it's all the same man," his friend answered, laughing. "The important thing is that the money came to Jerusalem."

Bar-Tov was describing the balcony's roof, which was made of galvanized sheet metal, supported by columns that served to channel water from the gutters into cisterns belowground. If the roofs of these houses, designed by the English architect William Smith, reminded one of the old city walls or a castle, the iron grilles on the windows were more suggestive of residences like those Smith and Montefiore were used to in London.

"The windmill which you see in the back was modeled on one in Kent, England," he explained. "It had a mechanism that was imported from England, the most advanced available at the time. It was to have provided employment and flour for the residents." He paused, and we all tried to take in the sight.

Today Mish'kenot Shannanim was a posh guesthouse for visiting artists. It took a lot of imagination to see these buildings as two solitary Jewish outposts on a windswept hill.

As if sensing the difficulty for the imagination, someone in the crowd declared: "For thirty years these houses stood isolated and alone, until Yemin Moshe began to grow."

We walked slowly along the path and stopped in front of the door marked *daled*—"four."

"But this neighborhood had another moment of glory, long after the original residents had left it. I refer, of course, to the days of the War of Independence, when the people of this neighborhood stood in the front lines, struggling for their survival, holding back the enemy who would otherwise have overrun the hills beyond."

Bar-Tov cleared his throat and continued: "One young man, the son of the neighborhood milkmaid, with Mauser in hand had become heart and soul of the resistance here. He stood alone atop a roof of one of the buildings of Yemin Moshe. He faced the Old City walls, from which the enemy was shooting, when suddenly he was struck by a bullet from behind.

"Who was behind him, my friends? Who stood at those buildings?"

He pointed to the large David Brothers building to the west, at the end of what was now Keren Ha-Yesod Street.

One of the Old Israelis answered quickly, almost as if his were a rehearsed refrain: "The British. Only the British could have been responsible."

"And they were very slow in permitting help to enter," Bar-Tov concluded. Then he turned and read the inscription on the monument in front of which we stood:

" 'Here in Mish'kenot Shannanim was born Avraham Michael Kirschenbaum—may the Lord revenge his blood—a son of one of the first families in this place. On the first day of Adar in 5708 [1948] he fell in the defense of Yemin Moshe in his solitary stand against the enemy in the War of Independence. He had lived but twenty-two springs.' "

The Protestant funeral across the valley Bar-Tov ignored, but the death of the young Jew Kirschenbaum was still recalled thirty-six years later.

We walked slowly and quietly past the rest of the buildings and out through heavy wooden doors, restored to resemble the original ones which opened from the wall that stood on the eastern edge of the neighborhood. There was a break in the traffic now on the road to Bethlehem as we crossed over it in the direction of Shamma, the next stop on our journey into the past.

Standing along the ridge overlooking the place where the Valley of Ben-Hinnom turns eastward, we were right above the new building of the Jerusalem Cinemathèque. But Bar-Tov disregarded it and the smaller building below which today had become the meeting place of the Jerusalem Chorus. He said nothing about the Arab boys playing ball on the floor of the valley. Instead, he began once again to describe something we could not see. And yet again it was these unseen objects from a Jewish memory toward which our attention turned and upon which our sentiments fixed themselves.

"Like Djoura el-Anav," Bar-Tov began, already staring down into the valley at what we took to be the place he was describing, "Shamma, or Sha'arey Zion, as it was sometimes called, was a neighborhood in which Jews, Moslems and Christians lived together. Founded in 1900 by Jews from Kurdistan and descendants of those from Spain—teachers, bakers, shoemakers and porters—it had about twice as large a Jewish population as Djoura el-Anav. In the beginning there were twenty-five families here. They called the settlement 'Sha'arey Zion' [the Gates of Zion] because it was so close to Mount Zion and to the Old City, but the Arabs who lived in the vicinity called the place 'Shamma.' "

"Why 'Shamma'?" someone asked.

"It's an Arabic corruption of the French for 'field of blood,' " one of the environmentalists explained.

"Yes, this was the place where the idol-worshiping Jews had thrown their children down to Moloch. So the field obviously became drenched in blood," a young man wearing a *kippah* added, and concluded, "We Jews later called it Emek Ha-Bachah [the Vale of Tears]."

"The life in the valley, below the road from Bethlehem and Hebron, was not easy": Bar-Tov was going on with his narrative. "In the winter, when the waters of El Rio Montefiore washed down upon them, the houses became damp and cold, while the earth around them became a heavy mud. And since the neighborhood lay in the ravine below Yemin Moshe and south of Djoura, waste and sewage from them naturally found their way into it. And my friends, as if this were not enough, thieves and robbers also discovered that what little there was of value here was easy to take, and they took it as often as possible."

"But that made the land cheap here," one of the old-timers explained, "and so people kept moving in—maybe eighty families or more lived here before the uprisings of '29."

"Maybe," the man in the khaki hat broke in again, "that was why Rabbi Mordecai Pereira, who lived here, was able to make a living by writing amulets and charms. When you have nothing else, you need your beliefs and your amulets."

This last comment seemed to arouse a few of the Orthodox near him, and they began to murmur. "Amulets and charms are not belief," I heard one of them say. But this was not the place or time for debates about the character of genuine faith; Bar-Tov continued his chronicle:

"There were two synagogues here, and they served as the real focus of community life."

"What else? Eighty Jews and only two synagogues?"

Even Bar-Tov smiled.

"Relations with the Arabs who lived at the southern edge of the neighborhood were quite good. Ya'akov Yehoshua writes that on the eve of Passover, Jews would send their Moslem neighbors *matzot*, while they would reciprocate on the night after the holy days' end with fresh loaves of bread, honey, cabbages and cheese."

"But then came the twenty-third of August, 1929," the man in the khaki hat said.

"Yes." Bar-Tov nodded.

"And from then on, the walls around the neigborhood began to crumble, while the divisions inside it quickly built up,'' the man in the hat continued. ''But even in my youth, after 1929, there was still a certain charm about the neighborhood,'' he concluded.

Bar-Tov picked up the story. He told us about the grove of trees that had stood there, and his childhood memories of them. How he used to escape from school every now and then and come to sit here.

''But by then, of course, most of the Jews had gone. Shamma was just too far from all the other Jewish neighborhoods in the new city.'' Now everything was gone.

We moved on toward the southeast. To our right, Bar-Tov pointed to the remains of a large aqueduct hewn out of the bedrock. Through here the water had flowed from the Hebron Hills by way of Solomon's Pools, near Bethlehem. The clefts in the stone were dry now, the pools little more than stagnant water. In today's Jerusalem, the water is pumped in from Rosh Ha-Ayin via the national pipeline. The cisterns and ancient aqueducts were now only relics of another time.

''What are those caves?'' one of the students asked, pointing to the large openings in the side of the hill.

Without stopping, Bar-Tov answered, ''That is the burial ground of the Karaites.''

The Karaites are a Jewish sect who refuse to accept the Talmudical-rabbinical traditions that characterize mainstream Judaism. Since their law forbids them to be counted in a census, no exact figures for their population were ever established. But of their numbers then of approximately seven thousand, there were today perhaps twenty-five families living in Jerusalem.

''It looks deserted.''

''The cemetery has fallen into decay and disuse; but in the last few months there have been some requests from leaders of the community for government assistance to clean it up.''

Weeks later, in search of the Karaites of Jerusalem, I found my way into the place in the Jewish Quarter of the Old City, opposite Nissan Bak's half-destroyed Tiferet Yerushalayim Synagogue and belowground, where the restored Karaite synagogue is located. To get inside, I knocked on the door of a member of the community who lived on the floor above. With pleasure she took me inside to a small museum which overlooked the floor of the place of worship.

''We are an ancient people,'' she assured me in perfect Hebrew, and pulled out a series of albums and facsimiles of documents which traced the history of her people to the dawn of Jewish civilization.

But what seemed to give her the greatest pleasure was the photos of Karaites from Poland.

"We too have an Eastern European past," she said, looking into my eyes.

I remembered reading reports of Karaite collaboration with the Germans. And as if she were reading my mind, she added, "—for which we suffered."

The synagogue, a large room with Oriental carpets hung around the walls, lacked many of the Jewish symbols I was used to seeing: the eternal light, the holy ark, the candelabrum.

"What they call a synagogue is no different from a mosque," an old Jew who lived around the corner had once told me as we stood on his rooftop overlooking the courtyard of the Karaites. Inside his apartment he had a giant painting of the Nissan Bak Synagogue in all its glory. "That was a true place of prayer."

Bar-Tov too seemed to disdain the Karaites; he did not linger for even a moment at the caves. As with the Protestants, theirs was not a past toward which he wished to direct our attention. He turned instead to the buildings on the ridge beyond the caves.

"In front of us are the houses named after Yosef Bey Navon, the initiator of the railway whose station is just over the hill behind us," he said, and stopped. He told us how Navon has persuaded a Swiss Christian banker named Frutiger to invest with him in these houses and in a variety of other projects. In the end, both of them lost a great deal of money. Navon ended up a broken man living in France; about Frutiger's destiny, Bar-Tov knew—or at least said —nothing.

There had been but two rows of buildings—about twenty-four houses in all—in which lived no more than ten Jewish families. In 1887, when the neighborhood was founded, it was just too far from the city to attract a large Jewish population. Many of the original prospective tenants forfeited their down payments and never moved in. And yet, ironically, because the place had been relatively devoid of Jews, here, unlike the case in Djoura el-Anav and Shamma, the houses had survived the fighting during the '48 war. In fact, one of the original settlers who came back after 1967 found his house and former Arab neighbors who greeted him with graciousness.

"So while the neighborhood was too far from the city to draw many Jews, if you sit here and look about, you will see how beautiful the place is and maybe understand why Navon and his partners believed that it might succeed in attracting those who still lived in the cramped quarters within the walls.''

The view was truly breathtaking. On the eastern horizon were the villages of Abu Dis and el-Azariya, what the Christians called Bethany, and beyond them the barren hills of the Judean Wilderness. On a clear day, a careful eye could make out the pale blue of the Dead Sea and the reddish mountains of Edom and Moab, in today's Jordan. Below, at the rim of what was once the City of David, the site of the original Jerusalem which King David had conquered and taken from the Jebusites, lay the village of Silwan. Its small square houses hugged the side of the mountain on the other side of the Valley of Jehoshaphat. Underneath some of them we could see the caves of the ancient necropolis. And to the north were the walls of the Old City, the Temple Mount, the silver dome of al-Aqsa and the golden Dome of the Rock. In the late afternoon, the sound of the muezzin calling worshipers to prayer could already be heard over the loudspeakers in the minarets. A brisk wind blew up from the desert and carried the sound away. I zipped up my sweater.

It was late; shadows already covered Mount Zion, which rose across the valley. In the waning light, three Arab boys were digging along the backside of the hill. ''An illegal archeological excavation,'' one of the Haganat Ha-Teva women called it, and smiled. ''They are hoping to find some ancient coin or shard which they will be able to sell to tourists.''

''And will they?'' I asked.

''It's not impossible,'' she replied. ''The past is very close to the surface here.''

CHAPTER
·5·

THE CITY OF DAVID

And David took the stronghold of Zion: which is the City of David.

II SAMUEL 5:7

I stood on a hill overlooking the Kidron Valley. For several hours I had shared memories, both personal and acquired, with the others on the tour, and now I lingered after everyone else had left, trying still to make my way into the provinces of the past. Silently, I gazed at the distant walls and domes, growing golden in the waning sun. For a few moments, I lost track of time and wandered at the crossroads of imagination and memory.

To my right, in the east, rose the Wilderness of Judea, into which the prophet Jeremiah had fled when the people of Jerusalem became too much for him. Behind me, to the south, was the road of the Patriarchs upon which Abraham, forefather of all those who now filled this land, had marched as he led his son Isaac here to Moriah, which rose majestically before my eyes. Across the valley from where I stood were the nearly three-thousand-year-old remains of the City of David, the ancient Jerusalem, and beyond them stood the two-thousand-year-old walls of the Temple Mount. A few of the steps upon which Jews had ascended to this holiest spot could still be seen. I had trodden upon them, in the footsteps of my ancestors, trying to imagine myself walking with the psalmist who had composed his many songs of ascent with these steps in mind. Below and to the west lay Gehenna, the infamous Valley of Ben-Hinnom, where in a hellish act of perverse worship, the followers of Moloch had thrown their children down in sacrifice. Beside me, not far from the remains of the ancient aqueduct, a young Arab shepherd tended his small flock which nibbled on the wild wheat and underbrush that grew near the caves in which the Karaites had once buried their dead. The panorama of the past stretched out over the present.

Once again a dry afternoon wind began to blow out of the desert. As I turned to leave, I noticed that I was not in fact alone. One of the older women who had been on my tour had, like me, stayed behind when the others had departed. She was leaning against a large flat stone on which the Karaites had rested their dead before entombment in the caves. A shifting breeze blew her fine gray hair into her eyes. She grabbed at it quickly, and then, as I moved in her direction, turned suddenly, looking straight into my eyes. Something in her expression aroused in me an unexpected urge to explain my lingering.

"I was thinking about all those who passed here before us and wondering if it is really possible to look at these places without recalling the past."

She nodded; a knowing smile lit up her face. "There are all sorts of attachments here. We Jews"—she took a deep, yawnlike breath that seemed almost a sigh—"cannot ignore the past." And then, after a moment's pause, she continued: "There is a story about two men who had been traveling together for a long time until they came to a crossroads. As they approached it, they saw that the signpost there had been overturned and now lay on its side.

" 'We are lost completely,' said the one. 'Without the signpost in its proper position, how shall we ever know where we are going?'

" 'But you have forgotten, my friend,' said the other, 'that as long as we know where we have been, we can correctly position the signpost so that we shall also know where we are going.' "

The woman smiled and caught at a flyaway strand of hair that the wind rising up from the valley beneath us was again blowing into her eyes.

"If you recall well the Jerusalem of yesterday, you will certainly better understand what you see about you and, more important, find your way to the Jerusalem of the End of Days.''

''And how would you suggest one go about doing that?'' I asked.

''Well, I suppose this afternoon's walk was a good start. Don't you think so?''

''Yes, but are there special places to go?''

''Go over there''—she pointed to the other side of the valley—''to the City of David. See where it all began. There you will see the depth of our attachments.''

''There are Arabs living there too,'' I said.

''Yes, I suppose you will see their ties as well. But remember, they came after us. They settled on top of our graves—sometimes even inside them, in the caves. And if you ask them where they are from, they won't tell you their fathers came from across the Jordan or down from the north, to find work or to escape disease. You see, they have chosen to forget the past.''

''But they know they have been here for generations.''

''Yes, but we know how to go much further back in our memory and in our attachments. But don't believe me; go see for yourself.''

And where is the City of David? On a hill below the Temple Mount, surrounded by the Valley of Jehoshaphat to the east, the Valley of Ben-Hinnom to the south and the Tyropoeon (or what some call simply ''The Valley'') to the west, archeologists have found the remains of an ancient city. In Egyptian texts from the nineteenth century B.C.E., the place is called ''Rushlamem.'' In the days of Abraham, when it was ruled by Melchizedek, priest of the God Most High, it was called ''Shalem.'' At the time the Israelites conquered the Promised Land under Joshua, the city was in the hands of an Amorite king, head of a coalition of mountain and plains rulers. Seemingly impregnable, it therefore remained independent and outside the boundaries of any of the conquering tribes of Israel.

At the time of David, the new Israelite king who had been ruling from Hebron, in the south, for seven and a half years, Shalem was controlled by the Jebusites. This Jebu-Shalem remained a fortified city, beyond the abilities of anyone—so its inhabitants believed—to take it. But David of Bethlehem, of the tribe of Judah, head of a new dynasty and coming out of a destructive and divisive war with the heirs of the first Israelite king, Saul, of the tribe of Benjamin, was determined to capture this place some called ''the stronghold of Zion'' and make it his new capital: Jerusalem. Then, in the words of the psalmist: "From out of Zion would come Torah [the law], and the word of God from Jerusalem."

To many scholars trying to decipher the past, the choice of Jerusalem was a logical one. Situated on the lowest part of the Judean mountains, it was naturally fortified by the deep valleys around it and the other mountains beyond. It marked the crossroads between the Road to the Sea ("Derekh Ha-Yam," the Hebrews called it) and the King's Highway (Derekh Ha-Melekh), which ran along the watershed. To pass between the two, traders and travelers had to come through Jerusalem, and so anyone who held this city in the mountains between the desert and the sea held power far beyond that of any local chieftain. Besides, being so close to the desert, down to which during times of emergency one could easily flee (as David himself had done during the days of his flight from the wrath of Saul), the city gave its inhabitants—and especially its leaders—an additional sense of security. Finally, Shalem was near one of the richest sources of water in the mountains, the Gihon Spring. Although erratic at times (a source of inspiration to the spiritually inclined who saw the hand of Heaven in its ebb and flow), the Gihon could bubble up three hundred gallons of water on a good day, enough to support a relatively large settlement.

For David, striving to unite the kingdom under his rule, there was one additional advantage to Jerusalem—a political one. Lying between the lands of Judah and Benjamin, the main contenders for the kingship, it remained outside the heritage of either. The new ruler did not risk angering any of his subjects or showing favoritism by making this city his capital. On the contrary, this act of daring conquest of the hitherto invulnerable city in their midst undeniably demonstrated, in the words of the Scriptures, that "the God, the Lord of Hosts, was with him."

And thus, although the Jebusites believed he neither could nor would take their bastion on the hill, David took it, enlarged it and, as reported in the Second Book of Samuel, "dwelt in the stronghold and called it the City of David."

For the Jews, exiled and wandering for two millennia but in their collective memory never forgetting Jerusalem, the City of David to whose remains they now come is more than a place; it is the epicenter of their right to return, and the archeologist who uncovers in it signs of their past is the prime agent of their claim. In Jerusalem, thus, archeology—at least for the Jews—is much more than a science : it is a search for roots, the quest after title. Their digging is the way they correctly position the signposts of history, and especially Jewish history.

Ask an Israeli archeologist to explain a site and he will frequently point out all the Jewish-oriented stones and structures first, and then in relation to them everything else is put into place. Stones are "First Temple Period" or "Second Temple Period"; towers are Hasmonean or Israelite. And while the Byzantines, Umayyads, Abbasids, Crusaders, Mamelukes, Ottomans and others are here, they are often marginal to his interest or that of his major audience, which remains directed toward Jewish national roots.

By law, if in today's Jerusalem anyone discovers an archeological relic of yesterday's city in the course of tomorrow's construction, such building must be stopped and the site examined by experts. If the find is significant, uncovering some important link to the past, it must be preserved.

But archeologists do more than unearth the past; they also lead the public through it. In both cases, however, they are in a sense doing the same thing : making the invisible apparent. Guided tours by the diggers, slide shows, lectures that reveal the finds in all their depth are among the most popular cultural events in the city. Where else would an organization calling itself Archeological Seminars turn out to be a touring organization, and where else but in Jewish Jerusalem could it have any hope of attracting anyone other than a small group of specialists ?

There are even those who come to Jerusalem in order to participate, if only for a few days or hours, in an excavation. Sifting through dirt on a rocky and hot hillside, they physically act out the drama of painstakingly uncovering the past and feel—in the words of one woman who did it—"as if I were visiting a world that for a millennium or more silently awaited my arrival."

Those who do not dig go to witness the results. For many of them, these infatuations with and visits to the subterranean city and the layers of life it reveals are also a way to establish ties to the place which their antecedents once called home. Under all of Jerusalem, covered by the detritus of history, waiting to be discovered, lies the heritage of an Israelite past. Beneath the refurbished walkway is a Byzantine street under which lies a Crusader archway which itself is atop a Roman roadway. And below the Roman road is the top of a Herodian wall from the Second Temple Period which itself is built onto a Hasmonean tower that is linked to an Israelite wall leading to the City of David which rests upon the bedrock. To the seeker of ties, these stones speak eloquently and with finality : regardless of the many generations of others who also made a life here, we were here first ; the place is ours.

Although the City of David had been explored by at least eight archeological expeditions—the two most famous being Charles Warren's in the late nineteenth century and Kathleen Kenyon's in the mid-twentieth—those were not enough for the Jews, whose need to know sprang from far deeper cultural wells than those of the others who preceded them. Already in the nineteenth century they had prepared the grounds for the quest by buying a good part of the hill from the locals (most of the money came from the Rothschilds). That purchase made possible what has gone on for the last eight years, during which Yigal Shiloh, an archeologist from the Hebrew University, led a team of people who picked over a part of a hill once called the Ophel, sifted its earth, cleared its tunnels and classified its stones.

When Shiloh began his excavation, he started digging along a hill in which his predecessor Kathleen Kenyon had excavated. In an area that came to be identified arbitrarily as ''Area G,'' Kenyon reported she had come upon some bones which were apparently part of a medieval cemetery. These she had removed, since they were of no significance to her archeological searches nor of any importance to the Jordanians, who then held the hill into which she dug. When he continued her work in the City of David, Shiloh wanted to uncover not only the area Kenyon had excavated but also its continuation farther down the slope.

But if the bones were of no significance to the Protestant Britisher Kenyon or to the Moslem Jordanians—or, in fact, to the scientist Shiloh—they were of primary importance to the *charedim*, the black-coated Orthodox Jews who had no interest in or need to know about the stones of the City of David but who saw themselves as guardians of the graves of their forebears who, awaiting the day of resurrection, lay beneath the soil of this hill.

Although the excavations touch both those who carried them out and many who come to gaze deeply at the results, giving them a sense of attachment to place and heritage, the search for the City of David was by no means a quest by the pious for additional holy sites. For them, those in the black hats and coats and those who live within the pages of the sacred texts, the power to find the place of the sacred rests not with archeologists but with the holy tradition. For them, no need exists to find the royal Tomb of the House of David and with it title to the land. The citations of Jerusalem in

Scripture and liturgy and the accepted traditions are all the deed the pious need.

As if to distinguish themselves from those who come to look at excavations in order to see into their heritage, the pious *close* their eyes when they pray at *their* holy places. For them, the site—something more than stone and soil—is seen not by the eyes alone, but in the mind and heart. The archeologist might call their Jerusalem mythic; they call his a sacrilege, as they call his archeology idolatrous.

And here the conflict over competing attachments to Jerusalem's past exploded. To the archeologists the bones hindered the search for stones, for deeper cultural roots. They aimed to enlarge their knowledge of the city's past. But to the *charedim*, more important than establishing the site of David's palace, uncovering the tombs of the kings of Judah or finding Bathsheba's bathtub was the requirement of safeguarding the sanctity of the eternal rest of Jews who came to this hill to await their resurrection in the footsteps of the Messiah. The past they protected was one they believed assured them a place in the world to come.

For those fired only by faith or the people who make their lives in the four cubits of the tradition, then, there is no need for archeology. To find the royal tomb they need go no farther than the traditional Tomb of David, which they fully believe sits atop Mount Zion. There they go to pray over a velvet catafalque housed in an arched room that sits above a deep cave inside which they trust lie the remains of the great king and his family. They need not see them; the *kabbalah* that they exist, a handed-down tradition, is sufficient. Protected by taboos which warn those who would dare descend and disturb the resting place of the holy that they risk the wrath of God and His defenders, this site has until now not been open for digs. To the people who pray here there is no need to excavate; they are not impressed by the findings of scientific archeology. In fact, they repudiate its right to determine the site of the sacred. That can be done only by those who feel the awe of the numinous.

For generations, all that remained standing of the Holy Temple was a portion of its courtyard's outer Western Wall—Ha-Kotel Ha-Ma'aravi. This became for the Jews the place of their greatest pieties, the spot where they mourned for Jerusalem and prayed to the God who once made this His abode. When archeologists excavated the continuation of the Kotel and later the adjoining southern wall of the Temple Mount, although a few *charedim* rushed down to pray here, they were outnumbered by the many others who chose *not* to extend the place of prayers to these sites, which are in fact no less connected to the Holy Temple than the sacred piece of the Western Wall where the pious still pray. And likewise, there are no worshipers along the unearthed steps to the Holy Temple. No rabbis hold forth here; no priestly blessings are offered where the psalmist sang his song of ascent. In these unearthed places, the priests are archeologists, their followers seekers of another sort. So those who find their birthright in traditions have their sacred sites, and those who find theirs in archeological discoveries have theirs.

But if the traditionalists find their sense of belonging in prayers and custom, how do those who find their links through archeology celebrate attachments at the digs? To find out, I visited and revisited the uncovered sites throughout Jerusalem, observing the observers. The challenge of the woman on the hill that I go see for myself rang in my ears. I looked for the way people "positioned the signposts."

First, and above all else, I witnessed the almost ritualized silent gaze of fascination and awe. To look upon the uncovered past is for many an act of singular importance and moment. For hours, for example, I found myself with others standing and staring at the seam in the city walls where the ancient Herodian stones meet those of a later era. Or I have watched as people approach with awe the remaining shred of a lintel through which once, two thousand years before, the Temple Mount was entered.

The vision must go beyond the material. The archeological witness must be able to see past the relic remains to their antecedent majesty or their ineluctable reality. A broken arch that juts out from the Western Wall cannot be seen just for what it is now, a ruin. Instead, with the aid of drawings and descriptions offered by the guide, the visitor must be able to see a grand stairway that once rose over it.

In the new archeological park inside the City of David is a room in which lie the charred remains of the destruction suffered during the Babylonian conquest in 586 B.C.E. "Imagine the agony here," the visitor is told as he stares at the ashes and works his imagination.

Not far away, beneath a house in the Jewish Quarter, are Israelite and Babylonian arrowheads found at the foot of an Israelite tower, remains of the fateful battle for the city after which would begin the first period of exile. "You can see why they fought here," the guide suggests as the visitor looks at the map explaining the strategic importance of the neatly piled stones in the remaining rampart. Around the corner stand the uncovered remains of a burnt house from the period of the Roman conquest of the city in 70 C.E. The identity of its inhabitants is known from inscriptions found inside the house and from textual references in the Talmud. Even the date of the fire, a month after the Temple's fall, is known. The broken pots and the arm of a Jew who died defending his home bear silent witness to the past, while the visitor gives voice to his feelings of attachment: "I can almost smell the fire and hear the sounds of the battle."

As if aware that they must learn how to look, the visitors are filled with questions, all of which try to give them a picture whose dimensions include time. How was it? What happened? Where could they hide? Each visit arouses curiosity whose satisfaction leads to the stores of collective memory. "I have got to read the Bible" and "I really want to learn more about what happened here" are phrases heard again and again. To learn is to make a pact with history, never to forget thee, O Jerusalem.

Seeing, however deeply, into the past is not enough. The visitor must be able to touch or at least be touched by what he sees. The body plays a large part here. People walk along old city walls, into ancient rooms, atop worn two-thousand-year-old paving stones, through restored shafts. There is even a tour through an ancient water tunnel dug in the time of Hezekiah, the last king of Judah, in which the visitors, candles in hand and soaked up to the waist in spring water, are asked to imagine the experience of those who originally cut through the stone and their joy at completing the task which would bring the water from the Gihon Spring to a pool inside the walls of the city. Tracing the tunnel with his feet and a candle, the visitor brings life to the wellsprings of the City of David. Walking where the ancients walked means becoming more than visitors; it means following in their footsteps and becoming their heirs. And that in turn means experiencing a connection not otherwise felt.

"People think," says archeologist Meir Ben-Dov, taking a group through the City of David, "that human nature was very different centuries ago or that the people then were not as smart as we are today; but when you look closely at the life they led, you discover they were not less intelligent than we and not so greatly different from us today."

We are more than heirs of the ancients; we are the ancients brought back to life.

And lest any visitor have difficulty imagining the contact, he or she is exposed to the personal touches that bring the archeological find into life. Following along the length of the Western Wall, the visitor is shown a barely legible inscription carved by an ancient pilgrim, who celebrates his arrival from some distant venue at the "place of trumpeting."

"Imagine," the guide says, "his joy at arriving at the Holy Temple in time to hear the blowing of the *shofar.*"

And through imagination, the joy becomes the visitor's own: "How exciting!" "Incredible!" "Imagine that!"

Moving beyond the inscription, visitors are asked to marvel at the huge size of the stones which Herod had hewn and carried to the Temple Mount. With great precision, the archeologists and their guides explain how each stone was moved, rolled on logs and laboriously brought from the quarry to the place of their piling. And if these explanations are insufficient, visitors need not worry: there is a plan to have one stone set up in a way that would allow those coming here in the future to see a demonstration of the method. Some would even be able to push the heavy stone themselves, to feel what the experience was like.

In many of the rooms that have been unearthed, accurate reconstructions have been added and visitors are asked to imagine themselves living here, using the hard stone benches for seats or lying on them as on beds. "Look," I have heard people say, "they decorated their walls too." Or "You know, I could live here too." And the unspoken, yet understood refrain to all such comments is "We are not very different from those who came here before us."

Nor is the visitor alone in these feelings. The archeologist, if he is to communicate his sense of vocation, must testify to these feelings. Lecturing before a packed house at the Rockefeller Museum about his work in the City of David, Yigal Shiloh says, "We were not able to find the bathtub of Bathsheba or the palace of the king, but we know more or less where they were. But we have made contact with the past in ways that are most striking. We encountered, for example, in a chamber filled with *bullae*, or seals, a kind of administrative archive, in which we found, among others, a seal bearing the name of Gemaryahu Ben-Shafan, who is mentioned several times in the Bible as a scribe at the court of Jehoiakim, king of Judah. You see, people left their names on the wall, so to speak, just as we do today."

Repeating the story of this find, Meir Ben-Dov evocatively adds, "Imagine, you find the seal of someone whom you have read about in the Bible. It gives you a feeling that cannot be described, a kind of trust in the past and connection to it.''

Reporting on his finds in the City of David, Yigal Shiloh notes that cult objects and fertility figures were found in abundance in this city whose only legitimate God was supposed to be the one who had taken the people of Israel out of Egypt and who had given them the law at Sinai. The prophets had railed against the people for abandoning this God in favor of idols of stone and wood. And here, in the archeologist's hand and before his eyes, is evidence for the righteousness of the prophets' cause.

To the modern Orthodox, those associating themselves both with the rational science out of which archeology emerges and with faith in whose domain archeology is insignificant, finds such as these are of the greatest significance, for not only do they give the sacred texts a real location in history—something the modern and rational side of these Jews needs—but they also provide supports for faith. In the discovery of the false gods lies a legitimation for the wrath of the prophets. And there is empathy too. Just as today the people fail to live up to the high standards demanded by the religion, so was it yesterday.

So the pious, the *charedim*, close their eyes to the digs and open themselves only to their own sources of faith. The modern Orthodox merge their faith with the evidence of the digs. And all the other Jews look to the excavations to make their claims and experience a sense of belonging.

But what about the local Arabs of Silwan, the village which has grown atop the debris that covers the City of David? To the archeologists and their followers who hunger to dig beneath their homes, they have become obstacles. But the local Arabs care not for the Jewish bones nor about their underground stones. Not drawn by any of the needs that bring the Jews to this hill, these Arabs seek rather to live out their lives without disturbing the patterns of existence which they have established over the last few hundred years. To some the archeological park is a nuisance, bringing buses and tourists trampling through their neighborhood. To others it represents an opportunity, and a few local residents have set up kiosks in their backyards selling cold drinks, postcards, candles for the water tunnel or ''antique coins.''

But perhaps nothing represents more clearly the difference between the Jewish attachments to this place and those of the local Arabs than the story of what happened when the archeologists, seeking to extend the area of their excavations, came to a home-owner whose house abutted a section of the hill being dug.

After months of negotiations with the archeologists, the owner at last agreed to allow them to dig in a corner of his property. But there were certain conditions. He would be paid a rental fee throughout the period of the dig. And when the dig was complete and the archeologists had uncovered all they wanted, they would rebury everything and return his backyard to its former condition. Having found their underground home of some unimaginable past, the Jews had to leave and give him back the home he and his forebears had lived in for generations.

And that is just what happened. The archeologists dug, discovered the structures of a small house from the City of David and a bit of its courtyard, took photos, made notes and then with reluctance covered everything once again. And that was that.

For there was nothing the Arab wanted from this place but to be let alone. He had played here as a child, and he wanted his son and grandson to play here as children. His favorite spot in all Jerusalem was here: his home. He wanted it undisturbed. Let the Jews find their attachments elsewhere. And if it happened that they and he held attachments for the same spot, his were on top. And to him, these were the only ones that counted.

I wandered back up the hill from the houses of Silwan to Area G and the ancient tower upon which the archeologists believed David's palace might once have rested. As it had been from my vantage point on the other side of the valley, the panorama of the past was everywhere. For generations my antecedents had prayed and hoped for the rebuilding of Jerusalem, the raising up and repositioning of its stones. But as I gazed now at the stones and ashes of David's capital, I realized that a Jew need not await the rebuilt city to experience a sense of triumph and resurrection; he could see in the discovery of its ancient ruins testimony to a glorious past. Uncovered remains could likewise arouse feelings of revival and transcendence: as the stones and ramparts had not been wiped from memory, so too the attachments of my people to the place were still intact. But they required the wiping away of what had been built up atop them in the meantime. That part had been left out in the story of the repositioning of the signpost.

As I walked away from the remains of the City of David, behind me walked two high school teachers from New Jersey who had been with me on this archeological tour. They were marveling at what they had seen.

"So what do you think?" I overheard one ask the other, as we neared the stairway that led away from the site.

"I'll tell you," answered the other, stopping for a moment to take a last look at the pile of stones so filled with meaning and history. "I'd love to see more. I'm dying to find out what's under the rest of the hill. I'd love to find the kings' tombs."

"Yeah," the other answered, "but Rothschild didn't buy the rest of the land, so we can't dig—that's what the archeologists say."

"But don't you think we have a claim anyway?"

"I guess. I guess the only claim we have for being here at all is that we are Jews."

"Well, when you think about it, isn't that enough?"

CHAPTER
·6·

HOLDING ON TO THE INHERITANCE

We have neither taken any other man's land,
nor do we hold dominion over other people's
territory, but only over the inheritance of our
fathers. On the contrary, for a certain time it
was unjustly held by our enemies; but we,
seizing the opportunity, hold fast the
inheritance of our fathers.

I MACCABEES 15:33–34

"The only claim we have for being here is that we are Jews." Several days later while I was driving along the highway between Tel Aviv and Jerusalem, the subject came up again. I pressed down on the accelerator and my little red Renault sped toward the Bet Shemesh junction. If I failed to build up momentum here, at the gate of the valley, the place the Jews called Sha'ar Ha-Gai and the Arabs, Bab el-Wad, where the road begins a steep ascent as it moves out of the flat coastal plain and into the terraced hills of Judea, the trip to Jerusalem would take quite a bit longer. Inexperienced drivers often discovered that a slow start here led inexorably to a belated arrival in the city at the top.

"Do you think the only claim we have on Jerusalem derives from our being Jews?" I asked.

The question was addressed to Menashe Har-El, the man sitting next to me. He was a biblical geographer. An energetic man with coal-black hair and eyes to match, he looked and acted much younger than his sixty-eight years. In the nineteenth century his family had come here from Bukhara, in Central Asia, returning, as his father and other Jews like him had believed, to the land of their forebears, closing at last the long chapter of Jewish exile and wandering. Coming as a very young boy, Menashe had grown up in the land of the Bible, in Jerusalem's Bukharan quarter, and held a deep love for it.

The Bukharan quarter was a neighborhood of wide avenues and once-stately homes. At one time, the Bukharans had been among the richest of Jerusalem's Jews. While many of them kept their homes in Central Asia, quite a few also built second homes in the Holy City, which they visited and to which they sometimes retired or sent their relatives to live. Throughout the neighborhood, which had fallen into disrepair after the Bukharan Jews lost their fortunes in the Russian Revolution, there were reminders of its former glory. Although now a school, a neo-Renaissance-style thirty-room, fifty-five-meter-long mansion—Ha-Ar'mon, or The Palace, it was called—built by one Elisha Yehudayoff still towered over its surroundings.

Yehudayoff had been extraordinarily proud of his home and had even prepared a special room in it for the Messiah, who, after resurrecting the dead, he was certain would be pleased to stop in to rest in this, the finest house in the neighborhood. Above the main staircase on the upper floor, Yehudayoff had inscribed a plaque with the psalmist's ageless promise: "IF I FORGET THEE, O JERUSALEM, LET MY RIGHT HAND FORGET ITS CUNNING."

On another building, a Bukharan Jew inscribed the stone sills of eighteen windows with the announcement

> I, HAJI YECHEZ'KEL—SON OF YA'AKOV HALEVI, MAY THE LORD PRESERVE HIM—A SERVANT OF THE LORD, MAY HIS NAME BE BLESSED, BUILT THESE HOMES AND THIS YESHIVA AND HAVE GIVEN THEM AS A TRUST TO MY FATHER AND MY CHILDREN, THAT THEY MAY ADMINISTER THEM AS THE CIRCUMSTANCES REQUIRE BUT NEVER SELL, PLEDGE OR MORTGAGE THEM UNTIL THE REDEEMER COMES, AND NAME THE BUILDING AFTER ME, THE YECHEZ'KEL BUILDING.

This was the Bukharan quarter in which Menashe Har-El had grown up.

For the mountains, and especially those of Judea, Menashe had a special feeling. Changing his family name from Babayoff to the Hebrew Har-El, meaning "mountain of God," he had also named each of this three children after a mountain: the boys were Sinai (where Moses had molded the people) and Nevo (where Moses had gone to die), and the daughter was Masada. And when at last he moved from Jerusalem, he chose to make his home on the outskirts of the city in Motza, a small village in the Judean mountains. In these hills, he believed, his people, the ancient Israelites, had found their first home in the Promised Land.

During his life thus far, Har-El had done a variety of things. Following in the footsteps of the biblical Joshua, he had scouted the land, becoming a land surveyor and field man. Before the establishment of the state he worked for the Haganah, and later for the Israel Defense Forces. Later, he assisted in the often-risky repatriation of Jewish refugees from Arab lands, a process that was part of the population exchanges which took place after 1948. Working undercover in some of the neighboring countries, he helped Jews escape from Syria, among other places. His Arabic was fluent. In time, he became a geographer and a professor at Tel Aviv University.

More than anything else, Har-El loved this land, and the Scriptures which he considered the key to comprehending his people's claim to it. He had written a number of books that traced the connection between the written word and the land, including his famous *This Is Jerusalem*. Now, at Tel Aviv University, he was teaching his last semester before retirement.

Often, during our drives back and forth to Tel Aviv, where I was also teaching, he would tell me something about the territory through which we passed. Once, he had reviewed for me the battles during the siege of Jerusalem in the days of the War of Independence. The road upon which we traveled was still strewn with rusting and bloodstained half-tracks and trucks in which Jews fighting to open the road to Jerusalem had been wounded or died. These vehicles, which the Israelis had transformed into memorials to those who had fallen in that combat, were for him unimpeachable evidence of the Jewish attachment to this land.

Always implied, in whatever Har-El said, was the assertion that the Jew was inalienably bonded to the land passing before our eyes.

And so when I asked him my question now, I knew pretty much what he would answer.

"What better claim could there be?" he answered with a question. "How many other people have a deed to their land as undeniable as the Bible?"

Although he was attached to the words of Scripture, by no stretch of the imagination could Har-El be considered an Orthodox Jew. For him, the Bible was not a code of law, as the rabbis argued, or a series of mystical commands, as the pious claimed. Nor was it even simply a great literary document, as some modern critics believed. It was very simply the epic and poetry of his people's past, the testament of its identity and its ultimate title to the land. To Har-El, Scripture was the basic text of Zionism.

Har-El quoted the texts with such ease that at times it seemed to me as if the words he repeated were his own. These words he saw reflected everywhere. The road along the mountain ridges upon which we drove was the image of Isaiah's prophecy: "And I shall make My mountains a way, and My highways shall be raised on high." And when asked to account for the settlement in the hills, he quoted Ezekiel: "And upon the mountains of Israel shall their fold be."

"From the mountains came our sense of strength," he said to me many times. "The Patriarchs, Abraham, Isaac and Jacob, refer always to El- Shaddai. Do you know what that means?"

"*Shaddai*?"

"Yes."

"Is that *shaddai* as in *shaddaim* [breasts]?"

"Precisely. So El-Shaddai is the God of the places shaped like breasts from which nourishment comes, from where there were springs of life-giving water and where some farming could be done along the terraces. El-Shaddai is the God of the Hills.

"You remember what the Aramaeans said when they had to explain their defeat by the Israelites: 'Their God is a God of the hills; therefore they were stronger than we.'

"All those terraces you see, they were cut and set in place by our forefathers, the Israelites who had sown grain, planted vineyards and grown olive trees along the ridges where they had made their settlements. We were the first to practice terrace agriculture in these mountains. We learned how to let the water from the upper terraces irrigate the lower ones. We made the hills bloom and give forth life. Study the Scriptures and look at the land—they leave no doubt where we come from or where we belong." To Har-El, the

Israelites, our antecedents, had completed the work of creation here. That gave them title to the land. And we, their children, inherited that title.

When once we passed some sheep grazing along the side of a mountain and near them saw a shepherd from a nearby Arab village who I suggested represented the original inhabitants of the land, Har-El objected that long before the fellahin came here, the Israelites brought their flocks to the hills. Why else did Ezekiel use the imagery of flocks upon the mountains in his prophecy to the people? And was David not a shepherd whose flocks wandered over the mountains of Judea?

"We came from Europe," I objected. "Didn't you come from Central Asia?"

"We *returned* from Europe," he corrected me. "We started out here." The Jews, he continued, had to remember who they were. The land and the Scriptures would reawaken in us a memory long suppressed by generations of exile. Thus would primeval attachments at last be aroused.

As if to give him an opportunity to arouse such attachments, I turned to the scenery around us. We were passing near the Valley of Ayalon, past Sha'ar Ha-Gai, and I thought of the lines from the Book of Joshua associated with the valley. The night before, I had helped my son Uriel review the tenth chapter for a test in school, and so the verses were still fresh in my memory. Why, I asked, did Joshua utter his famous words "Sun, stand thou still in Givon; and thou, Moon, in the Valley of Ayalon"?

"If you are ready to listen," Har-El began, "I shall tell you." That was his way of saying that if I was prepared to leave behind the asphalt highway and forget about the new cottages of the villages we passed and pay attention to another time which fell along the lie of the land, I might understand and see something otherwise invisible.

"I'm ready," I said.

He began with the first line of the chapter: "Now it came to pass, when Adoni-zedek, king of Jerusalem, heard how Joshua had taken Ai and had utterly destroyed it; as he had done to Jericho and her king, so he had done to Ai and her king; and how the inhabitants of Givon had made peace with Israel and were among them; that they feared greatly because Givon was a great city, like one of the royal cities, greater than Ai, and all its men were mighty ..." Har-El's deep voice gave life to this epic. "Wherefore Adoni-zedek, king of Jerusalem, sent unto Hoham, king of Hebron; Piram, king of

Yar'mut; Yafia, king of Lachish, and D'vir, king of Eglon, saying: 'Come up to me and help me, and let us smite Givon, for it has made peace with Joshua and with the children of Israel ...' "

Outside the car's window were the mountains and fields where all that the text described had taken place. Under the effect of Har-El's description, peppered as it was with Scriptural quotation, the present melted away under the increasing immediacy of the past, and though I kept my eyes on the road, I found myself visualizing that earlier time. It was a process that became increasingly easy with practice. One had only to alter the focus of one's consciousness from the visible to the imagined. The more one knew about the past, the easier it was to imagine and the more visible it became. And because this kind of imagination revealed Jerusalem to the inquiring eye, there was an added incentive to learn history and share in the collective memory.

"And the men of Givon sent unto Joshua to the camp at Gilgal, saying: 'Slack not your hands from your servants; come up to us quickly, and save us, and help us, for all the kings of the Amorites that dwell in the hill country are gathered together against us.' " The battle came to life, with Joshua pursuing the kings into the setting sun.

"Joshua needed the sun to stop so that he would not be blinded in his pursuit of the kings, who had run toward Beit Horon." As we drove in the same direction, I could immediately comprehend the point of Joshua's prayer for the sun to stand still. Reconstructing the battle as we drove, Har-El showed me precisely where the sun had had to be and where each army must have stood, calculating the precise hour of the attack. "At no other time would the stopping of the sun have been crucial to Joshua."

Although I could not see the soldiers, and the remains of Givon were half-destroyed by time, the past had a sudden immediacy here that was striking and undeniable.

"It's really incredible how you can see these past events here," I said, trying simply to show my appreciation.

Perhaps my reaction struck him as fulsome, or maybe he just wanted to make a point, but he shot back with impatience and mild contempt in his voice, somewhat offset by his paternal choice of words; it reminded me of Tavio's reaction on the first night of our guard duty:

"My friend, you look at the land, and that is good. I am happy you are interested; I wish my students were as curious and appreciative. But your remark reflects your naïveté, your distance from the reality of your own history. How could you for a moment believe that you could see anything here without at the same time witnessing the past? And not just any past, but ours—the Jewish past? Maybe other tourists look at these places and they see a nice hill, or a pile of stones, a wall, a broken cistern, a spring, but a Jew looks at these places and he sees Abraham, Isaac, Jacob, the prophets, kings, exile and redemption—the whole of Jewish history and peoplehood. That is what attracts him.''

To be sure, Har-El was not just a local booster. He knew the sites were not in themselves what attracted observation; there were more beautiful places to be seen elsewhere. The Alps were more impressive than the mountains of Judea; the Old City walls of Jerusalem had their parallels in many other medieval cities. Other places had springs and cisterns. But what attracted a Jew to these sites—their glory—was embedded in Jewish collective memory.

As for Jerusalem, the Romans had tried to wipe out its Jewish traces, but they failed. Later, after the Romans—from the first century until the beginning of the fourth—came the new order of Christianity and the Byzantines. But as Har-El was quick to note, the Eastern Christians came from a world whose capital was Constantinople. ''These Christians never were natives of this country,'' he explained with conviction, drawing out each word so that I would not miss its significance. ''And when they walked this country, they did not know the language of its inhabitants. They did not know Hebrew or Aramaic. They remained outsiders.''

And yet, paradoxically, as Har-El admitted, these outsiders had designated many of the holy places, spots at which the children of the original inhabitants now gathered to pray. The Tomb of Rachel, perhaps today one of the holiest of Jewish shrines, had been a Byzantine ''discovery.''

So too it had been with the Arabs. They likewise had long-held traditions about holy places. And in many cases, their designated spots became the places to which the Jews flocked in prayer. Nabi Samuil, the burial place of the prophet Samuel, on a hill northwest of the city, was a site the Moslems designated but which the Jews venerated as well.

But that was just the point. ''After the destruction of the Second Temple,'' Har-El explained, ''nobody knew anymore where the holy places were.'' And so the foreigners found them—or more precisely, *founded* them. But the Jews made a more important contribution: they transformed the attachments and memories of others into something with transcendent meaning.

For Menashe Har-El, Israelites were everywhere he looked. They lived; they left their marks; they pulsed in contemporary Israeli consciousness. The fact that Rachel's Tomb was, after all, a Byzantine discovery or Nabi Samuil a Moslem one and that there was another, non-Israelite side to this place seemed a relatively unimportant detail in Har-El's scheme of things. The crucial fact was that no one cared more about these places than the Jews whose history was so ineluctably implicated in them.

There could be no mistaking what was happening here. Har-El's arguments were but another—perhaps the most extreme—illustration of the same assertive act of attachment to this place that I had witnessed on my Haganat Ha-Teva walks or seen in Nahalat Shivah or heard from Tavio. There was a line from the Book of Maccabees that Har-El liked to quote; he had used it as the epigraph to his book about Jerusalem. To him it said everything; its verity was undeniable: "We have neither taken any other man's land, nor do we hold dominion over other people's territory, but only over the inheritance of our fathers. On the contrary, for a certain time it was unjustly held by our enemies; but we, seizing the opportunity, hold fast the inheritance of our fathers."

I thought often about the price that Jewish attachments to the land exacted. On no day did I think about them more than on the the fourth and fifth days of the Hebrew month of Iyar, the month that follows the holy days of Passover. With nighfall on the fifth— a warm spring evening in Jerusalem—on Mount Herzl, near the tomb of the founder of modern Zionism and the graves of the soldiers who have fallen in defense of the state to which it led, the festivities of Independence Day—*Yom Ha-Atz'ma'ut*—begin. This is the day to celebrate the return to the "inheritance."

Situated on the western edge of the city, Mount Herzl—unlike the Temple Mount, Mount Zion or the Mount of Olives, and far away from them—has no religious past or even an identity older than the modern state. Its name and significance are inseparable from modern Israel, and hence its importance in the celebration of the new holiday that marks the establishment of the new state.

In a country where most holidays begin as holy days, mandated by the Torah and shaped by religious traditions, this is one of the two national civil holidays without such roots (the other is Jerusalem Day, the anniversary of the reunification of the city). And so, unlike the case on holy days, the commemorations do not start in the synagogue; they begin here. Songs are sung, soldiers march and the Speaker of the Knesset announces the start of what is essentially a state holiday. On this day, the nation expresses ties to the land, but it does so without the trappings of formalized religion. Although a few modern Orthodox synagogues have taken to reciting a special liturgy that associates the events of 1948 with the intentions of Heaven, most citizens see the anniversary of independence as a secular holiday and not a religious holy day.

As if to emphasize this fact, the celebrations shy away from the religious. During the evening come fireworks, and then the downtown streets fill with children bopping one another over the heads with little plastic hammers that emit a whistle with each blow, while in private homes there are social evenings and parties. On the morrow, as the people go out to tour the state whose rebirth thirty-seven years ago they are recalling, they move out of their homes into ''the exceedingly good land,'' picnicking in the parks they have planted and hiking through its retimbered forests. To pass Independence Day without a picnic would be like celebrating Passover without a *seder*.

But if on the fifth of Iyar the nation celebrates the day on which it declared its resolute will to be liberated and reborn in the land of its forebears and the successful struggle for its life, on the fourth, *Yom Ha-Zikaron*, The Day of Memory, it recalls the tax paid on that inheritance. For the Jewish people, the juxtaposition of sorrow and celebration, death and life, is not new. For them, joy is presaged by sadness, redemption by sacrifice. The coupling of the death of six million and the rebirth of the state has been burned into Jewish consciousness. The Day of Judgment, *Yom Kippur*, is always followed by *Sukkot*, the festival of happiness, and *Sim'chat Torah*, the day of rejoicing in the law. Apocalypse and redemption drip from every page of Jewish history. And now, in a kind of repetition compulsion, they are played out once more. First the depths of mourning and then the heights of rejoicing. First the flag is lowered and then it is raised. And that is why the celebrations begin at a military cemetery.

Yom Ha-Zikaron is heavy with the shared memories of those whose children fell in the wars that have become the benchmarks of Israeli national history. On the eve of the fourth of Iyar, at eight, The Day of Memory is ushered in with a two-minute blast of sirens throughout the country. As they did the week before on *Yom Ha-Sho'ah*, the day of recalling the Holocaust, all Jews throughout the country stop in their tracks and stand silent while the electronic ram's horn calls upon them to remember. And in the plaza in front of the Kotel—that symbol of destruction and renewal—a torch is lit, prayers recited and a *shofar* blown. In synagogues, the memorial prayers repeated at the morning service recall the names of the departed. This year, a young boy, barely past thirteen and bar-mitzvah, tearfully recites the Kaddish for his father, lost last week in Lebanon and lying now in the Judean Hills.

During the morning hours, at eleven, the country will once again pause as the two-minute blast is repeated. The main streets will suddenly still as buses stand in place; cars will stop, their drivers standing next to them. The men pumping gas will lay down their hoses and with their customers stand in silence; the grocer will stop counting out his customer's change, while the carpenters building closets in a new apartment across the street suddenly cease their sawing. Everywhere the Jews are silent as people listen to the same sirens which on other occasions have announced the beginning of wars but today remind them of their cost.

And after the silence comes an outpouring of memory. On radio and television come testimonies of loss, additions to the collective record of survival. There were no undistinguished lives; the best and most promising were killed. A poet mourns his fallen brother —"the more creative one," he explains; a mother describes her son, the source of her inspiration. A father collapses into sobbing, de-scribing the way his son, the soldier, made sure always to leave behind the little pocket money he gave him "because he thought we needed it more than he did." A sister tearfully tells the national audience about her brother, who alone among the family never complained and always brought joy into the house, until the day he brought death.

And over Galei Tzahal, the army radio service, comrades-in-arms share stories of those they have lost. "When you're fighting, a little door closes inside your brain," one explains, "and as your friends fall around you, you're able to go on. If that little door didn't close, we would all break down on the spot. But then, when the fighting is over, the door opens, and the memories pour out and overwhelm us with the sense of our loss."

"I could not believe my brother Nissim was dead. I was sure that I would get a call from the hospital saying it was a mistake, and he would come home smiling as he always did. And then they brought home his boots and his clothes, but still I could not believe it; I thought maybe they were someone else's. And then I saw him, and I kissed his forehead, hoping he would get up and smile and tell me not to be sad, that he was all right." The voice over the radio starts to cry; tears flow onto the listener's cheeks. "But he didn't get up; he just lay there on his back. Only that morning he had given me money to buy some new shoes, but in the end I spent it on his flowers."

"Time is no healer," writes reporter Eliezer Whartman in *The Jerusalem Post*, remembering his son Moshe who fell in 1975. "Time may assuage the grief, but the wound never heals." Like others who remember and share their memories, on this day he sees his son everywhere.

A son calls his mother to find out how she feels this morning. "Excellent," she answers. How is it possible? he asks himself; for four years she has ceaselessly mourned his fallen brother, Yossi.

"Are you sure you're all right, Mother?" he asks.

"Yes," she explains, hearing the unspoken question in his voice. "Last night I dreamed about Yossi."

"That is what it means to be a mother who has lost her son," the son concludes: "to live and pray for the nights that you can see him in your dreams."

The shared memories are everywhere. Over the radio, in the newspapers, in the silence. And then even the newcomer finds that without his noticing it, he has absorbed them, and the loss of others has become his own.

"I look at my six-year-old son," writes one mother in this morning's newspaper, "when I pick him up at the kindergarten. And then I look at all the other boys in his class, all of whom will someday be soldiers, and—God, forgive me—I cannot help wondering which of them will live beyond the next eighteen years."

And on his way home from school, my son Uriel tells me, he was stopped by a man who, placing his hands upon his head, blessed him with long life, praying that he might not join the sacrifices which are no longer offered only at the Temple altar. The Third Temple, the Midrash says, will be built of fire. On this day of shared memories and sorrows, the future and the past mingle in one vision.

Amidst all the testimony and tears, Jerusalem is silent, the flags on all the public buildings and many of the private ones fluttering quietly in the soft spring breezes. Places of entertainment are closed by law. In many windows memorial candles burn. And all of us who are left feel the guilt and sadness of survival.

On a hilltop just outside Jerusalem, in Kiryat Sha'ul, where Saul, the first king of Israel and fallen soldier, established his capital, a military cemetery now stands. "We are one in our sorrow," says the government minister. "And today our memories are drawn to the stone monuments and mounds of earth where lie those by whose merit we still live, the best of our sons.''

A father, his voice dissolving with each word, reads a letter from his son who lies in one of the fresh graves. His last words, scrawled while standing at a lookout post near the melting snows on Jebel Baruch in the Shouf Mountains of Lebanon: ''Enough killing.''

And that too is holding fast to the inheritance of our fathers.

CHAPTER
·7·

TREES OF LIFE

*Understanding the form and pressure of . . .
natives' inner lives is more like grasping a
proverb, catching an allusion, seeing a joke—or
. . . reading a poem—than it is like achieving
communion.*

CLIFFORD GEERTZ,
Local Knowledge

*B*y profession, Yisra'el Hershkovits, a short, almost stout
man in his forties with a pencil-thin black mustache and
wearing a lacquer-stained and sawdust-covered coat, is a wood
turner. He turns pieces of wood—disks and dowels—into an *etz
chaim.*

Literally, the words mean "tree of life." The reference is to a
verse in Proverbs: "It is a tree of life to all who grasp on to it,"
the "it" being the holy Torah. Searching for a term to describe the
decorated staves onto which the sacred scrolls are rolled, tradition
settled upon the term *etz chaim* which neatly combined metaphor
and reality. Like his father before him, Yisra'el has for the last
twenty-odd years crafted his trees of life for scrolls all over Israel,
the United States and wherever else Jews roll and read the sacred
Scriptures. He fell into this work when, after completing his army
service, he agreed to help his father out in the workshop for "a
short time."

"I am still here only temporarily," he explains as he stands sanding the end of a disk. And then he half-laughs and adds: "But then, we are all here temporarily, no?"

His practiced hands produce finely crafted designs as he embosses the *kaftor v'ferach*, button and blossom, which were part of the ornamentation of the Holy Tabernacle, onto his own creations. Of course, only the names remain; no one really knows what those buttons and blossoms looked like in the tabernacle which Bezalel crafted for Moses in the wilderness. But by using these ancient terms to describe his own decorations, Yisra'el somehow endows them with sacred associations and embeds them in another time. And thus he translates the past into the present.

Yisra'el is good at what he does; he is an artisan, and so the work of his hands is much in demand. He never lacks customers.

"Once, when the Prime Minister went to visit Egypt," he tells me, "I was asked to prepare a special case as a gift for Sadat, and on another occasion a miniature ark for the Queen of England."

But these special jobs are not really the ones that attract him most. Rather—although he is no hasid himself and often expresses a studied cynicism toward those who appear to him overly swept up by the charisma of one or another rebbe—it is from the making of a new *etz chaim* for a scroll that the Lubavitcher Rebbe, the Rebbe of Ger or the head of some other hasidic dynasty has commisioned for use in his synagogue or yeshiva that Yisra'el draws his greatest pride.

"You better clean your eyes," he told me one afternoon a few days later when I walked in and found him energetically buffing the silver-filigreed edge of a particularly ornate stave. "This is going to the Belzer Rebbe." His entire body reflected pride as he jumped about completing the trimming on his tree.

To be sure, Yisra'el turns out other items as well, including beechwood cases for the scroll of Esther (the *megillah*) and handcrafted wooden noisemakers, both used on the *Purim* holiday. He also makes an occasional *Hanukkah menorah* as well as *mezuzah* cases of all shapes and sizes with which Jews mark the doorposts of their homes and the identities of their souls. (He knows, he once explained, the variations demanded by each of the hasidic sects: one likes a plain rectangular case; another, one with a hole through which to see the parchment inside; a third wants beechwood engraved with an image of the Western Wall; a fourth requires cases with rounded edges—the possibilities seem endless and the differences nuanced and minute, but Yisra'el knows them all.) These other products are, however, sidelines—he calls them "special orders," in an English phrase that has entered his polyglot vocabulary—diversions from his essential craft which centers around the *etz chaim*.

"I make things people kiss," the wood turner says, summing up his craft, and then he chuckles.

In fact, he is right; most of what he turns out in his dusty little hole-in-the-wall workshop ends up treated with great reverence, circumspection and even a kind of devoted awe by the religious. And even those somewhat less than complete in their attachments to religion look upon these objects—*tash'mishey kedushah*, as they are called—as mystically endowed with sanctity.

His shoes usually covered with sawdust or wood chips and the air smelling of lacquer or burnt wood, Yisra'el sits (or more often, stands) with a soldering iron, burning flowers, buttons and Jewish scenes into the disks which will hold the parchment in place. Or else he walks to the back of the shop and drills holes into which to fit handles, bells or little silver crowns that adorn the fruits of his labors. Then again, he may come to the front and form a rounded handle out of a spinning dowel.

It is not his practice to make an entire *etz chaim* at once. Such "trees of life" do not blossom into existence so simply. Rather, one day he embosses handles while on another he decorates disks, cuts dowels or lacquers wood. The branches of his trees grow almost in isolation from one another. And then, when the order (in Hebrew the word is *haz'manah*, which can also—and perhaps more appropriately in this instance—mean "appointed time" or "invitation") for the *etz chaim* arrives and it must make its rendezvous with the parchment which the scribe has completed, the parts are quickly, as if by wizardry, fitted together.

In a single set of motions, the plain and profane pieces of beechwood become in his hands a sacred object, ready to be wedded to the scroll. Together then, the scroll and poles which are now a Torah are ceremoniously brought into the community which will regularly read and roll it. Often, especially when the Torah is a new one, it will be carried in a ritual procession into its destined synagogue ark with all the pomp and formality of a wedding. But by the time his trees are under a *chupah*, the "wedding" canopy, Yisra'el is already turning out new dowels, disks and poles for another *etz chaim*.

To the uninitiated who come in looking for some sort of quick transaction, he usually responds by saying that he is not looking for work and has more than enough to keep him busy. But if the visitors begin by exchanging information—telling him who they are, where they are from and what moved them to come to him, so that he can get a grasp on their lives—he at last consents to take on a *haz'manah.* Yisra'el's willingness to accept an order comes out of the establishment of a relationship, never in its absence. He works for the people he knows, acting on their behalf in the fulfillment of their needs.

"And when will it be ready?" the overly impatient and uninformed outsider might ask on occasion.

Yisra'el never knows. "It will be ready, with God's help, when you need it."

"Money?"

"There will be plenty of time for that." And there always is.

Dealing as he does in the margins of the sacred, Yisra'el has a special way of talking about his products too. These are not items to be treated or considered like any other piece of wood. Coming into his shop, a client, asking about the cost of an *etz chaim* at the conclusion of a long conversation (one could not jump to such crass questions right away, for that would destroy the friendly relationship just affirmed), might receive an answer like this:

"It depends what you want. You can get the *'zeh kailee'* [This is my God] or you can add to it *'v'anveyhu'* [and I will glorify Him]." The use of the quotation from Exodus is the wood turner's way of distinguishing between the simple and the deluxe-model staves. To his customers, the meaning of the quotation is unmistakable. "I'll take the whole verse: 'This is my God, and I will glorify Him,'" the customer might conclude, ordering the silver crowns atop the buttons and blossoms. In the ordering of *tash'mishey kedushah,* poetry comes naturally.

The wood turner and his work stand between the sacred and the profane. "The things I make are not in themselves holy," he once explained, "but they are able to somehow contain holiness."

A bit of the Jewish scholar himself (we met and became friends in a Talmud study circle we both were part of in the Holy City), Yisra'el understands the full significance of his work; sancta and the equipment to grasp their meaning are made in the same shop.

But there is more to the wood turner's in-between-ness. "People always think," he told me another time, "that I am one of them. The Belzer hasidim come in and they say, 'You're one of us, so make us an *etz chaim,*' and the Gerer hasidim come in and say, 'Nu, you're from ours, so make us a *mezuzah* for the rebbe,' and the Satmar, the Reb Arelach and all the rest do the same thing.''

But what about those who are not part of that world of hasidic dynasties and ancient pieties? The carpenter from the shop around the corner, the auto mechanic who painstakingly rebuilds transmissions nearby, the young kibbutznik who passes through selling eggs fresh from the farm, the retired X-ray technician who lives across the street and who needs someone to help him read the official letter from the tax-revenue office, the tinsmith taking a break from cutting metal, or the folk artist come to borrow a tool likewise find Yisra'el and his place a good port.

And for the cultural anthropologist from the university looking for the world of Jerusalem pieties, the wood turner and his workshop offered an opening I could never have found on my own. For me, Yisra'el became a guide into the world of religious Jerusalem.

Located on Rabbi Joseph Hayim Sonnenfeld Street, on the fringe of the industrial zone of the Beit Yisra'el quarter, down the lane from an open-air fruit and vegetable market, the wood turner's workplace abuts on one side the synagogues, yeshivas, scribes and Torah scholars of neighboring Me'ah She'arim. On the other side, Yisra'el's shop is but one store in a block filled with craftsmen: carpenters, automobile mechanics, tinsmiths and locksmiths. Across the way, there is an open-hearth oven where an Iraqi Jew hand-bakes long flat bread as did his fathers for generations before, while in the other direction, across from the Mir Yeshiva, is a tiny three-room glass factory where artisans blow creations that, judging from what may be seen in the museums, are not too different from those their antecedents crafted in an earlier millennium.

But the wood turner is not a carpenter, and people who enter looking to buy a table, stool, bookshelf or some other profane piece of woodwork are quickly directed to one of the other workshops around the corner. Nor is he a holy man, and those who buy the wooden *mezuzah* or *megillah* cases he makes are sent in the other direction to one of the scribes in Me'ah She'arim for the sacred texts and the pieces of parchment that go inside the case and complete its sanctity. Cases, yes; contents, no.

So Yisra'el's shop, like its proprietor, stands precisely at a crossroads of what the locals refer to as *gash'miyus* (material needs) and *ruch'niyus* (spiritual needs). That perhaps is also part of what makes it more than just another place of business or workshop but rather a kind of bridge or border-crossing point, one of those curiously liminal places where inhabitants of separate realms are likely to meet and feel momentarily at ease with one another. The secular and religious, the hasidim and those who abide by other orthodoxies or none at all can come together in the shelter of Yisra'el's trees.

And thus, on his way to review some mystical text in the yeshiva, a kabbalist who is also a scribe may stop in to pick up a *megillah* case for a client. At the same time, a cabinetmaker from next door may drop in for some of the Turkish coffee always brewing on the little hot plate in the corner. They may encounter an artist buffing his latest creation on one of Yisra'el's machines, while three little boys on their way to the vegetable stands to pick up onions for their mother stop in to gawk at the wood turner's hands and his noisy lathe, powerful drill, smoking soldering iron or hissing shellac gun. A boy from the Mir Yeshiva at the end of the street, on a break from his *lernen*, comes in to rest his mind from the twists and turns of Talmudic logic and argument, while an old man and woman arrive to order an *etz chaim* in memory of their parents on the thirty-fifth anniversary of their passing. All have come from their separate worlds to see the wood turner. But once there, they meet one another and touch, even if only for a moment, in this station at the crossroads hosted by this man who works in the margins of each of their worlds.

"I am," Yisra'el once simply put it, "perfectly located, right in the middle."

Like many of his visitors, I too was drawn toward the eddy of existence that churned around this little shop. Here, I somehow felt, an otherwise invisible junction of Jerusalem would reveal itself to me. Sitting there for hours day after day (Yisra'el understood from me that anthropologists look upon such time investments as perfectly legitimate), I began to discover that in many ways these visitors and the worlds they brought into his shop meant as much to the wood turner as the work of his hands, and perhaps more. On occasion, when I stole a glance at him from the doorway without his noticing, I saw that when he worked alone, his face took on a kind of dull look, almost signifying boredom, and his body expressed fatigue. His hands worked almost automatically. But when a visitor came in, he would light up. His hands would add just a bit more to the flower he was burning into the wood. His eyes would twinkle, and his entire body would take on a poise which suggested he was ready to encounter humanity to its fullest. And then, I knew, he would become far more than a wood turner. On those occasions, when he became a social worker, a counselor, a mediator, a collector and provider of information, and a gatherer and narrator of stories, he—more than the staves in his hands—was the tree of life which everyone grasped.

"I work best in the company of visitors," he once said.

To Yisra'el, conversation was no less a craft than turning wood; it required special expertise. "You have to know to whom you are speaking," he once explained. "Some people, if you tell them too little, you tell them too much—they fill in the rest. You have to know how to listen, when to say nothing. In other cases, you have to talk a great deal in order to say very little. And you have to know when to be deaf—that's when I like to turn on the drill. And then there are people who need to be told a great deal, so that they will see things in the right way. So you always have to know to whom you are speaking."

Conversation required background knowledge, something Yisra'el had accumulated over many years. Although he lived now in Kiryat Sanz, one of the somewhat newer Orthodox neighborhoods on the northern fringe of the city, he had grown up only meters away from his shop, in Me'ah She'arim, in the triangular court known as the Hungarian Houses. Inside this stronghold of Central European Orthodoxy, he had shared a tiny two-room flat with his parents and four brothers and sisters. The neighborhood and all those whose lives orbited about it, the personalities, conflicts, old gossip and new scandals were in his blood and tissue. He knew who would talk to whom and to whom one said nothing, who were natives and who were newcomers—what locals called in Yiddish the *geboreneh*, those born into the tradition, and the *gevoreneh*, those who having lived another kind of life at first had now found a way back to the tradition. And of course, he knew who remained beyond the pale, the contaminating outsiders. He knew how to read the endless announcements that were plastered all over the walls of the neighborhood—that is, he knew where to look for the small print and the code words that were the subtexts of many an innocent-seeming notice.

Whenever a stranger came into his shop, Yisra'el, like a native of some genealogically obsessed tribe, easily and quickly located him among relatives or acquaintances. Only when he had made the connection did the wood turner seem to relax and commit himself to further dealings with the visitor.

That social knowledge remained one of his most prized possessions, and he used it daily. It was not unusual, for example, for me to be sitting in his workshop and listening to him chat—what he called "having a *shmooes*"—with one or another visitor and then, when the caller had gone, Yisra'el would slowly but surely fill in the social, historical and religious context out of which the man (only occasionally did women enter his shop alone) came.

Day after day, I watched people enter. Then, patiently, I would wait for their departure to discover to whom I had really been talking and what there was in the person's biography that would bring him to life for me. The wood turner guided me and turned the world around for me as he twirled the disks on his lathe; he embossed stories into my memory while he burned ornaments into his trees of life.

During the days and weeks I sat with Yisra'el, I continued to watch the scene that passed before and through the door. A small woman who stopped to read one of the posters stuck on the wall outside his store—posters that served as a basic medium of information exchange in the neighborhood—provided *opsprechen* (exorcisms), Yisra'el told me, for those troubled by dybbuks and other evil spirits. A raggedy wanderer who traveled the streets of this and other neighborhoods was, I learned, not what he looked to be, a homeless man, but rather a Jew who had taken to wearing sackcloth and ashes in mourning over the continued presence of the greater part of his people in exile. Yet another who rushed in for a *mezuzah* case one morning was a man, Yisra'el assured me, who had written a book that, because it contained an endorsement from someone affiliated with the Ministry of Religion and the office of the Chief Rabbinate, had been shunned by the local community, who officially denied the authority of the state and its religious officers. Close to excommunication by the locals because of his book, the writer had to leave the neighborhood for a number of months "until the controversy died down." Even now, newly returned and setting up house again, he remained "suspect," "strange," haunted if not hunted.

In Yisra'el's workshop, debates were often completed that had begun within the walls of a house of study. One day around the holy day of *Sukkot*, a yeshiva student came in and began to discuss the merits of spending time searching for the perfect *et'rog* (citron) with which to fulfill the commandments of the upcoming festival. Was it desirable, he wondered, to spend time looking for a yellow, unblemished, "perfect" *et'rog* at the expense of time spent in study and review of the Talmud?

"The rebbe says that it's better to spend just a few minutes getting the *et'rog* in order to spend more time *lernen*."

"And how much time do you spend shopping for a car?" a red-headed hasid who was already in the shop asked, adding: "And shopping for a car is not a *mitzvah* that the Master of the Universe asked you to accomplish." He cocked his head as he spoke. "Certainly you should spend as much time and give as much care to finding an *et'rog* as you do buying a car. That's what I do."

"I bought my car in just a few minutes," Yisra'el offered.

"Ah, but you thought about it for weeks, years," said the red-head.

"Oh, so," the yeshiva boy concluded, "I thought about my *et'rog* for days. But I bought it in a few minutes."

In this sort of small talk, among the turnings of wood, worldviews were discovered and a people's ethos expressed. Here in the interstices of existence Jewish moods and motivations were quietly explored.

Over time, I came to realize that while I liked to watch Yisra'el work, I came more to discover some of the cultural vistas of the neighborhood that opened before my eyes, to hear stories and debates and explore the moods and motivations that emerged in the process. For the anthropologist in me, finding this place where neighborhood tableaux came to life before my eyes was like stumbling upon some hidden doorway to an invisible kingdom. The little shop and the street outside its door were the windows on endless dramas. As local Jerusalem passed by or came in, Yisra'el would narrate, the people would perform, and I would watch and acquire memories.

Although most of the time I could discover the entire world outside Yisra'el's shop from my perch on a stool inside the workshop, every now and then he would take me out "for an experience." If I was there in the afternoon, at dusk, when he received the call to recite the *min'chah* prayers, he would take me along. The call always came from the Russian Jew in the store next to his— "The Formica," he was called after the specialty he turned out. The Formica was a pious man, waking up each day in the morning darkness to get to the Western Wall for study and to complete his morning prayers with the rising of the sun. Gathering the workmen in the surrounding shops, he had organized a small congregation in one of the carpentry shops. In another hole in the wall where, among other things, pulpits were constructed, the sawdust and wood chips were swept away and a temporary synagogue was created.

Every regular participant at the carpenters' *min'chah* had a special spot from which he prayed. Yisra'el's was in the corner, behind a power saw. As they entered the little shop, the place and the men seemed to become transformed. From a shelf behind some two-by-fours, someone would pull out an old shoe box filled with prayer books, while another man took one of the new lecterns from the rack, dusted it off and made a place from which the service would be led. A few of the worshipers rinsed their hands in ritual ablutions; others changed out of their work coats. But it was not just these physical changes that marked the transformation. There was also something in their faces as they closed their eyes, kissed the prayer books they took in their hands and turned their devotions toward where the Holy Temple once stood, a place not so far away, that made the atmosphere in the shop change.

As I watched these rough-handed craftsmen whisper their prayers, I could not help wondering whether they were imagining that they might someday be among those who would help in the rebuilding of that Temple. Surely the builders of that place would come from among these men or those like them, believers with the proper skills.

At first I thought that I alone noticed the change in atmosphere in the shop. But then I saw how easily this quiet gathering of worshipers drew the attention of passersby. On most other occasions people walked past the carpenters' shops without so much as a glance inside; the noise of saws, lathes and hammers did not turn a single head. But the silence before or the quiet hum during the prayers was different; hardly anyone went by the shop without entering or at least slowing down. In the din of this industrial district, the hushed devotions of prayer were far more striking.

The congregation, a mix of Ashkenazim and Sephardim, had one custom that everyone adhered to scrupulously. During the cantor's recitation of the Kaddish, which they repeated in its extended Sephardic version, whenever he came to the words *revach v'hatzalah* —profit and salvation—they all echoed these words in unison. Every so often, especially around the end of the month, just before everyone's bills came due, the refrain was recited a bit louder than usual and with perhaps a bit of extra feeling. And then, in spite of themselves, a few of the men would break into a self-conscious smile or giggle.

Besides taking me to pray with the carpenters, Yisra'el took me other places as well. Once, he took me to Batei Ungarin, the Hun-

garian Houses, to see the little apartment in which he had lived as
a boy. We walked a few steps down from the street into the courtyard, into a space where every effort had been made to leave things
as unchanged as possible. Except for the cemented cover to the
cistern, which had since been replaced by indoor plumbing, and the
added floors on some of the buildings to accommodate growing
families, life here had not become altered too much in the hundred
or so years since the neighborhood was built by Jews whose origins
were in the Jewish villages and hamlets of Hungary. Ascending an
outdoor staircase, we walked through a small wooden door into the
two rooms that had been his father's apartment. A small sink stood
on one side of the entry, next to a little stove. On the other side was
a toilet. The high arched ceilings made the small space feel larger
than it was. Some light from the street came in through the tall
windows.

"This, which is now the kitchen," Yisra'el said, "was once actually outside. But in later years we built an addition to the house
so that there would be indoor plumbing." He quoted a Talmudic
saying: "Who is a rich man? He who has a bathroom close to his
table." And indeed, in this tiny apartment, the bathroom and
kitchen were side by side.

"You know, in the old days, going to the toilet here was no
pleasure, especially at night. We used to take a candle that we put
inside a can. On one side of the can we made holes and the other
side we left open. That way we got light but the wind didn't blow
the candle out on the way to the outhouse."

"And what about Sabbath?" I asked, trying to visualize the
experience. By the Jewish laws which enclosed this neighborhood,
no carrying of flames was permitted on that holy day.

"On Sabbath we walked and sat down in the darkness. And more
than once, we got to the outhouse and opening the door were scared
half to death when a cat jumped out or we felt a scorpion climbing
slowly up our legs."

Once before I had heard a story about the pleasures of indoor
plumbing in Jerusalem. The memory came from Moshe Sonnenfeld,
grandson of one of the famous rabbis of the city. But now, as I
looked at the toilet in Yisrael's boyhood home, I thought of it again.

In 1873, after coming to Jerusalem from Europe, Moshe's grandfather, Rabbi Joseph Hayim Sonnenfeld, became one of the guiding
spirits of Jewish life here. He helped organize the Bet Din, the
Jewish court of law, as well as what was called *Va'ad Ha-Ir
L'K'hilat Ha-Ash'kenazim*—the City Council for the Ashkenazic

Community—which among other things stood for a complete separation of the Orthodox and non-Orthodox in the city. Rabbi Sonnenfeld was the spiritual protector of the tradition for many of those whose offspring now made their homes in Me'ah She'arim and its surrounding neighborhoods. The street on which the wood turner's shop stood had been named after him. Although he was one of the founders of the Hungarian Houses, a settlement which made life outside the walls possible, Sonnenfeld himself never lived outside those walls. From the moment he set foot inside the Old City of Jerusalem, he took pains to make certain that he would never again leave it for more than thirty days at a time. He kept his vow.

But remaining tied to a residence inside the Old City meant that he would have to suffer the physical hardships which came with life in the primitive and cramped quarters within. To soften the hard life in his later years, his son decided to give him a special gift. No longer would the great rabbi, father and grandfather have to stagger through the cold Jerusalem nights to get to the outhouse on the other side of the courtyard, far away from his bed. The grand rabbi would get an indoor toilet.

How, his son wondered, would the old man, who regardless of his great stature in the eyes of the community lived a modest personal life, react to this gift, this extravagance? To find out, he came to visit his father on the day the plumbing was completed and then surreptitiously followed him on his first trip to the new facility.

When the old man came out and washed his hands, the son heard him mumble the traditional blessing thanking God for having allowed His human creations control over the cavities of their bodies. Then, in Yiddish, he heard the rabbi whisper an additional prayer: "Master of the Universe, I beg You, please do not charge this pleasure against those I may have merited and that await me still in The World to Come."

"Such was the heavenly pleasure of having an indoor toilet in Jerusalem," his grandson concluded.

As we stood in what had been his childhood home, I told Yisra'el the story.

"Oh, the day we completed the kitchen and toilet and brought in the plumbing," Yisra'el explained, "was a day of great rejoicing."

"And water?" I asked. Although in the beginning, Jews had been able to settle in Jerusalem because of its several springs and the many cisterns built in and around the mountains, since the growth of the modern city and its increase in population, water had become increasingly scarce and precious.

"Water we guarded with all our might," he answered. "We learned to take showers the special Jerusalem way."

"What was that?"

"You don't know? So you're not yet a true Jerusalemite. First you make yourself wet; then you turn off the water and soap yourself completely. Finally, you take a quick rinse. To this day, we still wash this way. Why do you think everyone so enjoys going to the *mikveh* [ritual bath]? Water, water, water." He laughed.

We began to walk back out of the courtyard toward his shop.

"You mentioned Sabbath," Yisra'el said. As we walked, Sh'lomo, the tinsmith, joined us. He was on his way back from the bank. Although orphaned while very young, he had grown up around the same courtyard as Yisra'el. To many of the old-timers in the neighborhood, Sh'lomo, a man in his fifties, was still known simply as "Reb Chaim's son," although Reb Chaim had been dead for more than forty years. Family counted for a great deal in these precincts.

"You know, we used to have just one oven for the entire neighborhood," Yisra'el continued.

"Yes, and on Friday afternoon everyone would bring his cholent pot," Sh'lomo added, his face lighting up. Cholent was the slow-cooking stew made of lima beans, potatoes, bones, spices and—among the relatively well-to-do—pieces of meat. Simmering overnight atop the low flame of the Sabbath oven, it was a staple of every traditional Ashkenazic family.

"Each family found some way to identify its pot. One put a little ribbon on the handle—"

"Another had a broken handle or a cover that was a different color from the rest of the pot," Sh'lomo broke in.

"And sometimes on Sabbath I would come to pick up the pot that my sister had brought over to the oven the day before."

"Some people tried to switch their cholent for another that looked or smelled a little meatier," Sh'lomo added, laughing.

"But—you wouldn't believe it—among dozens and dozens of pots, the man at the oven always knew exactly which was whose. I remember once or twice reaching for the wrong one only to be stopped and told, 'Not that one; that one over there with the yellow string.' "

Later, when I would walk the alleyways and courtyards of the

Hungarian Houses on Friday afternoons and smell the aroma of cholent, chicken soup, potato pudding and gefülte fish that wafted out of the windows, I recalled these reminiscences. Memories of a past I had not been party to but only learned about at second hand had through the stories I had absorbed nevertheless found their way into my consciousness and ignited my imagination.

There was another occasion on which Yisra'el took me out of his shop on a trip into the world outside his doorway.

"You know," he began one afternoon, "there's a group of men in the Kolel America who study Mish'nah every evening between *min'chah* and *ma'ariv*. This class has been going on since before I was born. For a year after she died, they *lernt* in memory of my mother, may she rest in peace, and so I feel a special attachment to them. Whenever they reach the end of a volume and celebrate a *siyum* [conclusion]—usually one of them comes in about a week beforehand to tell me the end is in sight—I bring them a little drink and some cake, and my wife bakes them a *kugel*. They are having a *siyum* tonight. Do you want to come with me? You'll see something that hasn't changed at all in more than fifty years."

The opportunity to enter into a realm of the Jerusalem past unmediated by someone else's memory was not something to be missed. "Of course I want to come."

Moments later, as if on cue, an old man in a musty black coat, unkempt beard and toothless smile walked through the door and picked up the noodle pudding—*kugel*—Yisra'el's wife had prepared. He said almost nothing, merely nodding as he trundled off up the street with his package in his arms.

"What is the Kolel America?" I asked after he had gone.

"Kolel America is an institution founded about ninety years ago by some Americans who came here. Not Americans like you"—he looked at me and smiled. "These people came from America but they had long beards and black coats; no one in America thought of them as Americans—but here they were 'the Amerikaner.' Like every other *kolel*, Kolel America was a charitable institution that collected money from some community abroad and distributed it among the locals who lived by the donations. That was, after all, how most of the Jews who lived here in the last century survived. That was the *halukkah*."

I had heard about the *halukkah*, the distribution which in a sense had been the pecuniary expression of the Diaspora Jew's symbolic longing for a return to Jerusalem. Those who returned to the land of their forebears survived on what those who failed to come sent them. One man's guilty conscience about his obligation to Zion was another's staff of life. In fact, for many Jerusalemites there was no other visible means of support beyond the money sent by Jews still living outside the Holy Land.

"So the Kolel America lived off the money from America. But it was tiny in comparison with some of the other *kolelim* whose support came from the great communities of Europe. Still, they had a large building right here on Me'ah She'arim Street. As a boy, on cold winter mornings I would walk the few steps across the street from our rooms to their synagogue and start up the stove so that at daybreak when the *minyan* for the morning prayers gathered, the chill would be gone from the room.

"I remember stumbling out of bed before the first light of day and slipping into the big, dark building. It took a while to light the coals and to take the chill of the night away. Sometimes I couldn't get the embers to light. And then at last the men came in and took their places in the benches. I remember the smell of the smoke from the stove and the smell of the old leather of their *t'filin* [phylacteries] as they wrapped them around their arms. And sometimes, if we were blessed with plentiful winter rains, the damp smell of mud became mixed in with it all. You know, there are memories that always come back when you return to some places, memories that are part of what you are when you return to that place.

"In the beginning, the Amerikaner established a large synagogue in Me'ah She'arim, right in the middle of the neighborhood. One door opened up on the main street and the other in the back to the marketplace and inner courtyard. The building is tall and large. But it turned out to be too big for their little community here. There were never enough other Amerikaner who came to join them. They didn't really have a rebbe who attracted many people. So they rented out the building to a larger group, immigrants from Pressburg."

"That was where the Chatam Sofer came from, no?" I asked. The Chatam Sofer, sobriquet of Rabbi Moses Sofer, had been the spiritual leader of the most traditional Orthodox Jews of Hungary. With a tremendous following particularly among Hungarian Jewry, he had become known throughout Europe in the nineteenth century as an opponent of any sort of reform in Judaism.

"Yes, and Rabbi Akiva Sofer [from the same family] used to pray there in his time, and so did I," Yisra'el added with a smile.

"It's a large building, but on the side is a much smaller room where the Amerikaner found themselves a place to settle.

"Actually, although they were called 'the Amerikaner,' the founder of the place, today a man of about seventy-five, was born in Jerusalem. But before coming here, his father had lived in America, had been a rabbi there. The son is called Reb Avraham Levinstein, and he has a brother—maybe you have heard of him—Reb Naftali Levinstein. They and their adherents are called 'the Amerikaner.'

"In any event, there are those who continue the activities of the *kolel*. They have a *gemilut chesed* [kind deeds] organization that helps the needy and offers all sorts of support." As Yisra'el became more and more engrossed in this history, his hands transformed the disk in his hand into a circle of flowers.

Later, at dusk—what Yisra'el referred to in Hebrew as *dimdumim*—and holding a bottle of brandy and some cake, we made our way to the little synagogue. After pulling down the steel shutter and locking up the workshop, he led me up the block. As we stepped inside the door and found ourselves within a cavernous and dark synagogue, I tried to imagine what it must have been like for a young boy to come in here alone on winter mornings to prepare the way for those few who would later come to pray. The solitude, bordering on loneliness, and the chill in the air were all I could think of now.

On the far side of the large room was another opening through which I could see light. We walked toward it. There, in what had once been an outer courtyard of the synagogue but had long since been covered over to make a small chapel, sat about ten or twelve men. They were all old, or at least looked that way, and as they leaned over the worn tables, several of them were holding their heads in their hands. Against the wall sat their teacher. He read from a timeworn, frayed copy of the Mish'nah, sliding his finger along the page while the others followed in their volumes. They had been waiting for Yisra'el before starting. But now that he had entered and was in the other room fumbling with the large paper bag in which were the cake and the bottle of brandy, they could begin. They sat up straighter, and the teacher leaned forward and began reciting the closing lines of the text. The few words they read went quickly, and soon the first part of the *siyum* was over and the celebration was set to begin.

"Say a Kaddish," someone called to Yisra'el, and he came in and stood next to a couple of the other men who recited this prayer in memory of the dead.

"Amen, amen," everyone answered at the conclusion of the Kaddish. "And now," one of the men in the back called out with gusto, "a *L'chayim* [To life]." Yisra'el pulled the bottle of brandy from the bag. The toothless man distributed a few shot glasses, while another man replaced the just-completed volumes on a shelf in the back of the room. After the first drink, Yisra'el heaped the *kugel* on a plastic plate and began to pass it around the room. A few of the men grabbed for the pieces. One asked if he could take a piece home for his wife. "*L'chayim*," the men called again and again, downing glass after glass and chasing it with bites of *kugel*. The food and drink brought rosy vitality to their faces; the toasts brought the room to life.

"For some of these men," Yisra'el had told me earlier, "this is the best meal they will have all week until Sabbath. And maybe even better than what they will eat then."

Yisra'el handed the teacher the plate with cake. The honor of its distribution would fall upon him. As he distributed knowledge to the soul, so he could hand out nourishment for the body.

In a few minutes, the entire celebration was over and books were once again being taken from the shelf and handed around the room. The time had come to begin the new volume of Mish'nah in the never-ending cycle of study that marked these men's existence. A few lines were recited.

"And the full meaning of this shall be discussed tomorrow night," the rabbi concluded.

As I reflected on what I had witnessed, I wondered whether there was any way I could translate the immediacies of this world into the metaphors of another, whether there was anything that these old men did which could ever be appreciated or comprehended by people who did not and never would share their existence. In actuality, there was not much for the uninitiated eye to see, nothing strikingly beautiful about their chapel or especially memorable in their celebration. These old men constituted one of countless such study circles that had for generations existed here in Jerusalem. But as I looked at Yisra'el and the pleasure in his face—he had photographed them and taped their service—I realized that they represented a memory of his own past, his own invisible Jerusalem. I had been wrong in supposing before coming that I would be able to enter the past unmediated by another's memories. Indeed, only through Yisra'el's memories—or what I imagined them to be—was this little episode at all worth recalling.

We finished the evening service. As we walked back afterward, Yisra'el turned to me and asked, "So did you enjoy it?"

Looking for something to say, I commented on how much of what I tried to see was filtered through his experience, as he had shared it with me. Yisra'el nodded. "Interesting what you see and what I remember," he said. He paused and then, after a few moments of silence during which he had apparently been thinking about what I had seen and he had not, he said: "You know, my anthropologist friend, we all see what we want to see," and then, correcting himself, added, "what we are *capable* of seeing."

CHAPTER
·8·

DAYS OF AWE

*Repetition has meaning . . . it alone confers
reality upon events; events repeat themselves
because they imitate an archetype—the
exemplary event. Furthermore, through this
repetition, time is suspended, or at least its
virulence is diminished.*

MIRCEA ELIADE,
Cosmos and History

*F*rom the days before *Rosh Ha-Shanah,* the Jewish New
Year, the onset of the Days of Awe, a time of reckoning
and self-search, until after the festival of *Sim'chat Torah,* the rejoicing over the law, by far the most interesting and active parts of
Jerusalem were the precincts of tradition, places where the presence
of yesterday alone gave legitimacy and meaning to today. To initi-
ate me into its ways, Yisra'el, the wood turner, invited me to join
him on the eve of the New Year at the Ger Yeshiva, where he and
hundreds of others planned to reenact the centuries-old practice of
offering *selichot* (penitential prayers) and reciting them in the
presence of the revered and aged hasidic eminence, the Rebbe of
Ger. In the waning hours of the old year preparation for the new
one begins.

Many hasidim, and those who orbit their world, still believe in
the miraculous powers of their rebbe. To them his mere presence,

and even more so his prayers, have the capacity to influence the powers on high. In the era following the destruction of the Holy Temple, whose ashes still smolder in Jewish memory, the rebbe has in the hearts of some taken the ancient place of the High Priest whose task at this time of year had been to ''atone for himself and for his people.''

''If you want to have a unique experience, to see a side of Jerusalem outsiders never discover, and feel something that you can feel nowhere else,'' my friend suggested the morning before, ''then come with me to Ger tomorrow.''

Of course, he did not really mean Ger, the city in Poland where the hasidic dynasty headed by the present rebbe, Israel Alter, had its origins. Rather, he meant the yeshiva in the Ge'ulah quarter, bordering on Me'ah She'arim, where, after the firestorm of the War against the Jews, the center of Ger hasidism had moved. Here in Ge'ulah (the word means ''redemption''), in another space and time, Ger had transplanted itself and renewed the process of spiritual repair.

''They begin at eight plus,'' the wood turner told me. ''Come get me and we'll go there together.''

At the time I did not yet realize it, but my friend was offering me not simply a trip to another location but a journey to another disposition.

That evening, on my way to pick him up, I took a wrong turn and got lost on the grounds of the Biblical Zoo. Driving around its perimeter, I found neither hasidim nor a rebbe but only camels and goats, neither of which were very much help in finding the street I was trying to locate. Finally, after circling about for endless minutes in a rising panic and encountering a series of dead ends, I managed to find my way out and with the redolence of Noah's ark still in my nostrils reached the appointed meeting place in Kiryat Sanz, an Orthodox neighborhood in the northwest corner of the city.

Named after Sanz, a little village in northern Galicia from which many of the original inhabitants came, this neighborhood—like Ge'ulah and Me'ah She'arim—where men all seemed to wear black coats and married women were never without kerchiefs on their heads, reflected another time and mentality closer to Eastern Europe than the Middle East in which it physically existed. Here the culture they nurtured had found a way to overwhelm and even deny geographic realities. The black gabardine kaftan and the fur hat, or *shtreimel,* the married men wore on Sabbaths and holy days might once have been at home in the cold of Poland or Russia, but these people had by an act of collective will brought it into the heat of the ancient homeland as if it were a natural part of the landscape. And by that collective will, places in this city were made to recall another. To some it might seem as if I were driving through twentieth-century Jerusalem, when in effect I was traveling from Sanz to Ger, moving between villages linked by an Orthodox Jewish tradition and locked in an association that transcended, indeed ignored, space and time. I was in a Jerusalem shaped by the ghettoes and *shtetls* of Eastern Europe.

Because I was late, Yisra'el was anxiously waiting for me on the corner; he worried that in the last minute he would have to catch a taxi in order to make it on time to Ger in Ge'ulah and his appointment with penitence and redemption. There was not a moment to waste if we at all hoped to find space to pray in the presence of the rebbe. As it was, he warned me, we would only manage to find room in the courtyard in front of the yeshiva, since the building itself would be packed to bursting with hasidim and other followers of their venerated leader.

I had heard a great deal about the Gerer Rebbe. Leader of what was perhaps the largest sect of hasidim in Jerusalem, he had become an important voice on the *Mo'etzet Gedoley Ha-Torah*, the Council of Torah Sages which acted as the official guide for political expression of the traditionalist Orthodox—the so-called *charedi* (pious) —community. A fifth-generation descendant of Isaac Meir Rothenberg, the founder of this hasidic dynasty and perhaps its most famous master, the present rebbe had continued the rationalist direction of the sect, emphasizing the importance of Torah scholarship over such alternatives as mysticism, song or missionizing as the primary instrument of personal repair, the activity which hasidim believed would bring about Jewish salvation and the days of the Messiah. If not all of his hasidim were personally up to fulfilling these demands of study, they nevertheless in principle were expected to revere the yeshiva and the endless review of sacred texts that went on there. And thus it was at the yeshiva, between the book-lined walls and in the presence of their rebbe, a small man in his eighties, that they ushered in the Days of Awe and murmured their penitential prayers.

Although I must have passed the Ger Yeshiva dozens of times during my days in Jerusalem, I nevertheless had no idea where it was. To the uninformed like me, it blended in with the other buildings around it. But as I would discover again and again in this city, one need shift his consciousness only slightly to discover a layer of life lying on another plane of existence that a moment before was beyond the horizon of perception.

Sitting next to me in the car and leaning forward with anticipation, Yisra'el guided me through the maze of streets through which we passed, taking every shortcut and alley that he knew in order to get us there in time. In the dark and after the fourth or fifth turn, I was completely lost, totally dependent upon his guidance. In retrospect, it almost seems as if this sort of confusion had been necessary to arouse within me the bewilderment with which I was to enter what was for me a new domain of the Holy City.

"Park here," he said suddenly.

"Where are we?" I asked. "This is just a dark side street. Is this where the yeshiva is?"

"*Tekef* [presently]," he said.

Locking the car—even in the "precincts of spirituality" one dare not forget about material matters, for the thief who comes to steal your car in Jerusalem is not always similarly immersed in the heavenly regions—we quickly walked a few meters until we came to the corner and Rechov Mal'khey Yisra'el, the Street of the Kings of Israel.

"Do you feel it? Can you see it?" my guide asked, padding rapidly ahead of me.

I *could* feel something. There was a palpable excitement in the air. Hasidim were rushing toward the large stone building across the street. Women wheeled toddlers, half-asleep, in the same direction. Cars were parked along the sidewalks everywhere.

"Look up at the women's section," Yisra'el urged, nodding toward the upper story of the building we approached. Although I could only catch a glimpse of the inside through the blinds, I could see from the way those at the windows jostled one another that the room behind them was packed.

I knew Rechov Mal'khey Yisra'el well, often wandering along it on my way to and from Me'ah She'arim Street, which served as its continuation. The shop at which I bought the caramel-flavored noodle pudding, Jerusalem *kugel,* that had become a staple of our Sabbath meals was here. Mrs. Rusenak's hat shop, where, under the front counter and hidden from the view of any but those in the know, the best selection of knit *kippot,* or skullcaps, could be found, was here. This is where I caught the Number 15 bus home. And yet, at this moment, I was undeniably disoriented and looked upon the streets around me as part of a totally alien universe.

To be sure, my confusion could be easily explained by the countless turns I had taken in order to arrive, by the fact that I had come upon the street by a pathway different from the one I normally took. Yet thinking now about my loss of bearings then, I prefer another explanation, somehow more appropriate. The neighborhood I knew was oriented around physical realities—buses, food, hats. But the street I was coming to this evening was attuned to a different kind of reality—prayer, self-reckoning, spiritual encounter. The season and a certain overpowering uniformity of thought and sensibility possessed all those around me; it had changed everything. What was otherwise an undistinguished square and not at all architecturally striking building somewhere in the middle of the block was, under the present circumstances, a doorway to another world, an entrance to a different time and another order of life. That aspect of the neighborhood was new and strange to me—and so of course I was lost.

Later, when the evening was all over, and I had watched the rebbe walk out and part the crowd like Moses sweeping across the Sea of Reeds, after he was driven away in his deep blue Buick, when all the hasidim had sauntered away, I suddenly looked around and instantly reoriented myself. No longer lost, I recognized every doorway and easily found the way to my car and from there home.

But that flash of recognition would come much later. Now, as Yisra'el and I hurried toward the yeshiva, I was still confused, and so I blindly followed along. On the corner, a kiosk that would normally be closed at this hour was open. The proprietor, aware of the special schedule of life here, knew that tonight there would be mothers looking to buy a lollypop or some other candy to keep their children quiet while their parents immersed themselves in acts of piety and devotion.

Crossing the street, Yisra'el and I walked down three steps into the outer courtyard of the yeshiva. Although little more than a pillar or two separated the courtyard from the street beyond, an invisible wall of sound seemed to enclose us as we entered; the noises of traffic were drowned out here by the voices of prayer above and ahead of us.

"Look—look at this." Yisra'el chuckled as he pointed to what must have been at least a hundred valises lying in a pile against the wall of the outer courtyard. They appeared to have been thrown by people who on their way to get near the rebbe had been in a frantic rush to be rid of their earthly possessions.

"They've come from everywhere, all over the world, to be near the rebbe tonight and in the coming days,'' Yisra'el said, perhaps exaggerating a bit.

We were late. The *selichot* prayers had already begun, and now there was hardly room to move into the courtyard. Yisra'el squeezed his way to a place near one of the outer walls; he leaned against it while he slipped a prayer book out of his pocket. Finding a seat at one of the many long tables that had been taken out of the study hall upstairs and placed in the courtyard was out of the question. From the windows above us came the cracked and sobbing voice of a hasid who was leading the service. We could not see him, but his broken cries penetrated the air, heavy with murmurs of petition and supplication.

''You hear that voice?'' Yisra'el asked. ''That is the very same *chazan* [cantor] who has led the *selichot* for years. You know, he's a man close to eighty.''

''He's not a very good singer,'' I said.

''Tsk,'' Yisra'el answered, clicking his tongue. ''You don't understand,'' he said, trying to sound patient in spite of what he clearly viewed as my naïveté. ''Don't you see, what is important is that he is the *same chazan* who has been leading the prayers and praying for the coming of the Messiah since the reign of the previous rebbe.''

In this corner of Jerusalem, the point was continuity—still to be able to hear the voice that had intoned the *selichot* for more than a generation. This Jerusalem eschewed emancipation from the past; it breathed in with memory and out with prophecy. Here the new was not the best. The cantor's great asset was his connection with yesterday, his capacity to evoke the feelings that had inspired *selichot* at Ger in the past. He gave voice to Ger's triumph over time.

Although knit into tight circles around the tables, the crowd still moved. But theirs was not a movement through space, from one point to another. Rather, it was a kind of back-and-forth motion. Part of it was physical, a swaying that accompanied the prayers; in the Yiddish vernacular that everyone here used, it was called *shokeling*. But there was as well another kind of back-and-forth motion. This one allowed the worshiper to move from the present to the past and back again, from ancient atonements to contemporary ones which reverberated with older ones.

Soon after Yisra'el and I had settled into our little space against the outer stone wall of the courtyard, I decided to explore the crowd and penetrate the wall of men pressing against me from inside. I wanted to get to and see the center of their attraction. There was something contagious in their desire to cleave to a spiritual center that was obviously somewhere else. Among hasidim, I knew, the most coveted places were those nearest the rebbe, where for believers the Divine Presence could be felt more immediately. For the moment, I wanted at least to try to reach that deepest point in the crowd, to see for myself what repentances were like there.

Standing at the margins of the courtyard, I watched the alms collectors slip into and out of the thickest masses of humanity. They moved with a fluidity that belied the density of the crowd. Surely, with the right determination, I could glide through as well.

"You'll never get near him," Yisra'el warned me, motioning upward with his head. Did he mean God or the rebbe? I wondered; but all I said was "We'll see," and I began to nudge my way through the crowd.

At first it was easy. In just a few moments I was able to push myself to the opposite side of the courtyard and found room under the overhang of the upper floors. Except for a half-dozen little boys of kindergarten age who ran around between the walls of this alcove, there was no one here. In a moment I understood why. Here the sound of the *chazan* could not be heard, nor could the place where the rebbe sat be seen. The ceiling was very low. A heavy emptiness filled the space, and from out of such emptiness repentances could not be aroused.

At the back were some stairs leading up to the main floor of the yeshiva. Each step brought me into increasingly dense packs of humanity. With difficulty, I made my ascent up the circular stairwell. Yet the harder the climb, the more determined became my effort to get to the top. At the first landing, a saprogenous odor of sweat-saturated gabardine and matted hair rose with the heat and filled the air. But curiously, rather than repelling me, as perhaps it might have done on other occasions (like all Americans, I had been taught to detest all body smells), it aroused in me unusually intense feelings of anticipation. It was as if, in my anthropological tracking, I had caught the scent of anxious repentance. I wanted to get closer. Elbowing past the bodies, brushing up against bony shoulder blades and grazing felt hats, I at last reached the vestibule and then, with a bit more effort, managed to get myself jostled to the doorway of the main room of the yeshiva. Standing now at the threshold, I could barely move.

Balancing on my toes and afloat in a sea of black and white, I rolled back and forth in the tide of the crowd, each member of which seemed to be trying to get a glimpse of the rebbe. But from where I stood all I could see was a swell of heads which like mine rose and fell or wobbled and lurched from side to side.

From somewhere in front of me, the *chazan,* whose voice I could barely hear from where I now stood, invoked the past, God's mercies and His primordial attachment to these His people. Then, in rising tones, he concluded with words echoing the time-honored petition:

"May Your servants find pardon today. Grace them with the nearness of Your affection as at the first. And whiten like the snow their rose-red sins. Deliver them from all evils in this year."

Around me, many of the same people who a moment before had been straining to see the rebbe closed their eyes, as if focusing on something else, imagined and interior. It was almost as if the blocked view on the outside deflected them to another, inside view, which in the light of what had just been recited they now strained to see. They turned from the rebbe's seat to another, higher throne. I closed my eyes too. In this quarter of Jerusalem, one could often see more clearly by closing the eyes than by opening them.

"Remember today the Covenant ..." I heard someone beside me whisper the words of the prayer which called out the powers of Divine memory. In my mind's eye, the only one with which I could for the moment see, these words flashed an image acquired after years of worship: the High Priest standing in the Holy of Holies, the inner sanctum of the Holy Temple. Who could forget that the prayers we recited tonight were but echoes of the rituals of atonement once carried out there, on the mountain nearby? Once again —this time in Ge'ulah, or was it Ger?—Jews were awaiting God's redemption. It was easy to lose one's orientation in the timespace of Jerusalem.

The congregation pushed forward and roared the traditional strophic response: "God, the King, who sits upon His throne of mercy, comports Himself with charity and forgives the sins of His people!"

My eyes flew open. There was no way to press myself any closer to the chair on which the rebbe sat. He was locked inside his inner sanctum, the swarm of his disciples.

"And the Lord descended in a cloud and He stood with him there and proclaimed the name of the Lord!" the *chazan* screamed at the top of his voice. The reference was to an event deep in our people's past, their atonement for the sin of the golden calf, but it seemed somehow appropriate to the sight before me.

"*Riboinoi shel Oilom* [Master of the Universe]!" someone behind me cried into my ear.

Startled by the sound, I jerked my head around. And then, perhaps because I had turned around too sharply or because of the press of the crowd and the close air around me, I lost my footing for a moment and began to crumple. But just as I did, someone brushed against me and spun me back around, while someone else leaned against me, propping me up so that once again I faced eastward, toward the rebbe and the Temple Mount. For that brief moment, physically swept up by the crowd, I felt myself emotionally swept up as well, and thrusting myself forward just beyond the doorway where I had been stopped, I closed my eyes tightly and with everyone else cried out at the top of my voice the next words in the liturgy:

"God save us, the King will answer us on the day we call Him!"

Now, when I reflect upon what happened to me in that crowd and at that moment, it seems beyond doubt that my strange vertigo and recovery were more than physical. Moving so swiftly from one image to another, pushed by the crowd and propelled by its desire to see and be near the rebbe and through him some otherwise ineffable past, I was set off into another orbit. All evening I had been moving in a Jerusalem that led breathtakingly from the Biblical Zoo to Sanz, from Sanz to Ge'ulah, from Ge'ulah to Ger, from Ger to the Temple Mount and the High Priest and from there to Sinai. With each jump, the seeds of some ancient tribal attachments began to germinate inside me, and my capacity to turn toward memories I had not known I could acquire began to grow. In the end I was no longer simply being pushed but was pushing myself. And then, finally, as an engaged participant I tore the bonds of my professionally disciplined distance and enabled myself to see through the eyes of others. For that instant, I passed beyond the boundaries of space and managed to get the inside view.

Moments later, having regained my balance, I returned to my place near Yisra'el against the courtyard wall. The descent was easy and uneventful.

"So did you get to the Holy of Holies?" Yisra'el asked, chuckling.

I nodded.

"And how far did you get?"

"Just beyond the doorway," I answered, thinking that I had probably reached my limits.

"That's a good beginning," he said, and then, before returning to his prayers, added, "we'll see how you do in the days to come."

In the days following my visit to Ger and until Yom Kippur, the holiest day of the Jewish year, Jerusalem had become, for me and for many other Jews, a place enveloped in the process of atonement. As the faithful turned their attention inward, visible Jerusalem turned into a Holy City whose outlines were molded almost completely around matters of faith. What was real was what one believed; no more, no less. Each synagogue and Jewish holy place became a portal leading to the Heavenly Court where, according to believers who now spiritually dominated the city, human destiny was decided. At the Kotel, the Western Wall, every psalter was in use as—from before sunrise until deep into the night—believers huddled against its stones and packed the cracks between them with tiny notes to God, requests for blessing, health, prosperity and happiness in the year ahead.

Mixed in with the hum of prayers was the chime of coins, as beggars made their way among the worshipers. The ring of the coins was the only sound needed to attract the attention of those prepared to give. A few supplicants carried letters, laminated in plastic and stamped with an official-looking seal, that certified them as collecting for an institution. No one ever bothered to read the letters. Other mendicants displayed their success in attracting funds by slipping bills in between their fingers: hundred-shekel notes between the first two fingers, five-hundreds between the third and fourth, thousands wrapped tightly around the pinkie.

As the crowd grew, so too did the number of beggars—men among the men and women among the women. Around and around they weaved their way. From above, the clink of their coins could probably not be heard and only the up-and-down movement of their hands would be visible, making it appear as if they were unwinding some invisible thread with which they were binding the throng together. And in a way, through the act of charity—of giving and receiving—that was precisely what they were doing.

In these Days of Awe, those who had perhaps been lax in coming to the synagogue during the rest of the year made a special effort and now came. Civil society, if not altogether replaced by the face of religion, at least put on much of its garb.

To be sure, few truly believed that the face the city had put on during these Days of Awe would remain upon it throughout the year; even in Jerusalem, holiness was hard to preserve *ad infinitum*.

But just as we sometimes put on special garments for special occasions to feel different without at the same time committing ourselves forever to dress the same way, so too the city tacitly permitted itself to don its blanket of holiness without having to promise it would never again remove it.

When the two days of *Rosh Ha-Shanah* arrived, the sound of the *shofar,* or ram's horn, could be heard floating out through the open windows of the crowded synagogues throughout the Jewish city, inaugurating the high season of atonement. On the afternoon of the first day, in line with an ancient tradition whose roots remain shrouded in mystery and folk belief, thousands of Jews from all corners of the city hiked down past the Gihon Spring to the pool of Shilo'ah, the only flowing water in Jerusalem, to recite the *tashlikh* prayer with which they cast away their sins. Singing God's praises and imploring His forgiveness, the Jew drops bread crumbs into the water, praying that as the crumbs float away into the deep, so too will his sins.

For generations Jews have practiced this custom near the various Waters of Babylon. In their exile, they have stood at rivers, seacoasts, ocean beaches and even beside reservoirs, wells and cisterns casting away their sins and praying for salvation and its reflection, the return to Jerusalem. After generations of wandering, to now cast away sins here in the City of David, in the valley below the mountain on which the Holy Temple once stood and from which the High Priest sent a scapegoat into the wilderness and with it cast away the sins of the nation, gave a new dimension to the custom; it brought Babylon to Jerusalem. Still fresh with the return to Zion, Jews thronged into the valley.

"Imagine," I heard a man say to a woman next to him as they walked down to the pool, "what it must have been like that day when the High Priest and the elders watched the scapegoat led off over there." He pointed toward the east and the bare hills of the Judean Wilderness just across the valley. In the days that followed, I would witness many more such imaginative flashbacks during which the practices of the present were seen in the light of the past.

And then would come *Yom Kippur.* The streets emptied of all unnecessary movement and synagogues filled with worshipers, reciting ancient appeals and arguments with which to mollify God. During these days time could be treated like space, losing its irreversibility as worshipers returned to their pasts and repented. In faith, yesterday can be remade in today's image while the present moment calls out future kindnesses promised to generations past:

"Our God and God of our fathers, recall the covenant made with our predecessors and do unto us as You have promised." The past is enlisted in behalf of the present: "Do not forget the covenant with our fathers and the promises of kindness You made to them."

Outside, an unearthly stillness; streets eerily devoid of cars, with only an occasional ambulance passing by swiftly and quietly, carrying those who have collapsed under the strain of the day to the sparsely staffed hospitals; the absence of motion gives the impression of the stopping of time. Since the afternoon before, the radio, the Voice of Israel, has been silent; only an empty hiss comes over the frequencies that normally fill the airwaves with news of life in the Jewish State. Today no Jewish papers are published, and Jewish stores remain closed. Atonement brings stillness, and what is still is stopped.

But if *Yom Kippur* is a day of stillness and stopping, the day before is quite the opposite, a whirl of anticipatory activity.

First comes the body. "Whosoever feasts on the eve of *Yom Kippur* receives merit as if he had fasted two days," the sages promised. On the eve of atonement, Jersusalem's streets are clogged with cars and shoppers; a kind of nervous energy seems to fill everyone. Tempers are short, and drivers honk more than usual to get around traffic jams; pedestrians push a bit more than they normally do. The open-air market in Machne Yehuda is a cacophony of sounds and a swirl of movement as everyone dances around trying to gather all the special items with which his family normally breaks fast so that tomorrow evening after a blast from the *shofar* marking the end of the fast, he will have them.

For the religious, whose footsteps, under Yisra'el's guidance, I pursue today, there is a full schedule to be followed. The morning begins early, with prayers in the synagogue or, preferably, at the Kotel. Even the eating on this day-before-the-fast has a frenetic quality to it as those living by the letter of the law rush about trying to fit in two large feasts before the evening. Then, sometime during the day, forgiveness must be sought among one's friends; God cannot forgive that which mankind will not. To appease one's fellow creatures, charity is distributed. In the afternoon prayer, the observant Jew returns to the synagogue and recites his first *Vidui*. The *Vidui* is a formal confession (to be repeated nine more times before the end of the holy day tomorrow) in which every Jew admits to the same list of transgressions. After the confession there are other penances that some make before their rush to dip in the *mikveh*, the ritual bath, where the body is lustrated before taking its part in the fast and atonement. Finally, at dusk, just before the onset of the fast, a last supper is eaten; parents bless their children and light the candles with which the eve ends and the holiest day begins.

In religious Jerusalem, the "eve"—Erev Yom Kippur—begins even earlier than this day-before. Late afternoon of the previous day is the time for *kapparot,* the time-worn practice of finding some scapegoat upon which to project one's sins. In the ancient days of the Holy Temple, this forlorn animal which the High Priest placed in the care of the *ish iti,* the man of the hour, was led out past the Hills of Judea, through the Valley of Ben-Hinnom—Gehenna—into the desert and a hill called Azazel, where its plunge to death was meant to redeem the entire nation.

And why a goat? With a goat the people of Abraham could repeat their forefather's primordial sacrifice, when on a *Yom Kippur* generations earlier, he substituted a kid for Isaac and saved the life of his son and the future of his people. For the religious Jews of Jerusalem, the primordial event is very much alive in the present.

The mountain, Moriah, on which Abraham offered up the first scapegoat still rises in the heart of Jerusalem. Atop it, however, the Temple no longer stands. The goat and the *ish iti* are but a memory; but scapegoating remains firmly anchored in Jewish consciousness. Seeking to ransom himself from punishment and spiritual darkness, a Jew may still perform *kapparot.* In place of the goat, he takes a chicken—a white one is preferable—which will be slaughtered instead of him.

Why a chicken? The custom emerged in ancient Babylonia, during the Jews' first exile from their holy land and Temple. There, fowl were more common than goats. And so, ever after, a bird, the legacy of the Diaspora experience, has been selected for a death that redeems.

The procedure is very simple. Following the recitation of verses from the Psalms and the Book of Job, the ill-fated chicken is waved up to Heaven and around the about-to-be-redeemed head—to confuse the powers of darkness which would descend upon that head—while these words are declaimed:

"This shall take my place. this shall be my substitution. This shall be my ransom. This chicken shall go to death, and I shall go to a good, long, peaceful life."

The genteel religious Jews of the finer neighborhoods in the city have substituted money for the chicken. They end their prayers by saying: "This money shall go to charity, and in return I shall go on to life.'' But the projection of evil and death in return for good, long, peaceful life is somehow lost, and the electricity of the exchange of life for death disappears in this civilized substitution. So some people—looking for a different alternative—give the money to the ritual slaughterer, who will use it for payment for those who still wish to sacrifice a chicken but cannot afford the price.

Jerusalem has quarters where the charge of the original exchange can still be felt—among them the *shuk*, the open-air market at Machne Yehuda. Here, amid the fruit and vegetable stalls, one can discover reflections and hear echoes of those ancient services upon the Temple Mount. The market becomes an altar, the shopper a supplicant, the butcher a Levite who assists the slaughterer, now a priest. And thus the prolongation of a moment from the distant past is carried to yet another limit.

Before *Yom Kippur*, during the Days of Awe, in the stalls where butchers normally sell chickens and meat, the *kapparot* in their traditional manner are still practiced. Surrounded by plastic crates in which hundreds of live chickens await their certain death, the butcher and the *shochet,* ritual slaughterer, like their predecessors, the priests at the Temple, await the offerings of the people and act as intercessors before God.

Lines have formed from early morning near those stalls where the chickens are best, without blemish, and the *sochet*'s price most reasonable. After negotiating with the butcher for the bird, the men will select a male chicken; the women, a female. From a distance, the transaction looks a little like a ballet. The buyer and butcher move close to each other. The bird, removed from its crate, is taken in hand and waved up and down, examined from far and near. The buyer nods. The butcher whirls around and places it on the scale behind him. There the bird stares blankly into a small mirror affixed to the wall, as if mesmerized by this first and last look at its living self, while the butcher and buyer, heads together, their arms in the air, their fingers waving, settle the price. Whisked off the scale, the bird is turned upside down, its talons tied with twine, and handed to its destiny. The buyer appears to bow, as he places the fowl into a sack for safekeeping; and then, rising in possession of his ransom, he turns to join the line of those waiting for a *shochet,* while the butcher steps to the side to deal with his next customer.

Slowly, the buyer shuffles toward the head of the line until at last he is face to face with the slaughterer. Again the arms and hands wave, again a deal is struck. And the buyer again bends low to pick up the bird, handing it to the man who will slit its throat. Together they hold the bird, and then the one takes it and waves it over the head of the other, the owner. Around and around, as the words of the prayer are mouthed. The ransomed soul steps back, and the *shochet* takes the bird in hand, turns it over and over, inserts his hand into its innards to make certain all is smooth and whole and that no unborn egg awaits life and then draws back its neck slowly, wets his fingers and finds the jugular vein. Swiftly and firmly he plucks a few feathers from the spot, and with a single motion takes the knife from his teeth. Its steel blade is spotless and without a nick, as the law demands, to make the slaughter as swift as possible. The neck is cut, squeezed, the blood spilled quickly upon the ground; and the bird, its life dripping away, is thrown upside down into a funnel. Shivering and heaving, the bird goes through the throes of death. As if growing heavy with the evil of its owner, it sinks ever deeper into the funnel. And then, suddenly, the talons —according to folk tradition, reminders of the talons of the angel of death who snatches away life—shoot up, as if grasping for their last perch in life. And thus they remain, frozen in horror that there is no more such perch. In moments the bird is stripped of its feathers, bound and bagged, to be eaten on the next day as part of the meal separating the feast from the fast of *Yom Kippur*.

On the days before *Yom Kippur*, the alleys of the *shuk* are packed with people who rush about stocking up on fruits and vegetables, fish, cheese, meat and any other things they think they might need for the coming days. Wherever a small crowd gathered about a stand, others would attach themselves to it, convinced that here quality is highest and price low.

Weaving his way through the crowds, a black-frocked and bearded man carried his basket of fruits and vegetables to a number of the stands on which hung signs reading: "WE SEPARATE TITHES FROM ALL OUR PRODUCE." The man was the collector for the poor. Receiving his quota of carrots, peaches, oranges, potatoes and anything else that grew, he would then recite a prayer over the remaining produce, certifying it fit for eating by the faithful, to whom all untithed fruits and vegetables were forbidden. If on other days the fruiterers might be lax in their tithing, throwing only the soft fruits, mushy vegetables or sour grapes into his basket, during these days before *Yom Kippur*, they scrupulously offered him their nicest produce. The roots of folk belief are deeply planted among the stands of the *shuk,* and on the day when the earthly Jerusalem begins its ascent to the heavenly regions, care must be taken to follow the dictates of moral and religious order.

''On all the ten days of repentance between *Rosh Ha-Shanah* and *Yom Kippur* one must be generous in giving charity,'' the sages suggested, ''but on *Erev Yom Kippur* be even more generous, for the merit of giving charity protects and defends one from evil decrees.''

Although they might not all be able to quote the source, Jerusalem's mendicants knew this rabbinic sentiment well. At all the places where the faithful might pass—the *shuk,* the Kotel, Me'ah She'arim Street, Ge'ulah, near the entrances to synagogues and other provinces of the Orthodox—their outstretched palms or the jingle of loose change flagged down potential donors. Leaving the *shuk,* I walked the city, focusing on the beggars whose ubiquitousness was one of the unmistakable signs of the season. One man, a regular fixture near the market in Me'ah She'arim, stood out. With his grizzled mien and the greasy woolen cap which he wore on even the hottest days, he leaned on a cane and waited for those he considered likely prospects. Then, spotting one, he began to shuffle after him, making his plea—Hebrew for the neighborhood's outsiders, Yiddish for locals.

''A little something for a poor man who needs money to get through the holy days, who wants to eat before the fast. I beg you, do not forget me.''

To those who handed him money, he responded : ''Be blessed ; be worthy to carry out other kind deeds.'' A few who handed him larger-than-customary donations were given kisses on the hand, a gesture that seemed to make most of them uncomfortable. Rushing past, one or two nervously wiped the beggar's spittle off their hands.

For those who passed him by without providing a handout, he had a barrage of curses, which in practiced exclamation he shot off in the seconds it took them to get out of earshot. Every so often, the cursed—stunned by the barrage—would wheel around and in reconsideration dig into their pockets and come up with some money. *Erev Yom Kippur* was no time to risk the denunciations of a poor man. Others, especially those who knew this man's tactics, crossed to the other side of the street in order to avoid him or rushed by quickly before he noticed them. A few turned and replied to his denunciations with expressions of shock or malevolent stares.

Another beggar—a mute—who had made his station the bench

near the first bus stop on Me'ah She'arim Street found a way of
shrugging his shoulders and extending his open hand that stopped
even those with tunnel vision. He had a childlike appearance, a
kind of bewildered innocence in his eyes that seemed to say: ''Isn't
this strange that I have been reduced to begging from you? I can't
understand what went wrong in my life. What has happened?
Won't you help?'' To judge by their expressions and the tender
way many passersby dropped some money into his hand, they
seemed more to be trying to comfort him in his puzzlement than to
provide him with financial support.

In the underground walkway that connected the central bus station to the other side of Jaffa Road, among others sat an old woman
reciting psalms while surrounded by picture postcards of sainted
rabbis, most of whom were holy men from Yemen, Morocco and
other communities that once were home to Jews in Moslem countries. To many of these Jews, the sainted rabbi was a power who
could intercede on high. For a donation, the old lady offered a
picture and a blessing. On *Yom Kippur Eve,* she sold out her collection.

Not far from her on the ground was another woman. Ageless in
appearance, she could as easily have been eighty as sixty years old.
There was no way to tell, and one got the feeling that even asking
her would provide no answer. She seemed too cut off from life, her
only connection to the living being her outstretched hand. Like all
the other married women, she had her hair totally covered. But the
faded kerchief she wore was too big and loose, and so it seemed
always to slip over the top of her glasses. Her mumbles for help
from a toothless mouth seemed as muffled as were her eyes by their
thick glasses with their heavily scratched lenses. But everyone knew
what she wanted; any words of pleading would be gratuitous.

Seated cross-legged, she would spread out her skirts and make a
sort of money sack out of them. Often she sat thus, lost in the
careful effort of trying to make out the numbers on the coins she'd
been given. Her head bowed into her lap, and sometimes she looked
as if she had fallen over onto herself and into a deeper sleep. Almost
invariably, when she had finally succeeded in making an accounting
of her collection, someone would toss a coin into the skirts and she
would begin her count again.

''If you want to see something from the past,'' Yisra'el had said
to me, ''then come to Sanz for *min'chah* on Erev Yom Kippur and
you'll see the old-time customs of Jerusalem.''

The "old time" that Yisra'el described was made of a mix of ancient Jewish practices whose origins were Talmudic but whose character was shaped in eighteenth- and nineteenth-century Europe. This old time had been brought to Jerusalem and grafted onto it by the Jews coming from Russia, Poland, Hungary—or more precisely, from the villages of Lubavitch, Ger and Sanz.

With three of my sons, I traveled to Yisra'el's apartment in Sanz.

"Wait until you see the plates," Yisra'el said, as we got ready to go the few blocks to the CHaBaD Synagogue. CHaBaD—an acronym for *chakhma* (wisdom), *bina* (understanding) and *da'at* (knowledge), the highest levels of knowledge in Jewish mystical tradition—was the name Lubavitcher hasidim had taken for themselves.

"Plates?" I asked.

"Wait—let me show you."

Taking down a book from one of the shelves in his living room, which—like so many other Jewish rooms in the religious city—also served as a library, he opened it and handed it to me.

"Read that," he said, pointing to a paragraph near the middle of the page.

"The community leaders of Medzibizh, the town from which the Ba'al Shem Tov, founder of hasidism, came, one year decided to abolish the custom of placing charity plates in the synagogues on *Erev Yom Kippur*. The noise of the *kapparot* money dropping into the dishes disturbed the decorum of the prayers, they believed. But the Ba'al Shem Tov opposed the decision. 'The sound of audible almsgiving,' he explained, 'dispels all unholy thoughts.' "

In the synagogue, which was really a row of rooms, the largest serving as the main sanctuary, the congregation was still forming. For today, the *pushke*, the box into which coins for charity were normally deposited, was put aside. In its place, as in many other synagogues throughout the city, plates had been set out on long tables to receive the *kapparot gelt*, the ransom money that had taken the place of the chicken which would take the place of the soul of the sinner. Carefully separated from any other currency and coins in the donor's possession, the money itself was reserved, dedicated for its special mission of redemption. Some people kept theirs wrapped up in the handkerchief which, thus laden, they had waved above their heads during the recitation of the *kapparot*. Others held it in special purses or separate pockets.

At the synagogue, the Lubavitcher hasidim who ran the place had taken one of the long tables around which they usually reviewed the venerated Torah texts and covered it completely with plates. So laden was the table with plates that some of the paper ones had to be folded and taped to its edge lest they topple over the side. Atop each plate were letters or signs naming the charity to which the money in that particular dish would be dedicated. Some of these looked generations old, the pictures of rabbis and orphans on them yellowed with age.

To the untrained eye there might appear to be no significant difference among the various plates. But judging from the varying amounts of money in each plate, it was clear that to the donors there were important distinctions. Some plates overflowed with coins and bills, while others held only a few shekels. A couple of men came in and began chuckling as they pointed to one of the nearly empty plates.

"You know why they're laughing?" Yisra'el asked me as he pointed to a particularly old-looking slip of paper on a dish. "Because this institution has been closed for nearly ten years."

Near the door, two young men were quickly surrounded by a few others who handed them money.

"These two are legitimate," the wood turner continued. "That one," he said, nodding toward the taller of the two, "goes around to the hospitals before every holy day and hands out money to those whose families at home need it."

Children gathered around the table with coins and bills their fathers had given them and placed them in plates of their choosing. While the fathers stood immersed in prayers, children argued as to which charity was most deserving or which plates most needed filling, those with many coins or those with few. One boy seemed to argue strongly against putting any money in a particular plate. He had heard the men talking about the bogus institutions represented on some of the plates. He too was going to demonstrate his savvy.

"*They* get money from everyone." He pointed to a dish near the far corner of the table.

"Maybe *they* need more than everyone," his father said, coming up behind him and dropping a bill into the plate. Thus, in passing and in the interstices of Jewish life, is the practice of charity taught and learned. Nevertheless, although taught on the run, these *obiter dicta* remain embedded in the memory long after the echoes of prepared sermons and ethical teachings have become stilled—or that, at least, is the impression gained from watching the behavior of the adults, for whom giving seems to be a natural feature of their communal life.

The service over, Yisra'el beckoned me out the door of the synagogue. "You want to see something you probably have not seen before?"

"What?"

"Malkus."

"What?" I was not certain I had heard him correctly. *Malkus* was flogging, a punishment once meted out by the courts in ancient Jerusalem. "Flogging," said the Talmudic sage Rabbah, "takes the place of punishment by death."

And the great exegete Rashi commented on this: "When a person transgresses the injunctions of his Maker, he deserves to die. But when he is flogged instead, that is a sign of the infinite mercy of the Creator."

According to the law, a maximum of forty lashes was allowed, but the rabbis, hoping to avoid the possibility of exceeding forty even by mistake, lowered the maximum to thirty-nine. And where the guilty could not withstand the maximum, he was lashed only to his limits, for flogging was meant to be not so much a means of retribution as an instrument of correction.

During the days when the great court of law, the Bet Din, was convened in Jerusalem, floggings were administered for all those transgressions for which the Bible prescribed *karet*—spiritual extermination: for violations of any of the "thou-shall-not's," for cursing and where the offender had not formally broken the law but had obviously transgressed. Two-thirds of the lashes were to be given on the back, and the remainder on the breast—but in most cases they were inflicted on the least vulnerable parts of the body. The offender stood in a bowed position, with the one applying the blows standing on a stone above him. And as the beating proceeded, it was accompanied by the recitation of verses from Scripture, admonitions and consolations. The flogging was carried out in public so as to have a maximum deterrent and humbling effect.

"Malkus," Yisra'el repeated. "You know what that is?"

"Yes, but I thought that was stopped ages ago."

"It was, but there are still some people who do it today, to remember the days when the Torah ruled here."

"Do they really flog people?"

"It's only a question of remembering," Yisra'el said as he led me to the porch in front of the synagogue. "Come—you'll soon see."

Men and boys shuffled into and out of the many smaller rooms along the side of the building. Every so often, one of the Lubavitcher hasidim would approach another and whisper *"Malkus"* in his ear. The two would then enter one of the rooms. I peeked into one and watched as the two prepared for this dramatic reenactment of a memory which at once celebrated the past and reaffirmed a religious view of its reality.

One of the men spread out a small towel on the ground on which he prostrated himself, dropping to his knees and lowering his head onto his elbows. His partner in the drama slowly removed his own belt, folded it into a loop, and standing over the man on the floor, administered what looked like lashes. When the one man had finished flogging the other, they exchanged places. The man administering the blows swayed back and forth and quietly whispered lines from the Psalms.

The blows were obviously tender and soft, with a kind of subdued but unmistakable pain nevertheless implicit in each lash.

"It almost looks as if it hurts them," I said to Yisra'el, "and yet the flogging is obviously symbolic more than it is real."

"It does hurt them," said a hasid who had overheard me, "from the inside."

"Why do they do it?" I asked, turning toward the speaker.

"To conquer the evil inclination, to cleanse away sin."

Citing the Rabbi Schneur Zalman of Liadi, founder of CHaBaD hasidism and author of its central text, the Tanya, he continued: "In the Book of Kohelet [Ecclesiastes], the fourteenth verse of the ninth chapter, the body is called a 'small city.' The Ba'al Ha-Tanya tells us that just as two kings wage war over a city which each wishes to capture and rule, to dominate its inhabitants according to his will, so do the two souls—the divine and the animal—wage war over the body and all its limbs. And so with our *malkus* we help decide the battle which tomorrow will reach its climax when we fast and try to forget our bodies in order to wrap ourselves into our prayers."

I watched the men get up. When the whole process was over, one of them—it was hard to tell which—uttered a loud sigh.

Says the Talmud: "A sigh breaks the body of a man."

They stood, replacing their belts and folding the towel. Finally, they shook hands with each other. According to the tradition, God can forgive a person only for those sins committed against Him; for those committed by one person against another, absolution can be received only from those who have been aggrieved.

"I ask," one man said to the other, "forgiveness for any transgression I have committed against you." And then they shook hands and embraced.

"Nu?" said Yisra'el. "Now let us go prepare for the Day of Judgment, which is almost upon us."

CHAPTER
·9·

ECHOES OF
CELEBRATION

*A man is surer of his faith when he sees to how
distant a past it goes back and what great
things it has inspired.*

EMILE DURKHEIM,
The Elementary Forms of the Religious Life

*I*n the Jewish Jerusalem, toward which Yisra'el had led and
pointed me, the past had been enlisted in the service of religious needs. The special cast its inhabitants put on that past became
especially clear on the evening that the holy season came to a close.

For over a month, from the days preceding *Rosh Ha-Shanah*
through *Yom Kippur* and into the festivals of *Sukkot* and *Sim'chat
Torah*, I had wandered mostly in the neighborhoods and among the
people for whom tradition was a way of life. Here, more than simply breaking up the work routines or adding an extra day of vacation, the holy days infused life with an alternative rhythm and
what the faithful called a *n'shamah yetarah*—extra spirit.

So powerful is the transformation that comes over those who thus
enter the spirit of the holy days and allow it to enter them that
when the last festival, Sim'chat Torah—during which the Jews
celebrate their having completed the annual cycle of reading the

Five Books of Moses—is over, they find it difficult to return to the routine. The next month they call Mar-Hesh'van—*mar* meaning ''bitter,'' bitter because no festivals fall during it. And so, before the onset of this quotidian bitterness, one more echo of celebration can be heard: *Is'ru Chag.*

Is'ru Chag, the code of law explains, is the day that follows the festival. No longer holy yet not quite mundane, this day-after resonates with the joy of the previous day, *Sim'chat Torah.* In the days when the Holy Temple was still standing, the faithful recall, additional sacrifices were brought and libations poured. It was an occasion of great celebration.

Said the sages: ''Whoever has not seen the celebration at the Holy Temple has not seen rejoicing in his life.''

In our time, wrote the author of the Jewish codes, all those who express joy on *Is'ru Chag* are thereby associating themselves with the actions of their forebears and following the prescriptions of the sages. They merit the appropriate reward. But more than that, the codes explain, he who rejoices on the night after the holy day attests by this that God's holy days are dear to him, for he can neither easily or suddenly tear himself away from them nor cease from rejoicing.

Is'ru Chag begins in the evening, with the formal separation of the holy day from the rest of the days. In Jerusalem, within the hour of the holy day's end, people gather to dance what are called the *Hakafot Sh'niyyot*—the ''second circuits.'' At this concluding go-round of the season, the dances that were part of yesterday's celebrations are repeated once more with feeling. Because *Is'ru Chag* is not formally a holy day, only its echo, the usual holy day prohibitions against the use of musical instruments are suspended at the same time that the atmosphere remains festive. So on *Is'ru Chag,* orchestras are assembled even as Torah scrolls are held aloft, and both are surrounded by circles within circles of humanity.

I went to the *Hakafot Sh'niyyot,* hoping that in the process and in the presence of others commemorating *Is'ru Chag,* I could witness the religious experience and the collective memory on which they were based. Watching from a distance would not be enough. Memories embedded in religious experience emerge gradually in the company of others, in the effervescence of collective celebration. They can be witnessed best with participation by the observer, out of merged consciousness and common circumstances. I would have to dance as well.

• • •

My children, exhausted with the celebrations of the last few days, were already asleep. Not wanting to leave them alone and unable to find a baby-sitter on this night when everyone seemed to be out for one more night of fun, my wife and I decided to go to Liberty Bell Park, where this year, as for several years running, the municipality had planned an "official" celebration. The park was a few blocks from where we lived, and that would allow our oldest son, who was in charge of the rest of the children, to come fetch us in case of emergency.

I had my doubts about this decision. A municipally planned *Is'ru Chag* celebration was not necessarily the occasion at which to catch a glimpse or feel the beat of the religious Jerusalem I was seeking. Still, I thought, perhaps I might learn from the formal festivities and what was missing from them something about the informal celebrations. Liberty Bell Park was at least a place to begin.

The municipality put great effort into its plans for these *Hakafot Sh'niyyot*. For a week beforehand, billboard columns and walls throughout the city had been plastered with posters by the dozens announcing this annual event. This was, after all, not just a celebration for the faithful, an end of the holy days, but also in a way the close of the national holiday period, the end of the summer and the beginning of the new year. The tourist season was ending. The winter rains, for which the faithful had prayed in the synagogue this morning, would—with the help of Heaven—begin in the coming days. Tomorrow life would drop again into its normal routine. Where else but the national capital, Jerusalem, should this boundary of national life and time be marked?

To someone looking for more than the shell of *Is'ru Chag*, the festivities at Liberty Bell Park were, however, not enough. Here, where every stone was new and it seemed every tree and blade of grass were newly planted, what went on seemed equally neoteric and ersatz. The *Hakafot Sh'niyyot* here were simply not authentic. Like the model of the Liberty Bell which the city fathers of Philadelphia had given to Jerusalem to be placed in the center of the park, what went on at the *Hakafot Sh'niyyot* here was only a pale representation of the original and even of the other reenactments I would attend later in the evening, closer to the sources, in Me'ah She'arim.

Located amidst the exclusive and rich neighborhoods Talbieh and Yemin Moshe and near the best hotels, the recently built park had become a place for many municipal festivities. Tonight, it drew people from all over the city. The surrounding streets, heavy with traffic, were filled with cars parked in every conceivable spot. Even the wide sidewalks of Jabotinsky Street were littered with cars, so that pedestrians had to weave their way between bumpers and around fenders as they neared the entrance to the park. There they were met by the green-uniformed men and women of the border patrol, who checked the bags of all those who passed through the park's gates. (Whenever there was a mass gathering in the city, security was increased and bags were checked for bombs or weapons, a reminder of the palpable tension that always exists just beyond the borders of the visible.)

"I have no bag," an American tourist from one of the nearby hotels called out to the dark beauty who stood at the gate checking all those entering. He flashed open his sweater; "Should I open anything else up?"

For a moment the serious look on her face betrayed a smile, and she answered in her heavily accented English: "You need open nothing else; I have seen all I want to see." The tourist shuffled past without saying anything more.

In the park, the stone paths were filled with entrepreneurs who had hauled out their supplies of *Sim'chat Torah* banners from their storerooms. Elaborately decorated flags made of folded paper cost three hundred shekels, while the more ornate ones, with several layers and additional prayers printed on the back, were five hundred. For the practical buyer who wanted something that would last more than a season there were plastic flags attached to little toy trumpets. When the child tired of waving his flag, he could blow on it.

Farther down the passage, in the middle of a large plaza near the copy of the Liberty Bell, a stage had been constructed. Here the program, called for 8 P.M., was now, at 8:30—on time, in Jerusalem terms—just getting under way. A few boys selling cotton candy stood at the entrance to the plaza, while a grizzled man worked his way through the crowd hawking taffy apples, a favorite of the season.

Surrounded by at least a dozen loudspeakers, the stage stood bathed in brightness from an array of spotlights. From my vantage point I could see an announcer—a kind of master of ceremonies—walking with microphone in hand and introducing all the dignitaries on the podium. Dressed in the colorful costume of his position, the Rishon L'Tzion, the Sephardic Chief Rabbi, was introduced. He walked toward another microphone and placed his mouth close to it. The distorted sound of his blessing pierced the air.

"A holy event, a holy people, a holy land, a holy city!" he cried out, as if unaware he had a microphone. As he shouted his blessings, the crowd kept pouring in. Few seemed to pay much attention to the words that blasted through the air; he stood too close to the microphone, and the volume of his voice was quickly becoming oppressive. Behind the rabbi, a group of elderly Jews dressed in the ceremonial costumes of their countries of origin—Bukhara in Central Asia, Kurdistan, Yemen—were being lined up by the stage manager. The announcer's mike was still on, and it picked up the directions they were being given as to how they would be dancing.

"And therefore," the Rishon L'Tzion was concluding, "we hope and pray that all of you who are here today, who are visiting this holy city this year, will be with us again next year in Jerusalem, a rebuilt Jerusalem, a complete Jerusalem, and may we see the redemption of all of Israel and the coming of the Messiah speedily in our days, and let us all say 'Amen.' "

The taffy-apple man was doing a big business; every other mouth seemed to be nibbling one of his round red treats. In some of the darker corners of the park, I could make out the shadowy outline of couples snuggling. A boy was unraveling a girl's long braid of hair. She shook it loose, and in the darkness it covered their silhouettes. I turned back toward the light.

The music began, and the men on the stage wobbled around in a small circle. The tune, one of the familiar international Jewish anthems, was neither from Yemen, from Bukhara nor from Kurdistan; it was one written in America by a rabbi born in Hungary. The words from the Psalms were familiar: "The Lord bless you out of Zion, and see to the good of Jerusalem all the days of your life."

Some teenagers, dressed in the blue-and-white uniforms of B'nai Akiva, the Orthodox Zionist youth movement, formed a circle near the back of the crowd and began dancing a hora. Faster and faster they whirled; tourists rushed over to snap pictures. The flash of the cameras from all sides lit up the circle.

"Ladies and gentlemen, straight from appearances in New York and singing some of his most popular songs there, I am happy to present Joe Amar!" the announcer called out.

"I've heard enough," my wife said. "I'm going home."

Together, we left Joe Amar's repeat performance from New York, the copy of the Liberty Bell from Philadelphia and the songs and tourists from America. While my wife turned toward home, I decided to go to Kikar Shabbes, the square in Me'ah She'arim where another set of *Hakafot Sh'niyyot* was supposed to be taking place.

Just across the street from the park was a bus stop from which I could get to my destination. I sat down on the bench. Beside me sat a young man in a brightly colored knit skullcap, a *kippah s'rugah* —a sure sign of his being one of the so-called modern Orthodox; the more traditional wore hats or black cloth caps. His arm was wrapped around the young woman next to him, his fingers playing with the tendrils of hair on her neck. Tonight was a special occasion, a Thursday night after a holiday. While Friday would normally be a regular workday, albeit shortened in the afternoon because of the advent of Sabbath in the evening, many places of business and institutions were giving their employees a *yom gesher*—a "bridge day"—off, so as to provide one of those rare long weekends in this country of six-day workweeks. For the Orthodox, who kept Friday nights as Sabbath—not an opportune time for a "night out"—and for whom, like everyone else, Saturday nights were the last evening before the early start of work the next day, this night was one of the few on which they could stay out late and not have to get to school or work the next morning.

The bus came quickly and I boarded, handing the driver my *kar'tisiah*, the card with twenty-five prepaid rides which the driver punched, and found a place near the rear door from which I, like everyone, would exit. Israelis might push and shove in order to get on the buses—"If we had been less pushy," one man once explained, "we'd have been thrown into the sea by the Arabs long ago"—but when it came to maintaining order inside, they were rather strict. Few people challenged the arrangement by which they would get on in front and off through the rear.

The bus passed through the major downtown intersection at Jaffa Road and Straus and King George streets. As they invariably did on weekend nights, teenagers had draped themselves along the metal bars that lined the sidewalks. Meant to keep pedestrians from crossing anywhere but at the crosswalks, these barriers had become hangouts for young people in search of company and with nowhere special to go. When they hung in place, it was almost impossible to walk down the street here, so thick had it become with bodies. Along with the recently converted mall on Ben-Yehuda Street, a block away, this section of town had informally become their meeting place, the bars becoming human hitching posts. Kiosks and fast-food places had taken advantage of this development and bloomed around the area. The overflow from the streets often poured into them.

On these streets the holiday could be felt, but there was no sign of the holy day. A few guitar players had set up their open cases and were entertaining the crowd in the expectation of donations. This practice had grown in the last few years. For a while most of the entertainers were Americans, but in time, some Israelis picked up the idea. They, however, were a far more motley group. A few knew nothing more about playing than how to strum two or three chords; they were beggars who had before simply held out a cup or palm. Now, with a cheap guitar and a few chords, they expected a big increase in their take. There were also those in search of souls, who had taken up the guitar as a vehicle for attracting the disaffected street people to the various ways of God.

"We want the Messiah now," one man sang to the tune of "This Land Is Your Land."

A few young boys gathered around him. The traffic light changed to green, and my bus moved on up Straus Street toward Me'ah She'arim. At the corner of Straus and the Street of the Prophets, instead of continuing north toward Me'ah She'arim as it normally did, it turned eastward and stopped. Getting off, I walked between the police barricades that had been set up at the intersection.

The Mitchell Theater, the movie house which separated the profane downtown area from Me'ah She'arim and the surrounding *charedi*, or pious, communities, and which was often a point of conflict between the two sides, was open, but few people appeared to be going inside this evening. For tonight at least, the pleasures the *charedim* offered attracted a far larger crowd than the movies.

Walking up the street, I passed at least a dozen parents pushing strollers or leading children in the same direction. A father half-ran with his son; he spoke to him in Yiddish: "Come, come, we're late." The boy, about eight years old, let go of his father's hand and began to run ahead.

At the crest of the hill, I could see the loudspeakers that had been set up in the square. They boomed with the sound of a political speech by an official of Agudat Israel, the ultra-Orthodox party, whose major source of support came from the *charedi* precincts, and which was the sponsor of tonight's gathering.

My route brought me from outside the neighborhood, so I ended up entering the square from the wrong side, coming in from the back. There I first came upon the band, made up of *ba'alei t'shuva*, newly Orthodox Jews from the Diaspora Yeshiva, an academy on

Mount Zion that specialized in turning Jewish nonbelievers into religious zealots. Once, these musicians had been more at home playing rock or folk songs; but of late, while they still played the same music, they had exchanged the original lyrics of these tunes for sayings of the rabbis or lines of Scripture. They could and also did play all the classic hasidic melodies. To the outsider, these boys, with their beards and earlocks, kaftans and hanging fringes, looked very much a part of the *charedi* community. But insiders, who knew everyone and from where everyone came, immediately recognized them as outsiders, and so, perhaps in order that they be heard but not seen, the organizers of the evening had found a way to conceal them from view. The band was squeezed in underneath and behind the stage.

The crowd, overwhelmingly *charedi,* was divided by sex: men filled up one side of the square; women compressed themselves on the other. A large sign directing each group to its own space was posted in front.

I walked through the crowd. My route had taken me into the women's section, and I could sense from the sidelong glances of those around me that they would be happier if I moved to the other side of the divide. Even the outsiders to the neighborhood, passing into a territory in which they knew they were only visiting, heeded the sign that divided the sexes. Joining the meandering line of men like me who were making their way around the women and toward the men, I walked away from my place near the stage.

Here and there, people seemed to be paying attention to the speeches being made from the stage, but most of those assembled in the square had come for something else. If you asked them why they were there, they of course would say for the celebration of *Is'ru Chag.* But there was something else. Tonight they could feel the press of the crowd; they could be absorbed in the people. Tonight offered a chance to see others and be seen, an opportunity to feel oneself part of something larger, a body politic. One could not but be impressed by the sight of their collective strength. The thousands of black-frocked men and kerchief-covered women, boys with knit *kippot* and girls with braided hair, old and young, who jammed the square celebrated their existence simply by displaying it.

The speaker on the dais sat down, and the band began to play. Once again, people turned their attention toward the front. A hasid in his fifties had climbed up onto the narrow space in front of the line of dignitaries. He took off his hat, under which was a black skullcap of crushed velvet. Sliding it rakishly slightly forward on his bald head, he began to dance in time to the music. Although he hardly moved his feet, his flailing arms gave the impression that he was in constant motion. Up and down and sideways they moved, bending at the elbows and then at the wrists. Every so often, he would open and close his fingers with a flutter, and the band would respond with some dramatic shift in the music, its tempo or timbre. He seemed at times to be juggling the air.

Behind him the elderly dignitaries, their faces masks of practiced indifference, hardly moved as he darted around in front of them. And just when it seemed he was about to back into one of them and fall into a lap, he lurched forward toward the front of the stage.

Suddenly he was handed an open bottle of beer. Placing it atop his head, he balanced it there while he continued his ever-more-frenzied dance. Faster and faster he moved, rushing from one to the other side of the stage in time to the music. A few of the dignitaries seemed to raise their eyes slightly. Again he leaned over backward, but the bottle remained perfectly balanced atop his head.

Another bottle was handed to him, and he placed this one on top of the other. Now with the two bottles sitting precariously atop his head, he pranced gingerly across the stage. A little of the beer inside sloshed over the top, but the bottles remained in place.

The crowd was totally absorbed in the performance. Children hung out the windows of the houses surrounding the square, while a few climbed onto walls along the sides. Many were raised onto their parents' shoulders.

Suddenly, a younger hasid jumped up on the other side of the stage. He too had a beer bottle atop his head and tried to keep time with the music. The curls around his ears swung wildly, and one must have hit the bottle, for it abruptly slid off his head. Managing to catch it, he slithered off to the side of the stage to the consoling applause of some of the crowd.

By now the older master had a new balancing act. On his nose he had poised two large chairs, one atop the other. And thus he glided across the stage. Back and forth he moved. By now even the elderly dignitaries watched him intently, flinching each time he came too close. When at last he got down on his haunches and leaned back, the line of dignitaries were moved to bend with him. And as the chairs on the juggler's nose began to waver, an elderly rabbi on the dais directly under them began to rise from his seat.

Throwing off the chairs, the juggler began again to flail his hands up and down and from side to side. He pulled up the tails of his long coat and tucked them into his pants. Back he leaned, until he was bent in half and his head rested at the black shoes of one of the rabbis behind him. Then, with a jump he stood erect, bent forward and jumped back. A voice boomed out: "Reb Riveleh Kreshevsky."

"What does all of this have to do with the season?" I asked one of the earlocked boys next to me in the crowd.

"Look in the Gemara," he said, referring me to the Talmud, which conferred on the practice all the authenticity he needed. "It was said of Rabbi Shimon Ben-Gamaliel that when he rejoiced on *Sim'chat Bet Ha-Sho'evah* [the Jubilation of Libation, a Temple festival coinciding with the third day of *Sukkot*], he would take eight flaming torches in hand and juggle them masterfully, without one ever touching another. And then he would balance himself on his thumbs in a way that no one else could—that was how he bowed!

"So there's nothing new here," my guide concluded; "it all belongs to the tradition."

On the stage, a singer who alternated his songs with various bird sounds was performing now. Leaving this strange nocturnal whistling, I decided to move farther into the neighborhood.

Bustling with traffic during the weekdays, tonight the streets were empty of all but pedestrians. In the moonlit darkness, the chiseled walls of the surrounding buildings seemed to hem in and enhance the darkness. No light came out of any of the windows. Everyone was either asleep or out. From a variety of doorways, wherever there was a synagogue, came the sound of singing and dancing. But above all others was the reedy sound of the clarinet. I followed it.

The streets were still damp from the morning's rain. For the last three days, since the eve of *Shemeni-Atzeret,* the concluding holy day of the *Sukkot* festival, on which the faithful began reciting their prayers for the life-giving winter rains, the intermittent early showers of the season had begun. The *yoreh,* Scripture called these blessed first drops. Little puddles filled hollows inside the first alley I entered. Here I came upon Yeshivat Ahavat Shalom.

Outside the small, unfinished building stood groups of young women and girls. Not allowed to enter inside, where the men danced, they hung at every opening, trying to get a peek at what was happening. So little space remained that a few were forced to stand in the fresh mud.

I pushed my way inside. The room was warm and crowded. In

the center, some men held a decorated wooden case inside which
rested the holy Torah scroll. But although it was clear from the
way the scroll was dressed that I was among Jews of Sephardic
origin—the Ashkenazim used soft mantles instead of hard cases
like the one before my eyes—these Orthodox Jews whose parents
came from North Africa had already taken on much of the outer
trappings of Eastern European Orthodoxy which dominated the
world of the yeshiva. They wore the black-and-white coats, and the
tunes they sang as they danced around and around were the same
ones I would hear this evening in some Ashkenazic synagogues.
From North Africa they had gone straight to Poland, even though
they lived in Jerusalem.

No people, Leopold Zunz, the great student of Jewish life, once
said, totally reverts to its ancient position. The return of exiles to
an ancient homeland and city had created a new series of combina-
tions, an ethnic mix. The stuff that held it all together here was
religious ritual, and the collective consciousness that bubbled from
that ritual. Here Jerusalem was being spiritually rebuilt. But that
I would discover only at the end of the evening.

Now, the celebration was just beginning; along the edges of the
room and at the outer rims of the circles, people were still moving
in and out. The centripetal force of the dance, when everyone in
spite of himself would be drawn into the circle, had not yet achieved
its full strength. For a while I stood taking in as much as I could.
There were five *hakafot* left to go. As the congregation moved toward the seventh and last go-round, the intensity would build. I
would come back later. I was not ready to dance just yet.

I edged my way around the circle and out the door, hoping to
penetrate farther into the neighborhood. Back out on Me'ah
She'arim Street, I joined the unending stream of walkers. Ahead
of me a line of wide-hipped women pushed baby carriages, their
husbands walking a few steps in front of them. And in little orbits
around each couple spun a pride of children. Again I could hear a
clarinet somewhere in the distance.

For a moment I thought the sound must be coming from the Mir
Yeshiva in neighboring Beit Yisra'el, and so I turned off at Sonnenfeld Street, passing the shuttered carpentry workshops and
dark glass factory. But the farther I walked down the hill, the
clearer it became that while there were lights burning in the yeshiva, the music was coming from somewhere behind me. So I
turned around and climbed the hill I had just descended, heading
toward Batei Ungarin.

Founded in 1891, Batei Ungarin had been the home of the *kolel*, or collection organization, that labeled itself Shom'rei Ha-Homot —Keepers of the Walls. Whether these were the walls of the Holy City or those which kept out the corruptions of modernity, I did not know. Many of its organizers had been followers of Rabbi Moses Sofer of Pressburg, the "Chatam Sofer," as he had been called. Although their rabbi never settled here himself, he regarded the establishment of a community of observant Jews in Jerusalem as a religious act of utmost importance. Here, he hoped, Jews would be able to fulfill the mandate of adhering to the ancient ways of their people. But these were ancient ways that had been reforged in the Europe from which the Chatam Sofer came.

"The new is prohibited by the Torah," Sofer had proclaimed. Where better than ancient Jerusalem to live out this truth? Who could believe that the new would ever penetrate its walls? To be sure, it was not a Jerusalem of the Middle East that he had in mind.

From the beginning, tenants in Batei Ungarin were assigned certain religious responsibilities which kept them anchored to the past. Attached to many of the houses were decrees which mandated ritual study, observance of commandments and a fidelity to the ways of the Chatam Sofer. Today, this trust still protects—some say overprotects—the neighborhood. Here the modern remains bonded in service to the ancient.

As I neared the archway leading into the courtyard, I could hear the sounds of an accordion and drums accompanying the clarinet. Stepping down the stairs, I rounded the corner and saw the courtyard filled with women. Some sat on the stairs; a few leaned against the old cisterns, long since covered over by cement. They chatted quietly.

The Chatam Sofer Synagogue was on the upper story. Along a narrow veranda on its side, some girls had managed to find space. They pressed their bodies against the wall—almost longingly—and craned their necks to get a glimpse through the windows. I passed underneath them and around the remaining groups of women, some of whom stood socializing in the courtyard chatting or sat on the stoops of the nearby houses rocking carriages back and forth, then climbed the narrow staircase that led up to the synagogue.

A seemingly endless line of men was ascending and descending the tight passage. Some of the men and boys tried to push their way up, while others carefully lowered themselves down the steep stone stairs along the outside of the building. But the mix of people—a curious blend of borrowed fragments of modernity and burnished relics of tradition—was unusual for this closed, traditionalist Orthodox neighborhood : black coats alternated with blue jeans, furry *shtreimels* with knit *kippot,* hasidic boys with earlocks and boys with sideburns, voices speaking Yiddish mingled with Hebrew speakers and even some who used English.

During the rest of the year, if outsiders dared venture into this fortress of insularity, they might at best be made to feel uncomfortable and at worst be chased out with insults and spittle. Tonight, however, they were drawn into the circle. Some young boys in blue jeans entered ; one wore a single earring. His friend tugged at his sleeve and mumbled something about their having to get somewhere else. But the boy with the earring appeared mesmerized by the sounds and sights all around him. A young hasid reached out his hand, and the boys were pulled into the circle.

Looking at the combination of faces and costumes before my eyes, I could not help wondering what it was we anthropologists meant when we termed people "exotic"; were the men in black coats and earlocks exotic, or were the boys in earrings and blue jeans? Who was stranger? And it occurred to me then, more clearly than ever before, that the concept itself was meaningless. In a world where borders could be crossed and timescapes rearranged, we were all exotic once removed from our natural habitat or informing context.

"You see all types here tonight." It was my young earlocked friend from Kikar Shabbes, speaking to me as if he had read my mind.

Inside the crowded room, everything seemed framed by the ubiquitous black coats and fur hats. In the front corner sat three hasidim who made the music : in the center a clarinetist who led the band, beside him an accordionist who seemed to move only one hand and on the other side a drummer whose hands moved so quickly that they sometimes seemed to strike all the drums at once. On the floor in front of them were circles within circles. In the innermost were the men with the Torah scrolls in their hands ; next came the older men, and finally, along the outer ring, the youngest ones. So packed was this last circle that if I let my eyes blur for a moment the scene appeared to become a single flesh, swaying first forward and then backward.

Song followed song, but although the melodies changed every time, each tune seemed to have the same fast tempo. Yet while the dancers' feet going up and down appeared to keep up the same quick pace, the circle itself nevertheless seemed to move in slow motion.

The repetition of the beat had a compelling quality, as if something ancient, embedded somewhere deep down in the collective unconscious of all those present, were once again presenting itself. And though I could not fully articulate what that memory was, I felt its presence as I pressed my way into the circle that passed before my eyes.

I knew the song now being sung; I had heard it earlier this evening in Liberty Bell Park: "The Lord bless you out of Zion, and see to the good of Jerusalem all the days of your life." But although the words were the same ones I had heard there, the timbre of the melody was different, as was its beat. What had been a formal, rather empty display of rejoicing pulsed here with a fervor that made the song seem altogether unlike what I had heard in the park.

"Do you feel it?" my earlocked friend asked, pulling me into the circle.

I did not need to ask what he meant, for he had already told me the entire evening was but a repeat of the ancient patterns of celebration that had their origins in this city on the holy mountain called Moriah where once the Temple stood. Still, when at last I got home that night, even though the hour was very late, I looked up the description the Talmud gives of the celebrations at the Temple. My friend had been right; there was a certain parallel between past and present for those inclined to look at things through the prism of religion.

"At the celebration of *Simchat Bet Ha-Sho'evah*," the text began, describing the celebrations that took place four days before *Is'ru Chag*,

> hasidim used to come before the people who gathered in the Temple courtyard, singing songs of praise and thanksgiving and dancing with drums in their hands. And the Levites, carrying harps and timbrels, trumpets and countless other instruments of song, stood along the steps: fifteen rows ascending [corresponding to the fifteen "songs of ascent" in the Psalms] from the women's courtyard to the upper one. And two priests with two ram's horns stood at the upper gate to the Temple, at the head of the stairs. Someone sang out and the horns were blown. Again someone sang out and again the horns were blown. And so it went, over and over.

Majestically they moved, half-marching and half-dancing, in a pulsating line, until they reached the Eastern Gate, which faced the Mount of Olives, from which, in the end of days, the Messiah and redemption were to come. Then they turned their eyes westward and proclaimed: ''Our fathers who stood on this place turned their backs to the holy place and their faces eastward, bowing to the sun—but we turn to God.''

So it was not just Eastern Europe that was being echoed here; ancient Jerusalem figured into the mix as well. Realities and recollections were laminated together.

There were echoes here that went back even further. Every so often a small man would appear at the front near the band and grab a microphone. Screaming into it, he announced the completion of the *hakafah*—the circuit of dancing—and then he would call all those who were to take part in carrying the Torah scrolls in the next go-round. First came all those named Abraham and then those named Isaac, Jacob and so on. The turns corresponded with the chain of Jewish being that began with Abraham, the first Jew. Hours later, it would end with all the *cohanim*, descendants of priests, and the *n'arim*, boys under the age of bar-mitzvah.

Each time the list of those to be called was recited, it seemed endless, with far more names than the number of scrolls there were to hand out.

''Who are all those people being called?'' I asked my guide. ''Are all those people here?''

''In a way,'' he answered. ''Some are; some were, some gave money; some gave blessings. They're all mentioned tonight.''

The call went out not only to the physically present but also to those who in one way or another belonged to this congregation, not only to the living but also to their forebears. After all, only those the congregation forgot were truly gone; the rest could live in the immortality of collective memory. Tonight, on the anniversary of great rejoicings, the sons and daughters could include anyone they wanted, from their forefathers to their own fathers. Here among the religious of Jerusalem, that was the meaning of the past.

I looked at my watch, and was shocked to discover that I had been several hours in this place without realizing it. It was nearly midnight. Pushing myself toward the door, I took one last look at the room. The men had begun another song, a line from the liturgy filled with the promise of yesterday and the vision of tomorrow:

"And our eyes will yet see Your kingdom, as foretold in the psalms of Your mighty David, anointed Messiah of justice."

Walking through the women's courtyard back up to Me'ah She'arim Street, I again found myself in the dark. The singing from the Chatam Sofer Synagogue grew more muffled with each step I took, and at last all I could hear was the melody carried by the clarinet. The Jerusalem into which I had entered since arriving in the neighborhood in a sense ignored its physical surroundings. Within its circles another world was being fashioned. As the dancers marched around with their scrolls, calling up their forebears and singing about past promises and future salvations, they wrapped up the present in the past and shaped it to an imagined future. This was the Jerusalem of the traditionally religious.

In this Jerusalem—freighted as it was with pasts and futures—normal time was being rearranged. And if these Orthodox Jews found the present least accessible or engaging, they could nevertheless make their way easily into the past or gain sudden access to the End of Days which everyone believed was sure to come. Maybe there was more. I had lost my awareness of time inside the synagogue. Perhaps, in a world where anachronism was the primary principle of order, one could also grab hold of a moment existing outside the flow of time as we know it—a moment that lasted as long as it reverberated in one's consciousness. Perhaps that was the special appeal of this Jerusalem.

I began walking again; one last stop remained to be made in this neighborhood. Near the end of the street, in an alley to the left, stood the large white stone building that housed the Toldos Aharon Yeshiva. The hasidim who were headquartered here were followers of the late Rabbi Aaron Roth—"Reb Arele," he was called in a kind of loving diminutive. Insiders called them the "Reb Arelach," Reb Aaron's.

In Hungary, Reb Arele had established a following around his charismatic personality and simple demand: no contact with the outside world. After immigrating in the 1930s and before his death in Jerusalem in 1944, he had once more established a following. The Nazi persecutions, Reb Arele had argued, were the result of the curse that contact with the outside world had brought. Only a reinvigorated isolation, a battle against the adulterations of the modern world, could protect Jews from even greater destruction. In the smoldering darkness of the aftermath of the Holocaust, this idea had offered some explanatory light for the faithful; and thus even in his declining years, Reb Arele had been able to build a new following out of the cinders.

As Jews who had ties to Hungary, the Reb Arelach found their way into Batei Ungarin. In Jerusalem, Reb Arelach's hasidim had brought together two traditions: the stringent interpretations of Jewish law and isolationist proclivities of Hungarian Orthodoxy along with the demand for purity which Jerusalem's religious atmosphere seemed to require. They took to wearing the golden-striped coats of the Jerusalem hasidim; during the week they wore coats with gold stripes on a black background, and on Sabbath the gold was against white.

And why did the Jerusalem people wear such golden-striped coats? I once asked a local.

"You know," he began, quoting the Passover Haggadah, " 'in each generation they stand over us to destroy us.' During the uprisings, the Arabs were ready to kill every one of us. But one thing they kept: they respected our holy men, as they respected all holy men. And if they saw a man with a long beard, wearing a golden coat, they were certain he must be one of the holy. So already in the days when we all still lived in the Old City, the hasidim of Jerusalem began wearing the golden coats. The Reb Arelach caught on to this idea."

The wives of the Reb Arelach were easily recognizable on the streets of the neighborhood. No matter how bright their print dresses might appear, or the sparkle of their ear studs, each one wore a plain black kerchief drawn tightly across her shaved scalp, and black stockings on her legs. Men in golden coats with wives framed in black—these were the Reb Arelach.

After their leader's death, a split occurred among Reb Arele's disciples. The larger of the two groups, those today known as the Reb Arelach, who fill the benches of the Toldos Aharon Yeshiva, followed the leadership of Reb Arele's son-in-law, Reb Avraham Yitzhak Kahan. A smaller group, known as Shomrei Emunim— "Guardians of the Faith," after the title of a book that Reb Arele had written—remained under the leadership of Reb Arele's son, Reb Avraham Hayim Roth.

Finding a wife was not always easy for these men. The isolation and the strict adherence to law are difficult to bear even in the domains of tradition. And so, unlike others in these precincts who found mates among sects different from their own, the Reb Arelach in the main married only within their own community.

As I approached, a few men stood in the alley leading to the entrance of the Toldos Aharon Yeshiva. If there were women about, I did not see them. Perhaps they were hidden in back. Toldos Aharon men and women were known to be punctilious about the separation of the sexes. Inside, the golden-striped coats, interspersed with a few that glistened in white on white, intensified a sense of having entered another world. Yet the brightness of the Reb Arelach's garb was undeniably set off by the dark look in the eyes of some that seemed to follow me as I weaved my way into the sanctuary.

Around the tables in the vestibule, behind a bookcase, through small groups of men huddled in conversation, I moved slowly toward the center of the room. There I supposed I would find the core whose power, radiating outward, held all these people together. But the center was empty. Or, more precisely, it was missing. The rebbe had not come yet, and at the center of the room I found nothing different from what I had seen at its periphery.

After the hubbub, the music, singing and dancing in all the other places I had visited, this room seemed eerily quiet. I wandered through the center as if lost in a dream. The groups of hasidim standing everywhere seemed to be murmuring in near-silence. Some sat on benches along the wall; others leaned over little *shtender,* or lecterns, on which they normally placed the books they ritually reviewed but which tonight served as hitching posts around which conversations were carried on. In a corner a man took off his *shtreimel,* revealing the bulky white knit cap he wore underneath. As he twirled the hat on his left hand, the fingers of his right played with its fur. For a while, I tried watching him unobtrusively. At each turn of the hat, his fingers were making twelve stops.

"Each time I put on my *shtreimel,*" a hasid had once told me, "I count the twelve tails on it, one for each of the tribes of Israel." That, I supposed, was the hasid's alternative to drumming his fingers.

If there was to be dancing here this evening, it either had not yet begun or was already over. In either case, I was out of synchronization with this world into which I had wandered.

In one corner sat an old hasid. His golden coat seemed more worn than those of the younger men who made up most of the crowd. It was wrapped loosely around him, revealing a yellowish-white undershirt and the gray hair of his chest. His beard was a shade of white perfectly matched to his undershirt, and his unkempt earlocks blended into it so that there was no way to tell where beard ended and earlocks began. His *shtreimel* was pushed back on his head. Slowly he slid it forward with his forearm while he scratched the nape of his neck. And then, offhandedly, he fluffed his beard, as if he were chasing moths out of it. But these motions seemed abstracted, for his deeply set, heavily ringed eyes betrayed an abiding look of fatigue and made him appear to have inwardly emigrated from the setting. He was, it seemed, somewhere else, beyond himself and this place. He was probably the worst person to ask what was going on here; but somehow his wizened appearance attracted me. The others, those more obviously anchored in the surrounding circumstances, had, after all, been of no help at all. So maybe this old man might enlighten me. Hesitantly, I approached him.

"Excuse me," I began, "but can you tell me when the *hakafot* begin?"

He continued to stare straight ahead without answering.

Again I spoke, a bit louder this time in case he had not heard me. "Do you know what time the dancing begins?"

He coughed heavily, his throat filled with phlegm. "Dancing," he wheezed, "comes later."

"When?"

"A question!" he replied.

There are some places in Jerusalem that no outsider can enter, even when the doors or gates are open. For me, the Toldos Aharon Yeshiva was one of them. I left.

Back out on Me'ah She'arim Street there were no more people walking ahead of me, for beyond Toldos Aharon there was nowhere for the people of this neighborhood to go. All that remained of the street from this point on was a row of stores, now closed. Ahead of me I could see the wide strip of a neighborhood border marked by the lanes of Shiv'tey Yisra'el Street. Beyond it was Musrara.

I could still hear music, but there was something different about it. It sounded totally different from what I had been hearing in Me'ah She'arim. It had a different lilt to it. Instead of clarinets, I could make out the sound of electric guitars. The sounds came from Musrara.

Divided by Shiv'tey Yisra'el Street, Me'ah She'arim and Musrara were worlds apart. Musrara—the name was Arabic; after the establishment of the State of Israel, the Jews had officially renamed it Morasha, meaning "heritage," but that name had never caught on. Earlier, under the Turks, people called the area Tlat el-Mutzabin—"the hill of the soap factories,"—for here the olive-oil soaps for which Jerusalem was known in those days were produced. For a time it had been a choice area in which to live. Its gentle hills caught the fresh breezes from the north and looked out upon the golden stones of Suleiman the Magnificent's Old City walls and the ornate Damascus Gate. But after 1948, when the city was divided, this had become a neighborhood in distress, a border settlement constantly being shelled by the Jordanians. Into it had moved those who had nowhere else to go, many of them immigrant Jews from Morocco.

For nineteen years, until 1967, Musrara had been all that separated the hostile Jordanian side of the city and the neighborhood of Me'ah She'arim. Like many urban border regions, Musrara had gradually evolved into a slum. The poor lived here. Some had taken over the large houses that Arabs fleeing to the east had abandoned. Into them moved several families with their many children.

Others moved into *shikunim* (large apartment blocks), not unlike the blocks on Stern Street in Kiryat Ha-Yovel, the neighborhood in which Tavio's Miriam had lived with her artist lover. On their eastern side, the one that faced the border, the *shikunim* had tiny windows surrounded with iron shutters that could be closed in case of shelling from the Jordanians. And the roofs were built like bunkers.

Like other such blocks, Musrara began to spawn social problems. While the older immigrant generation remained attached to and sustained by the salvations of their faith, filling little synagogues that sprang up in the area, their children, disappointed by the damnation of their circumstances, often turned to crime. And then came the Six-Day War in 1967.

Suddenly, a neighborhood that had been among the least desirable to live in once again found itself located on prime land. Within a few steps of the Old City, close to downtown, convenient to all sorts of roads leading into and out of Jerusalem, Musrara had a new future. But its residents, frustrated by their past, rebelled. They would not be moved and removed. Organizing themselves into what they called ''The Black Panthers''—the name alone came from the United States; everything else was locally inspired—the young people of the neighborhood began to make demands for improvement.

In time, some of the original Black Panthers entered Parliament as members of the Communist Party, while others joined the Establishment or made their way into another life. Others left. Some returned as contractors and carpenters to rebuild the houses that had been blasted away by the years of shelling. A variety of programs of assistance were launched. The most ambitious of them, organized through ''Project Renewal''—a semiofficial government program drawing funds and involvement from Diaspora Jewish communities and investing them in Israeli ones—twinned Jewish sections of Los Angeles with Musrara. A deserted school building was transformed into a community center, a new *mikveh* was built and a house which for nineteen years had served as a bunker on the frontier became a museum. Yet in many ways, Musrara remained the same, a struggling border community. The borders had changed and bullets were no longer directed from the Arab side, but the ecological lines which separated the community from its surroundings were no less real now than before.

Musrara still retained the brashness of a slum. Its young people were toughened by life, and its old were weakened by the loss of their authority. Little synagogues, most of them Sephardic and Moroccan in style, dotted the neighborhood. But they were filled mostly with the aged or with young people who occasionally accompanied them as an act of charity.

Tonight, however, Musrara's streets were echoing with music. I crossed over into Ha-Homah Ha-Sh'lishit, the street named for the ''third wall'' of the ancient city. Three or four large stones, remnants of the ancient ramparts of the Old City of the Second Temple Period, stood a few steps away, in front of a Bible school for Christian Arabs.

For a few moments I stood on the corner in front of the Romanian Patriarchate. In one of its windows two bearded monks in blue cassocks and large square black caps looked out. Following their line of sight, I came upon a few people gathered in front of a stage that had been constructed outside the door of a small synagogue. ''HEICHAL PINCHAS,'' read the sign over the door.

The assortment of people seemed a perfect reflection of the character of the neighborhood. A few people in their sixties and seventies sat on folding chairs. The men wore beat-up straw hats and threadbare suits; the women were in oversize print dresses and knotted, henna-dyed hair covered with loosely tied kerchiefs. They sat side by side. There was none of the strict, almost obsessive separation of the sexes here that had been the case across the way in Me'ah She'arim.

By far, the bulk of the sparse crowd were women in their forties and fifties. A few of the older ones held what were probably their grandchildren by the hand. The others, singing loudly, clapped their hands in time to the music, animating the older people near them. They seemed almost like cheerleaders. Many of the men who had accompanied them were inside the nearly empty synagogue; a few held drinks in their hands, while others nibbled on cakes.

Along the edges of the crowd, languidly leaning against cars or smoking cigarettes, were the young people. Three or four boys flirted with two girls in a corner, and then slowly the entire group sauntered off. Little by little, they moved down Shiv'tey Yisra'el Street and out of the music's reach. Even if the band was electrified, these were not the sort of tunes in which they were interested.

On the stage, a man in his forties with slicked-down gray hair, wearing a double-breasted suit with a narrow European cut, crooned "Barcelona." As if standing before a huge audience, he dived around the stage with microphone in hand, entertaining the people on the block. His eyes grabbed hold of and stayed with the women who clapped and sang in the area just in front of the stage.

"Thank you, thank you very much," he said when he had finished his song. There was a faded professionalism about him that reminded me of singers who, after the end of their career, had taken up performing in backwater theatres. Compared with the flow of activity in Me'ah She'arim, this street in Musrara seemed but a backwater.

"Another one!" one of the women called. "Yes, another one," the woman next to her repeated.

"*Mi Pi El.*" The singer began the words of a popular *Sim'chat Torah* song: "From the mouth of God may Israel be blessed."

Again the women began clapping. A few began to sing along with him. Some of the older people began to nod off in sleep. A teenage couple wandered off arm in arm. "We'll go to a movie; this place is dead," I heard the girl say.

How different this scene was from what I had seen in the Batei Ungarin, where the faithful and their visitors crowded inside the boundaries of the synagogue, where the old had seemed polished, augmented by the presence of the new. Here, on the street outside the synagogue, I saw a series of borrowed fragments, exhausted relics of tradition, sapped of most of their vitality by a present which hovered over everything. To the young here, the past was "dead." I turned back to Me'ah She'arim.

I continued walking until I reached the Ahavat Shalom Yeshiva, where I had stopped in several hours earlier. It was nearly midnight, but the girls still stood outside in the mud. If anything, the group had grown in size. Only the mothers with their baby carriages seemed to have left. I pushed my way past a few sweaty young boys who, with their shirttails out and sleeves rolled up, were handing around a large bottle of orange soda from which everyone was taking a swig.

Inside, the room had gotten very hot. Dust filled the air.

"Which *hakafah* is it?" I asked.

"The last," a red-bearded man near me answered.

In the center of the larger of the two circles of dancers stood a tall young man of no more than twenty. He wore a long-sleeved white shirt, drenched in perspiration. The band was playing a song whose refrain was "Jerusalem." The song prophesied the return of the exiles to the city and the renewal of the services at the rebuilt Holy Temple. With each mention of the name "Jerusalem," the young man in the center closed his eyes tightly and raised his hands toward the ceiling. Then, while the song was repeated over and over, he began to grab the hands of young children around him and pull them up with each refrain. And each time he lifted them, they seemed to jump higher while around them the crowd, borne by their example, began to dance ever more wildly, until at last the entire floor seemed to shake, and no one inside the room was left outside the circle.

The tune was contagious, as was the rhythm of the dance. But it seemed to me that the words as much as the music were what attracted everyone to the dance. There would come a time, the lyrics announced, when all the exiles of our people would return and once again life would be ordered simply around a divine service. No anxieties, no questions, no decisions—only the service of God. That was the messianic age for which these people longed; or that, at least, was the message of the song.

"In Jerusalem, in Jerusalem, in Jerusalem" were the words being shouted. This had become the center; the Torah scrolls were dancing about it. Here was the power of collective fantasy animating collective life. For the few moments of this dance, everyone in the room seemed pulled into a single, common imaginative vision. The dance was a drama, a restatement and a reaffirmation of a past that would reconnect with a future. It provided a passage from the metaphors of one kind of life to the immediacies of another.

"To Jerusalem," the crowd at Ahavat Shalom sang. And then, without a pause, they began the song with which the *hakafot* traditionally end, the timeless prayer of Diaspora Jewry—for generations the only kind of Jewry there was.

"Next year in Jerusalem, a rebuilt Jerusalem," everyone sang. As long as a single soul remained in exile, as long as the final Redemption had not yet come, the prayer still needed to be recited. "Next year in Jerusalem." They repeated the words over and over, their eyes closed in on the future, their feet jumping into and out of the past.

CHAPTER
·IO·

BLACK MARKET

*As an "island" culture, a minority embedded in
and subordinate to a majority group, the shtetl
functions always within a conditioning
element. In certain areas and in certain
situations it is absolutely influenced by the
"ocean" culture, as an island is coast-carved,
storm-tossed and occasionally inundated by the
surrounding waters. At any time its general
climate is affected by them. Yet to a large
extent it leads a life of its own.*

MARK ZBOROWSKI AND ELIZABETH HERZOG,
Life Is with People

With the holy days over, I began, like everyone else, to think about the mundane realities of life. One of those had to do with money. Living like other Israelis, I found that my monthly income in shekels was never enough. Although I tried, throughout the month, to preserve its value, the hyperinflation of the local economy made that nearly impossible. What a thousand shekels would buy on the first of the month cost twelve hundred by the thirtieth. And so I learned to treat my university paycheck like butter in the hot sun: something had to be done while it was still fresh to keep it from melting away.

One of the methods people found for holding on to what they had earned was transforming shekels into another currency which could be trusted to keep its value over time. Among the most popular was the American dollar. With dollars in hand, one could later buy back more shekels than it had originally cost to get the dollars. The

thousand of the beginning of the month became twelve hundred by
its end. In Jerusalem, there were several ways to do this. The legal
one involved a variety of bank schemes that allowed a person to
deposit money into accounts linked to the dollar.

A second, semilegal path involved going to the Arab sections of
the city to one of the authorized money changers. These money
changers had been in the eastern part of Jerusalem since before the
arrival of Israeli sovereignty and law. Some people argued that
their profession had a longer history than the Old City's wall.

Trying to disturb as little as possible the pattern of life that the
Arabs had established here, the government decided after 1967 to
permit these establishments to stay open. Formally, they were authorized only to change dinars, the Jordanian currency earned by
residents of the territories who moved back and forth across the
bridges to Jordan, into shekels. In fact, they did a big business
in dollars, Swiss francs, British sterling and any other currency
that locals wanted to exchange. And much of the time, they paid
a rate far more favorable than the banks. By law, Israeli citizens
were not allowed to conduct business with the money changers.
Although quite a number of Jews refused to do business with
the Arabs, claiming the profits went to support the P.L.O., many
did.

Yet a third money-changing operation existed: the black market.
Although other cities had far more active illegal currency exchanges, Jerusalem had its own underground, districts where foreign currency could be clandestinely bought and sold. One of them
was in the neighborhoods surrounding Me'ah She'arim.

Among the people who on the holy days danced with Torah
scrolls and who sang about the coming of the Messiah and the
rebuilding of Jerusalem, who remembered the Sabbath Day to keep
it holy, there were also those who during the week speculated in
dollars, francs and pounds sterling. My friend Yisra'el was not a
speculator, but he knew who they were. As I sat in his shop, he
would point to them all as they passed by the open doorway. An
aged man leaning on a carved cane, his pockets suspiciously bulging, was one of the oldest money changers in this neighborhood. He
was the "Establishment." A much younger man, a yeshiva student,
was a runner, specializing in turning foreign bank checks into cash
—in between his studies in Talmud, of course.

"He has a family to support, six children" was the easy explanation. "And he is learning in the yeshiva all the time." With his
black-market activities, he could supplement the small allowance

the yeshiva gave him and the help he got from his parents and in-laws.

"And the law?" one might ask.

"And the learning?" came the answer in the form of a question.

Among the big operators—those who made more than a meager livelihood from their illegal money changing—was a woman I shall call "Zusha." Zusha had managed to build up a successful operation with a reputation for efficiency. To look at, she was not at all the image of a black-marketeer. When Yisra'el pointed her out to me once, as she trudged up the hill and past his shop, I could not believe that she was the famous Zusha. Short, stooped, a faded kerchief atop her head, her thick feet dragging along in cracked blue slippers, she often padded through the streets of Me'ah She'arim, Beit Yisra'el and Ge'ulah, her arms loaded with bags of groceries.

"Zusha—now, there is a story, an entire book," Yisra'el said to me, hardly looking up from the disk he was carving.

"How do I meet her?"

"Change a lot of money."

But tracking down Zusha was not easy. Anyone who needed to ask for her was suspect—the revenue men and undercover police, masquerading as potential customers, often tried finding black-marketeers that way. To avoid them—those whom the locals called *malachey ha-chabala*, "the angels of terror"—the old woman did business only with those she knew, insiders, members of the community. The business she did with outsiders came through the intercession of insiders, and then only if she was reasonably certain they could be trusted.

"So how do I find her?"

"If you have enough to change, and you make contact with the right people, she will find you."

With some guidance from several locals, I took forty hundred-dollar bills, rolled them up in my pocket and began wandering about a number of doorways in various courtyards throughout the neighborhood. Where once I had followed the sound of music and dancing, I now followed a different trail. In some places my inquiries as to who could change money for me were ignored, at others I was given shrugs of the shoulder and at still others I was quietly told that the amount I wanted to exchange was too large; no one carried around that much cash. At last, I was tapped on the shoulder by a red-bearded, black-coated runner who in a whisper told me he would make the exchange.

Pulling me gently into an alley, he held his hand close to my pocket and murmured in a barely audible voice: "Give me the money."

"And you'll give me the change?" I asked.

"No, I'll get the bills for you."

"But I don't know you; how can you expect me to give you the money?" I protested. "Not that you don't look honest," I added quickly. There was no point in antagonizing the man who would help me find my way into another of the invisible regions of the neighborhood. For a moment he stared at me, obviously trying to determine whether or not he was being set up for an arrest. And then, evidently deciding my objection was sincere and legitimate, or seeing something in my face that he trusted, he said, "Wait here."

He rushed out of the alley, the hem of his black coat flying up behind as he scurried away, and turned into the gate leading to the market in Me'ah She'arim. In a minute or two, he returned puffing and out of breath. "Come with me," he said, accepting for the moment the firmness of my refusal to part with my cash.

"I'm not sure she'll let you in, but we'll try," he said. "She" could only be Zusha. I said nothing, afraid he would balk at my knowledge.

In a walk that bordered on running, we rounded corners and turned up alleys. I thought I knew my way around the neighborhood, but by the time I had made four or five turnings, I was lost. Suddenly, on a small back street, we came upon the old woman with thick feet in cracked blue slippers—Zusha. She was talking to another old woman who to me looked to be her mirror image. Had I seen the two old women thus on the street chatting in Yiddish, I might have thought they were talking about the rising price of chickens or some other innocuous matter. Nothing about them stood out more than their utter compatibility with their surroundings.

"Wait," my runner said, and then, slowing his gait, he approached Zusha cautiously and whispered something to her. Barely moving her head or changing her position, she glanced at me out of the side of her eye. The other woman looked me over too in exactly the same way.

At that very moment, a short, thin, bearded man with scraggly gray earlocks and bright blue eyes and wearing a black coat at least a half-size too big for him stepped out of the doorway in front of which I was standing. Instinctively, I turned in his direction. He looked at me and I at him. A flash of recognition lit up his face.

"Sammy!" he called to me in English, stretching out his hand to shake mine. Only people who had known me as a young boy called me by that name.

"Dr. Lurie," I answered in surprise, recognizing the eyes beyond the beard and earlocks and the voice inside the black coat.

A psychiatrist who for years had worked for the United States Navy in Chelsea, Massachusetts, Dr. Lurie had been part of my youth. Coming from a totally nonobservant, assimilated American background, he had wandered into Judaism and gradually been drawn toward Jewish Orthodoxy. In time, he had abandoned his entire past, including his wife, family, profession and everything outside the boundaries of religion. For a while, during his transition, he had served as president of the little Orthodox synagogue in which I had grown up. And then one day, he had collected his navy pension and simply left town. Later we heard that he had left America and was in Jerusalem.

"What are you doing here?" he asked me.

"I live here now. And you?"

"A little of this and a little of that," he answered, his English still inflected with the broad *a*'s of his Boston accent. For a few minutes—while I forgot what had brought me here—we talked about the people we knew, about who was still living in Boston and who had gone. And then he disappeared into the streets of the neighborhood. Remembering now why I was here, I looked around, expecting to find my guide and Zusha, but both of them were gone.

Disappointed that I had apparently spoiled my chance to enter the underground world of the black market, I was still somewhat relieved. The last few minutes of running around in dark alleys had aroused in me an anxiety about this whole plan. After all, to get my story I was risking four thousand dollars. Maybe this coincidence was a sign from Heaven that I had best leave the earthly Jerusalem alone and stick instead to its more spiritual regions. I turned back in the direction of Me'ah She'arim. Suddenly, someone tapped me on the shoulder. It was my red-bearded runner.

"Come; she says it's all right."

Rather than closing the door on my transaction, Dr. Lurie's warm greeting had been enough to convince Zusha that I was not an undercover revenue man.

"Stop here," the runner said, turning in at a doorway near the corner of the street and going a half-flight up the dark stairwell. "Show me the money," he demanded in a soft voice.

Thinking we were about to enter Zusha's, I pulled out my wad of bills and gave it to him. He counted them quickly, and before I could say anything or even become slowed by my anxieties (which had not yet risen to their heights again), he put the forty green hundred-dollar bills into his pocket.

"And my shekels?" I asked as he turned to descend to the street.

"Come," he answered, and ran down the stairs. Again we went up and down stairs and around corners. As I rushed behind him, I couldn't help wondering if the old woman with the cracked slippers ran up and down these as well.

At last we stopped in front of a little alley. Ignoring us, three little children played on the low stoop that led up into it. "You wait here. She won't let you in. I'll be back in a moment," the hasid said, and disappeared into the path behind the children.

Before I could collect my thoughts and express my protest, he was gone. I stood alone in the little street, staring dumbly at the children on the steps. What have I done? I thought. How do I know the man has not just taken my money and run out of the alley from the other side? And if he has, what recourse do I have? To whom could I complain? The police would be of no help, since the entire transaction was illegal from the start. I did not even know the name of my hasid, nor could I describe him very well. He had a reddish beard, a black coat and hat and a white shirt. That described about fifty percent of the people on the streets around me. What I had, at best, was a very expensive, somewhat unbelievable story, suddenly cut short by my naïveté and carelessness. I began to pace back and forth in front of the stoop. I was getting very hot; beads of sweat formed on my forehead, and the back of my shirt was wet. And on top of everything else, I had to go to the bathroom.

The minutes passed excruciatingly slowly. Other hasidim went into and came out of the alley in front of me. A few looked at me suspiciously as they passed. This had to be Zusha's place, I thought. Surely my runner would return.

But as the time continued to pass, doubts again crept into my mind. Maybe the men going in and out were simply wondering why I was standing around here, alone, in front of a private apartment building. Maybe they were right to be suspicious. At last, it occurred to me that I could at least see if the alley was a dead end; that way I would know if there was any point to waiting here at the entrance.

Walking up the three steps that led into the little path and around the corner, I discovered that indeed the alley did end inside, at the foot of a steep and narrow stairway, the top of which I could not see. There was no one there. I returned to the street. Again, the minutes passed slowly. I sat down on the curb. More black-frocked men walked out. Finally, the tension grew to be too much. Unable to hold out any longer, I stepped into the alley and slowly climbed the stairs. There was a half-open door at the top. I peeked inside. If this was not Zusha's, at least I might be able to find a toilet.

What greeted my eyes was beyond belief. There in front of me stood dozens of black-frocked men with neatly stacked bills in hand. On the other side of the table, making change and handing out the packets of bills, sat Zusha on a little kitchen stool. This was nothing more nor less than a bank. Not state-controlled or internationally regulated, it was nonetheless a nerve center of local underground banking.

Stunned and disoriented, I looked from face to face, trying to find my man. But all the faces and black coats suddenly looked alike. At last, my man, standing at the front of the long line, saw me. So did Zusha.

"Out! Out of here immediately!" she screamed in Yiddish. The message was for me, but she addressed it to him. She seemed afraid or unwilling to look me in the eye; but everyone else in the room turned around. Dozens of pairs of eyes stared at me—some in curiosity, others in anger or fear. Zusha's outburst had startled them all. Spontaneously, I took a few steps backward.

Rushing over, my hasid handed me bundles of bills. "Take this," he said, his hands trembling, his voice insistent.

"What is it?"

"Most of the money; I'll give you the rest elsewhere."

"You're coming with me?"

"Yes, yes, of course. Now go!"

"But I can't walk through the streets with this," I protested. My arms were overflowing with the green thousand-shekel notes which were then the highest-denomination currency available. The government printing office had not been able to keep pace with the inflation, and small bills were still being used for large transactions. People came and went to the banks with shopping bags.

"Give me a bag," the hasid asked, running back to Zusha.

"First take him out," she said, still not looking at me.

But now that I had held some of the bills in my hand, my nerve had returned; I was not going out again without my money. She threw him a little paper bag, and the hasid quickly stuffed the bills into it.

• • •

Later, when I told him the story of my exchange at Zusha's, my friend the wood turner laughed and told me, "You think *you* were nervous. She is even more nervous. The angels of terror have tried to catch her several times. In her room there she has a chute down which she throws all the money, if she thinks someone is coming. More than once she has left the city on a trip—not a pleasure trip, I assure you."

Several months later I heard from Yisra'el that the police had raided Zusha's. But when they got inside, she was ready. The room was empty of people.

"You want dollars," she had reportedly said; "come—I'll show you dollars." Then she had taken down three books from the case on the wall. From inside one ragged copy of the Psalms she pulled out a ten-dollar bill. From another, she withdrew a twenty, and from her frayed *Tzena U-re'ena* (Go Out and See), a Yiddish commentary on the Bible traditionally reviewed by women, she took a five. The police fined her ten thousand shekels, then about twenty dollars.

"She'll finance the rebuilding of the Temple," Yisra'el said, chuckling; "but in the meantime ..."

"Come, we'll finish elsewhere," my hasid said as he handed me the bulging paper bag and nudged me out the door. Zusha resumed her counting.

"Where are we going?" I asked as we descended the narrow stairs leading from Zusha's.

"Somewhere we will not be disturbed."

Cutting his way through the alleys and streets of the neighborhood once again, he led me to the *shtibblach* in Beit Yisra'el. In this little network of undistinguished one-room synagogues on a narrow street behind some grocery stores, he found a small, deserted chamber. At this hour of the afternoon, no one was here praying, and those who sat reviewing the Torah texts were either napping or eating lunch, the big meal of the day. Spiritual Jerusalem had vacated this space; the *shtibblach* could now be reserved for the earthly and profane. Now was the time for private business.

Leading me inside, he closed the door and withdrew a wad of bills from somewhere inside his black coat. Then, reaching in again, he brought out a small calculator and computed the exact amount coming to me.

"Let's count," he said, "and we'll see what I still owe you."

I began to flick through the bills, but there were thousands to be counted. I would have to count past a million and a half. Never in my life had I actually counted that high. My fingers moved slowly. They still trembled from the anxiety acquired along with my cash. Now *I* was afraid of the angels of terror or someone else stumbling into our countinghouse.

"Do you want me to count while you watch?" he asked as I fumbled with the green notes.

"Please," I said after my first hundred thousand. I could not cope with the counting, even though the bills were neatly stacked and Zusha had seen to it that all of them were facing the same way and that each pile of fifty thousand was held by a little rubber band —just as the banks did.

I handed the money back to the hasid. His fingers flew as he flicked past each note. I marveled at his speed, barely able to keep my eyes focused on what I watched. Seeing my look of unbelief, he smiled at me sheepishly and explained, "It goes faster if you're used to it."

I sat quietly watching. Perhaps my face betrayed a shadow of lingering anxiety, or perhaps he simply wanted to reassure me. In any case, he stopped counting for a moment, looked at me and said simply, "You can relax. Here we'll be all right. Don't worry."

I had always known that for Jews the synagogue served as a sanctuary. For generations, in the Diaspora, Jews had gone to their houses of prayer and study, places where they could assemble in communal intimacy, where the threatening world governed by outsiders rarely entered. In many ways, the synagogue remained the last ghetto, the inner sanctum of community life. Never had I imagined, however, that in Jerusalem, the capital of a Jewish state, such a Jewish ghetto could still be experienced. Yet here and now, inside the *shtibblach*, I felt the sense of anxiety and security which signaled the separation of "us" from "them." We were the Jews, the insiders, struggling to carry on our business unmolested by them, the outsiders, the "authorities," the "angels of terror, may their name be blotted out!"

The curse, which I heard many times in these neighborhoods, was the same one Jews had for generations used whenever they referred to their enemies. And here, this time, it was being used against Jews.

I thought for a long time about this feeling of separateness that I experienced so vividly that day. Echoes of it were everywhere in these precincts. Here, for example, people not only dressed differently from the rest of the Jews in Jerusalem, they also spoke in a different language. For them modern Hebrew, which they knew and used when they had to, was anathema. It demeaned the status of Hebrew as *loshn koydesh*, a holy tongue to be reserved only for study and prayer. For them, Yiddish was the language of mundane reality. And as if the separations of dress and language were not enough, each Friday afternoon with the onset of Sabbath, the people I was now among put up barriers which physically separated their neighborhoods from the rest of Jerusalem. Beyond these barriers no cars could enter and only those outsiders who were willing to abide by the rules of life here would dare venture.

They did not watch television, had their own newspapers, seldom spent much time out of their neighborhoods. They were, very simply, an island culture, a *shtetl* inside the ocean of Jerusalem and the Jewish State. The outside world came in, but the people here spent much of their energy keeping it out, rejecting its legitimacy and undermining its authority. Intruders were sometimes pelted with stones and hurled invective.

To the people who lived in Me'ah She'arim and the neighborhoods like it, modern Israel, the Zionist ideal of a national revival in this land, was flawed. It had been brought about by the ungodly. Only the Messiah sent by God would renew the settlement here. The state the Zionists had created imposed its authority by power. So the people here still waited for the Messiah, and in the meantime they found holes in the power of the State.

Throughout these precincts there were signs warning residents that whoever cast a vote in the elections or took part in the official affairs of government was distancing himself and the community from messianic redemption. Those locals who considered themselves defenders of the city—*neturei karta*, as they were called—were certain that a state founded and led by Jews who did not share their fear of God, who did not observe all His commandments in the way they did, deserved no cooperation or involvement. In short, no secular Zionist entity could ever hope to bring about the desired national redemption. Only the Messiah, God's holy emissary, would be able to bring into being a genuine Jewish state. To vote in Zionist elections or participate in a secular government was ineluctably to deny this religious understanding, and hence to defer the coming of the Messiah. "Zionist" was synonymous with "Nazi-onist," in that both undermined the reign of the Kingdom of Heaven.

In these neighborhoods, army service was avoided like the

plague ; most of the men exempted themselves by studying in yeshivas. Most of the primary schools—all private—accepted no money from the Ministry of Education. Collections for these came from abroad or from individuals, but not from the State.

But all this was not new. In Jerusalem, the religious community antedated the State. Some Jews had been here for generations, unwilling to be torn away from the remains of their Temple. During the nineteenth century, they were joined by others : from Lithuania, they came at the urging of the great scholar Elijah, the Ga 'on of Vilna ; from Russia, they came on the advice of their hasidic leader, the late Rebbe of Bratslav, Nahman, grandson of the Ba 'al Shem Tov. These and others like them came because to them the return to the Holy City would bring about the age of Redemption, the coming of the Messiah. A time for which they would wait and for which they would prepare by religious activity, by study in the yeshivas and prayer in the synagogues. Slowly but surely, they began to fill the Jewish quarters of what was still an outpost of the Ottoman Empire. Although some became shopkeepers and money changers, many had no visible means of support ; they lived off the *halukkah*, charities collected from abroad from their home communities and disbursed through *kolelim*, collection organizations. Largely ignored by the secular Zionists who began coming in the early part of the century and who founded the modern state, these Jews learned to live in the Holy Land as they had lived in all the countries of the Diaspora, to live in a state within a state.

And when at last, in 1948, the state within which they lived became Israel, the pattern of their life did not change. They still felt themselves to be a minority, a ghetto community in a sea of "outsiders." Those laws the outsiders established which they could not help keeping they kept. But whenever they could, they created a separate community with its own rules and regulations.

Money changers they had been in the Diaspora, and money changers they remained in the Zionist State. Zusha and the others like her were following in a long line of those who served their own community.

The two Jewish communities—the one in Me 'ah She 'arim and its precincts and the one that emerged out of the Zionist dream—were side by side, but by no means did they have the same aims, nor was their Jerusalem the same place. It would take the Messiah to bring them together.

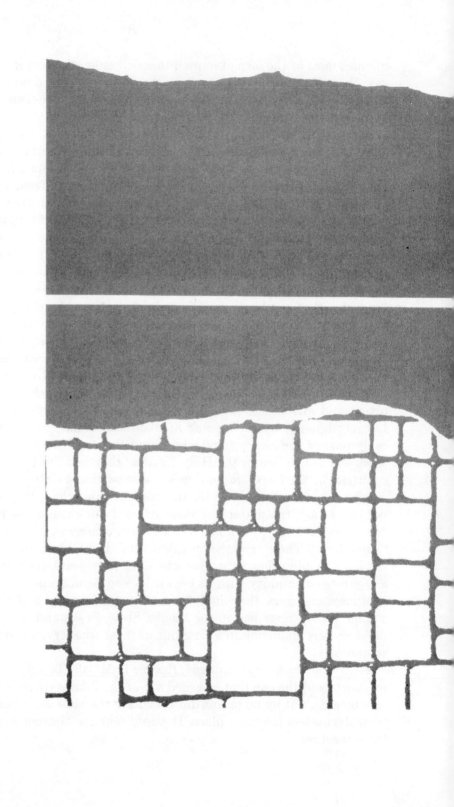

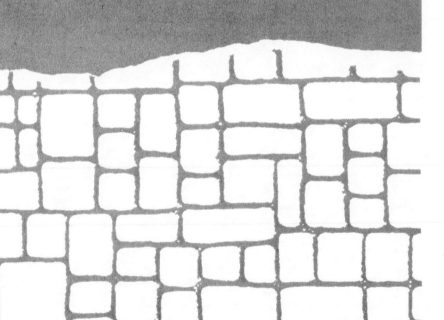

PART

•2•

CHAPTER
·II·

OLD GLORIES

*I will remember. When I come to the place, I
shall know.*

THOMAS WOLFE,
Look Homeward, Angel

What's past is prologue.

WILLIAM SHAKESPEARE,
The Tempest

*I*n the Christian Quarter of the Old City, inside the Church
of the Holy Sepulcher, perhaps the most sacred shrine of
Christianity in Jerusalem, there is a spot, marked by a stone ball,
which is said to represent the navel of the world. Omphalos
Mundi, it is called. And as the Foundation Stone on the Temple
Mount is believed by Jewish tradition to be the place from which
the universe radiates, so for Christianity this is said to be the
center.

So to discover the Christian Jerusalem, it seemed wise to begin
at the center. Here, perhaps, one could discover what remained of
the ties that attached Christians to the center. But for a start, I
needed a guide.

"Haganat Ha-Teva," Tavio suggested when I asked him if he
knew someone who might lead me into the area. The Society for the
Protection of Nature in Israel had a cadre of guides for all occa-

sions and all neighborhoods. Surely, he told me, I would find someone appropriate there.

"I don't really know the Christian holy places; they're not really
part of my Jerusalem," he explained, and then added, "You know,
for many years—not so long ago—a Jew who even dared to walk
in the vicinity of the Holy Sepulcher was risking his life. Most of
us avoided it and passed through the Moslem neighborhoods instead. There it was far safer for us."

"Yes, but isn't it safe for Jews now?"

He laughed. "Today we're probably safer in the church than in
the Moslem Quarter. But why should I give the Christians the
satisfaction of my interest? Maybe they thought all those years we
only wanted to get inside their holy places, to desecrate them or
who knows what. So now let them see that even when we *can* go in,
we don't care to. Let them have their churches; we have Jerusalem."

Tavio's lack of interest notwithstanding, the next morning I went
to the Society's offices inside the old Russian Compound. There,
between what had formerly been the Compound's community oven
and its canteen, in what was once a storeroom, sat Mr. Brandeis,
who I had been told would be able to put me in touch with a guide.
A slender, gray-haired man in his late sixties, seated on a straight-
backed chair behind a plain metal desk, he listened quietly as I told
him of my interests.

"If you want to learn about the Christians in Jerusalem," he
answered, "start here."

"Here?"

"What do you think this building was?" he began. For a few
minutes we talked about the Russian Compound and its history. It
was an important part of the recent Christian history of the city.
During the nineteenth century, as the political currents leading the
European powers to this backwater of the rapidly failing Ottoman
Empire became more powerful, Russian Christians—like many
other European pilgrims (including Jews)—began making their
way to the Holy City. To assist them in their pilgrimages, the countries from which they came saw to it that travel taxes were lowered,
shipping lanes opened, steamship companies organized and hospices
built.

Brandeis reached into a weathered-looking wooden file cabinet
and pulled out a large magazine filled with photos of the building
and pilgrims who had stayed here at the turn of the century. Dis-

covered accidentally in an old storeroom of the Compound by Joe Schadur, a transplanted New Yorker from Queens who now lived in Jerusalem and worked for the Society, the pictures showed throngs of Russian pilgrims filling the courtyard in front of where we sat. Most appeared to be farmers and peasants, the women's heads covered in long babushkas and the men all long-haired and bearded. Disembarking from their long sea voyage, the faithful ignored the surrounding locals and placed themselves in the care of their Orthodox monks and priests, guardians of the holy sites. In one memorable photo a group of about two hundred posed, knapsacks on their backs and walking sticks in hand, ready to set out on their journey to the holy sites. In front stood the holy men, and at the edge of the picture, half out of it, as if in impatience to get started, a Russian kavass, acting as their security guard, sat astride a white horse. For many of these Russians, the pilgrimage was the great event, the crowning glory of their lives.

Describing their arrival, an English observer, Adela Goodrich-Freer, wrote:

> At Jaffa every pilgrim devoutly and repeatedly crosses
> himself on setting foot in the Holy Land; many a bearded man
> stoops to kiss the sacred soil, while tears of real emotion are
> falling from the eyes of men and women alike. Most of them will
> walk the forty miles, the nearly three thousand feet of ascent
> between this and Jerusalem.

I thumbed through the album of photos. There were pictures of hospice rooms, the furniture that filled them, people at prayer or lining up with their kettles for breakfast. One full-page photo depicted a huge room in the women's dormitory filled from wall to wall by simple cots; at their edges sat peasant women of all ages. Thrown into the narrow aisles between the beds were mounds of sacks: clothes for the long voyage and pilgrimage. At the side of the room, in the darkness, stood a dark-eyed, hairy monk—the only man in the picture. A smile seemed to play across his features. Come from the Motherland, this was his flock, and he their shepherd, protector of their holy places.

In its heyday, during the last years of the previous century and until the outbreak of the First World War, the Russian Compound had been a kind of city within a city. The Imperial Treasury of Russia granted the Church in Jerusalem five hundred thousand rubles, to which the Russian people added another six hundred thousand in order to buy the ten acres of land (a former Turkish firing range) just outside the city walls. Here they built their little outpost of Mother Russia on the holy soil of Jerusalem. In addition to dormitories for men and women, the Compound housed an infirmary, dining rooms, an apothecary, a canteen and a cathedral as well as the headquarters of the Russian Consulate. And being exempt from the local Ottoman laws—the Turks had since the Crimean War increased the capitulations they were offering the European powers (including Russia, which had formally been defeated in that war)—the Russians had even established their own court of law in the Compound to which their nationals were subject and in which alone they were tried and judged.

In the Compound courtyard, huge water cisterns honeycombed the ground. In a city where water was scarce and a cistern a symbol of established presence, these structures were of unmistakable significance. Later, at the end of the century, when the Sergei Building, in which the visiting elite would be lodged (and where Brandeis and I now sat), was raised to the west of the main Compound, bathhouses were built. Since the lavish baths built by the Romans two millennia before, Jerusalem had not seen their like.

Like other Christian pilgrims—the Templars of the German colony, the French housed in Notre Dame, the Austrians from the hospice in the Old City, the Italians, the Spanish and others—the Russians were gone now. Their pilgrimages over, these Christians had all returned to their various homelands, leaving behind their monasteries and hospices and a few religious to care for them. Few pilgrims came to stay in these places anymore. When they came, they went to hotels instead. Conrad Hilton and his ilk had supplanted the monks, priests and nuns as innkeepers. Indeed, where once the turrets of the Russian Compound had been the tallest buildings outside the Old City walls, today the tower of the Hilton Hotel in Givat Ram is the outstanding feature of the new city's skyline.

As for the Russians, these days they hardly come at all. Only a few anti-Communists remain in the Old City. And of course, Jewish immigrants from the Soviet Union have come. The First World War, the Bolshevik Revolution and later, after 1967, the break of diplomatic ties between the U.S.S.R. and the State of Israel had all led to the Russians' abandoning the Compound. In their place, the Israeli police and the city jail were headquartered in the main area of the Compound—as had been the British before them—while the

Sergei Building housed the Agriculture Ministry and Haganat Ha-Teva.

There was a kind of vanished glory about many Christian sites like these. Buildings with a Christian past still stood, but Jewish Jerusalem was flowing around them, seeping in, filling their insides and covering over much of what was Christian about them. In many cases, all that remained was the Christian names. Terra Sancta and the Collegio San Antonio, still the property of the Christians, now housed departments of the Hebrew University. They were now integral parts of Jewish Jerusalem. With no Christian pilgrims to fill their rooms, the owners were happy to find someone to pay them rent. The great temple of the German Protestant Templars, now the property of the Armenians, stood in the heart of a middle-class Jewish neighborhood, as did the old Ratisbone Monastery. On the land surrounding the Greek Orthodox Monastery of the Cross stood the white pavilions of the Israel Museum. Rumor had it that the sole monk living inside had run off with a Jewish girl several years before. It was sometimes hard to remember that these places were once outposts of the Kingdom of Christ.

"You have a guide for me?" I asked Brandeis at last.

Putting away his album and methodically turning his little notebook to the proper page, Brandeis, whose Hebrew still betrayed the accents of a German Jew, a *yekke*, told me of a woman named Ricarda Schwerin.

"Who is she?"

"She is one of our guides, formerly a photographer, very knowledgeable. You will find that she is more comfortable in English than in Hebrew—or in German, if you speak that."

Ricarda had been living in Jerusalem for almost forty years, since her immigration from Germany, but she had never managed to master Hebrew. She was a stickler for being on time, Brandeis added.

Another *yekke*, I thought. The *yekke* was the German Jew, that precise incarnation of Germany who among Germans was considered a Jew but among Jews represented everything that was German—everything except, of course, the unspeakable cruelties and horrors.

"Does she really know the Christian Quarter?" I thought that seeing the Christian Quarter through the eyes of a Jew would provide something less than a full view—but then, in a city where Terra Sancta had become a branch of the Hebrew University, what else could I expect?

"I would not have recommended her otherwise," Brandeis answered, and assertively handed me a small piece of paper on which he had written her telephone number. "I am certain you will be quite pleased."

That evening I called her. At the other end of the wire a thin voice, speaking precisely and in a matter-of-fact tone, answered my inquiries. Ricarda's speech had none of the cadences of Hebrew in it or even the inflections I associated with an Israeli's English. She offered no informal niceties about how she was looking forward to meeting me or glad to be of service. After we had discussed all the particulars of my interest and her fee, she concluded simply : "On Thursday morning, meet me outside the Lions Gate at eight exactly."

"How will I recognize you?" I asked.

"*I* will find *you*," she said. "Stand at the right side of the gate on the outside of the walls. And be on time; we have much to cover."

Ricarda was a *yekke*, all right.

On the appointed day, I set out for the Lions Gate at about a quarter past seven. Ricarda had succeeded in making me anxious about being late. I knew the way. If I kept up a good pace, the trip from my apartment would take a little more than half an hour. That would allow me a few minutes to linger on the way at anything that caught my interest.

Moving toward the Old City and coming out of the Valley of Ben-Hinnom, I walked up King Solomon Street. At the end of it, rising like the sun ahead of me, were the golden walls. Passing them at the northwest corner, I crossed Jaffa Road and headed east, down into the valley some called the Tyropoeon. To the careful observer, even the traffic along the newly asphalted avenues paved into the valley could not obliterate the profiles of the ageless hills and vales.

Another outline of a far less distant past—but no less important to the local inhabitants—could also be discerned. Although more than seventeen years had elapsed since the reunification of Jerusalem, the markings of the now-torn-down border barricades could still be seen along two pillars of the French Catholic hospital against which they had stood between 1949 and 1967. Not far away, at what was once the edge of no-man's-land, the holes left by Jordanian shells fired during those years still marked the former Barclays Bank building. In Jerusalem, the past is not soon or easily obliterated.

After 1967, the road leading down into the Tyropoeon had been renamed *Ha-Tsanchanim*—"The Paratroopers"—by the conquering Israelis. Beyond the Damascus Gate, in the cleft of the valley, in what, when the city had been divided, had been the center of the Arabs' downtown, the same street was called Suleiman Road, named after the Turkish sultan who had built the walls that now surrounded the Old City. But for generations, from at least the days of the Bible, the whole stretch of road had been called simply "The Valley"—*Ha-Guy* in Hebrew; *al-Wad* in Arabic. Many locals still used these names.

As I descended into the valley, Notre Dame, with its large refurbished hospice, rose on my left. Built just outside the walls in 1887, this fortresslike structure had once been the last stop outside the Holy City for many French pilgrims who during the previous century had made the arduous journey across the Mediterranean and up through the hills of Judea. Here, in this city among the mountains, they hoped to retrace the steps of their Saviour along the Via Dolorosa from Gethsemane to the place of Golgotha and the Holy Sepulcher.

To serve its citizens, the French Government—which had assisted the Church in building Notre Dame—in 1889 requested the Ottoman ruler, Sultan Abdul Hamid, to provide them with easier access to their holy places inside the city walls. Granting their request, the sultan broke through the walls just across from the entrance to Notre Dame and had a new gate built there, at the ridge of the valley. To some this gate was forever after known as the Gate of the Sultan, and to others, Bab el Abdul Hamid, but most people referred to it simply as the New Gate. In Jerusalem, something built about a hundred years ago could still be called "new."

For nineteen years Notre Dame sat on the frontier between Jordanian and Israeli Jerusalem. Sitting thus in the line of sniper fire and hostility, it had gradually fallen into disrepair, a casualty of the uneasy and incomplete armistice. Now, with the removal of the barricades, Notre Dame was after many years getting a face lift, and people were going in and out. Most of those I saw this morning were local Arabs who worked there. Like the Russian Compound these days, it too stood largely empty of pilgrims.

Passing through the thick crowds that were streaming into and

out of the Damascus Gate, the major northern opening to the Old
City, I began to hurry. Though the press of humanity here was
fascinating, I knew there was not enough time to watch its ebb and
flow if I was to make it in time to my rendezvous. I moved eastward
toward the Lions Gate and my meeting with Ricarda.

For a while I stopped near the corner of the walls to watch the
sheep-and-goat market which this morning, as it had been every
Friday morning for generations, was carried on by the Arabs. It
would take many more visits to begin to decipher the order under
what appeared to the casual visitor as a milling crowd of fellahin
and bleating sheep and goats. I watched for a few minutes, captivated by the sight. But there was not enough time to stay more than
a few minutes. I would have to come back again for a careful and
sustained observation.

It was getting close to eight, and I turned the corner toward the
Lions Gate. There was no mistaking it; on either side of its double-
tiered arch (a relic from the sixteenth century and the end of the
three-hundred-year Egyptian Mameluke period, when gates were
built with high, pointed arches on their external side and flat,
straight ones inside) were a pair of lions in stone relief facing each
other. Poised on three legs, each one extended his front paw toward
the other.

There is a Moslem tradition, Ricarda would explain later, that
these lions are older than the rest of the gate and were brought here
by the Caliph Omar more than thirteen hundred years ago. Then,
according to the legend, when centuries later Suleiman the Magnificent was having the current walls and gate constructed, in a dream
he saw two lions which threatened to tear him to shreds if he failed
to hurry the work on the city wall. When he awoke, he decreed that
these lion reliefs were to be added. And in order to associate the
walls' building with his nocturnal visions, he added the nearby
Arabic inscription which proclaims that this gate and the wall
around it were built by his order.

At the edge of an old Moslem cemetery and overlooking the Valley of Jehoshaphat to the east and Gethsemane beyond it, the gate
leads down eastward toward the City of the Dead, the ancient Jewish cemetery on the Mount of Olives. On the inside, it leads to the
Via Dolorosa.

There are those who refer to the gate by other names. Some
Christian Arabs call it Bab Sittna Miriam—''the Gate of Our Lady
Mary,'' referring to a tradition that it leads to the tomb of the
Virgin Mary, situated among the other hoary gravesites in the ne-

cropolis. Others call it Bab e-Riha, the Jericho Gate, because from here begins the road down to that most ancient of cities.

In the time of Jeremiah, there was a gate at or near this place known then as the Gate of Benjamin, for from here began the road to the territory of the tribe of Benjamin. When Nehemiah refers to it, he speaks of the Sheep Gate. Through here, during the time that King Solomon's Temple stood on the hill to the west, sheep headed for the sacrificial slaughter would be brought first for washing in the nearby pools of Bethesda and then led up to the priests who ministered at the Temple.

There are those who say that the name ''Sheep Gate'' comes from the fact that the Arabs hold their sheep-and-goat market here once a week. But for a long time that market was held at the next gate over, the Flower, or Herod's, Gate. Moreover, as Ricarda would argue later, ''Ask yourself why the Arabs chose to have their sheep-and-goat market here. They are far more protective of traditions than most people. What we see today is probably all that is left of a far more ancient tradition of bringing the sheep and goats through here.''

''I believe you are waiting for me.'' The sound of German-accented English behind me was startling. ''I am Ricarda.''

She was thin and short, barely over five feet in height and with a slight hunch to her back. Her blond-gray hair was clipped close to her head, and her tanned face was covered with lines. She stared at me through steel-blue eyes. And when she spoke, she appeared hardly to open her thin pink lips. Sometimes, she paused to roll those narrow lips inward over her teeth. Although she was clearly in her late sixties or even into her seventies, there was an energy about her that belied her years. When we began walking, I was struck by the quickness of her pace. Under her arm she carried a large leather sack that looked as weathered as she; some rolled maps stuck out of the top of it. On her feet she wore khaki canvas shoes from which the tops of her brown socks stuck out. She had rolled the tops of the socks down to prevent them from sagging. Around her neck was a gold medallion, her official designation as a licensed guide.

''You have been looking at the gate?'' she continued, skipping all the social niceties again.

I nodded.

''So, then let me tell you about what you have been looking at.''

She proceeded to tell me about the gate and about its various incarnations throughout history. Then, as we moved under the archway and into the Old City, she added, almost as an after-thought, "There are those who call it Saint Stephen's Gate, after the Basilica of Saint Stephen. *Ja*, but that is really incorrect, since the basilica is far closer to the Damascus Gate than it is to the Lions Gate. If you remind me later, when we get over that way, I shall point out its silver dome."

We walked a few more steps and stopped for a moment. Ricarda turned back toward the gate. "Perhaps for the Christians what is most important about this gate—of course, beyond its closeness to Gethsemane—is that it opens onto the Via Dolorosa.

"But you mustn't believe all the stories about the various Stations of the Cross along the Via Dolorosa. *Ja*?" She took a few steps and then stopped. "You know about the Stations?"

"Aren't they the stops that Jesus is supposed to have made on His way from His judgment by Pilate until His crucifixion at Golgotha?"

"*Ja*, but the truth is they are almost completely imaginary. We can't really know where He walked and where He stopped. All we know, and some people are not even sure of that, is that He passed from the garden of Gethsemane, which is at the base of the Mount of Olives, to somewhere up there." She pointed in the direction of the Church of the Holy Sepulcher. "We know little, if anything, about what happened on this road or even if this was really the road. These matters are covered by all sorts of religious beliefs. People believe what they choose to believe."

"Do you think that matters to the pilgrims?" I asked.

"Not really. They are in any event going on an interior journey, *ja*? Jerusalem is something they imagine more than it is a place they visit. Shall we go?"

She was impatient to begin.

"*Ach, ja*," she said, stopping suddenly, "I had better tell you that there are those who call this the Galilee Gate because according to the Acts of the Apostles, men from Galilee came down from the Mount of Olives and entered the city here after the ascension of Jesus. Well, whatever its name, there is no question that we have just passed through a very old doorway and have embarked upon a route that will take us in the footsteps of the ancients."

This last phrase sounded a bit too practiced. I felt a touch of disappointment at the thought that rather than an inside view, I was about to be given "Guided Tour #101: In the Footsteps of the Ancients."

But Ricarda was not the sort of person one simply abandoned; I followed her. Our next stop, just inside the gate, took us into the courtyard of the Church of St. Anne. Passing under the arch and through a vaulted entrance, I found myself captivated by a small but exquisitely laid-out garden. Someone had obviously given great attention to it, for it was verdant with a wide variety of bushes, trees and flowers each of which, though different from the others, found sufficient space to grow. The total effect of this harmony amidst difference was at once striking and strangely peaceful, especially when compared with the noise and dust at the sheep market just meters away on the other side of the walls.

Upon reflection, there was something else striking about the garden. The different plants so neatly placed together silently elaborated a message. It seemed a parallel to the Old City, filled with neighborhoods of all sorts that like this garden were at once different from each other and yet pressed together within one set of walls. In the context of this city, a garden like this one could not but point beyond itself.

From inside the church next to the garden there came what sounded to me like a large choir singing in English. I stepped inside for a look. But instead of encountering what had sounded like the Mormon Tabernacle Choir, I discovered only fifteen black men (who I later learned were Americans on their first tour of the Holy City) singing at the top of their voices.

"How great Thou art!" they sang, their deep voices and rich harmonies bouncing off the walls and echoing through the cavernous dark room. A white-cassocked wisp of a monk slipped in quietly from his place near the stairs at the back. Like me, he was drawn in by the men's singing. We stood there in the church for a moment, side by side, along with a few others who had tiptoed in, and listened spellbound. And then, in a burst of vibrato and four-part harmony, the song was over, the spell broken. Picking up their cameras and following their guide to the altar, the singers reverted to tourists and began snapping pictures. Sighing, the monk pattered back down the stairs, and I backed out the door.

Ricarda was gone. Neither interested in showing me the garden nor attracted by the singing, she had instead walked to the far side of the courtyard and stood above the sun-drenched remains of the Pools of Bethesda.

"Come here," she said, waving at me. "I thought you had run away."

"No," I answered, "I was just caught up in the sights and sounds of this place."

She turned to the pools, which were now little more than deep pits surrounded by stones, crumbling bricks and broken pillars. A lizard ran into a cleft in the rocks. "What you see before you is far more significant. These pools have been important to at least two of the peoples who live in this city. For the Christians they are the site of Jesus' miraculous healings."

She reached into her bag and withdrew a small leather-bound book from which she now read in English:

" 'Now there is in Jerusalem by the sheep market a pool, which is called in the Hebrew tongue Bethesda, having five porches. In these lay a great multitude of impotent folk, of blind, halt, withered, waiting for the moving of the water. For an angel went down at a certain season into the pool, and troubled the water: whosoever then first after the troubling of the water stepped in was made whole of whatever disease he had.' "

She closed the book and returned it to her bag.

"Here, all here," she said simply, stretching her arm across my field of vision.

In the deep excavations above which we stood there was almost no water to be seen. The road paved across and atop the valley to the north, silt and shifts in the groundwater had over the centuries changed the reality here so that the only liquid that still collected here after the winter rains was mixed with waste that bubbled up from broken pipes in the vicinity.

"Unfortunately," Ricarda added, "nothing stays the same. Healing waters are today lost in the cesspool that you see here." She signed; old glories had given way to the decay of neglect.

"Why the name 'Bethesda'?" I asked.

"*Ja*, well, that is not completely clear. Some say it comes from the two Hebrew words *bet*, which means 'house,' and *hesed*, which means 'mercy.' But others, those who connect these pools to an earlier period, to the Jews and their washing of sheep in the time of their Holy Temple, say that the name comes from *bet* and *zayit*, which means 'olive.' This part of the city and the olive groves beyond were once called Betzayita." She paused, and we gazed down into the brown cavity. "*Ja*, there is also an explanation that comes from the report of a French pilgrim that fish were once kept here and because people hunted for the fish here—the Hebrew for 'hunting' is *tzayad*—these pools became known as those in the Bet Tzayad.''

''Why were the sheep washed here?''

''I'm not certain about all the laws, but I believe they had to be prepared for the sacrifices. You know, the Temple was just a few meters south of here. Some say the pool they washed the sheep in was where the parking lot across the street now stands. It's hard to know these things; they were so long ago.''

She turned northward and pointed. ''Later the Byzantines built a basilica here. If you cross the wooden bridge you will see some of its remains, including a fine mosaic floor. Come—I shall show it to you.''

She walked briskly across the remains and stopped in front of the mosaic, protected from the sun by a fiberglass roof.

''Watch,'' she said, sprinkling some water from her canteen over a small section of the floor. Cleansed suddenly of their dust, the colors in the stones appeared to jump back to life.

''This floor can only hint at the magnificent church that once stood here. We can only guess how beautiful it was. Imagine.'' She sprinkled another few drops on the mosaic as we moved away.

The place is still beautiful, I thought, but said nothing. Ricarda was already past the garden and out the archway, on her way back to the Via Dolorosa. I caught up to her just as she turned into a doorway that led to the First Station of the Cross, what is known as the Praetorium, or Court of Law.

''I could show you all these Stations, but I don't believe you are interested in them. After all, you are not on that kind of pilgrimage, *ja?*''

I said nothing.

''But this Station is special. Come.''

We walked through the church and followed a blue sign that pointed to something called ''LITHOSTRATOS.''

''I am taking you to the paving stones of the ancient Roman city,'' Ricarda whispered; the narrow hallway was cluttered with tourists and pilgrims, each group apparently with its own guide who knew how to tailor his explanations to his listeners' expectations.

Descending from the street entrance to the level of the Roman city, we came at last to a low-ceilinged room. Ricarda pointed to a small engraved design on the floor here. Its outlines were barely perceptible.

''This is an ancient game. We're not even certain what it was called; some call it 'the game of the king.' We don't know exactly how it was played. What we are fairly sure of, however, is that the loser lost his life. Here,'' she continued, ''are some photos of the dice that went with it.''

''Why is it so important?'' I asked.

''To some Christians it is important because it is believed that the Roman guards played this game with the man who called Himself 'King of the Jews.' And when he lost, they crucified Him.''

''Our Lord was brought here.'' The voice belonged to a guide who was bringing in a group behind us. I turned to watch him. These were the same black men I had seen before at St. Anne's. ''And this is the game the Romans played with Him.''

''Here?'' one of the men asked. ''You mean Our Lord actually walked along these stones?''

''It is indeed very likely that the 'place that is called the Pavement' of which the Book of John speaks was here. And here is where, after he had judged Him, Pilate had Him scourged to please the Jew—'' The guide suddenly saw me, or at least the skullcap atop my head, and seemed to catch himself. He continued: '' —the rabble outside. And from here they took Him in His crown of thorns. I am quite certain you all know the verse in the fifteenth chapter of Saint Mark.''

''Come,'' Ricarda said; ''we shall continue on to something that will interest you more.''

We turned and climbed some stairs and walked out through a small souvenir shop in the church. Once again we were on the Via Dolorosa.

''You know about the Antonia?'' she asked when we were outside.

The Antonia (named after Mark Antony) was a fortress built by Herod. His reign having been imposed upon the Jews by the sovereign Romans, Herod wanted to be both loved by his subjects and secure in his domain. So while he had refurbished and enlarged their Temple, which in the days of Ezra and Nehemiah had been rebuilt far more modestly, he had also built the Antonia a bit higher up on the hill. Here, on what at the time of that first rebuilding had been the site of the Hananel Tower and slightly to the north of the Temple Mount, Herod placed his magnificent palace of marble and gold. Although he said it would protect the Temple from invaders who might come from the vulnerable northern border (where the land lay higher than the walls), the fact was—and apparently his subjects knew it—that he needed his fortress more to protect himself from the people whose ''Fortress was the Lord.'' From the Antonia, Herod, the son of a Jew and an Idomenean woman, could look out upon the multitudes of worshipers who would gather on the Temple Mount. From here he would see if anyone was rousing the people to rebel in the name of the Lord.

''Of course, today,'' Ricarda pointed out, ''it is our soldiers who look out over the mountain to watch the Moslems.''

Herod—or, more precisely, the architects, engineers and slaves who did his building for him—had etched his memory and ensured his immortality in the stones of this city. Of the Temple he refurbished, the rabbis said in the Talmud: ''Whoever has not seen Herod's building has not seen a handsome building.'' But the Antonia, perhaps his crowning achievement, with its bathhouses, halls, courts and towers, was largely destroyed. Today only its cisterns and some of the stones of its towers can still be seen. On its remains there now stands the Omariyeh Boys' School.

''I suppose that you do not want to go onto the Temple Mount,'' Ricarda said.

''That's right,'' I answered. Like many other Orthodox Jews, I remained bound by a rabbinic dictate that forbade any but the purified priestly class (of which there were none today) to set foot upon the mountain for fear we might mistakenly wander into the Holy of Holies where, according to tradition, the sanctity of God's Presence still hovered. I was not certain whether I believed in this, but I knew that I would not challenge this public prohibition.

''Well, I shall try to get you as close as is possible. You shall have Herod's view; he too did not set foot on the mountain.'' She looked for the caretaker she knew who had promised her a quick entry and peek this morning.

We entered briefly. The tall cypress trees and golden Dome of the Rock were striking. I wanted to linger here, but after a few moments Ricarda urged our departure.

''They don't like us to stay here too much. I told the guard you would give him some money if he let us take a peek, but I think we ought to go now. You can come back on your own later, *ja?*''

''So where do we go now?'' I asked.

From the school, she led me to the Alexander Church. The door was locked, and we were about to leave when a black-robed Russian Orthodox monk came around the corner. Ricarda knew him, and the two greeted each other warmly.

On his head the monk wore a floppy velvet cap that reminded me a bit of some of the skullcaps I had seen in pictures of nineteenth-century German rabbis. A sparse brown beard ringed his cherubic features, and a gold tooth glistened at the side of his mouth when he smiled. Like other monks, I supposed, he had come to this holy place to pray, meditate, and follow a spiritual path closed to others who pursued the mundane life. He may well have done that, but few of his flock came anymore. And so these days, after reciting his prayers, he pursued another vocation: selling souvenir postcards and collecting entrance fees from those unbelievers like me who wanted to visit the remains of the Herodian city wall that had been uncovered within the walls of the church. He smiled sheepishly as I handed him my shekels and he gave me back a stamped receipt.

"These stones prove," Ricarda told me, "that the site on which the Holy Sepulcher stands was originally outside the city."

"That would make sense," I said. "By Jewish law, which was strictly observed in Jesus' time, there was no burial within the city limits. So if he was buried on the site of the church, that would have to have been outside the walls of that time."

The truth was that no one knew for sure that the Church of the Holy Sepulcher was the actual site of the burial, any more than anyone knew where Mohammed had ascended to Heaven and spoken with the angel Gabriel or—much as I was unprepared to admit it—where Abraham had bound up his son as an offering for God. But that was not surprising: what people believed, what had made its way into the collective memory and now constituted a reality far more compelling and powerful than the events recalled was what often counted most in Jerusalem. History was not all that remained of the past or even necessarily the best way to understand it. The holy places I was visiting were spiritual reference points. Religious memory evoked places not necessarily as they were, but in its own image, as it supposed they must be.

At last we arrived at and entered the Church of the Holy Sepulcher, a network of chapels and religious domains. "There is a great deal of controversy about who is in control of the church," Ricarda began as we passed through the plaza in front of the main doorway. "But the status quo law has kept some order here."

Affirmed in 1878 by the Congress of Berlin at the conclusion of the war between Russia and Turkey, the "status quo principle" established that no changes would thenceforward be made in the holy places. Everything would remain for the time being exactly as it was. For generations, this vague rule had kept relative peace around the holy places. Thus, for example, when the Greeks bricked over one of the two doors through which the church was entered to control the crowds, that change was fixed in place after 1878, no matter how awkward or curious the stones may have appeared to subsequent generations of visitors—silent testimony to the status quo principle. Eighteen seventy-eight had frozen things in place, and of course those who held no control over any holy place at that point in time still had no control.

"Look," Ricarda said, pointing above the church door: "even that wooden ladder above us [she pointed to the right-hand arch, where a short ladder leaned against the building] has been left exactly as it was when the law was passed."

"Does it have religious significance?"

"If it didn't then, it will sooner or later, I am sure." She laughed a dry laugh that soon evaporated into nothingness.

We entered the church, and she turned suddenly to greet a short gray-haired man in a worn-out gray suit and thick spectacles who sat near the door. A policeman stood next to him. The old man leaned forward and stretched out a trembling hand. I shook it too.

"This is Mr. Nusseibeh," she explained. "For generations the keys to the front door were held by a Moslem family, the Nusseibehs, so that no one Christian sect could banish any of the others."

The old man smiled and nodded, falling back into his seat. As we continued into the church, Ricarda detailed the rivalries among the various Christian groups who saw themselves as guardians of the holy places. By giving a Moslem family the keys, the authorities hoped to neutralize the rivalries and maintain the status quo inside. Since the implementation of the plan a few generations earlier, it had more or less worked, although every so often a Greek Orthodox monk would attack an Armenian for encroaching on his space or Copts fought with Abyssinians.

"But Mr. Nusseibeh, as you can see, is an old man—in his eighties. Soon he will have to give the keys to his sons, as the law stipulates. But that will not be easy."

"What's the problem?" I asked.

"His sons have other aspirations in life. They do not wish to be keepers of keys who sit idly at the church door. There is no future in that for a young Palestinian."

"So someone else will sit at the door," I said.

"You forget the status quo. Any change here threatens to change everything. You may think the past is not so fragile, but if you think that, you do not understand anything about Jerusalem," she said.

Exploring the church was for me a series of bends and turns. We would turn into one or another room or grotto, bend low through one or another opening, climb or descend one or another flight of stairs. Ricarda was careful to explain the significance of every nook and slab of marble, but there was a certain remoteness in her account. She was not caught up in the competition of beliefs that seemed to reverberate throughout the many chambers of the church. The Omphalos Mundi was just another spot. Places like this, I thought, were better seen under the guidance of believers.

When we went down one staircase leading to the cave or quarry over which this basilica had been built, I was struck by the thousands of crosses etched on the wall by the generations of Christian pilgrims who had made their journeys to this last earthly resting place of their Saviour. The roughness of the engravings, the smoothed edges of the lines evoked for a moment the images of bent and robed medievals who, broken in body but whole in spirit, had found the place of their fervent prayers. In the cold air of the grotto, I felt a chill.

"According to an old superstition," Ricarda said as we descended, "children begotten in the church would be children of good fortune. With that in mind, some pilgrims turned these dark corners into a brothel. I have seen that written somewhere."

From the Church of the Holy Sepulcher, Ricarda led me through the neighborhoods of the Greek Catholics and Greek Orthodox. Whatever the rivalries between these two, the little whitewashed houses and courtyards in which they lived side by side, the inscriptions on the lintels, the crosses, the language of the inhabitants all transformed their little corner of the city into an outpost of their native land.

Coming out of the narrow alleys of this Greek enclave, we found ourselves inside the Jaffa Gate and heading toward the Anglican Christ Church on the other side of the road. This, I had been told, was a site worth seeing because its consecration in 1849 marked the renaissance of European interest in the Holy City. The bishop who had come here to missionize among the locals was a convert from Judaism. He hoped to convert Jews, and so he had built a church devoid of most christological symbols. Perhaps most arresting was the Hebrew of all the inscriptions on the wall. Reading the Lord's Prayer or the Principles of Faith in Hebrew made their sentiments seem closer to the ancient religion of the Hebrews. If in tracing Jesus' footsteps from Gethsemane to Golgotha one was struck by the Jewishness of this Christian Saviour, here one was touched by the similarity of Christian sancta to those of the synagogue.

"Does this place missionize much anymore?" I asked Ricarda.

"When the English built their church, it started all the others missionizing. And it awakened in the Jews and the Moslems the need to hold fast to their own faiths." Christ Church's days of glory were over almost as soon as it was built.

Outside the church, we stood at the edge of the Armenian Quarter. Ricarda took me inside. The Quarter was really little more than a large monastery; it certainly did not cover twenty-five percent of the Old City. I had already learned from Victor Azarya, a Hebrew University sociologist who had written a study of the Quarter, that the people inside were the offspring of refugees who had come here to find sanctuary during the period of Turkish oppression and genocide in the early part of the century. Although they still lived inside the monastery—greatly outnumbering the twenty to thirty monks there—they were not pilgrims. Most of them were not even very religious. It was curious. Here were the only lay Christians in large numbers still to be found on the grounds of a monastery in Jerusalem, and they were there as refugees rather than pilgrims. Indeed, as Azarya told me, the residents went through all sorts of avoidance procedures to keep out of the way of the resident priests and monks. And if they sent their sons to a seminary, it was never to the one inside the church here. Living in Jerusalem, they turned in their hearts toward Armenia and Mount Ararat. If the day ever came when their homeland in Armenia was open and free, many, if not most, would return. Or at least, so they said.

We watched the black-hooded monks shuffle through the dark Church of St. James. At a later date, I would return to listen to the haunting melodies of a service here; but now Ricarda introduced me to Kevork Hintlian, one of the lay officials inside. He showed us through the museum, once a dormitory for monks and now a treasure-house of Armenian memories, and then showed us out. It was getting near noon, and we were both a bit tired.

Ricarda took account of this. "Do you want to continue still, or have you had enough?"

"I wouldn't mind a coffee," I said, "if you would join me."

"Well, it's not necessary," she answered, "but if you like, there is a place we can go to not far from here."

There had been a certain melancholy about Ricarda's descriptions which had grown throughout the morning. Although she demonstrated a good knowledge of the sites, there was something about her and the tone of her descriptions that struck me, an expression of lost hope and abiding pessimism, a kind of *Weltschmerz*. Every-

thing she showed me was, from her point of view, past its moment
of glory. Things were always worse or getting worse. Beliefs turned
out to be myths; historic sites were now ruined remains; beauty
had given way to destruction. Was there something of her own past
that was injecting itself into her tour? I had felt and heard it in
the asides, the little commentaries about things getting worse.
Again now, I was aware of the tinge of pessimism in all her descriptions. I wondered about it. It was time to take a tour of my guide.

"You are from Germany?" I asked.

"I am from Jerusalem; I was born in Germany," she answered
precisely.

The waiter, an Arab in a raggedy black-and-white kaffiyeh,
walked over with our coffee. The sweet liquid that Israelis called
botz—the word for mud—came with a heavy mudlike sediment at
the bottom of the tiny cup in which it was served. He had heard
this last exchange.

"You are from America?" he asked me.

"Yes."

"I lived there twenty-five years, in New York," he said. "But I
decided to come back here. This is my home."

Ricarda looked at him, rolling her lips over her teeth.

"Are you happy to be home?" I asked him.

"I could not be anywhere else."

"But it's not what you expected," Ricarda added.

"What is?" the waiter said, and walked away.

There was that note of pessimism in Ricarda again. I took a sip
from the little cup in front of me.

"Have you lived here long?" I asked her.

"Since the early 1940s."

"Ah," I said, imagining her escape from the Nazis.

"It is not what you think," she said quietly.

"How do you know what I think?"

"I am not a fool," she said, and sipped her coffee. "You think I
fit the model of the *yekke*." She took a drink of coffee and put the
cup down almost empty. "But I am not a *yekke*."

Ricarda rolled her lips over her teeth and sat quietly. I said
nothing and looked at her while taking tiny swallows of my drink.

"What do you mean?" I said at last.

"You really want to hear?"

"Yes."

"In Berlin, my husband and I were students. He studied interior
design and I, after some other work, concentrated on photography.

We had met as students in Walter Gropius' Bauhaus. You heard of the Bauhaus?''

I nodded.

''*Ja*, it was probably the most exciting place to study at the time.'' This was the frontier of artistic thought in Europe, beyond the reach of anything but the principles of excellence.

''And then the troubles started; the outside world pushed its way into our lives. Around us poverty and extremism—two diseases that feed on each other everywhere and always—grew. And so in addition to being students, my husband and I became Socialists as well. To be a Socialist among Fascists was dangerous; we were arrested, and for a time were held in a concentration camp.''

Ricarda played with her cup, swishing the little liquid that remained in it around and around over the mud at the bottom.

''The horror that would come later in those camps had not yet fully fermented. *Ja*, but there was enough to darken a lifetime of dreams. With some good luck and some money we managed to scratch out of the ground, we found a way to escape from the camp. There was a chance to come to Palestine or France. My husband, convinced that the Nazi boots would yet march into Paris, decided we should come here, and I agreed. We were promised passage aboard a boat headed for Jaffa, and although we did not get exactly to the port, late one night we jumped off the deck and were smuggled into Tel Aviv.

''After congratulating ourselves on our good fortune in remaining together and escaping, we settled down to rebuild our lives. But nothing was easy, *ja*? It was terrible here. For a time we lived in Tel Aviv. But for us there was nothing there. We had no money, and the skills we did have were not needed.''

''When did you come to Jerusalem?''

''After nearly a year of living on scraps, finding odd jobs that allowed us to live a bit longer in our rented rooms but never really getting out from our debts, we decided that we would come here. Someone had told us that Jerusalem was a place where we would be more at home.''

''If you were Socialists, why did you not try a kibbutz?''

''We were Socialists, not farmers,'' Ricarda explained. ''And we were not Zionists.''

''So why did you come here?''

''There were very few choices available for people fleeing Germany and the Nazis.''

She rolled her lips.

"We chose this one. Many others would have lived had they been able to make the same choice. But no one was offering them a refuge, and there was no State of Israel to take them in."

"As it does the Ethiopian Jews now," I added.

"I suppose."

"Was Jerusalem the right choice?"

"*Ja*, well, who knows? What is true is that I am still here, and I think I shall never leave." She paused.

"Would you like some more coffee?" I asked.

"No"—she let go of her cup—"but have some if you want it."

"Go on."

"*Ja*, well, the trip to Jerusalem in those days was not like today. There was a road but no highway. We bumped over the mountains for hours until at last we came in sight of the city. Can you believe me, can you understand me, if I tell you that the sight enchanted and repelled me at the same time? It was dirty, poor, but still it had a beauty radiating from its walls and stones that even in our broken state we could not help seeing. I think for the first time in years we felt we could stop running.

"Still, there was no work for architects, interior designers or photographers. And even if there had been, we had not the materials that would help us do it. No money, no connections, nothing."

"Surely there must have been need for building."

"*Ja*, there were some architects working, but much of what was being done here was traditional, done by amateurs. Conrad Schick, who had built so much in the last century, was—in case you don't know it—a Protestant missionary from Germany who wandered into architecture. It's true that you can see one or two Bauhaus-style houses in Rehaviah. One stands on the corner of Arlosoroff Street, near the Bank Le'umi. But for the most part, engineers or draftsmen did the work of architects. As for interior design, that was pretty much can-as-catch—how do you Americans say it?

"But my husband found a way to trade on his skills. At first he arranged with our new landlord to fix up all the carpentry around the house. That took care of our rent for a time. For everything else, we lived against our debts.

"*Ja*, and then as more and more people came in from Europe, my husband at last came upon an idea that helped us get a start. A number of Jews coming from Europe had been more fortunate than we were, and they came out with possessions. You know, they had many of those large pieces of furniture that they had had in the large flats in Berlin and elsewhere. And then they came here, many of them moving into Rehaviah. But the little flats they got here could not accommodate the large furniture. People were heartbroken to discover that the belongings they had struggled so to bring along with them were too big for their flats here.

"My husband went around to these people and offered his services. He told them he was an interior designer—many of the Germans had heard of the Bauhaus, of course—and he could cut their furniture down to size so that it would fit into their new flats and still look as good as it had before."

A commotion began on the street in front of the café as a young porter, pushing an upright piano through the streets, scraped it along the side of one of the gleaming Mercedes taxicabs. The driver and porter argued as to who was to blame, while around them a small crowd gathered. A policeman from the Kishleh, the nearby jail, was walking over. Dispersing the crowd, he managed to calm the situation. The porter moved off, the cabbie found a passenger in the crowd and Ricarda—whose attention, like mine, was grabbed by the little drama—returned to her narrative.

"Not all the German immigrants had the money to pay my husband for his work, but everyone who hired him had leftover blocks of wood that he cut away from their bureaus and chests. Often he took these in place of payment."

"What good were they?"

"To a designer like my husband, they were worth more than money. He and I took the fine mahoganies, oak and cherry woods and began to carve toys out of them. No matter how poor people are, they will buy toys for their children. *Ja*, and especially after the troubles they had been through, many parents wanted to ease the burden of the changes on their children by buying them toys. Our wooden pieces were highly desirable and, what is probably more important, indestructible; and they were beautiful."

"You want some more coffee?" the waiter asked us.

"No," Ricarda said.

"You, sir?"

"I would like some squeezed orange juice, please."

"Only one?" the waiter asked.

"All right, I'll have one too," Ricarda answered.

The waiter walked over to a boy in the corner and passed our order on to him. Taking two oranges from a plastic basket on a nearby shelf, he cut them in half and put them in a large hand squeezer. In a few seconds, the nectar from these golden blossoms of Jericho—that was where many of the vendors of the Old City got their citrus—dripped into the glass underneath.

The boy took two more oranges and filled another glass. We watched him silently from our table on the other side of the large room. I could already taste the sweet juice. Outside, the bell of the date-palm-juice vendor could suddenly be heard. I turned to watch him walk past the archways of the café.

"I'm sorry that man didn't come by a minute earlier," I said, pointing to him as he walked by with his urn and bell. "I wanted to try his *tamar hindi*."

"You have to develop a taste for it; too sweet for me," Ricarda said.

The waiter brought back our juices. Ricarda and I took long swallows, and then I asked her to continue.

"So the wooden toys made money for you?"

"They helped us climb out of debt."

"And things got better."

"They might have, but the world outside would not let us alone. The war in Europe followed us here, and then our own War of Independence, which brought with it the siege. Life here became a continuing struggle."

She finished her juice and rolled her lips. Then, in the same matter-of-fact tone she had used throughout her story, she continued: "My husband was killed. We had by now two children, a son and a daughter."

"How was your husband killed?"

"He was hit by a shell."

"So he had at last become a Zionist?"

"No," Ricarda said drily. "I told you we were neither of us Zionists. He fought only to defend his family, because he realized that if he did not fight, we were all in danger. And there was nowhere left for us to run away to. This was our last home on earth."

I thought of the Zionist arguments for a Jewish homeland. We had to have a homeland—so one such argument ran—because in the end no one else would have us; that was the lesson of Jewish history over the last two thousand years. Home was where they took you in when no one would anywhere else. For a people, home was a homeland, a state. For the Jewish people, home was the land of our fathers, the one promised to Abraham, where our Temple had stood, where our people had shaped its earliest consciousness, the Land of

Israel. Here, when no one else would take us in, we would be welcome—citizens under the Law of Return which made every Jew a native of Israel. Here we would die fighting, for we knew we should never again be dispossessed. There was nowhere else to go. Ricarda's husband might not have been a Zionist, but he died fighting for a Zionist, a Jewish, cause.

I tried to explain the logic of my argument, trying to sound earnest without becoming maudlin. Ricarda glanced over at the Arabs sitting behind me.

"They fought too," she said pointedly.

"They attacked," I said, hoping no one around me would hear. I was eager to let that enmity fade away, but the history had to remain clear.

"Look, I understand what you want to say, but you don't understand something very basic," Ricarda said. "I told you I was not a *yekke.*"

"What has that got to do with anything?"

"I am not a Jew," she said, and paused; and then continuing, added: "You see, that makes all the difference."

I was thunderstruck. Her destiny had been so wrapped up with the Jews: Socialism, concentration camp, Palestine, death in the battle for Jerusalem. And now she was a guide here. Trying not to appear nonplussed, I began rolling the juice glass between my palms. Maybe I had misunderstood her.

"You mean you are an atheist?" I asked.

"That's true, I am an atheist, but I am also not Jewish. I am a German."

"But the concentration camp?"

"I told you I was a Socialist."

"But why come to Palestine, then? And why were you given help by the people who ran the boats?"

"My husband was born a Jew."

"And what about your family?"

"They had given up on me when I married. I have no idea what happened to them, nor they to me. I was written off, a black sheep."

"And how did the Jews treat you?"

"Well, there have been difficulties all along. They wondered when I did not mourn the *shivah.* And many times I have been asked why I have no *mezuzah* on my doorpost. You see, I left the Germans but I did not come over to the Jews, and that is hard to comprehend. Especially here. I am not sure I understand it myself."

"Did you want to become Jewish?"

"Why should I?"

"Are you an Israeli citizen?"

"Oh, yes. Otherwise, I would have no nationality whatsoever. Look, I am an Israeli. My son serves in the army. I love this country —less now that it has taken on the imperialist doctrines of Begin, Sharon and some of the others, but still I feel it is my country. And I am bonded to Jerusalem eternally. I have, as you Americans like to say, paid my dues, *ja*?"

"Yes, probably more than most Jews."

"Well, that probably is of no importance to anyone."

"What did you do after your husband was killed? Did you use your training at all?" I asked her.

"Yes. For a long time I was a photographer. Some of the portraits of the country's leaders are mine. There is a well-known picture of Golda that I did."

"And why don't you take pictures anymore?"

"Well, I'll tell you. One night someone broke into my flat and stole my cameras and my developing equipment. And so I stopped."

"Just like that?"

"Just like that." She smiled ironically. "I had had enough, at least as far as the powers of darkness were concerned."

"And what happened to your pictures?"

"The Israel Museum received most of them, those that were not stolen with the cameras."

"And now?"

"And now I give tours; other people take the pictures."

"What about your children?"

"I tried to raise my children. But it was not easy. And finding the right schools was not easy. And then when people learned that my children were not celebrating the holidays along with everyone else, that made things even harder. Do you know what it is to be here and not to go to your family for the Passover *seder*?"

"No," I answered, "but I have lived in a place where nearly everyone celebrates Christmas and I do not."

"Yes—well, then, imagine."

What was it that made me surprised to find out that Ricarda was a Christian? As we sat in silence for a few moments, I realized that it was not just that she had traveled a path parallel to the Jewish road in history but that I had come to think of Christians as people who visited here but did not settle, who loved the idea of Jerusalem but made their homes elsewhere.

"Do you find it odd," I began, "that in all these Christian places we have visited and some others I have been to on my own there is no one really left? I mean besides the monks, priests and nuns. And the Armenians are refugees waiting to go back to Armenia. Where are the pilgrims? They have all gone away."

"*Ja*, well, nothing stays the same—even here." To Ricarda, history seemed very definitely a one-way street.

"But you are not leaving?" I asked.

"No, my life is here," she said, standing up to take her leave of me, "but I look forward to no salvations."

After I left Ricarda and her one-directional view of history, I wandered on my own back toward the Jewish Quarter. Throughout the ages, the Jews had lived all over the Old City, especially in places close to the remaining Western Wall of the Temple. But over time, the largest concentration had been in the southeast corner. After 1948, the Jews had been removed to the west, and the Quarter had fallen into destruction. Those synagogues not destroyed under Jordanian rule had been put to use as stables or storerooms; many were filled with dung. Jewish homes were turned into wrecks. The neighborhood had become a wasteland.

Returning in 1967, the Israelis, many of whom had grown up in the Quarter, came to renew what had fallen into disrepair. What could be restored, they restored. What could not, they rebuilt. The dislocations of history could be repaired, they seemed to be saying. Old glories could be brought back to life.

Batei Machseh Square, once the largest open space in the Quarter, the plaza where the Arabs had assembled the remaining Jewish inhabitants on the day they were to be expelled from the city, was among the places first restored. Although the Rothschild Houses, a hospice and hostel for the poor still standing in 1967, could be repaired, the rest of the square had to be razed and rebuilt completely. As the place was being rebuilt, someone thought of a famous narrative in the Talmud, some lines of which were then engraved along the wall at one side of the square. It was a story that somehow seemed to me an alternative view of history to what I had just heard from Ricarda. In a way, it seemed in the spirit of resurrection that still stuck to the sites in the Christian Quarter—a spirit that Ricarda had somehow avoided throughout the morning.

I walked toward the engraving, recalling the story in the Talmud. I wondered what Ricarda would have thought of it, and for a moment I imagined myself repeating it to her :

"Shortly after the destruction of the Second Temple, Rabbi Akiva, the man who learned to read only in his fortieth year of life but ultimately became among the greatest scholars Jewry has ever known, was walking atop Mount Scopus, along with other equally great rabbis. From their viewpoint his companions believed they could still see the smoke rising from the heaps of ashes and destruction atop the Temple Mount, and so in mourning for the loss of majesty at this most holy of sites, they rent their clothing.

"When they reached the point closest to the Temple Mount, they suddenly saw a jackal run out of the place that had once been the Holy of Holies—the most sacred spot of the Temple, where the High Priest alone could enter and then only once a year on the Day of Atonement. Seeing this, they all began to weep in despair—all except Rabbi Akiva, who smiled.

"Stunned at his reaction, his companions asked the reason for his smile, and he answered—you know we Jews have always liked answering questions with a question—he answered : 'And why do you cry ?'

"So, rabbis and scholars that they were, they began to quote verses from the sources. Pointing to the spot from which the jackal had come, one of them—I think it was Rabban Gamaliel, but I'm not certain—said : 'This is the place of which the Holy Scriptures warned that the common man who even so much as dared to draw near it would be put to death, and now jackals stroll upon it. How can we not weep ?'

"To the rabbis, the jackal was the visible proof of the denial of all God's promises to His people, a portent of worse things to come, the end of hope, proof that the glories of the past were gone. But for Akiva, who continued to smile, it was quite the opposite. Turning to his companions, he said : 'Why, that jackal is precisely the reason I can smile. Do those very same Scriptures not tell us through the mouth of Isaiah that God shall take as witness of His deeds Uriah the priest and Zechariah, the son of Berechiah ?

" 'Now,' continued Akiva, 'we have always been troubled by this verse.' The others, happy to be swept up in Talmudic dialogue, nodded. 'What, we wondered, could Uriah, who comes from a far earlier period of history, have to do with Zechariah, who comes much later ? And yet the word of God had coupled their prophecies.

" 'And what had each one seen ? Through Uriah, the Almighty

had promised that Zion shall be plowed like a field and Jerusalem be in heaps; and the Temple Mount deserted as a wooded hilltop.

" 'And,' Akiva added, 'so it is now, as jackals wander among the heaps on what is only a wooded hilltop.

" 'But in the book of Zechariah we find the prophet speaks otherwise.' "

The quotation from Zechariah was the lines engraved on the wall. I walked over to read them. In the bright afternoon light of the plaza, children, already home from school, ran everywhere. Some were playing soccer, the most popular game of the season. A few were riding bicycles and playing tag. A small group of tourists was shuffling into a café at the far end of the square. On one of the benches, near a small playground set up in another of the corners of the place, an old man sat reading the afternoon paper and holding a cane between his legs.

I turned to read the writing on the wall.

> THUS SAYS THE LORD OF HOSTS: "THERE SHALL YET SIT OLD MEN AND OLD WOMEN IN THE SQUARES OF JERUSALEM, AND A MAN LEANING ON HIS STAFF BECAUSE OF HIS MANY YEARS. AND THE PLAZAS SHALL BE FILLED WITH BOYS AND GIRLS PLAYING IN THEM."

Turning to look again at the fulfillment of Zechariah's prophecy, I imagined myself concluding Akiva's story for Ricarda: " 'Until the prophecy of Uriah had been fulfilled, I feared that the prophecy of Zechariah might not come to be. Now that we see that Uriah's prophecy has been fulfilled, we may be certain that Zechariah's promise will also come to be.'

" 'You have comforted us, Akiva,' the others said. 'You have comforted us.' "

I turned to watch an old woman walk a little girl to the slide in the playground across the square. Jerusalem was a place where history is not a one-way street; here the resurrection of old glories still seemed possible.

CHAPTER
· 12 ·

MONKS

A religious man respects the power of God's creation to bear witness for itself.

THOMAS MERTON

"What will you drink? Arak, wine or ouzo?"
The speaker was a Greek Orthodox monk, Brother Cornelius, but the question was not the sort I would have expected from a member of a monastic order. Cornelius, however, was not anything like what I imagined a monk to be. He eschewed solitude, embraced the active side of life, disliked formal church services but loved God in nature. Instead of the pallid complexion of the contemplative, he had the ruddy suntanned features of an outdoorsman.

He was born in Jerusalem, where his father had moved after a dispute with an older brother about some cows they had jointly inherited. Having begun a new life here, the father in time lost his wife. At sixty-two, he remarried, this time a poor sixteen-year-old Greek orphan, Cornelius' mother.

As a boy, and even as a young man, Cornelius—or "Costa," as

he was then known—had not felt called to the religious vocation. Had his destiny unfolded according to plan, he would probably have taken over his father's business, a bakery in the Old City's Christian Quarter. But after an accident in the shop, his father lost a leg to gangrene, and the bakery had to be sold. With that, security in Costa's immediate future quickly evaporated. At last, the old man died, and although the widow took to cleaning houses, there was never enough money for the family, and soon Costa found out how to make his way on the streets.

With little schooling and largely illiterate, in time he found himself work as a cleaner and handyman. Life was mostly a case of catching an odd job here or there in the increasingly crowded and dirty walled city. During the Second World War he worked for the British Army and learned the little English he knew, but for the most part, Greek and Arabic remained the languages of his daily discourse. A fellow conscript taught him how to write and read a little of the street Arabic he had learned to speak well enough.

Following the departure of the British and the war of 1948, he found himself—like many in the Jerusalem Greek community who lived inside the walls or in the eastern, non-Jewish neighborhoods of the city—inside the Jordanian sector of Palestine. He returned to being a handyman and cleaner.

"One day," Cornelius continued his story, "my good friend—today he is barber—give me a paper: how you say, a magazine. 'Take this and burn it,' he say to me."

"What was it?"

"It was Communist paper. I don't know what it say. First, I don't read. Besides, I don't even know what is this 'Communism.' I never interested in politics. But he is my friend—a Greek—and he is in trouble, need my help. He is afraid to carry the paper on street. He think no one notice me with paper because everybody know I not political. So I take it, put it under my arm and go to find place to burn it."

On his way, Cornelius—apparently an object of suspicion by the tense authorities still not used to policing the city they had just wrested from the British and Israelis—was stopped by the Jordanian police. Discovering the pamphlet, they arrested him as a Communist. His protests of innocence and ignorance were useless, and he was thrown into prison. For three years he sat locked in the Kishleh, the jail just inside the Jaffa Gate near the Citadel of David.

"I still hate to walk near the place," Cornelius added. "It was a terrible life in this jail. Dirty, dark, tiny rooms. The food is horrible. The Jordanians don't care what happen to you inside. And in a time, you too don't care.''

Released at last, he tried to go back to his work as a handyman. But the police, convinced that he was dangerous, continued to harass him.

''Every time I get a job, they arrest me. So what happens? People give me some money to go get paints or cleaner, brushes or rags. Then before anything, the Jordanian police arrest me for a few days.''

In those days, food in the prison, laundry—all expenses—were charged against the assets the prisoners had. ''Each time I come out of prison, no more money, no job, nothing.''

His clients, increasingly uninterested in his excuses, were convinced he had spent their money on himself, on a drinking binge or on other excesses. He was, after all, someone who had been in jail and was known still for his gusto for life and its pleasures. Finding work became harder and harder. The only sure thing in his life became the arrests, and they were intolerable.

''So I become a monk.''

Cornelius told his story to me while I sat inside his room in the Great Greek Orthodox Monastery of Constantine and Helena, which stands inside the Christian Quarter of the Old City. After my trip with Ricarda, I had become convinced that the only way I would understand Christian attachments to Jerusalem—or at least, to its holy places—would be by talking with the monks and priests who had made the Holy Place their places. I wanted to talk to Christians for whom there was no other home save this one.

For a Jew, closer to Orthodox Judaism than to Orthodox Christianity, however, making contact with a monk required an introduction. That came about almost by accident, when a local anthropologist, Jeff Halper, and I, on a walk through the Christian Quarter, decided to stop into the monastery.

Long before, I had come to Halper for help in finding my way into new corners of the city. An American from Minnesota, a dropout from Hebrew Union College, the seminary for Reform Jewish rabbis, he had come to Jerusalem originally to write his dissertation about urban neighborhoods. In the process, he married a local girl, moved into a house in the Nachla'ot quarter, the area in which he did his research, and had become part of the human landscape of the city. In the parlance of the discipline, his colleagues would have said simply: ''Halper went native.'' Although he completed his degree and had for a time been a lecturer at Haifa University, now he gave tours of the city for the Society for the Protection of Nature, taught extension courses at a variety of educational institutions and was hard at work writing a historical anthropology of Jerusalem in the nineteenth century. With him, I hoped, I would meet people whom alone I would never discover.

As we walked north in one of the bazaars of the Old City, along a narrow lane filled with souks selling religious souvenirs, sweets and meats, we passed a Greek-owned barbershop—that of the same barber who had been the cause of young Costa's going to jail. Across the way stood the Constantine and Helena Monastery. Offhandedly, Halper mentioned a monk he knew whom he thought I ought someday to meet. "He's open and talkative, not at all like what you might expect to find in a convent," he added.

"Could we meet him now?" I said, pouncing on the opportunity.

"I suppose so. Let's find out."

He turned back and opened the door of the barbershop. The owner greeted him in English. In the non-Jewish quarters of the Old City, Jews who did not speak Arabic always found English a far more congenial language of discourse than Hebrew. The latter was far too politically charged; it symbolized Jewish dominance, something most of the locals in the eastern part of the city and those who wanted contact with them liked to deemphasize. So except for those whose business affairs brought them into contact with Jews, few East Jerusalemites spoke Hebrew fluently.

After the obligatory niceties, Halper asked the barber, "Is Costa in the monastery now?"

"Yes, yes. I see him before." He razed a few hairs off his customer's neck. "But you know, don't ask for 'Costa' in there. Call him 'Cornelius.'" That was the name Costa had taken when he joined the order, and that was how he was called inside.

We crossed the lane from the barbershop and walked up the alley steps toward the monastery, seat of the Jerusalem Patriarch and local headquarters of the Greek Orthodox Church. The Church had once been among the richest landholders in Jerusalem. The neighborhoods of Talbieh and Rehaviah, the famous King David Hotel, the Y.M.C.A. and even the Israel Museum and the Knesset stood on lands once owned and later, in the cash-flow problems following the First World War, sold by the Church. Even without the hope of meeting Cornelius, I would have wanted to see this place.

The large, thick brown metal doors to the monastery were closed. A smaller door carved out in their center was, however, open. But to enter it, we had to bow deeply. As we walked through it, I wondered whether this door was purposely made small by the Church fathers to ensure that all who set foot into their territory would always lower their heads upon entering. It would not have been unusual, since in this city, form often followed faith rather than function.

Once inside, we found ourselves in a large, rather dark courtyard. All the writing on the posted signs was in Greek. We might still have been in Jerusalem, but we had without doubt entered another domain. Apparently, although the monastery insiders dwelt in Jerusalem, they had remade it into an outpost of Greece.

While I stood just inside the gate, Halper walked toward the back of the dark space and approached a cage within which sat a small bald-headed man in a shapeless brown jacket.

''Is Cornelius here?'' he asked in English.

The guard was not certain which Cornelius we meant; there were several. ''Do you know where is his room?'' he asked at last.

''Yes,'' Halper answered.

''So go up yourself and see.''

Leading me, Halper walked from the dark entrance into an even larger, far brighter courtyard, and then under a series of arched ceilings. At the last one, some Arab laborers were stripping off the blue-and-white paint on the walls which over the years had faded. In two sections, the Jerusalem stone underneath had already been fully exposed, cleaned and renewed. Later, Cornelius would point with pride to this work for which he, as overseer of the laborers, felt responsible.

The space inside the walls was mammoth but labyrinthine: tunnels leading to archways and courtyards within courtyards. After a number of turns we came at last upon a particularly large garden in which a variety of fig and olive trees and bushes had been planted. As in many other places throughout the Christian Quarter, dotted as it was with monasteries—Greek Orthodox, Greek Catholic, Coptic, Franciscan, Ethiopian, Russian Orthodox, Latin Orthodox and others—the contrast with the dirt and noise outside in the souks was striking. One passed from a life ruled by the immediacies of commerce to another far more ephemeral, formed by symbol and fashioned by faith. In the one everything was covered by noise; in the other silences dominated. One was embedded in the here while the other seemed, at least to an outsider like me, part of the hereafter.

Ascending a wide staircase into the main building of the monastery, we entered a cavernous dark and empty hall. The echo of our footsteps was all that broke the silence here. Continuing slowly past a dingy-looking row of toilets, we approached a line of plain brown doors. Halper knocked on one. "I think this is his room."

No one answered. "Cornelius," he called softly, as if a loud voice would somehow desecrate the place. No answer. There was no one around to ask.

"Could he be upstairs?" I wondered, moving toward a circular staircase in the middle of the corridor.

"I don't know. He once told me that he's supposed to be in charge of the Arab laborers, so he could be anywhere." We wandered back to the toilets to look for a sign of life there, but there was none.

With no one here to host us, we had penetrated as far as possible into the convent. There was no point to lingering any longer; sooner or later the guard would come around and chase us out.

"Well, maybe we'll come back another time," Halper suggested.

Turning and walking down a few steps, we began making our way back to the entrance when suddenly we saw a tall, heavyset man who looked to be in his sixties trudging toward us. He dragged the heels of his shoes; later I would notice that he had caved them in.

"It's him; it's Cornelius."

We made our greetings and I was introduced. The gray-cassocked monk held out a large, callused hand and invited us into his room, which turned out to be a curious mix of the temporal and the sublime. Inside, the sacred seemed swallowed up by the profane, or at the very least by the mundane.

"I am sorry about mess," he said upon opening the door.

The room was large, but much of its space was taken up with piles of dirty-looking clothes and boxes, many of them filled with bottles. One corner, in which his bed stood, seemed a kind of oasis of order. Above it, a few large color photographs of himself were on the wall. A bayonet from an army rifle hung there near snapshots of his sisters, one of whom lived in Russia and the other in the United States. Along one wall was a painting of the Virgin; near the door, another of a saint. On a small table next to the bed stood a big but old Grundig radio. In the opposite corner was an ancient-looking refrigerator standing next to a modern television set. On the floor everywhere were cases of liquor, while on a table nearby stood half-empty bottles of ouzo, brandy and arak. Between the refrigerator and the table was a beautifully carved bench, perhaps a pew from a church. Atop it were more piles of clothes, pants inside out and shirts whose sleeves appeared knotted. The entire heap was peppered with black sock balls.

In another corner of the room, behind a kind of shower-curtain arrangement, Cornelius kept his kitchen. Near the door were some hooks on which hung three of the large black caps the monks wore and a variety of gray and black cassocks.

Finally, where I might have expected to discover icons or devotional prayers, what caught my eye most was a handmade poster adorned with postcards and snapshots of girls around which were penned greetings written in German, English, Spanish and French.

Seeing my eyes scan the room, Cornelius explained somewhat sheepishly, "I not expecting company." He laughed.

Underneath his cassock, which he now pulled off, Cornelius wore a bulky-knit green turtleneck sweater. He threw his hat on a hook on the wall. His straight gray hair shone with perspiration. Sitting on the edge of his bed, without the hat or cassock, he looked quite different, and acted far more relaxed. Now he offered us the drinks and in answer to questions, unfolded his story.

Neither a refugee from life nor a man in obsessive pursuit of holiness, he had never sought to abandon the profane world in favor of the solitary, sacred life in a cloister. Rather, he had in effect fallen into his vocation because there was nowhere else better for him to go. But although he entered the convent, he had still found a way to allow the vitality of the outside world to which he was so attached to seep inside. The life of the street and the outdoors still flowed in his veins and pulsed in his blood.

After joining the order, he was sent first to the Mar Saba—he called it St. Saba—Monastery in the Judean Wilderness. Built into the mountains on the edge of the Kidron Valley which goes out from Jerusalem, this place east of Bethlehem and about thirty kilometers out of Jerusalem was established in the fifth century by the monk Saba who had gone from his native Greece on a pilgrimage to the Holy Land. Although by the end of his life, Saba had established fourteen monasteries and four hospices, this one—where for years he had lived a hermit's existence—alone carried his name. Here he had been interred. For fifteen hundred years, the spot over his bones and opposite the cave in which he lived his solitary life had been revered as a holy place.

Cornelius' time at Mar Saba was not one of unmarred joy. Set off in the desert without electricity, running water or much company except for the dozen or so monks who lived there or the pilgrims who came on feast days, he lived a fairly solitary life.

To be sure, he had not been the first to experience the seemingly interminable confinement of this place. Describing his visit to Mar Saba in the late nineteenth century, Charles William Wilson, Royal Engineer in the British Army and one of the foremost explorers of Jerusalem, wrote in his *Picturesque Palestine*: "The convent is considered by the Greeks almost a penal one, and scandal says that all its inmates except the superiors have been sent hither for heresy or other offenses. Of heresy certainly they must be acquitted, so far as their knowledge goes, for they are profoundly ignorant...."

But if Cornelius, like many of his forebears, betrayed an ignorance about theological and ecclesiastical matters, he all the same held on to and over the years nurtured a certain naïve faith. "I don't know much about the Church, but I know how to feel religious," he explained.

"In the things of God," Cyril of Jerusalem had once written, "the confession of no knowledge is great knowledge."

Still, the life inside Mar Saba had been far too constricted for Cornelius. "From the fourteenth of January in 1952, I live there for eight years, fifteen days and three hours," he said, and took a great swallow of arak.

"Was it like prison?" I asked.

"You say it," he answered, smiling.

"Why did you stay?"

"And where else to go?"

But for all his time in the monastery, Cornelius was not totally subdued.

"Once, I have an argument with the Superior. So they send me to St. George's."

East of Jerusalem and five kilometers west of Jericho, standing at the end of Wadi Kelt, St. George's was another monastery built into a mountain in the Judean Wilderness. Here he stayed for only six months. And then he was sent into the Sinai to Santa Katerina.

"The worst was Santa Katerina. Too far from everything. Thank God I stay there only three months. Then I come here."

"Let's talk about Jerusalem," I said after a sip of my drink. Had it changed over the years? I asked.

"You mean since the Jews?" he replied, and then without waiting for an answer, continued: "You want me to tell the truth?"

"Of course."

He looked at my glass. "You want more ouzo?"

"No, thanks."

"What's the matter? You drink too much for poison and not enough to get drunk." He laughed. "No matter."

"Jerusalem?"

"Okay. Well, it's not as nice as Toronto. Toronto I like very much. Milwaukee even better. Good beer." He smiled slyly.

For a moment I felt a crush of disappointment: even the monks, I thought, would rather be in places other than Jerusalem. Cornelius laughed when he saw the consternation on my face. Here was a monk born and raised in Jerusalem, a guardian of its holy places, and he tells me he likes Milwaukee! This was not exactly what I had expected to discover. I pressed on.

"But Jerusalem, how has it changed?" I was seeking the locally anchored recollections of a native. Cornelius was, however, too much enamored of the present to linger very long in the past. Besides, for him the past was not bathed in nostalgia; it was something from which he was still trying to escape.

"Now it much better than in Jordanian time or when I am growing up. I tell you the truth. It much cleaner. You know, when I am a boy, people piss in street. Then they wipe themselves on walls. I not like this kind of dirtiness. So I put pepper on walls. Next time somebody wipe himself, he scream because it burn him."

He laughed and lit a cigarette.

"You know it so dirty, I lose my eye because water dirty. Look: you see this eye"—he pointed to the right one—"is glass."

"How about the people?"

"I like all people—only not the Gush Emunim and the Mafia."

Gush Emunim were the Orthodox Jewish settlers who had formed a religious attachment to the land acquired since the Six-Day War in 1967. Through its settlement they hoped to bring closer the day of the coming of the Messiah and the redemption of all Jews. The presence of nonbelievers in the holy places was to some an impediment to the fulfillment of their messianic hopes. Cornelius knew that he and the world he inhabited were one such obstacle.

"The Mafia?" Halper asked. "Who do you mean?"

"The Jewish terror, the Arabic terror." They too looked at people who did not share their view of the future as obstacles.

If we entered the realm of politics, I was certain walls dividing us would quickly block any bridges on which we could meet. Quickly, I changed the subject.

"And how has the monastery changed over the years?"

"Look," he said pointing to the radio, television set and cases of liquor. "In the old times, we not allowed to have this. And we get one bottle to drink a week. Now we have how much we want. Radio, television. We get our freedom."

"Why?"

"Patriarch knows that no one would become monk if you live like in prison."

Later, I would meet another Greek Orthodox monk, Michael, whose attitude was quite a bit different. One of two monks who lived in the Monastery of the Temptation, sometimes called the Quruntul, he yearned for more restrictions, for freedom from the obsession to be free.

Built onto the side of a sheer cliff west of Jerusalem and overlooking the oasis of Jericho, the Quruntul was where, according to some Christian beliefs, Jesus had been tempted by Satan and had fasted for forty days. In the fourth century, monks had taken to living in the natural caves that dotted the cliffs. A hundred years ago a small monastery and chapel had been built over one particularly large cave in which, according to tradition, was a stone on which Jesus planted Himself and remained throughout the temptation.

Having climbed up the steep hill to get to the monastery from the spring below, I met Michael, who pattered about the dark caves in slippers. A young man in his thirties with a smile that lit up the darkness, he had been born in Greece but had already been in the Holy Land for twenty-three years. For a little over two years he had dwelt in the Quruntul, his only companion an older monk and the occasional visitors who came during the few hours each day the monastery was open to outsiders. Although the facilities were modest in the extreme—water from cisterns, small cots and tiny cells carved into the cave—things were changing. During the last year, at the urging of the Patriarch, electricity had been brought into the place.

Was he pleased with the improvements? I asked.

"I don't like them," Michael explained. "They completely change the atmosphere of the place."

"You mean that now you can have radios and television here?" I asked, thinking of Cornelius' room and what I had seen in it.

"Of course, and why not?" Michael replied. "If the power is here, it's too tempting not to use it. Then there is nothing that distinguishes this place from the city. And then, if that is the case" —he smiled and played with his slipper on the stone floor—"you might as well be in the city. There's no reason to be out here." And as for the city, it had already forfeited much of its sanctity by slipping into the twentieth century.

"But aren't monks prepared to deal with temptations?" I asked, half-smiling.

He shrugged his shoulders, smiled and said, "There are other, more important liberations."

"So we free now," Cornelius explained, taking a long drink of arak.

"But tell him what you think is the best part of your new life," Halper interjected.

"You mean Helgart?"

"Yes."

Helgart was a German woman whom Cornelius had met in Jerusalem around Easter time several years earlier. He was always stopping to talk with women whenever he walked the streets. Later, I would watch him in action, striking up conversations with every pretty girl we passed as we strolled through the streets of the Old City. On that Easter night, he told us, he had come upon Helgart and a woman friend. Their money had been stolen and they were thrown out of the hotel in which they had been staying. With no place to go, they were invited by Cornelius to come with him. He found them room in his cell.

Months later, at Easter time when I met Helgart, she told a different version of the events leading to their meeting.

"Angelica and I were sitting in a café inside the Jaffa Gate. It was seven in the evening, and we were watching Cornelius, who was there also; he was talking to tourists.

"We wanted very much to talk to him too, but we were a bit afraid. And then, when it looked as if he were about to leave, Angelica forced me to speak, and we asked him a few questions. He was friendly, so alive that we were very much attracted by his company. The next day we met him and he showed us around."

Both versions of the story ended the same way: the friendship stuck, and since then Helgart, who lived in Cologne, had come to Jerusalem fourteen times and Cornelius had been to visit her as well.

On the way to Germany—a trip to which he always happily looked forward—he would go aboard the airplane clad in a cassock and monk's hat. After takeoff, the monk ambled down the aisle to the lavatory. Inside, he removed his hat and cassock and exited looking to all the world like a tourist. ''The stewardess see a monk come into plane, but somewhere in the air, he disappear.'' He laughed.

''And often I call her in Germany. The monk in charge of the telephone is good friend. He let me talk all I want.''

Helgart was a friend to warm his bed—another part of the world outside the monastery which Cornelius had managed to draw into his life.

''How's your knee?'' Halper asked.

For years, Cornelius had been suffering from some sort of bone problem. When at last his left leg had become intolerably stiff, he went, at Halper's advice, to the Hadassah Hospital on Mount Scopus.

''The doctor in Mount Scopus he want to cut my leg. He say the two bones come together at knee and rub each other. They need to be separated.''

''So did you go for the operation?''

Perhaps recalling his father's amputation, the monk decided there had been enough leg cutting in his family.

''No. I go to Bedouin instead; I believe in their remedies.''

For years, Cornelius had been close to the Bedouin. In those matters on which the Church was silent, Cornelius had chosen to align himself with the ways of the Bedouin. He worked with them and spoke their language. And he had assimilated some of their ways, especially their medicines and remedies.

''What did they do for you?''

''The healer, he take a long nail, make it red-hot and bang into my knee where I feel the pain. See?''

He rolled up his pants to reveal several black circles which the burning nails had left along his leg. There were two on either side of the knee, looking a bit like vacant, malevolent eyes. Three others surrounded his ankle.

''And this helped?''

''Oh, yes. Very good. Look!'' He stood and walked around the room. ''I able to walk good now. And if it stiff sometimes, I take glass like this.''

He reached for a glass from the cupboard near the refrigerator.

''You know this cure?'' he asked.

He wadded a piece of paper and, lighting it with a match, threw the burning ball into the glass. Quickly, he turned the glass over and pressed it hard against his knee. The fire went out, and as the smoke curled around inside the glass, the skin was sucked up into it, forming a vacuum at the edge. Cornelius let it rest there a few moments and then, with a loud pop, pulled it off.

"Ah, it's good!" he laughed.

"What does it mean to be a monk?" I asked.

"Eight thousand six hundred and twenty olive trees."

"What?"

"I am responsible for eight thousand six hundred and twenty olive trees. I take care of trees. To me, a man serve religion with his hands, not just in church. I work with trees. I see them grow. I see the olives get ripe, make them into oil. This bring me closer to God.

"Some days I go out on my tractor to the fields. We have many fields around Jerusalem, almost all the way to St. Saba. I work with the trees; I help them grow. This means religion, no?"

I looked at this simple man who had the mark of his vocation clearly marked upon his brow. On his forehead where his rectangular hat normally rested, I could see that the line of his suntan ended too. For Cornelius there was no special religious and ecclesiastical side of life; instead, the whole of his life was very simply located in religious precincts, and for him that was enough. Where he planted his trees, there he planted and nurtured his faith.

"You want to see my gardens here?" he asked.

"Very much."

"We go. And then if you have car we go to St. Saba. Today is the feast of Saint Saba."

"All right."

As we headed toward the door, Cornelius grabbed his gray cassock and black monk's cap from the hook by the door and threw them both on.

"Come—I show you."

We walked back through the courtyards, stopping at the large garden. He was right: there was something in the greenery that exuded, if not holiness, a sense of quiet separation from the surrounding profanity. And if he had made that greenery bloom, he could perhaps in some way have remained in contact with the Spirit that nurtured it.

From the garden, we wandered up to the roof above the Church of the Holy Sepulcher. Here, in the year 326, Saint Helena had discovered what she claimed to be the site of the True Cross, and here, less than ten years later, a basilica had been dedicated. Over the years, as pilgrims made their way to this shrine on the spot where most of Christendom believed their Lord had been buried and later resurrected, additional chapels had been added. Today, the complex of chapels inside the church, and Golgotha, which had been absorbed into it, was a three-dimensional maze of holy places atop and beside one another.

"There are different jurisdictions here, are there not?" I asked.

"I no understand. Speak more slower," he answered.

"There are different monks and groups who keep control over different parts of the church."

In Jerusalem's Christian holy places, the various sects had more or less divided their control over the sancta. The basic rule of order revolved around cleaning. Whichever group was responsible for cleaning a particular spot in the chapel would try to claim dominance over the sacred site. So monks were always trying to extend the sweep of their brooms beyond their borders. Those who held adjoining territories were always the ones who entered into the greatest disputes with each other.

"Yah. Copts, Catholics, Ethiopians, Armenians. With Armenians is a real problem. They clean a place once, they think it belong to them forever. I once get my head cracked by Armenian priest who try to keep me from cleaning our section of chapel. But don't worry, I put him in hospital for five days."

"Where are the Ethiopians and Copts?" I asked as we walked along the roof.

The quarrel between these two groups for control of a section of another roof over the church was legendary. Once, when one of the groups had gone to their prayers, the other quickly took over a piece of their territory and changed all the locks so that when the worshiping monks and priests returned, they found they could no longer get into their old places. (When I once asked one of the soft-spoken Ethiopian monks about this episode, he giggled with embarrassment and said simply: "Someday, maybe, we shall be able to build a chapel large enough for everyone.") A temporary solution had been found based on the "status quo principle."

"The Ethiopians and Copts are that way," Cornelius mumbled, waving his arm over his shoulder in the direction of a beige dome with a cross atop it. He was not particularly interested in their holy perch.

Many times I had visited the Ethiopian roof, one of my favorite places in the Christian Quarter. Driven from the inside of the church to the roof during a nineteenth-century religious dispute, which took place before the status quo principle had taken hold, these quiet Christians had built a new sanctuary above the holy places. Inside a small gate, also manned by an Arab guard, I found what appeared to be a replica of a small village in Ethiopia. Around a few eucalyptus trees which grew on the roof, the black monks had constructed tiny one-room huts that looked as if made of dried mud. Inside each cell were a simple cot, a small table and a crucifix on the wall. A slightly larger dwelling was used for communal eating. The two nuns who prepared the food for the twenty or so monks who lived there had separate modest quarters of their own. In a few corners were some rusty-looking pumps from which they all got their water. Along one wall were some bells by which they called themselves to prayer. Finally, through a tiny door which made the visitor bow low to the floor, one came to their two chapels, one above the other. The whole place was an oasis of peace in the sky above the souks and bazaars of the Old City and the street leading to the Damascus Gate.

When I visited them during the winter afternoons, I often found a few of the monks sitting on benches around the dome. There, in the light of the sun and the brightness which the cupola reflected, the black-skinned and black-clad men would warm themselves. The sight was always quietly striking.

I remember the first time I entered their chapel on the roof. Although far smaller than the massive building the Church had built on Ethiopia Street in the western, new part of the city, this was their holiest place. George, a tall, dark-bearded monk with a gentle smile, who had been here for twelve years since his arrival from Africa (to which he believed he could never return), had shown me through the chapel, pointing out the Bishop's gold-and-purple throne. Standing before the inner sanctum in which the Bishop offered the symbolic sacrifice of faith, he proudly displayed the sacred book whose handwritten parchment pages were cut in the shape of a cross and whose words were all in Ge'ez, the liturgical language of the Ethiopian Church.

"Are you happy living here?" I asked him.

Smiling, he answered: "And where else could we be?"

And then he explained how, according to Ethiopian tradition, his people draw their origins from the union between the Israelite King Solomon and the Ethiopian Queen of Sheba. Had not Haile Selassie (who had escaped to and lived in Jerusalem when the Italian Fascists invaded Ethiopia) called himself "the Lion of Judah"?

"And when the Queen of Sheba heard of the fame of Solomon because of the name of the Lord," read the Scriptures describing this visit in First Kings, Chapter 10, "she came to Jerusalem with a very great train, with camels that bore spices and gold very much, and precious stones; and when she was come to Solomon, she spoke with him of all that was in her heart."

As I looked around the little Ethiopian chapel, my eye was caught by a painting that memorialized this fateful meeting. In the picture, showing a bejeweled Sheba and a bedazzled Solomon, I noticed suddenly that among the king's retinue stood three men dressed in the garb of hasidim. The hasidim, of course, had their origins in nineteenth-century Poland. But to the "abuna," the holy men of this church, they somehow represented the authentic Jews, witnesses to the union of two peoples. "The capacity, variable among peoples as it is among individuals, to perceive meaning in pictures," wrote anthropologist Clifford Geertz, "is, like all other fully human capacities, a product of collective experience which far transcends it."

With Cornelius we walked to the edge of his part of the church's roof. For a moment we stopped at a grating.

"This is where I pass the holy fire to the Patriarch," Cornelius explained. "Everybody think it's a miracle, that the fire come from Heaven. But"—he laughed—"the miracle begin here with me."

We moved toward the edge of the roof and looked out silently on the vista beyond. The view from the roof was extraordinary. In the distance were the red mountains of Edom and Moab beyond the river Jordan. And to their south, a touch of the blue Dead Sea. Below were the courtyard in front of the basilica and the remains of an earlier Byzantine church. Pilgrims, priests and tourists wandered in and out. Beyond stood the spire of the Lutheran Church of the Redeemer. Behind me were the belfry and ramparts of Terra Sancta, the Franciscan convent and Notre Dame. The private verandas of bishops and patriarchs were all around along the edge of the roof. Two grates were over holes which opened onto the holy sepulcher below, and the faint smell of incense wafted up through them.

"Ready to go to St. Saba," the monk announced suddenly.

We left the convent and threaded the narrow streets toward my car, which stood parked just outside the Jaffa Gate. Once inside it, I put on my skullcap, which on Halper's advice I had taken off before entering the monastery. "They might think you are one of the Gush Emunim, if you leave it on," he explained, "and then we'll never get inside."

When we were seated in the car, Cornelius turned to me. "You do one thing for me," he said. "Take off the cap at St. Saba." In this country, even when barriers come down and prejudices seem to disappear, they have a way of quietly reappearing.

The ride to Mar Saba soon took us on the main road to Bethlehem. Here for the first time I saw a reminder that in less than a week it would be Christmas. In Jerusalem proper, the Christian holy days were hardly noticeable except to those who searched for their signs. Besides, each Christian group celebrated Christmas on a different date. Over the road, just outside Bethlehem, hung a sign which in English wished everyone a "MERRY CHRISTMAS." A few of the nearby telegraph poles were festooned with lights.

"For the tourists," said Cornelius.

As we moved south through the warm December afternoon sun along the route that Joseph and Mary must have traveled a little less than two thousand years before, I thought that all my acquired American associations of Christmas with snow were totally wrong-headed. They had nothing to do with the original locus of these events. They came from a Christianity that had long ago separated itself from the realities of Bethlehem, Jerusalem and the Holy Land and had instead embedded itself in European and American landscapes.

Here in late-December Bethlehem, the temperature was mild—sweaters-only weather. A white Christmas was the last thing one expected here. Reindeer were nowhere to be seen. And then, what about the stable versus the inn? None of the houses here looked at all like the crèche scenes I had seen on the New England lawns of my childhood. And as I recalled some of the two-thousand-year-old houses that I had seen—those from the Second Temple Period, the time of Jesus' life—it dawned on me that the difference between the "inn" and the "stable" two thousand years ago was probably negligible. The inn was likely no cleaner than the stable. The only difference between the two may have been the animals. Given the sorts of people who stayed in inns and who traveled the dangerous roads outside walled cities in those days, the stable, with its sheep and goats, may in truth have been the safer of the two places to give birth. How foreign were my borrowed conceptions of the dawn of the Christian experience! How right was the argument that suggested that when something is "remembered" several times, the memory itself becomes more powerful than the event it recalls.

"Turn east here," Cornelius said, and I veered off the main road, passing along the outskirts of Bethlehem and into the neighboring town, Beit Saḥur. With each kilometer we moved farther east from the watershed, and the earth grew increasingly barren as we headed toward the wilderness and in the direction of the Dead Sea. But in the valley—really a dry river bed called *wadi* in Arabic or *nachal* in Hebrew—where the water rushed down when there was rain in the higher elevations, vegetation grew.

"Those are my trees," Cornelius said, pointing to a grove along the side of the hill. He knew each tree, which were his and which someone else's. They marked the way for him far better than any road signs.

"Sometimes I used to make the trip on a donkey, before I get the tractor."

The road grew narrower and narrower, hardly wider than my car —but it was still two-way. A car coming in the other direction would force me to turn halfway into the shoulder. I concentrated totally on my driving.

We were beyond what Israelis called "the green line," the armistice line that held between 1949 and 1967. For the last few months, there had been increased problems with stone throwing by the locals, especially the young boys. Each time we passed a concentration of houses in front of which stood a group of boys, I silently shuddered in fear that a stone would come flying through my windshield.

Cornelius waved to everyone, and many of those we passed waved back. His bearlike figure was familiar in these parts. At Ubeidya, a small Bedouin village about eleven kilometers outside Beit Saḥur, Cornelius told me to turn east onto a tiny, hilly road that made the one we were coming off seem like the king's highway in comparison. This would take us straight to Mar Saba. But the six or eight kilometers that remained were by far the hardest. The sun was going down much faster than I expected; the ride was taking longer than I'd hoped. I wondered if we would have to drive back over this treacherous path after dark.

"Ubeidya," the monk explained, "is settled by children of the servants who long years ago come to help to build the monastery."

I let my mind play with the name Ubeidya. How true it was, I thought, that a place could localize a memory and evoke feelings. Just the mere passage and recitation of the name had been enough to get Cornelius going on to a story about a distant past. The name Ubeidya sounded very much like the Hebrew word *eved*—"servant." That, I mused, was how the village had got its name. The local fellahin frequently kept alive memories through the names they gave to places; often archeologists were drawn to a place they thought would yield some relics precisely because the local Arabs had a name for it that echoed the ancient one.

Cornelius waved to an Arab who, squinting as we drove by, suddenly noticed the monk inside. His face broke into a smile, and then he waved back and yelled out a greeting as the car flew past. "I know everyone here," Cornelius said.

"Here you be careful on the turns," the monk warned me. I slowed down, needing no further warnings. The hairpin curves were about 140 degrees at some points, and the incline at least 45. To make things a bit more challenging, little pebbles were strewn across the pavement so that if I tried to slow down by braking, I found the wheels rolling out from underneath me. Pumping the clutch and downshifting, I forged ahead, fired more by my adrenaline that by anything in my car's engine.

As we passed the last Arab house and headed toward the shining desolation of Judea, I found myself wondering what it must have been like for Saba walking out here in the fifth century, alone, driven by some religious devotion I could not even begin to fathom.

"You know, sometimes I walk myself to here from Jerusalem," Cornelius said as if reading my mind.

"How long does it take?" Halper asked incredulously.

"I lose a little the time, but I think over four hours."

"Why do you do it?"

"It is good exercise; I like to be outside. Why not?"

Cornelius had told us that he did not like going to church, that he could get "closer to religion" when he was out taking care of his trees. In spite of my being impressed with his garden in the monastery, the argument, at the time he made it, had sounded to me a bit self-serving: a monk who enters the order to escape harassment by the police, who smokes, drinks and sleeps with a woman did not seem to me to have a very strong case to make for getting "closer to religion." But gazing now at the boundless landscape before my eyes, at the hills of Judea and beyond to the red mountains of Edom in the distant Transjordan, I suddenly had second thoughts about the sincerity of his faith. Didn't another monk—Father Louis, better known as Thomas Merton—once explain that "a religious man respects the power of God's creation to bear witness for itself"? In those terms, Cornelius was a religious man.

The road twisted sharply; I slowed down the Renault to a crawl. Below us I could see at last the cupola of Mar Saba, on a precipice overlooking the Kidron Valley.

"There it is. Now I show you the place where I spend many years." We growled down the last few curves in low gear.

"What about the skulls?" Halper asked. He wanted to see the catacombs of the monastery where the remains of martyrs and holy men are kept. Those who had been here in life spent their eternity here, waiting for the Second Coming.

"Why not? I show you that. I show you St. Saba too."

Stopping inches away from the cliff's edge, we parked next to another car, the only other sign that the outside world had made contact with this place.

Stepping out into the clear air of the desert, we followed Cornelius toward the convent door. As we approached it, the chapel bells suddenly began to toll, shattering the silence.

"They call the monks to prayer now," Cornelius explained. "Come—we go in."

The little door—the only entrance into the compound—was locked; Cornelius tugged on a rope that was attached to a bell on the other side. Again and again, in a sort of syncopation with the prayer bells, he pulled the cord.

"It's a good thing we're here with you," I said. "I would never have dared ringing at prayer time." What I did not realize then but would discover months later when I tried to penetrate a Greek Orthodox holy service on my own was that not only would I not have dared ring the bell, but it was only with an insider like Cornelius that I could allow myself to have such an inside look at a world so foreign to my own.

"No problem," Cornelius said. "Someone answer the door in a minute." He rang a few more times.

"A little iron-barred door is the entrance," wrote Charles Wilson describing his visit here in the 1880s, "where travellers must present their credentials before admission, and where they are carefully scrutinised by the janitor." That was a hundred years ago; it could have been today.

On the other side of the door we could hear the shuffle of feet and the mumble of something in Greek. Cornelius rattled back an answer, and the door was swiftly unlocked to reveal a young monk in black cassock. With his robes unfastened and his efforts to stuff his long brown hair under his hat, he looked a bit like someone in a nightshirt and nightcap who had just been pulled from bed unprepared. Grunting a greeting to our escort, he looked at us with suspicion and then said something in Greek. Cornelius' voice betrayed impatience; he waved his arm as if sweeping the young monk out

of the way and then led us down the stairs toward the central
courtyard of the building.

"He ask me if you Orthodox; but I tell him it none of his business."

"I am Orthodox," I said with a smile, putting my finger on the
skullcap I had a few minutes before folded into my pocket. Halper
winked; Cornelius ignored the joke.

Reaching the bottom of the wide stairs which descended gently
to a lower terrace, we passed what must have been the oldest monk
in the place. Slender and stooped, with slits in place of eyes and a
face framed by a wisp of gray beard, he looked to me more like a
Zen Buddhist than a Greek Orthodox monk. Shuffling slowly across
the open space toward the chapel, he fumbled with the hood on his
cassock. Cornelius greeted him and he responded with little more
than a silent movement of his lips.

Later, reading the account of American travel writer John Lloyd
Stephens, who had visited this place in 1836, I visualized this old
monk again. Gazing at the monastery for the first time, Stephens
had come across what could only be described as this man's double,
an "old white-bearded monk, leaning on his staff, and toiling up
its sides." Either little had changed here in a hundred and fifty
years or else this place had a way of transforming insiders in an
endless set of reflections and shadows.

We crossed the courtyard, ascended some stairs and moved toward the outer wall of the monastery, the whole of which was built
into the stone of the cliff. From here we would be able to look down
into the abyss of the Kidron.

"How many rooms are there here?" Halper asked.

"More than hundred and ten. But it not help—there still no
place to go here. And no women."

From the beginning, Saba had been convinced that the presence
of women in this place would pollute its character, and they had
therefore always been prohibited from even passing beyond the
doors of the monastery. It was a rule that differentiated this place
from most of the other Greek Orthodox monasteries in and around
Jerusalem.

The view from the portico of Mar Saba was awesome. In the late-
afternoon sunlight and beneath the still blue sky, the bright sandstone of the surrounding mountains glowed brilliantly. Cornelius
pointed to the caves in the hill on the other side of the gorge.

"There is cave in which Saint Saba lived."

The land around was just as Charles Wilson had described it:

"bare, wild, and desolate." Below the convent where we stood, a wall clung to the steep face of the ravine on which the buildings hung. From a distance, the sandstones of this man-made structure, like the ones at the Quruntul and St. George's, must have looked like an extension of the wall of the ravine carved by the Kidron. But as one got closer, the fortress was unmistakable; the eye could make out buttresses and battlements, the one protection against nature and the other against man.

Coming into this same wilderness, Edmund Wilson had called this place "subduing and dreadful." He was wrong. Life here was neither subdued nor filled with dread. Perhaps what was most remarkable about this place and the people who had lived and continued to live here was their obdurate survival. Amidst desolation and near the Dead Sea, life had established itself and, relying only on its faith, clung with a quiet tenacity to the side of a rock. About the monastery, in clefts of the mountain walls or against some battlement, caper bushes or other small plants had taken root, as if in conspiracy with their human neighbors against the wasteland and death.

"Are there any hermits left in the caves?" Halper asked. I thought immediately of the wisp of an old man we had seen before.

"No more. The last ones were at St. George's."

Once a week, on Sundays, these ascetics would come down to the chapel. The rest of the time, their only contact with the world was the little basket of food each one hoisted up into his hole.

Cornelius started talking about the last of those hermit monks.

"One of them, he die and no one know it for a day until they notice he did not send down his basket again."

"Why would someone want to be a hermit monk?"

Cornelius looked at me with surprise: "Why not?" Cornelius had a way of using these two words to avoid becoming entangled in existential dilemmas. To life, to destiny, to God, he said, "Why not?"

Later, Michael, the monk at the Quruntul, would offer a different answer to this question. Quoting the *Timaeus,* he said simply: "It is hard to find the Maker and Father of the Universe, and having found Him, it is impossible to speak of Him at all."

Nearly six hundred feet below us in the *wadi,* a gush of frothy water passed on its way toward the lowest point on earth, the Dead Sea.

"Where does the water come from?" I asked.

"Some of it comes from the spring in Silwan." Another man—

Foutius was his name—was speaking. He stood with us looking down at the water that had bubbled up from the ground at the Gihon Spring in Jerusalem.

That spring, in the City of David, emptied its water into the pool of Shilo'ah, or what the Arabs called Silwan, through a long tunnel dug in the eighth century B.C.E. by laborers working for Hezekiah, king of Judah. The digging of this aqueduct was one of the legendary accomplishments of ancient Jerusalem. Over a length of 533 meters and with a gradient of more than 2 meters, two teams of laborers hewing stone at opposite ends of the valley had miraculously met in the middle and completed the tunnel. Thousands of years later, in 1880, an inscription on the tunnel wall celebrating this achievement was discovered and deciphered. "THIS IS THE STORY OF THE BORING THROUGH," it read.

> WHILE [the diggers lifted] THE PICK EACH TOWARD HIS FELLOW AND WHILE THREE CUBITS [remained] TO BE BORED [through, there was heard] THE VOICE OF A MAN CALLING HIS FELLOW, FOR THERE WAS A SPLIT IN THE ROCK ON THE RIGHT HAND AND ON [the left hand]. AND ON THE DAY OF THE BORING THROUGH, THE TUNNELERS STRUCK, EACH IN THE DIRECTION OF HIS FELLOWS, PICK AGAINST PICK. AND THE WATER STARTED TO FLOW FROM THE SOURCE TO THE POOL, TWELVE HUNDRED CUBITS. A HUNDRED CUBITS WAS THE HEIGHT OF THE ROCK ABOVE THE HEAD OF THE TUNNELERS.

The water flows on from Silwan into the Kidron. I had always wanted to see what became of it. Now, as I stood on the edge of Mar Saba looking down at the flow, I thought of its beating heart at the Gihon Spring.

"Do you take your drinking water from here?" I asked Foutius.

"No, it's too dirty here. On the way from Jerusalem, along the narrow valley, it picks up all kinds of dirt and sewage. That is why it looks so frothy."

From ancient times, the narrow walls of the Kidron Valley had served as a conduit for the sewage of Jerusalem. Looking down into the waters, I tried to imagine what they must have looked like when they flowed with the blood of the sacrifices on the Temple Mount or when they were filled with the ashes from the fires of Jerusalem's destruction. But this monastery was no place to evoke Jewish memories.

"We get water here from cisterns," Cornelius explained.

"Unfortunately, this has been a poor year, as was last year. Very little rain," Foutius added.

"Will the drought chase you away?" I asked.

Foutius smiled. "It will just make life a little bit harder."

"Do you live here?" Halper asked Foutius.

"Not now; I have come only for the holy day tomorrow."

"But he live here once," Cornelius said.

Like Cornelius, he had spent eight years here. But he, as I later learned, was a man with higher education, a science teacher with a graduate university degree, a soft-spoken man with almond-brown eyes who was only now beginning on the path of becoming a monk.

"You miss it?"

Foutius half-smiled. "Sometimes." Then, turning to walk back inside the convent, he added with a giggle, "But not as much as Cornelius."

"Come—I show you more," Cornelius offered.

He took us back into the courtyard. The space was trapezoidal, with a small cupola in the middle over the sanctuary where the bones of the saint once rested. Two stone hatches with metal rings were set into the limestone floor. There was some fresh-looking cement around one of them.

"Here we bury the monks," Cornelius explained. "We bury one not too long ago. Here." He pointed to the fresh cement. Laid on stone benches, the bodies were covered with limestone and then, later, after decomposition, the bones were moved to grottoes and cases inside the chapel at the other end of the courtyard. Each monk had a special monastery to which he was attached and where he would go for his final rest. However much he might not have liked it here, Cornelius was wedded to this place forever. When his day came, he would likely be returned to its crypt.

A young boy in blue jeans appeared from one of the doors. For the holy day, a few young seminarians had come from Greece to assist in the preparations and service. While Cornelius spoke with him, arranging some refreshment for us, I noticed the owners of the other car I had seen outside. Two men, one with camera and the other helping him carry his equipment, were setting up a shot in the courtyard. The photographer looked at me tentatively and, making a sudden connection, greeted me softly in Hebrew. The unexpected switch into Hebrew, like a shift of consciousness, provided a momentary escape from the world of Mar Saba under whose charm I had fallen. The brief encounter and interchange in Hebrew articulated—if only for a moment—that bond between kin which language allows and which somehow transcends the boundaries of place. Thus, we having touched each other, I asked him quickly what he was doing here. Before moving into one of the other terraces, he answered, speaking softly: "Like you, we came to peek at another world."

He smiled.

"*Shalom,*" I replied. And then we floated apart in different directions, expatriates tied together by a common fascination for the foreign but each exploring it in his own way.

"You take coffee?" Cornelius asked us.

"Thank you."

"Come—the boy will prepare it while I show you more."

We went into a long dark room in which the walls were lined with dark wooden tables and benches. There were candlesticks all around, but the little light that came in through the windows was enough for now. Along the simple wooden tables were clay jugs which were meant to hold drinking water when there was any. Cornelius had turned a few spigots of cisterns as we passed them on the way, but they were all dry.

A hooded monk came in and said something in Greek to our host and left quickly.

"They start to pray now."

Cornelius took us up the stairs to see where he had lived for his eight years, fifteen days and three hours. That wing of the monastery seemed deserted even now, when visitors and seminarians were here.

"Are there many monks here?"

"Less and less. It is very hard to find those who want to follow this way."

"Would you be a monk again, if you could relive your life?" Halper asked.

"I don't know. Why not?" To Cornelius there was little or no point to second-guessing personal destiny.

"Will you take us to the bones?" Halper asked. He wanted to see the assortment of skulls of all the monks who had once lived here.

"Why not?"

We returned to the courtyard. From the small chapel in the northwest corner the sounds of the monks at prayer filled the stillness of the late afternoon. A few latecomers from among the semi-narians were slipping in. Cornelius took us in the direction of the chapel, which I would later learn was dedicated to John of Damas-cus, who for a time had lived here.

After the bright outdoors, my eyes took a few minutes to get used to the darkness inside. Like every other room here, this one was lit only by candles. But unlike all the other men inside the chapel, who stood hovering over hymnals atop lecterns or were seated in pews, attentive to and involved in the liturgy, Cornelius was absorbed in his role as guide. He led us to see the cases filled with skulls that stood in a small alcove at the rear of the chapel. The more important ones were all arrayed in two neat rows in narrow cases lining the walls. Above the cases, inside a cave recessed into the wall and covered with a glass door, were more skulls. These were stacked in a heap. The darkness of the cave made it hard to see them, so Cornelius took a candle from nearby and held it up to the opening so that we might see inside.

"Is this where you're going to be in the end?" Halper asked him.

"Who knows?"

In less than half a year he would in fact begin the journey that would bring his bones to join his brothers here in the wilderness. Now, however, death was something he mentioned only in passing, and only in reply to our curious questions.

Halper pressed him for details about the procedures for remov-ing the skulls from the crypts and their placement here. Cornelius was not terribly interested in the whole matter and spoke instead about fourteen thousand martyrs killed by the Persian invaders and buried now inside the cave. I too was quickly losing interest in the discussion, feeling drawn rather to the living monks who stood behind me tunefully reciting an ancient liturgy. The service was quite different from any I had ever witnessed before. Several monks stood around a small pulpit reading their chant from a large book. Later, at Quruntul, I examined the volume—the words Greek, the print in various colors. The younger monks and a seminarian held up a candle for the cantors. Their tenor voices seemed to intone long, rising and falling melodies. More than a recitative but not quite a song, the tune had a kind of luminous quality that elicited a sense of awe.

Across the small room sat the Bishop on what looked a bit like a throne. From here he seemed to direct the service. I turned my full attention to it. Behind me Cornelius droned on about the skulls, and without thinking I tried to quiet him with a "Shush." Somehow the drama I watched held me and demanded a devotion that moved me to still all disturbances.

From Michael at Quruntul I would subsequently learn a little bit about the prayers. "When we pray," he explained, taking me out of the chapel to the cave for our profane conversation, "we face the east, toward the rising sun. As the light comes from there, so comes from there the light of our faith. Seven times a day we pray, often at night or in the very early morning."

Suddenly Cornelius came into my line of sight; he was leaving. As he neared the door, the Superior, raising the hooked staff he held in his hand, called him over. He whispered something in his ear. Why, the Bishop asked, was Cornelius wearing his gray cassock? For this trip outside the walls of his convent, he should have worn his black one; the Superior was not pleased. Cornelius made what appeared to be a reverential bow and backed out the open chapel door. I followed him.

"Where will you drink," he asked, "inside or outside?"

The inside was a small room with no windows. There was still light in the courtyard; from here we could better hear the services. "Outside," I answered for both of us. Cornelius directed the seminarian working in the little dining room to prepare a small table for us outside, while we went to see the crypt in which, according to our guide, the saint lay entombed.

This far larger chapel was permeated with the smell of incense. Although candelabra and votive lamps hung everywhere, the overall impression remained one of darkness—a stark contrast to the cathedral of the outdoors in which Cornelius worshiped and which had so enveloped us as we stood on the portico overlooking the Kidron. We walked to a rectangular glass-faced case against a wall in the center of the room. Underneath royal-looking robes, there appeared to be something inside, but just exactly what was hard to determine in the darkness. Adorned in gold trim and red velvet was what Cornelius told us was once a body. I could make out litle more than the robes. (Later I read that the body of Saint Saba had been moved to Venice long ago, and so to this day I still do not know what I saw.) Around the outside of the case were amulets, charms and a variety of other personal possessions that pilgrims visiting this holy spot had left as offerings.

"What are these?" Halper asked, holding up one of about a dozen watches hanging along a cord suspended above the case.

"Oh, you know, the pilgrims they come and they want to leave something valuable to them as a blessing for Saint Saba. So they leave the watches.''

The image of the abandoned timepieces in this timeless shrine seemed particularly fitting. Confronting the ancient, sacred past represented in the case inside this chapel in the wilderness, the pilgrims had been suddenly moved to an act of sacrifice. And what could they give? What had value in the outside world but here suddenly seemed appropriate for leaving behind? The watches were perfectly suited for offering. In this place, they ceased to be watches; they became instead deposits of faith, votive offerings, timely sacrifices. I fingered the watches, as if they would somehow reveal the feelings of those who had so spontaneously left them here. Fastening upon these fragments of forsaken modernity suspended above this relic of embraced tradition, we were at once enveloped by an eerie stillness. And even for us who were not pilgrims, the present seemed for a moment strangely more remote than either the past or the future. In the darkened, silent chamber, death and life mixed together.

''Come,'' Cornelius said, breaking the spell and calling us back to our senses. ''We have our drink.''

As we left the sanctuary, a few pilgrims passed us on their way in. They headed straight for the case, around which they huddled, crossing themselves. One man pressed his lips against the glass and kissed it.

Returning to the courtyard, we found a small table set with three cups of coffee, three glasses of brandy and three sweets. The monk quickly downed his brandy (including a tiny fly that had drowned in it) ; Halper chewed on the gooey candy, and I sipped the coffee. In the background, we could still hear the luminous voices of prayer coming from the chapel of John of Damascus.

The brightness of the surrounding hills was beginning to fade; in about an hour it would be night. Recalling our ride and anxious about repeating it in the dark, I suggested we begin our return. Cornelius stood and swallowed another brandy. As we receded toward the door, we could hear someone ringing the bell outside. The same monk who had let us in rushed ahead of us and opened the door, letting in some Arabs, their heads covered in white and flowing kaffiyehs. Greeting Cornelius, one man warmly grasped his hand and embraced him.

''Old neighbors,'' the monk explained later. I thought of the Greek pilgrims who had passed us earlier without a sign of recognition. It was curious how the monks—in principle here at the holy places to represent their Greek coreligionists—in effect establish a greater feeling of closeness with the local Arabs. In belief they may be Greek Orthodox but in life they have become a part of the local human landscape.

Just before we reached the door, Cornelius stopped and turned suddenly toward a plant growing out of a crack in the stone wall. Hardly more than a solitary weed, it blossomed almost as if out of its own will to survive. In the dry air of the desert, its sweet, minty odor was triumphant witness to the enduring power of life even in the face of barren rock. Cornelius, the tender of gardens and trees, tenderly pulled off a sprig of its leaves and handed one to each of us, a memento of our visit.

We spoke little on the ride back to Jerusalem, as if the silence of Mar Saba were still with us. It was getting cold now, and as we sped back to Jerusalem, I turned on the blower for a little heat. The sweet smell of the mint from Mar Saba filled the car.

At last we arrived at Jerusalem, descending into the Kidron and ascending again to the Jaffa Gate. Gazing at the ramparts of the wall around the city, I saw as if superimposed upon them the rounded cupola and stones hewn and set in place by monks at Mar Saba. Both visions preserved enough of their reality so that for a moment I was not sure which sight came from my mind's eye and which stood there before me. At that moment, I uncovered what was for me a heretofore invisible artery that ran back and forth along the Kidron, between mountaintop and desert, which connected this Holy City, obdurately surviving the wilderness of history and endless conflict, with that testament to unyielding life in the Wilderness of Judea from which we had just come.

"We go again," Cornelius promised as he stepped out of the car.

We did not go again—at least, not in the way that he and I imagined we might. Several months after our visit to Mar Saba, Cornelius died suddenly. By early spring, already entombed in the rocks underneath Mar Saba, he was part of the eternal landscape of Judea. For all of his wanderlust and love of life outside the convent, Cornelius had at last been returned to its boundaries. Only pilgrims and visitors get to leave; the monks and priests abide in these places forever.

After Cornelius' death, I imagined he had gone out of my life forever. But I was wrong; there would be one last occasion on which I would encounter him and his world.

A few days after the Greek Orthodox Easter, when I had acutely missed Cornelius on my trip (about which more later) to the Holy Sepulcher, Halper, who had informed me of the monk's death, told me that Helgart, the "widow" (she called herself that half-seriously), was in town. She was eager to meet Cornelius' friends. She called him "Costa," for it was not as a monk that she remembered and loved him.

"Do you want to meet her?" Halper asked.

"Why not?" I said, hearing Cornelius' voice as I used this his favorite expression. Two days later, we all met at a café downtown.

In her early forties, with clipped brown hair and a tanned, healthy-looking complexion, Helgart was fleshy, broad-shouldered, and well groomed—not at all the image of a woman I expected to have been involved emotionally with an alcoholic, illiterate monk in his sixties. But she had been, and from everything she said it became clear that she had loved him sincerely.

For a while I listened to her reminiscences, looked at photos that she had collected over the five years she knew Cornelius. In a few minutes, as I flipped through the pictures, I could trace the transformation of the young Costa, a smooth-faced and handsome boy (inside the old monk she had always been able to see that young Greek Pan), into the robust, one-eyed, bearded monk who, beneath his cassock and in his heart, flirted with the world outside the convent to which he still felt attracted but to which he knew that as a monk he could never fully return.

"Why do you think he continued to be a monk?" I asked, handing her back the pile of photos.

"Where else could he go now? It was too late to be anything else. But still, you know, he was too young to die," she said of this man twenty years her senior who had taken her very far from her life in Cologne as a secretary. Her eyes shone as she spoke, the tears just beneath the surface of her tough Teutonic front. She sipped her drink.

"How exactly did he die?" I asked.

"It was sort of strange," Halper began. "One night in March he had begun bleeding profusely from his nose."

"This was not the first time," Helgart broke in.

She continued the story, telling me that when the bleeding began, the brothers—as they did with all the sick monks—took Cornelius to St. Joseph's Hospital in East Jerusalem. High blood pressure, the doctors said, from too much alcohol. For four days they dried him out in the hospital until one afternoon the nurses heard a delirious screaming coming from his room: someone was chasing him, he cried out. Rushing in at the sound of his shouts, they found the window open and Cornelius lying dead on the ground outside.

"Who gave you the news?" I asked her.

"Costa's friend."

"The barber?"

"You know about the barber?" she asked.

"Yes, he told us how the barber had given him the pamphlet that ultimately led to his arrest."

"Yes, the barber called me. They were always the closest friends." She paused and took another sip from her drink.

"At first, I didn't want to come this year," she continued. "I thought it would be too hard without Costa. But now I am glad I came. Talking to all of his friends, I have discovered that he is still very much here, and that makes it easier, you know?"

Helgart spoke of the many brothers in the monastery who, like her, missed him and through their shared memories held on to him.

"You know, many of them were far more educated than he was, younger, and so on, but they all loved him, looked up to him in a way like a father or at least an older brother. They took all their problems to him because he always had a clear answer. They really ... loved him," she concluded.

"Why not?" said Halper.

"Why not?" We laughed, hearing Cornelius speaking the words.

Would we like to meet one of the other monks, perhaps to share some of those memories? she asked. She knew some of them; maybe they would talk to us openly.

"Whenever you can arrange it."

Two days later, on a Friday, we met—Helgart, Halper and I—at the Jaffa Gate and walked to the convent. Helgart appeared to know all the storekeepers and neighborhood locals. On Saturday she was to return to Germany, and so as we headed to the monastery, she said her farewells to all those we passed whom she knew.

When we arrived at the door of the convent, we learned that the archimandrite we had planned to meet was not there. But as we stood at the gate wondering what to do, another priest Helgart recognized came out the door. They greeted each other warmly and spoke briefly. The priest, wearing a black cassock over a deep blue robe, appeared to be in his late twenties, with a light brown beard and thick straight hair that reached to just over his collar. Helgart introduced him to us.

"Evlogios was a good friend of Costa's. He is going now to the St. Gerasimus Monastery, near Jericho. Would you like to come?"

I thought of my trip to Mar Saba with Cornelius and of the magic of that inside view. "We go again," he had promised, and now that promise would, in a fashion, be fulfilled.

"Why not?"

In a few minutes we were in my car rolling down the mountains of Judea, past the dry red earth of Adumim and descending swiftly into the wilderness. Here the tribe of Benjamin had established its inheritance, and here Jeremiah had wandered, pondering his prophecies for his people, depressed and alone. Here the Essenes had traveled to escape the evils of impure civilization and had headed for their ascetic life in Qumran, and here the Roman legions had marched, as generations later would the Arabs, on their way to fight my forebears for the city on the hill behind us. The Judean Wilderness had swallowed up all that history; only collective memory and human consciousness kept it alive. And even that was in danger in the face of new imperatives: today a new urban settlement, Ma'aleh Adumim, challenged the memory of the past and the barrenness of this place with lines of ultramodern apartment blocks and newly planted trees.

We passed on beyond Ma'aleh Adumim, back into the empty landscape. Nearby, a Bedouin girl of no more than ten or twelve years followed a flock of goats which nibbled on the brush that, nourished by the winter rains, still clung to the sides of the hills during these first weeks of spring. In less than a month, together with the heat and sun, these animals would strip the vegetation and return the land here to desert. "The Bedouin bring the desert with them wherever they go," I had once heard someone say.

Halper was asking our priest questions about his life. Evlogios answered in halting English. He had been born in a small Greek coastal village, into a family that was not especially religious.

"So what made you choose to enter the monastery?" I asked.

"I come one time to the holy places, here to Jerusalem, and I so like it, I decide to become a monk. Later they send me to Russia to study in Leningrad." He had spent six years there, studying, visiting the museums, exploring the interior world of his faith.

"And then, before six years, I come here, where everything begins for me."

"And now?"

"And now I am here. This is my home. I love it very much."

"And if the Patriarch were to ask you now to go somewhere else?"

"Now, this would be very hard for me, very hard, I think. I do not know."

I wanted to ask him to tell me more about what had inspired him, to explain to me the nature of the experience he had had upon first coming to Jerusalem, to know if he yearned at all to be elsewhere, to return to Greece. And I wondered whether he would someday rediscover the outside world as had Cornelius and find out that it was too late to go back.

But even had he been able or willing to express the character of what he had gone through, his poor English and my nonexistent Greek made it impossible for us to plumb such depths. There were simply no words available to us that would make comprehension possible. As was the case during my encounter with Cornelius, I would have to let what I saw bear witness for itself.

Outside, we dropped past the sign marking sea level. From here on we were descending toward the Dead Sea. Beside us, the white mounds of the eroded plain rose up like the walls of a canyon.

In less than half an hour we were at a junction near the floor of the valley, where one road turns north toward Jericho, "the oldest city on earth," according to an old milestone, and the other turns south toward the Dead Sea, the lowest point on earth. Between the two is a small stretch of pavement leading straight to the Jordanian border. At one time, and perhaps someday again, one could stay on that road and in about an hour reach Amman, once the center of life of the ancient kingdom of Ammon and today the capital of the Hashemite kingdom.

"Turn here," Evlogios said when we were meters away from the border. He pointed to a rocky road that led northward into the flat, white plain. In the distance, throbbing in the heat rising from the sands around them, I could see the limestone walls and silver dome of St. Gerasimus.

"Ach, *ja*," said Helgart wistfully, "there it is."

This onetime solitary outpost of faith had over the years found itself amidst encroaching civilization. A short distance away, to the northwest, sat Jericho. And just a few meters from the walls of the monastery was Bet Ha-Aravah, a few stucco houses at the beginning of the unpaved road, built on the ruins of a kibbutz that had been founded in 1939.

The founders of the kibbutz had sought to tame the desert here, painstakingly flushing away the salt that had penetrated into the deepest layers of earth so that the soil could again nourish life. Slowly they had achieved success and made this wasteland bloom. But then came the destruction of war and the partition of the land. The kibbutz had to be abandoned. By the late 1960s when the Jews returned to it, all signs of what they had built and grown had been destroyed by those who had taken over the land. Although the site had been reclaimed, today Bet Ha-Aravah was only an outpost, a lookout near the Abdullah Bridge, a forward position at a hostile border. On the other side of the highway, replanted kibbutzim once again brought life to the desert, blanketing the white sands with large, square green fields that held back the sand and thistles.

Passing the few buildings of Bet Ha-Aravah, we bounced on toward St. Gerasimus, the place that the Arabs had named Deir Hajla. Here, near a place where the faithful believed Jesus had stopped on His way up to Nazareth, Gerasimus had in the fifth century established his monastery. Only pieces of a mosaic floor from that ancient sanctuary still remained inside the fortresslike building that now marked the spot. The present structure was about a hundred and fifty years old. A spring was nearby, but the water the single monk who lived inside used was collected in two large cisterns, one of which marked the center of the fortress.

"Turn," said Evlogios again when we came to another fork in the road. This time I drove onto a dirt path that was softer but less bumpy. It led right up to the steel door of the monastery. Without the little breeze created by the movement of the car, the air down here was oppressively thick with heat. Quickly we got out of the sun and entered the convent.

"Only one man lives here?" I had asked incredulously on the way down.

"Yes."

"Is it not lonely?"

Evlogios smiled thinly. There was no answer to a question such as this.

"You will see," Helgart said from her seat in the back.

Inside the monastery, the heat did not feel nearly so overwhelming. The shadows cast by the walls and the grape arbor strung across a large part of the inner courtyard took the sting out of the sun. In the middle of the courtyard was the opening to the large cistern.

Under the arches lining the inside walls, Chrysostomos, the lone priest, had created small aviaries behind chicken wire. The soft chirping of the little birds inside perforated the silence without disturbing the sense of calm which almost immediately enveloped us as we entered.

"*Ach, mein Gott*," said Helgart as she looked up to the veranda at the man who stood there looking down at us, "it's Jesus."

Halper and I looked up to see a man in his late thirties standing barefoot and bareheaded, with long black hair and beard, wearing a flowing black robe that hung loosely on his tall and narrow frame.

"Doesn't he look like Jesus?" Helgart repeated.

We walked around to the steps and up to the veranda. Near the first corner were a human skull and some other bones atop a shelf.

"One of the former residents," Halper laughingly suggested. The others, we later found, were piled behind a small chapel in one of the rooms downstairs, their hollow eyes forever staring eastward.

Chrysostomos was seated on a wooden armchair built into the space between two pillars. The chair, part of a one-piece arrangement that included its mate and a table between them, forced him to sit in a half-reclining position. With his feet crossed, his body relaxed and the fingers of his right hand loosely curled around a cigarette dangling from a long holder, he leaned back languidly and looked calmly in control of his world.

For a long while we sat in silence while the Arab workers—a boy in his teens and a grizzled older man—softly slipped past us every so often. Chrysostomos was master of his fortress. With a few words in Arabic, squeezed out of his mouth in between cigarette puffs, he ordered the boy to bring us cold orange drinks. After we had sipped these slowly and silently, the boy wordlessly collected them and then brought out small cups of Greek coffee. And had we stayed, Helgart later told us, we would probably have gotten some freshly caught rabbit for lunch.

On the ledge of the veranda were five or six jars that held the carcasses of snakes and scorpions Chrysostomos had caught around the monastery. The eyes of one of the small snakes (caught just this morning, Evlogios told us) still sparkled.

"What are they floating in?" I asked. Evlogios translated the question.

"Ouzo," said Chrysostomos, his face betraying a shadow of a smile.

"Ach, look down there," Helgart said, pointing to the cat in the courtyard. It nibbled on a snake still wriggling with life.

As we watched it in silence, a young woman in her twenties, wearing a denim jumper over a work shirt, her wiry blond hair in a braid, slipped in quietly and sat on the bench without being introduced.

"You would like to see the church?" Evlogios asked after a while.

"Yes."

He waited a few more minutes while Helgart finished her drink and then rose and led us into the large chapel. Chrysostomos stayed outside, chain-smoking and painting icons to be sold or later given away to pilgrims.

Like all the other sanctuaries I had seen in Greek Orthodox churches, this one had an altar in the east set off from the main prayer room, a few rows of thronelike armchairs, candle stands with lit and unlit tapers stuck into the sand around them, lecterns upon which were some hymnals and frescoes or other paintings everywhere. The stale smell of incense filled the air.

Halper and I spoke with Evlogios for a while about the nature of the Greek Orthodox service, the differences between it and the Jewish one we knew: the Greeks, the priest told us, needed only two people present to say the liturgy, while according to Jewish law we needed a minimum of ten adult males. Jews needed a community present; Greeks needed only to know the community existed somewhere. For us life was always with people; for them solitude was quite a bit easier, or at least so it seemed.

"I show you the candle room," Evlogios said, taking us to where Chrysostomos made votive candles. With windows that looked out over the sparkling wasteland near the Dead Sea, the room was littered with candles and crushed tapers. The smell of them saturated the air.

Evlogios took us through some of the other rooms and then led us back to our place on the veranda, where again we sat with Chrysostomos. The young woman in the denim jumper spoke now. Where were we from? she asked. She, it turned out, was an American from Oregon who had come here "to serve the Church."

"Are you going to be a nun?" I asked.

"That"—she pursed her lips and flashed an enigmatic smile—"is between me and God."

Ignoring this little exchange, which he may or may not have understood, Chrysostomos busied himself in painting an icon he held in his hand.

"Mein Gott," Helgart said with a laugh, "you ask so many questions! I have been here before and it never occurred to me to ask all these things; I just sat here enjoying the blessed silence."

After a while Helgart began to talk about Cornelius, and Evlogios, taking out the Greek passport he had in his breast pocket, showed her two photos of the dead monk that he kept inside it. One was a particularly formal-looking one in which Cornelius' glass eye had been touched up to look real.

"I make this one a big one," Evlogios explained. "We put it in the room where are the pictures of all the other brothers."

Helgart wanted to buy one of Chrysostomos' candles to light in Costa's memory. We waited until the Arab boy brought what turned out to be two packs of them and an icon, a gift from a friend to the bereaved widow.

Helgart took the candles. "Do you want some?" she asked us in the car. "I need only one."

"No," Halper replied for both of us. "We're staying. You'll need them more, to remember what is here."

"Are you sure?" she asked again.

"We're staying; we're sure."

CHAPTER
·13·
IMAGES

*The innocence of the eye is the whole point
here, the cleansing of the doors of perception.*

VICTOR TURNER,
Image and Pilgrimage in Christian Culture

*The world as illusion and the world as reality
are equally undemonstrable.*

ANTONIO MACHADO,
Juan de Mairena

*T*he invitation that arrived in my December mail from the
Israel Interfaith Association, a local counterpart of the
National Conference of Christians and Jews—with Moslems included, although they seldom participated—read: "Members and
friends of the Association are cordially invited to a Social Gathering celebrating the holidays of Hanukkah, Christmas and the Birth
of the Prophet Mohammed, all of which fall this month."

The event was to take place in the students' lounge of the Reform
Jewish Hebrew Union College on the evening of December 26, the
day after the last night of Hanukkah and (in one of the many
traditions celebrated in Jerusalem) the second day of Christmas. A
sparkling white building next to the King David Hotel and overlooking the Old City walls, the college stood very near to what had
once been the border between the Israeli and Jordanian sectors of
the city; it seemed a perfect gathering place for a group such as

this one. To many of the Jews who controlled the religious life of the city, Hebrew Union College—indeed, any non-Orthodox institution—was, if not strictly speaking a non-Jewish domain, undeniably beyond the boundaries of traditional faith. To the Christians, well represented in numbers this evening, Hebrew Union College was, on the other hand, perhaps as close as they could get to the precincts of Judaism. And if any Moslems came—the only obvious Moslems I would see that night would be some of the Arab construction workers completing a new wing of the College—then this building on the front lines of the western side of the city was a place they could unobtrusively visit. The invitation went on: "At this meeting our friend Mr. Traugott Fasch will present a slide show on MY JERUSALEM—A PERSONAL APPROACH TO THE INTER-RELIGIOUS NATURE OF THE CITY. Traugott, born in Germany, has for many years been seeking to comprehend the spiritual secret of Jerusalem and its meaning to the followers of the three faiths. He expresses his search by study of Scripture, by writing and photographing. The slides which are of unique quality will be accompanied by readings and explanations in English. Those who attend this event are promised a very special experience."

When we made our way to the students' lounge, in an annex at the back of the College, my wife and I found the room filled with more than sixty people. Most of them appeared to know each other, and they stood or sat in small groups chatting. What looked like eight votive candles lit near the window turned out to be a reminder of the Hanukkah lights. The fried-in-oil jelly doughnuts, a traditional Hanukkah treat that recalls the miracle of the oil associated with this Feast of Lights, were in abundance. People sipped coffee and tea or nibbled on doughnuts and tangerines.

Moments after our arrival, a quiet rush of movement signaled the start of the formal presentation. After offering brief words of greeting, the evening's chairman introduced Traugott—the name in German means "trust in God"—as someone who had countless times visited Jerusalem. "Although he lives in Germany, he does not let a year pass without a visit." And then, the short introduction and polite applause over, Traugott stood before us in front of a large white screen.

Traugott had soft red hair tied in a ponytail that fell down his back. His narrow, curly beard framed a thin, almost gaunt face. A plain white shirt hung loosely on his slender frame, its sleeves a touch too long so that they overlapped the heel of his palms. He was probably in his early thirties or maybe late twenties; it was hard to tell exactly. His lips were delicate, and he spoke softly in German-accented English.

"I have been to Jerusalem for the first time in 1975 and I suppose like many of you I have fallen in love with her." Throughout the evening he spoke of the city in the feminine.

"Fourteen times I have come back. And always I walk through the city—the Old City, the new city and the Mount of Olives. Many times I walk the whole night, just to be near her, to feel her, to watch the sun rise in the Judean Wilderness from my place on the Mount of Olives. And I take pictures."

He paused for a moment, as if framing his speech with concentrated silence. My first inclination had been to dismiss him as a throwback to the hippie era. Besides, I was a bit put off by the idea of a German who would show me, a Jew, a son of Holocaust survivors, a view of Jerusalem I had not seen. These were not days for sympathizing with Germans; a delegation of members of the Green Party from the Bundestag had just come across the Allenby Bridge from Jordan. They dripped with hostility, refusing at first even to pay the customary visit to Yad Vashem, the Holocaust Memorial. I had not thought very much about them until I heard the accent and cadences in Traugott's words.

But there was something soft and disarming about him. Perhaps his quiet voice, slender build and calm demeanor conquered my resistance. Maybe it was something of the obvious control he had over the audience. He was mysteriously charming.

"I do not walk in order to take the pictures. But when I see something that touches me, I take a picture.

"When I think about Jerusalem, I think also that this is where the Holy Temple stood. Now, according to Jewish tradition, it was not God who dwelt in the Temple, it was His name that lived there. As it is written in the thirty-third chapter of Second Chronicles: 'In Jerusalem shall My name be forever.' "

The idea Traugott presented was striking; it left God in His place while allowing Him to inhabit another, to share Himself with humanity.

"God continued to live in His everlasting abode, but He came to the Holy Temple to live through His name. So they say that the Temple was a meeting place between the spirit and the matter, a gate between Heaven and earth." Traugott paused, allowing the silence to return. Then, when it had swallowed us up, he continued.

"And Jerusalem is also the place where Jesus was crucified and where, according to Christian tradition, He rose up in spirit. So you see for Christians it is also in Jerusalem that matter and spirit meet.'' Again he drew in his breath and was still.

''And Jerusalem, the Moslems believe, is the place where the prophet Mohammed set off on his steed on his journey to Heaven, to the realm of the spirit.''

Again he paused. Then he fumbled with some index cards that he held in his hands. The audience remained silent. In a moment, he continued: ''Now, I believe, as I suppose that many of you here do, that the person is also a place where matter and spirit meet. And so it is easy; it is natural that a person shall fall in love with Jerusalem, for the two are kindred. They are in many ways the same.''

He sucked in his lips. ''I don't know if I express myself clearly, if you catch my ideas of how I can feel a love about, for Jerusalem.''

No one spoke. Next to me I noticed one of the nuns who had come to the meeting clasp her hands together and stare at the floor.

''I have prepared some slides I have taken to try to give you a sense of how I am feeling about Jerusalem and how I see that the three faiths—the Jewish, the Christian and the Moslem—can live together here. There will also be some music which I hope will help you feel something extra about the pictures.''

He walked toward the middle of the room and sat down next to the slide projector. A few people politely applauded. And then the lights went out.

The music began with the theme by Vangelis from the film *Chariots of Fire*. On the screen, the throb of the cymbals and the gossamer notes of the piano were juxtaposed with visions of golden domes, cupolas, spires and shining stone walls set against the deep blue of the Jerusalem sky. Each slide appeared for half a minute, dissolved and gave way to the next. Traugott said nothing.

There was nothing really unusual about the process itself. But the photos and the music did create a mood, gave the feeling of traveling outside the real world. Traugott's vision of Jerusalem, as exposed in the slides and presented as a series of dissolving images, took on a metaphorical quality. They seemed to suggest that the boundaries which were so real outside in this city could be dissolved by imagination. Image supplanted, or at least redefined, reality.

Every so often when a striking slide lit up the room, the audience would murmur their appreciation. The shots were remarkable, worth thousands upon thousands of words. This German was an artist, and his love—perhaps even more, his respect and awe—for Jerusalem was unmistakable.

The picture frames trained our attention on images and expressed the ideas packed into them. Three shots of the same flowery wall near the municipality: in the first, three boys in knit skullcaps walked, almost unaware of one another; in the second, three Ethiopian monks in blue cassocks and black caps pressed together, looking like one body with three heads; in the third, an Arab—perhaps a gardener, or just a man taking a walk—wandered among the flowers, his checkered kaffiyeh billowing in the breeze.

Two photos taken near the holy Western Wall lit up the room. The first captured a Lubavitcher hasid in black hat and coat; he was one of those who spend time near the Wall trying to prevail on Jewish nonbelievers to return to the ways of tradition. In the first frame he was talking to a soldier who wore one of the cardboard skullcaps distributed at the Wall—an obvious sign of his estrangement from the traditions of Judaism. Both men stood near the Wall, the hasid talking, the soldier, half-turning to the Wall and half-facing the other, listening—one imagines wordlessly. In the next photo the hasid had taken off his jacket and rolled up his sleeves; his arguments seemed almost audible. The soldier had turned slightly more toward him and now looked directly into his eyes. How quickly repentance ripened in Traugott's slides.

In another slide, the Western Wall stood deserted. ''The rain was falling,'' Traugott explained, ''and so no one was there.'' The plaza glistened, the golden light of the spotlights reflecting off every stone. Looking at the image, I knew that the Wall was not deserted; the worshipers were inside Wilson's Arch, where in the shelter prayers and psalms continued to be recited. But Traugott was, after all, a foreign visitor to this holy place of my people; how would he know? Besides, he was right; in his picture no one was there, only the unearthly glow of the water and light.

The music now shifted to the soft voice of the singing rabbi Sh'lomo Carlebach, chanting a line from the psalmist: ''O God, save us.'' Over and over images of traditional Jews filled the screen until at last we saw a picture of a Jewish father and son. The father's beard shone; the boy's earlocks flew in the wind. Both had their eyes closed, their faces bathed in the reflected light coming from the Wall. The boy buried his head against his father's body, and the father's arm dropped down to cradle it. ''O God, save us.''

Traugott came to the end of the first carousel of slides. We sat for a moment in the white light of the blank screen. Coming slowly forward to the front of the room, he stood silhouetted and announced : "I have asked Mrs. Ben-Horin to read to us from Psalm 122."

A stocky woman stepped toward the front, her silhouette replacing his against the screen's light. She moved over to the side as Traugott began to project his next slides. Views of the city walls, domes, minarets and spires shined in our eyes. But the perspectives were again unexpected, the reality of the image again transformed to a poem. And then, to make the point unmistakable, the words of the Psalm—as if expressly written for the occasion—overwhelmed the images.

"Shir Ha-Ma'alot," a song of ascents, the heavy Mrs. Ben-Horin began in lilting Hebrew :

> I rejoiced when they said to me :
> "Let us go unto the house of the Lord."
> Our feet are standing
> Within your gates, O Jerusalem ;
> Jerusalem, that is built
> As a city connected together.
> Whither the tribes went up, even the tribes of the Lord,
> As a testimony to Israel,
> To give thanks unto the name of the Lord.
> For there are set thrones for judgment,
> The thrones of the house of David.
> Pray for the peace of Jerusalem ;
> May they prosper who love you.
> Peace be there within your walls
> And prosperity within your palaces.
> For my brethren and companions' sakes,
> I will now say : "Peace be within you."
> For the sake of the house of the Lord our God
> I will seek your good.

Mrs. Ben-Horin melted back into the audience as the light of the slides faded. As he had used silence to frame his words before, Traugott began to use darkness to frame the light of his slides. At last, out of the blackness, he kindled a slide of the Old City ramparts lit in the golden spotlight of evening. From the perspective of the camera, the tower of the Dormition Church on Mount Zion, which is outside the walls, nevertheless appeared to be stationed atop them.

"Look," Traugott noted, "how much the spire looks like a British bobby."

"More like Kaiser Wilhelm," someone in the audience called out. After a pause, Traugott—somewhat reluctantly, it seemed to me—admitted: "Yes, also he looks like Kaiser Wilhelm, who donated the money for the foundations of the church."

There is no mistaking the Kaiser's image. The cupola with its cross on top looks like his helmet. The two clocks on the tower and the rectangular window between them are his eyes and nose. The gable over a lower window forms his drooping mustache, while the rest of the tower outlines his erect bearing.

"But I think," this German friend of Jerusalem added, "that there is one more image that best suits the view here. It is recalled with a line from verse six in Isaiah sixty-two: 'Upon your walls, O Jerusalem, I have appointed guards, all the day and all the night.' " In Traugott's images, a church on Zion protected the City of David. And all was well.

At last we were shown a picture in which the outline of the Shield of David, a cross atop the Church of the Holy Sepulcher and the crescent atop the dome of a mosque were superimposed. The perspective was just too perfect for our interfaith gathering, and at last someone broke the silence to ask where this picture had been taken. Was there really a place where one could stand and behold these three symbols so perfectly in line?

"There is no place where all these three symbols of faith can be seen at once," Traugott explained. "But I have taken two pictures on the same place on the film to show this to you. In Jerusalem, some scenes must first be imagined in the heart and the mind before they can be brought into clear view and recalled."

CHAPTER
·I4·

EASTER

*The basic axiom underlying what we may
perhaps call the "religious perspective" is
everywhere the same: he who would know must
first believe.*

CLIFFORD GEERTZ,
The Interpretation of Cultures

Ricarda, Cornelius and his brother monks, and Traugott were not my only contacts in Christian Jerusalem. One evening, when I came to walk my tour in the Mish'mar Ez'rachi, I found myself paired with a woman who would reveal yet another aspect of this city.

Tavio had a cold that night, and so I was assigned to go around with a new volunteer, a recent immigrant. In her mid-thirties and wearing a kerchief over her hair, she looked to me like one of the many young Orthodox Jewish women from Brooklyn or Queens who seemed always to be moving to Jerusalem. Who else, I thought, would cover her hair this way? Her name was Jean.

But as we began walking and talking, I very quickly learned how wrong I was. Jean was not from Brooklyn or Queens; she had come to Jerusalem from Durban, South Africa.

"How big is the Jewish community in Durban?" I asked. Most

of the Jewish South African immigrants I'd met had come from Johannesburg; a few were from Cape Town. I knew none from Durban.

"I imagine it's quite small," Jean replied, "but I really don't know. I'm not Jewish."

That was unusual. South African Jews immigrated to Israel in relatively large numbers. But South Africans of other faiths—I had never heard of any coming here.

"Is your husband Jewish?" I asked. trying to figure this woman out.

"Oh, no," she said, "we're both Christians."

We walked a few steps down the block in the direction of the Yemin Moshe neighborhood. "We may as well start our tour down there," I said.

"If you don't mind my asking," I continued after a few moments, "what made you come to Jerusalem?"

Jean was quite prepared to answer my question. "You're not the first to ask, I assure you." We passed the entrance to Liberty Bell Park.

"My husband and I are both quite attached to the Bible. We always have been. We read it every night."

"Is he a minister?"

"No, we're both teachers. We work over there now." She pointed to St. Andrew's Scottish Church. "Our students are mostly U.N. people, children of the UNIFIL troops."

"Did you come at the request of the United Nations, then?"

"No, nothing like that. We were getting quite troubled about life in South Africa, and one night as we read through the Scriptures, we came to a series of verses that seemed to us to point the way."

"Do you remember them?"

"Quite well. The first was from the twenty-sixth chapter of Matthew, verse eight: 'To what purpose is this waste?' It was a question that seemed to sum up our feeling of distress. We closed the book and talked about the point of our lives, where they were leading us. And then my husband gave me the Bible and asked me to open it and read aloud the verse on which my eyes first fell. So I opened up the book."

"And what did you read?"

"The fifth chapter of John, verse eight: 'Rise, take up thy bed, and walk.'

"And then my husband took the Bible and he turned it to Second

Corinthians. 'Are they Hebrews? so am I. Are they Israelites? so am I. Are they the seed of Abraham? so am I.'

"So we came here."

"Why especially Jerusalem?"

"Because it was here that our Saviour had spent His last days on earth. And here we would be upon His return."

The rest of the evening Jean talked to me about her experiences in this city. She loved the place. She could feel Christ everywhere. And she was happy to be among the Hebrews, the Israelites, the seed of Abraham. In fact, she added, since she felt this way as a Christian, she could not imagine how a Jew who came here could ever think of leaving. "It's all so much more alive for you, after all, isn't it? I mean, we have our churches and hopes, but so much of the rest is yours."

"Are there no difficulties?" I asked.

"Well, of course, there's the language, but we're learning slowly. And then there's the calendar."

"What do you mean?"

Jean explained that at first it was hard to adjust to a place where the Jewish holy days were the state holidays and where the Christian ones seemed to pass almost unnoticed. But that was all right, she said. In practice she and her husband had found that it forced the religion back into the heart. "You have to think more about Christmas when you don't see it bandied about in every shop window and doorway. Though I must admit not all the parents of my students see it that way. They object to having to adapt their lives to your calendar."

"Are there no times that you feel your holy days get some notice here?"

"Well, there's Easter. But then, that's because it is so close to Passover, I suppose. Then too, Easter is the Jerusalem holy day, isn't it? Christmas happened in Bethlehem, but Easter—all that was here. Have you been here for Easter? Wait, you'll see."

My impressions, as a Jew, of the one whom Christians call their Saviour had always been rather troubled. To begin with, I could not look upon Him as a Divinity. Nevertheless, because I grew up in a Christian society much of whose culture I had absorbed into my own spirit, neither could I dismiss Him completely. Thus, Jesus of Nazareth became for me a shadowy figure, a symbol of others' faith to be gazed upon with fascination from afar who could, however, never quite touch me.

And then, like Jean, I came to Jerusalem and encountered another Jesus. This was a Jewish boy born in nearby Bethlehem, a local who had walked these streets. At Gethsemane, by the pools of Bethesda, in the room of the Last Supper atop the mountain now called Zion, along the Via Dolorosa and finally at Golgotha and the site of the Holy Sepulcher, a different Jesus from the one I had imagined in America appeared. Here at last I discerned a Jesus who was not an American Protestant, but someone much closer to me, a local Jew appalled by the hypocrisy and vulgarity he saw about him in a Jerusalem dominated by Rome and its minions. Here I discovered a Jesus who generations after His passing was still palpably present, about whom Jerusalemites still seemed to share memories and whom they talked about—in the words of the nineteenth-century traveler John Lloyd Stephens—"as a man with whom they had been familiar in his life. . . ." This was a Jesus even an unbeliever like me could understand, sympathize with and touch.

But this Jesus with Whom I had made my peace was, I knew, far from Jean's Saviour, the Christ to Whom my Christian neighbors turned in their prayers and Whose eternity beyond time they celebrated on the days of His birth and of His resurrection. "My conviction is that a native has the whole consciousness of his people and nation in him," Thomas Wolfe had argued in *Look Homeward, Angel*. To know that Jesus, I would have to follow in the footsteps of Christian believers—if that was possible. I did not think myself capable of going further, but I would try.

Jean was right. In Jerusalem, Easter, the great celebration of life over death, the festival of the liberation of spirit, was the best time for such an encounter. Christmas, after all, was celebrated to the south, in Bethlehem, at the Church of the Nativity; but Easter had happened here, in Jerusalem, at Passover time. Seated at His Passover *seder* in a room on Mount Zion, Jesus, sensing that an end was near, had turned to His disciples and, pointing to the wine on the table, proclaimed it His blood, while the *matzah* on the table He called his body. And then shortly after, He had been scourged, taken to Pilate, wreathed in thorns and made to bear His cross to Golgotha, where He was crucified on a Friday. He became the paschal sacrifice. Then on Sunday, in the words of a Christian pilgrim of the last century, He "disarmed death of all its terrors." And the great adventure that is Christianity began.

As there is disagreement among Christians over when Christmas falls, so too believers are at odds about the precise day on which their Saviour rose. In this season of holy days, when the death of winter gives way to the blossoming of spring, each group has found its own day of new life to celebrate. A week after the Catholics and Protestants of Jerusalem celebrate Easter, the Greek Orthodox have their own commemoration of the Resurrection.

When he had taken me through Mar Saba, Cornelius had briefly described for me the practices surrounding this day. The ritual of the holy fire was foremost: on the day before the holiest one, the Patriarch, standing inside the Holy Sepulcher, would light the first candle—for years, the "miraculous" fire from Heaven was handed to him through a hole in the roof by Cornelius—and then in a flash the other monks and pilgrims, in bursts of enthusiasm, passed the flame from candle to candle. Later, on Easter, the Patriarch led a procession through the streets of the Christian Quarter into the Holy Sepulcher.

This Easter, I had hoped, Cornelius would be my guide. As he had taken me through Mar Saba, so he would lead me into the Holy Sepulcher. But only days before the beginning of the festival, I learned that Cornelius was dead. Already his body had been encrypted in the mountains beneath Mar Saba, and in a year his bones would join those of other monks he had shown us in the cases and catacombs of the monastery. With Cornelius in the hereafter, I would have to go in here myself. Still, Cornelius had told me enough so that it was to the Greek Orthodox Easter I decided to go rather than to any of the others.

Two days after the end of Passover—what we called "Pesach" —on the Greek Orthodox Easter Sunday—what they called "Pascha"—I entered the Old City through the New Gate, weaving my way around the Franciscan monastery that hugged the inside of the walls. Ahead of me a brown-cassocked Franciscan descended slowly into the Valley and in the direction of the Church of the Holy Sepulcher. Later I would see him again, offering the Mass in the little area inside the church that had been set aside for the use of his order.

Inside the city walls the Valley became twisted into alleys and crooked, narrow paths. Following them carefully, I soon found myself in front of the Greek Orthodox convent. Today, the street here was alive with people, all of them speaking Greek. From every window and lintel flew the blue-and-white flag of Greece and the red-and-white one of the Patriarchate. On all the stores nearby, signs in Greek had been pasted on the windows and doorposts. The same merchants whom in the past I had heard hawking their wares in English or German or Hebrew, depending on the tourists coming through the bazaars, now spoke in Greek. Prices, although still quoted in dollars—everyone's favorite currency these days—were also being given in drachmas. It seemed as if the entire network of streets surrounding the convent had been transformed into an outpost of Hellas.

Clutches of old women in black dresses with black kerchiefs covering their knotted gray hair wandered the souks, chattering in Greek and searching for some rosary or cross to take into the church with them, there to be newly consecrated. Walking with them, a few of the older monks, their black caps tightly bracing their long hair, their beards neatly groomed, had taken it upon themselves to shepherd the pilgrims through their shopping. They knew where to stop and shop and where not. The wise shopkeepers had long ago learned how to show their respect for these men of the cloth, and those who had not would learn now as they watched the line of shoppers pass them by.

In front of a number of the shops were neat stacks of white handkerchiefs on which were printed images of the Saviour. These were for use by the faithful as shrouds, to cover the face of the dead with an image of the Resurrected. Then too, I saw some of the worshipers using them to sop up the rose water poured on the Stone of Unction, the marble slab atop the spot where believers say Jesus' body was anointed before burial.

For a time I threaded my way through the groups of Greek pilgrims, past a few Greek Orthodox Boy Scouts in uniform who, having finished their earlier procession to the church, were now rolling up their banners and going elsewhere to celebrate the holiday in other ways. As I observed the shoppers, most of whom seemed to be elderly—although here and there an old mother or father appeared to be accompanied by a son or daughter—I began to allow my imagination some free play.

After years of saving and planning this pilgrimage, some of these Greeks had traveled from their little villages in the hills or coastal fishing communities to at last enter the sacred precincts of Jerusalem, here to celebrate the rising of their Lord. A few wore little badges on their breasts, given to them by the priests who had organized the trips. Along with the rosaries, crosses and portraits of the Saviour they had purchased, they would become cherished family heirlooms, the palpable tokens of what might be the religious highlight of their lives.

Yet although their devotions directed them to the church, they could not help becoming caught up by the rhythm of the market-place. And then, as they descended from pilgrimage into tourism, quite a few, having found and bagged their beads and religious articles, began shopping for shoes, blouses and other bargains that were not to be had in the village back home. And their cassocked escorts ceased being spiritual leaders and became instead shopping guides. And Jerusalem was no longer just a holy city but a grand bazaar.

Wandering thus among the shoppers and my imagination, wondering where to turn next in my search for another image of Jesus, I noticed amidst the crowd a group of women clutching long tapers. Like a jet stream, they flowed past the eddies of shoppers with a striking sense of purpose reflected in their gait and visages. The sight wrenched me out of my reveries and reminded me of what I had come to see. Convinced that by mingling with them I would float in the right direction, I slipped in at the end of their line.

In moments, I found myself standing in the square in front of the Church of the Holy Sepulcher. Although later in the day as worshipers poured in from all sides it would become much fuller, already there were people in all parts of the plaza. Besides being Easter for some, it was Sunday for everyone. Nuns—some wearing the round-domed headdress of the Armenian Church, others wearing the square pillbox hat of the Greeks and still others in the black wimple of the Catholic habit—were everywhere in evidence. There were men here too, but the women far outnumbered them.

Just inside the door of the church in an anteroom sat Mr. Nusseibeh, keeper of the keys. Shriveled up inside his gray suit, he chatted with several of the policemen who had come today to help maintain order. Behind his thick glasses, Nusseibeh's eyes twinkled at the activity. This was his busy season of watching. He knew all the priests, where each one would turn and whom he would lead.

Ahead of me, the women with the tapers in hand were sweeping by him toward the vestibule where, beneath some hanging candle lamps, lay the marble marking the place of the Stone of Unction. A few of them began to weep, while others threw themselves upon the spot. One woman passionately rolled her forehead atop the moistened slab, kissed it and crossed herself. A second took out a rosary from her handbag and rubbed it in the fluid on the stone. Another came in and, falling to her knees, kissed the place on which the body of her Saviour had been anointed, crossed herself and then repeatedly made the sign of the cross on the stone. Reaching over her, an old nun spritzed more rose water for the pilgrims yet to come.

Behind her an old woman in black shuffled in and with great difficulty lowered herself to her knees and then, prostrate, began kissing the stone, her tears dripping into the tiny pools of fluid that had collected along its edges. Then, raising herself with excruciating slowness, she took out a kerchief from her sleeve and began to swab the stone. Although her hand trembled, she stretched her arms out fully and energetically—as if she were wiping the floor in her own home—trying to absorb as many of the precious drops as she could. And when the cloth was heavy with them, she pulled a small flask from her bag and, unscrewing the top, squeezed some of the holy liquid into it. Carefully she replaced the top and put the bottle in with the other treasures in her bag. Then, pulling her skirt up above her knees and unrolling the long blue stockings she wore underneath, the old woman took what moisture was left in her kerchief and rubbed it upon her swollen, arthritic joints. Finally, withdrawing six or seven strings of beads from her handbag, she rubbed these along the stone, holy rosaries which, thus consecrated, would impart a special sanctity and added vitality to the prayers of all those who used them. And then, in a parting gesture, she knelt again, crossed herself and kissed the stone.

In 1836, after gazing at pilgrims who had reached this place, John Lloyd Stephens had written: ''The infatuated Greek still kisses and adores this block of marble as the very stone on which the angel sat when he announced to the women, 'He is not dead; he is risen; come see the place where the Lord lay.' '' As I watched the old woman hobble away into the shadows of the church toward the place of the sepulcher, it occurred to me—as it had in Mar Saba— that in the hundred and fifty years since Stephens' visit not much had changed here. The tableau of pilgrimage remained stretched on the frame of long-held tradition.

I followed the old woman, still hoping that in the footsteps of a believer I might witness a sight I could otherwise not see; but in the crowded darkness, I lost her. Instead, I found myself among congregants who had come to say Mass with the Franciscans. A few were lighting tapers which they placed along a ledge outside the sepulcher. The chapel, such as it was, was hardly more than a few meters of open space. A larger chapel, curtained off behind the monks, was set aside for the Greek Orthodox service. All the benches were filled, and worshipers had brought along small folding stools which they set up and sat on in alcoves nearby.

I walked around the sepulcher to the other side to get a better view. The Franciscans were using the eastern opening. In the western one, a solitary Coptic priest lit tapers and affixed candles along the ledges of the wall. His congregation would be here another time ; now his job was to keep the flame of faith quietly alive. A few meters farther, an Ethiopian monk, relegated by the status quo law to a chapel outside the main church, stood quietly looking at a crucifix near the Chapel of the Apparition, mumbling prayers. He tilted his head to the left and wrapped a coverlet about his shoulders. In the darkness, his eyes shone with a gentle piety.

Passing him, I came back around to the Franciscans in time to hear an organ from somewhere up in the balcony piping out the opening melody of the Kyrie. I looked up at the sound and saw rays of sunlight drop down from the glass dome at the center of the basilica over the sepulcher. The five Franciscans who stood facing the tomb sang the opening words of the Mass while another, facing them and robed in red and white, answered. The chanting rebounded through the cavernous room, disturbed every so often by the sound of benches being moved from the nearby Greek Orthodox chapel where the spirit of prayer was still being prepared. Watching and listening for a few moments, I stood behind an Armenian monk who like me had become transfixed. And then, as the Franciscans sang the Gloria, I felt myself backing away from the congregation. However beautiful the melody and impressive the ceremony, the sentiments here glorified a Divinity not my own ; I could not stifle the sense of estrangement nurtured by years of Jewish life that welled up inside me. And being an unbeliever, I suddenly felt like a voyeur instead of an observer. When a moment later a group of tourists passed near me, I melted into line with them and moved away.

Peeking into the Greek Orthodox chapel, the Katholikon, I found it filled to overflowing. Still the worshipers poured in, and each one found someplace to sit or stand. A few monks were consulting with the police about just where to place the barriers around which they would march later. One of them walked to the center of the room, the Omphalos Mundi—Navel of the World—as if to make certain the entire universe was properly aligned. I slipped out the door and fell back into the darkness.

''We'll wait till they're through and find a quiet chapel to say our Mass.''

The familiar American drawl caught my attention ; the voice was that of an American priest, leading about a dozen of what must have been his parishioners through the church. Looking a bit dazed and overwhelmed by the panoply of traditions through which they weaved their way, they seemed to try to avoid being touched by any of the hundreds of others who were marching through the large rotunda. "Alvin, stay next to me!" one of the women called to her spindly, gray-haired companion. Each held a taper he or she would light at the sepulcher, and most of them also dangled a camera around the neck. The priest's was the largest, and it rested securely upon his ample belly. He was in shirt sleeves with a stiff white collar.

"Here, let me get a photo of y'all here," he said, shepherding his small flock toward the side of the burial chamber. They stood stiffly in a little group.

"Now we'll have somethin' to show 'em back home in Charleston," their pastor said with a smile after he had snapped the picture.

Behind them I could hear an Israeli guide explaining to another group of tourists why he knew it was impossible for the sepulcher to be the place where a garden had stood and where the grave of Jesus might have been. "Would *you* have planted a garden here? Do you believe anyone did?" he asked. "I don't think so—but of course, we don't know for sure," he concluded.

There were some who did. As if to answer him, a few meters away the faithful lined up at the mouth of the tomb to receive Communion from the Franciscan priest. He who would know must first believe.

Turning toward the door, I slipped past the Stone of Unction, on top of which someone had placed five white lilies. Dewy water, like nectar, dripped from their petals onto the slab. For all of the wiping by the worshipful, the marble was still moist and the air was filled with the smell of incense and rose water. Amidst the prostrate, I walked out into the bright Jerusalem sunshine.

In the square, the crowd had thickened visibly. A few people— some of those staying at the convent, perhaps relatives of the monks and priests—stood atop the roof of the church and looked down. Next to them an Israeli soldier standing guard adjusted his red beret and said something into his walkie-talkie. I stood at the edge of a small group of black-clad Greek women. On my other side, a ruddy-complexioned man leaned on a carved walking stick. In front of me, a stunning, rather tall German woman wearing a stylish outfit with a label that said "SPLENDOR IN THE GRASS" stood scanning the crowd. Her lush blond ponytail swished past my cheek each time she turned her head, the fresh smell of her soaped skin a welcome contrast to the thick odor of incense and rose water.

Suddenly the bells atop the church began to peal. Beating rhythmically, they grew louder and more insistent by the moment. With the sound, a palpable change came across the crowd, as all eyes turned toward the stairs that entered the square from the west. Thus we stood, all eyes on the stairs, our hearts beginning to beat in time with the bells. Then, after what seemed an interminable wait, we saw a slow procession of priests and monks led by a young robed seminarian carrying the holy banner atop a silver staff. Marching in two parallel lines along the sides of the stairs, the monks, with their cylindrical caps, were clothed in black cassocks, while the priests, their caps jutting out slightly at the top, were robed in gold.

The bells had grown very loud and drowned out the voices of the marchers, who had begun to chant something. A few broke out of the line and began to wave toward the bell tower, signaling to the one in charge of the ringing to cease. But apparently caught up in his service, he remained oblivious to their motions and kept up the tolling. The old man near me lifted his cane and shrieked something. Soon others in the crowd were waving and yelling to the bell tower. For years, Cornelius had been in charge of this task. Now he was dead. Obviously this year's ringer was new on the job.

While the bells went on ringing, the last ones in the procession continued marching down the stairs. A few threw flower petals into the crowd. And then came the Patriarch, robed and crowned in gold, a jeweled scepter in his hand. His freshly shampooed long white beard glistening, he stood looking out over the crowd while the others tried to silence the bells. At last the ringing stilled, the chant began again and the Patriarch, his eyes flashing from behind his gold-rimmed glasses, marched regally forward. Again flower petals were thrown from somewhere as the entire party entered the church and turned toward the Katholikon and the Navel of the World to begin the holy service.

With the entry of the Patriarch into the church, the crowd began to divide. Those who had come only to see the pageantry, who were attracted by the spectacle, who had focused their cameras on the action and snapped at every movement, turned now toward the gates leading out of the square. Some headed west toward the souks, and others went out to the east and the open spaces of the Muristan and the al-Jedid market.

Still in search of the spirit that moved the believers here, I resolved to stay and stepped forward with those who followed the procession into the church. After all, I had already been to a Greek Orthodox service with Cornelius during my visit to Mar Saba. But as I came toward the lintel, recalling my brief encounter with the Franciscans I felt suddenly alone in this crowd of worshipers. Without Cornelius in whose wake I could follow, I was held back. The barrier was not external. On the contrary, the crowd pushed me forward; it was easier to let myself be forced inside than to slither out of line. What held me back was something interior, something that forced me to shorten my steps and let the devout stream past me on all sides. Try as I might to share the desire and devotions of the pilgrims around me who pressed into the chapel, alone I could not. The procession had led to a place into which only the faithful could pass. The Saviour whose Resurrection they were celebrating, whose memory awaited them inside, was not mine. He who would see must first believe.

Reaching the limits of my ability to view and envision, I moved out of the stream of believers flowing around me. I would remain outside, no matter how hard I tried to participate. And so with nothing more for me to see beyond the door, I turned away.

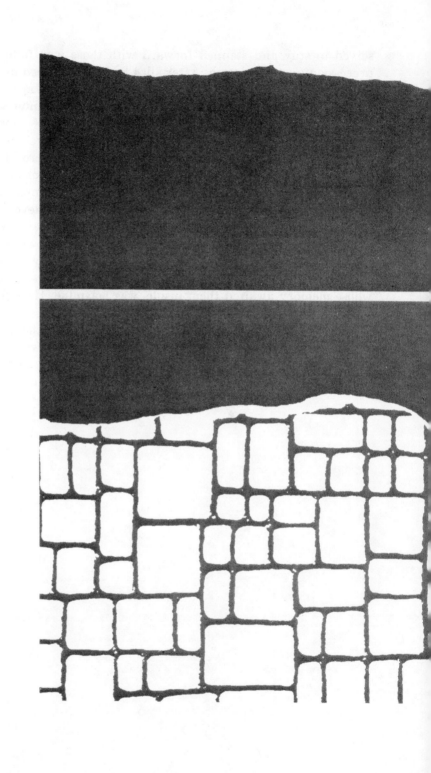

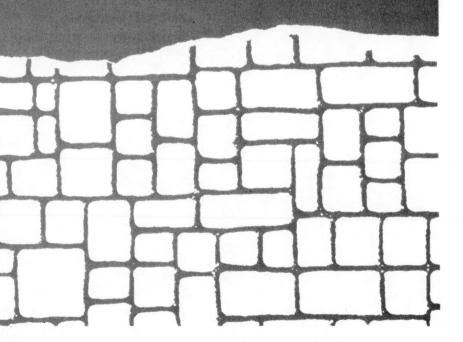

PART

•3•

CHAPTER
·15·

THE CHILDREN OF ABRAHAM

In the same day the Lord made a covenant with Abram, saying: Unto thy seed have I given this land, from the river of Egypt to the great river, the river Prat.

GENESIS 15:18

"If this land was promised to Abraham's children, then remember, we Arabs are Abraham's children too."

The speaker was Samir, a cabdriver from Jerusalem, a native of what the Arabs call al-Quds—"the Holy." I was concluding a long walk through the alleys and streets of the Moslem Quarter, where I had been wandering for days, trying to get a feel for al-Quds. After nearly six hours this morning, I found myself near the Damascus Gate, feeling as if my feet were crumpling, and so I decided to treat myself to a cab ride and jumped into Samir's bright green car, which stood among the twenty-odd other taxis parked at the stand outside the gate. As we drove toward the western, Jewish part of the city, I struck up a conversation—every Arab cabbie speaks some English. How, I asked him, did he feel about the change in life here since 1967? He looked into the rearview mirror and into my eyes for a moment; perhaps the skullcap on my head made him think I was one of the group of young Orthodox Jews trying to establish Jewish settlements in the Moslem Quarter: "My father and his father before him have lived here. This is my home, no less than it is yours." And then he invoked Abraham, our forefather-in-common.

The memory of Passover, recently celebrated, was fresh in my mind. Maybe that was why his remark made me recall a *midrash* I had recently retold my children at the Passover *seder*. After the Israelites had crossed through the parted waters and while the Egyptians drowned behind them, the angels on high began to sing songs of praise. "How can you sing songs of praise," the Almighty asked, interrupting them, "when my creatures below are drowning?"

How could I celebrate the liberation of my people, the beginning of the journey of the children of Isaac and Israel to the Promised Land that Passover represented, and remain insensitive to the national consciousness of my cousins the offspring of Ishmael and Esau? They were as much a part of the vista of this city as the ramparts of the Ottoman wall or the camel sauntering along the edge of the Mount of Olives.

For one living as a Jew in Jerusalem it was relatively easy to avoid al-Quds, since although the physical barriers between the Arab and Jewish sectors of the city had come down after 1967, the cultural and social ones seemed still pretty much intact. Friendships across these barriers were nearly nonexistent; schooling was separate. There were two independent centers of town, which had developed individually between 1948 and 1967. Each had its own shopping district, and for the most part Arabs and Jews moved in separate orbits.

There were language barriers as well. Arabs spoke Arabic predominantly, while Jews spoke Hebrew. And although each group learned the other's tongue in school, neutral English (a residue from the days of the British Mandate when both groups lived under the domination of the Union Jack) was the most common linguistic bridge between them. But neither Arab nor Israeli wanted to abandon the tongue of his people to talk with the other. So conversation was minimal.

Arabs read their own newspapers, went to their own movies and cafés, attended separate schools and even used their own bus lines from their own central bus station (although for some reason everyone seemed to use Arab-owned-and-driven taxis). And Jews had their own press, centers of entertainment and places to shop. They seldom if ever rode the Arab buses. And only if they wanted bargains or exotic souvenirs, or if the Arabs had something unavailable on the other side of town, did the Jews come to buy in al-Quds. Arab doctors performed the illegal Jewish abortions—but almost no one talked about that.

To be sure, Arabs did come to work for the Jews. Since 1967, they had by and large taken over the building trades—even the most fervently Zionist settlements found themselves dependent on Arab construction workers and stonecutters. And without the Arabs, the garbage in all of Jerusalem would not be collected. In short, where there was menial labor to be done, the Arabs did it. Things had changed a great deal since the idealistic early days of Zionism when even the lowliest job was done by Jews, and "head of the street sweepers' union" was the formal title of Shraga Netzer, one of the most powerful political operatives in the country.

I had not started out to avoid the Arabs. In the beginning, I was genuinely interested in talking with them, in discovering the nature of their attachments to Jerusalem. After all, in many ways they were part of what made this city seem so different from any place I had ever lived in before. With their checkered kaffiyehs atop their heads and gray or white jallabiyehs hanging from their frames, their fingers wrapped loosely around worry beads, leaning on carved walking sticks or sitting in little nooks among the souks of the Old City while smoking ornate water pipes topped with pungent-smelling tobacco, the men seemed to symbolize the distant and timeless Levant. Among the women, those who were veiled and robed, who carried their packages—no matter how large or bulky —perfectly balanced upon their heads, quietly but unmistakably reflected the survival of yesterday inside today. And even the children, astride their donkeys in the alleys behind the walls or herding their goats and sheep along hillocks on the sides of the Kidron Valley, recalled the image of the ancients whose lives are the stuff of Bible stories.

And so, in the early days of my Jerusalem stay, I had taken to walking about the Arab Quarter of the city, hoping I would find the Arab counterpart to Tavio, Cornelius, or Yisra'el, a person who would show me his side of Jerusalem and share his memories. I had had this desire again this morning. But after six hours of walking, I had found nothing—until I came upon Samir. But Samir had nothing more to tell me beyond what I have here repeated.

Normally, in my search for al-Quds, I headed first toward the area around the Damascus Gate, the major Arab artery into the heart of the city. Fridays were the best days to go, for on this day the gate pulsed with a heavy stream of people who went in and out on this, the Moslem Sabbath. Here they came to do their last-minute shopping in the open-air markets, and here they thronged to worship in the silver-domed al-Aqsa, the Friday mosque that stood on Abraham's mountain, next to the spot on which the Jews' Holy Temple once stood.

On Fridays the pattern of traffic in front of the Damascus Gate, situated in the crease of the valley, was different. The trucks usually loaded with produce from the Arab-owned fields and farms throughout the territories were all parked for the day along Nablus Road. The fellahin had come to town to shop and pray.

The Damascus Gate was the hub of everything here. Once it had opened onto gently sloping hills which I had seen in so many pictures that I could by now almost make them out beneath the busy intersection choked with cars going east toward A-Tur, west to the Jewish sector and north toward Ramallah and Nablus. According to most archeologists, the site of this opening goes back two thousand years to antiquity, when it was part of an interior wall of the city. Underneath it are the uncovered remains of the triple Roman gate through which the city—then called Aelia Capitolina—was entered after the Roman conquest, just over two millennia ago.

Over the current Ottoman arch the Arabic reader can still decipher the following inscription:

OUR LORD THE GREAT SULTAN AND BRILLIANT GOVERNOR, SULTAN OF THE STRANGERS, ARABS AND PERSIANS, HAS COMMANDED THE CONSTRUCTION OF THIS BLESSED WALL ... SULEIMAN THE SON OF SALIM KHAN, MAY ALLAH PRESERVE HIS REIGN AND HIS KINGDOM.

But as with the reign of the Romans, all that remains of the Sultan's kingdom is the stones and the inscription. On the wall, the Israelis have built a promenade. At its entrance an Arab boy collects the tickets of the tourists who want to walk the walls and climb the ramparts. I had taken that walk many times.

Coming down from the walls one morning, I stood on the steps to the gate and looked around. At the taxi stand, here since the days of the British, a few drivers chatted quietly. One of them buffed his shiny red Mercedes and adjusted the feather on its aerial. Behind him, a stocky man wearing a red fez and leading himself with a hand-worn walking stick trickled down the steps that led to the gate. He was followed by an older man, distinctively robed in a flowing black cloak with gold trim, his jallabiyeh showing from underneath, his kaffiyeh neatly wrapped about his head, who walked hand in hand with a young man—perhaps his son—in Levi's and a black windbreaker. Three little boys chased one another through the crowd, eventually disappearing among the people entering through the gate. An Arab woman tightened the silky white kerchief on her head and grabbed the hand of the child by her side.

Friday was the day when a flea market was set up on the steps, and I often stopped to watch. Along a particularly wide landing, a fellah in a tattered jallabiyeh was spreading out white and black sheepskin rugs for sale. Another prepared to sell Duralex glasses from France (one of which he repeatedly dropped on the pavement to demonstrate their unbreakable quality). A third was spreading out nuts and raisins in large wicker baskets. An ancient-looking brass scale and some stones with which each customer could weigh his purchases rested nearby. Near the huge metal doors to the gate, two women arranged fruits and vegetables for sale. They would use their ample breast pockets for holding the money. Next to them, a boy who sold slices of sesame-seed candies and peanut brittle was polishing the blade of his wide knife with a white rag. Everywhere there were sponges, tablecloths, toys, fruits, shoes, clothes and dishes being readied for sale. For the Jewish tourists there were even *menorot* and knit skullcaps embroidered with Hebrew. For the locals there were Arab newspapers.

In the turning of the gate, the Arab money changers—in a Jewish capital, in one of history's countless ironies, money changers are Arabs—counted out their dinars, dollars, francs and shekels. Fridays were a busy day.

The day began early here, with the first call to prayer before sunrise. Later, the main noontime prayers, held once a week in al-Aqsa, would begin. That allowed for all the time in between to meet with those one had not seen all week. From the morning, the owners of kiosks and shops were preparing their wares for the largest crowd of the week. In the Nepal Café, just inside the gate,

Mustafa prepared the water pipes he rented out to his customers and the cards with which they usually played a version of gin rummy. At the squeezer, new grapefruits and oranges from Jericho were piled, and in the back, sweet Turkish coffee was being brewed.

Across from the gate, the latter-day notaries, twentieth-century scribes, as on other mornings, set up their typewriters on little tables or wooden crates along the road. They made their living by providing help to the illiterate or those with some official form to fill out or who needed translation of a document written in a Hebrew or English they could not comprehend. Friday, a day off from work, was a good morning to get this kind of thing done. In Omar al-Faja's "Public Relations Office," two men sat at the ready near a typewriter and stared off into space while they waited for clients. One of them puffed languidly on a Farid, the cigarette that only Arabs smoked.

At the corner, near a bagel vendor who was setting out his round rolls, a few young porters with their wooden hand trucks were also waiting, hoping someone with a purchase too large to carry would hire them to wheel the merchandise through the narrow alleys of the Old City and home. On other weekdays, their fathers or brothers waited along the wall on Nablus Road, near an open field, in hopes that someone driving by would stop and offer them a day's labor. Today, however, the elders were off, and only the young boys released from their schoolwork prepared to hire themselves out. Many of them would work in the Jewish neighborhoods or settlements that were being built on lands once under Arab control. Day laborers took the work where they could find it, and settlers took workers wherever they could get them. The politics of the business was for another time.

The center of al-Quds was fascinating. Although it was located only about a kilometer to the west of the Jewish downtown, it was clearly in another cultural hemisphere. Here in Jerusalem one could walk in less than half an hour from a contemporary Western city, along the edge of a monastery whose architecture still reflected the battles and salvations of a previous century, past pockmarked reminders of wars of Armageddon and liberation, near gates left by superstitious Turkish sultans and end up in the Levant and another time. To my eyes, this place had a vitality unmatched by any other spot in the city. At all hours, there were people here.

And during the summer, in the watermelon season, at the place where today trucks were parked, temporary kiosks and little booths were constructed where men stayed up all night guarding their piles of melons against pilferage. During Ramadan, which this year fell in midsummer, when for a month Moslems fasted all day and ate at night, these kiosks were the center of al-Quds life.

Sometimes, when I drove through here on my way to the Hebrew University on Mount Scopus to the east, the sounds of a Haydn quartet or Mozart symphony on my car radio while outside my car window were scenes that might have greeted an Ommayad caliph, I felt as if I were in a time capsule, a bubble passing through from some other universe. And then, struck ofttimes by the absurdity of my self-enclosedness, I would—even in winter—roll down the window of the car and allow the sounds and air of one world to mix with the other so that they congealed into a single experience. It reminded me of one of Traugott's trick slides.

Along the street, in a manner typical here, walked two Arabs, one man loosely draping his hand over the forearm of the other. At my feet, collapsed in a pile on the sidewalk, two old women enclosed from head to toe in the black chadar, the veil of Islam, held out their hands and with practiced cries—pleas to passersby and Allah (just in case)—begged alms, while next to them at small pushcarts stood men selling sesame-seed rolls and spiced eggs.

I walked toward the Lions Gate. It was Friday, a good day to see the sheep-and-goat market. Bedrock swathed the base of the walls here. I followed it past Hezekiah's Cave, an ancient quarry for the stones of the city (and some say those of Solomon's Temple). Just beyond it was Herod's Gate. Across the street was a hill—al-Sahira, the Koran called it—within which Arabs have for centuries buried their dead. In the local dialect of Arabic, the hill's name came to be pronounced "Zahira," which means "flowers," and the gate opposite, although originally named for Herod, came to be called Bab al-Zahira, or Flower Gate, by the people of al-Quds. In the gate's cleft, a small-time grocer and a cassette dealer had found niches from which to scrape out a living.

But if once this entrance had been identified with the mighty Herod, it was hard to see why now. More like a side path into the Moslem Quarter, this was not a major opening to the city. For centuries it had been sealed, and when, upon taking control of the city, the British opened it, they somehow never managed to renew its days of glory. A rank odor of urine and putrefying garbage wafted from the large dumpsters that stood behind the gate. I moved on quickly.

Reaching the northeast corner of the city, I came upon the sheep-and-goat market. Over the course of weeks, I had returned here repeatedly, trying to decipher the patterns of exchange, so different from anything I knew. While their kin were hawking toys, dishes, rugs and raisins farther to the west, these herders were practicing the ancient commerce their forefathers had carried on for generations. For a moment as I gazed around me, it seemed that seller and buyer were frozen in time, and I had along with them entered some timeless suspension. Watching from various corners and at last summoning the courage to wander in among the men and animals, I tried to absorb as much as possible. It was difficult; this was not a place for bystanders. You either had business here or got out. But there were always some tourists about, snapping pictures—so I brought a camera behind which I could stand and watch.

Gradually, as I observed the give-and-take, the shadings of the present showed up against the outline of a past I could only imagine. A few of the owners of the larger herds had brought their merchandise in trucks. Many of the animals were crowded against the wooden rails which held them on the truck beds. Others had led their flocks here on foot and had secured them with ropes and sticks. Each man had marked his stock with a special-colored dye. The shepherds-turned-businessmen, for that is what they were on market day, spent much of the time huddling or crouching in small circles. A few of them used little scraps of paper for their figuring, but most—as I supposed they must have for generations—simply scrawled numbers with a stick in the dirt. In their hands they held a variety of notes: Israeli shekels or Jordanian dinars, both of which were legal tender here. In one or two cases I saw what I thought were American dollars, but the hands that held them moved so quickly that I could not be sure.

A few women wandered among the men, but they stood out simply because of their small number. And none, as far as I could see, did any buying or selling. (Later—from a shepherd's son who was taking a degree in anthropology—I learned that although they formally owned no flocks, some of the women did have a controlling interest in many and used the men as their sales agents.) Occasionally, one or another would histrionically grimace or complain when the man she was dealing with was angry, or else display a kind of quiet satisfaction when the transaction went well.

Although I understood none of the Arabic they spoke, it was easy enough to tell when a deal had been struck. Examining the mouth of the animal, looking behind its ears, palpating its chest, the potential buyer would then begin a long process of bargaining over the price. Sometimes this required his walking away from the seller in what appeared to the outsider like anger or at least disgust, while the former put on a show of offense at the initial offer. Sooner or later, however, in apparent reconsideration, one of the two would change direction and move toward the other. Now would begin the final round of dealing. At last, the drama of their haggling complete, the two shook hands and exchanged money.

Then the pair walked toward the purchase, the poor animal oblivious of this sudden turn in its destiny. Sometimes the buyer lifted it with his arms around its belly, or else—if it was a goat—he might hold it by the ears so that the animal was forced up on its hind legs, and then the two—man and beast—seemed almost to dance away together. At times, the buyer (or his son) would pull on a rope tied around his new possession's neck and lead it away, or use a stick to get it into his herd, and then he would push the rumps of the last animals, all the while yelling encouragement or warning—it was often hard for me to tell the difference.

Amid the crowd walked a tall, grizzled-looking man in a white turban and wearing a huge tin urn on his back and a belt hooked with drinking glasses, which he rinsed from a pitcher of water held in his hand. While everyone else did sheep business, he hawked *tamar hindi*—date-palm juice. In his hand he swung a heavy brass bell. To those willing to pay the few shekels he charged, he offered his sweet concoction in a rinsed glass.

There was something strangely terpsichorean about the way he worked. Because the urn was strapped to his back, with the spout coming over his shoulder, he would have to bend his entire body in order to get the dark brown fluid into the glass. From afar, it looked as if he were dancing to the sound of the bell and then, as he poured the drink, he bowed low before his customer, straightening up swiftly when the liquid bubbled up to the rim of the glass. Although it was in payment that the other extended his hand, from a distance the bills were not always visible. And so at that moment, the two seemed engaged in some silent *pas-de-deux*. And then, with the buyer handing back his empty glass, which the vendor with a few quick movements flushed and rinsed, the ballet came to an end.

For a long time I wandered al-Quds seeking someone to be my guide. But I do not speak Arabic, the language of the locals, and they chose not to speak Hebrew, the language of the conqueror. My English marked me only as a tourist, and with tourists you don't get involved in conversation except to sell them something. So I found no one.

Endlessly I searched, sitting in the cafés and meandering along the streets of the Old City and outside the Damascus Gate. I visited Arabs who lived in Shuafat, along the road north of the city. With the Interfaith group I made some contacts. In the Rashadiyeh school for boys, I shared time with some Arabs who were learning to play the oud, a stringed, lutelike instrument. In the Mulaweyeh school for women in the Harat al-Sadiyeh neighborhood just inside Herod's Gate, I watched girls learn embroidery, hairdressing and cooking. I sat with merchants in the bazaars of the Old City, sipping sweet mint tea and chatting about life in this city. But whenever I tried to evoke the past, asking about attachments to Jerusalem, I was turned instead toward small talk at best and at worst toward politics and Palestinian national aspirations and greeted with formulaic statements about military occupation, Zionist racism and Israeli injustice.

Once, I learned of a Mrs. Assali who might—if she trusted me— answer my questions and reveal her feelings toward Jerusalem. I made all arrangements for an interview. But at the last minute, she refused to meet me. How could I, a Jew, and one who wore a *kippah* like the "zealots" who sought to settle and annex the West Bank, be trusted? She would not talk with me; a letter would have to suffice:

"I don't think that my feeling is different from anybody else's feeling of attachment to her place of birth," she wrote in her careful and delicate script.

> However, there is something that distinguishes the place and not
> the feeling. I experience here a sense of elation and pride in
> being able to say "I'm from Jerusalem." This is the feeling of
> the authentic Jerusalemite who inherits, as though genetically,
> this awe toward the timelessness, pricelessness and universality
> of the city.

But after the June war of 1967, the city was united by the military occupant and proclaimed the eternal and indivisible capital of Israel. The mere pulling down of walls does not unite peoples. A queer feeling of alienation possesses me whenever I step behind that wall. If I ever go to the western side of Jerusalem, I do it to visit the home I was born in. It is still there, a standing witness to the injustice done to me and to thousands of Palestinians driven from their homes. One can never forget or forgive. Jerusalem remains my home, and it remains the *Qibla* of thousands and millions of Arabs, Moslems and Christians, who see in it the spiritual embodiment of their existence.

At the moment we are forcefully subjected to the rule of "might is right," but there will come a time when that would no longer be valid. A feeling of inferiority and guilt will keep haunting the Arabs until they regain their right and presence in Jerusalem.

She had nothing more to say, wanted no further contact. I began to give up hope. And then, one afternoon, I met Salim Khoury. I had gotten his name from the Interfaith group. Others whom I had contacted on the list given me failed to show up for appointments. But Salim Khoury came.

A teacher of English in the Rashadiyeh school, just outside the Damascus Gate, Salim also wrote poetry—in English—about Jerusalem. On a spring afternoon when the city was withering under the desert heat rising up from the Dead Sea, we met at that enclave of the West which sits upon a peak east of the Old City, the Hebrew University on Mount Scopus.

At first, I wondered how I would recognize him; we had never met. Although I did not expect a kaffiyeh and jallabiyeh, I hoped for someone who would resonate the past, an Arab to fit my imagination. "I am fat," he had told me simply when by telephone we arranged our meeting and I asked how I would pick him out.

Arriving early, I stood at the entrance to the faculty-club café where we were to meet. This afternoon the place was crowded with a group of Polish-speaking Holocaust survivors who had come to refresh themselves while on a tour of the campus. In corners, here and there, professors and their guests sat knotted in conversation. On the lookout for my rendezvous, I roamed through the crowd. At last, near the door, I saw a lumpy, thick-girthed, slightly balding man with a thin mustache and tentative expression. His eyes scanned the room.

"Salim Khoury?" I asked. Dressed in a wrinkled suit jacket too small at the shoulders but a size too big in the sleeves, he stretched out his hand to shake mine. Stuffed into a white shirt, yellowed by too much wear, and sporting a wide, long-out-of-fashion paisley tie, he looked less like the exotic Arab of my imagination than like the schoolteacher he was. As we walked toward one of the couches for our conversation, I tried to hide my disappointment in his drab and colorless appearance. And then, in silent consolation, told myself that we were, after all, born of one generation, Abraham's children raised after the Second World War. Perhaps that would make possible an understanding between us; perhaps it would get us away from clichés and formulas.

"If you want to ask questions," he began, after I brought over some coffee, "I am ready to answer."

"Would you tell me about your attachment to this city?" I asked, hoping this poet could take my stiff questions and fill them with his songs of Jerusalem.

"I am born in Jerusalem," he began slowly in a slightly accented, soft-voiced English, "at a hospital which is now the Russian Compound, on August 8, 1940. So I grew up a Christian Arab in Jerusalem. I love Jerusalem. I live in a house in which I have a panoramic view of Jerusalem, when I stay awake to contemplate it." He offered me a Farid cigarette and then lit his own.

He continued, the smoke escaping from his mouth and rising up his nostrils: "From my side, I was the son of an electrician. When my father died by an accident in Amman, I had to take over the support of my family, and I left the Friars' school near the New Gate." He stopped, waiting for another question.

"How has Jerusalem changed since you were growing up in it as a young boy?"

"When I was a boy taking classes at the Friars', our neighbors the Israeli soldiers were just five meters distant, and they used to shoot into our classrooms. Nineteen forty-seven–forty-eight was the most difficult period. I stayed three months at home. When the city came together, I went to the Hebrew University, and then I ended up teaching at the Friars' College—so you see how the cycle completes itself. I suppose therefore, if you think about that and you look at things now, you must say that it is better.

"But there are those who think back to their affiliation with

Jordan or with what they think is in the future. So they are trapped between the past and future, and they are stagnant; they are waiting for solutions. They are parasites on the past and fantasizing about the future, and so they cannot face the facts.''

Having witnessed the heavy price that his people had paid for their too-great attachments to the past, Salim was not about to luxuriate in nostalgia that would only arouse a feeling of loss and frustration. *He* was facing the facts. Unlike the Jews I had met for whom memories—both acquired and inherent—were the roots with which they implanted themselves in the soil and amid the stones of the Holy City, the Arab who chose to recall the past could only be confronted by his severance from it. To long for what could no longer be retrieved, to think back to what was now unthinkable was fantasy, something not to be shared with an American Jew in a *kippah* who, sitting at the Hebrew University, obviously called Jerusalem his own.

If there was anything to be said to one like me, who by his person represented the powers that be, it was that the current economic downturn in Israel and the new levying of taxes were taking a higher toll on the lives of the Arabs, who were losing jobs and having to pay higher taxes at the same time. And if I really cared about the Arab experience in Jerusalem, *that* was what I should know and write about. Salim saved his lyric memory for other occasions; he confronted me now with the rhyme of current realities.

''Now we are suffering from taxes, inflation. This has made the great difference during the last two years. I want to give you facts.'' And he laid out some of the economic problems.

''Only economy matters?'' I asked at last.

''You know, I was from the beginning against the barbed wire and against dividing Jerusalem. For many years I was promotional director at our tourism bureau, and I always said to our tours at the Mandelbaum Gate, 'Pray for the peace of Jerusalem.' We don't want Jerusalem in pieces; we want Jerusalem in one complete peace.

''Just two weeks before the 1967 war, I sat with a friend near the New Gate. And I felt, I told him, that soon it will be open. And really after two weeks there came the war, and the gates did open.

''You know, I was the first one to visit the west side. Still there were some barbs, not all of them removed. I wanted to see the other side.'' He drew on his cigarette and took a sip of his coffee.

''How did that come about?''

''It is an interesting story. On the second day of the war, I heard knocking on my door. 'Who's there?' I said. The answer was 'Miz'rachi.' He spoke to me in Arabic. He asked, 'Where is Ibrahim?' Ibrahim was my father. I tell him that he has passed away. He says that they used to work together in the Ramallah broadcasting station. And he said, 'I thought that it's my duty the first thing to come and visit you because I used always to think of you.'

''And this,'' Salim concluded, ''is a proof to you that friendship, you know, ever lasts. And this Miz'rachi was an officer. He took me on a whole tour through West Jerusalem.''

To Salim this story showed the power of friendship and attested to his willingness to cross boundaries. But perhaps because I was a Jew, I heard in it something else: Even before the guns of the Six-Day War had stilled, the Jew, Miz'rachi, was out trying to revive memories, to reconnect himself and reestablish ties with Ibrahim Khoury in the east. The conqueror was taking his old colleague's son to his own side of the city. The tour of Jerusalem had begun. The efforts to bridge the no-man's-land, the vacuum of history, by acts of witnessing, the process of taking it all in, had begun. But the Arab, though open and friendly, remained at best passive and at worst blind to the process. He was taken; Miz'rachi was in the driver's seat. It was not long before Salim discovered that even with the physical barriers dividing the city removed, the road between the east and west was not two-way.

''And do you now know your way about the western side of the city well?'' I asked.

''I have not been back many times since.''

''Why not?''

''We are related to this city,'' said Salim. There was no need to belabor the details. ''We are not like the Jews who are trying everywhere to uncover their Jerusalem in order to find their roots. Maybe that is your concern, but we know where we are. Let me be frank with you. Jerusalem is the heart of the West Bank, you see, because all of us who live there flow through it. It's very important to us.''

Miz'rachi had to come to the east at the first opportunity, while the bullets were still flying. In the middle of the war, Miz'rachi had come looking for Ibrahim Khoury, to remind himself of past ties.

That was as important as the physical conquest that preceded it. Every Jew I had heard or watched establish a tie to this place had knotted it with references to the strands of history. That I had seen on my Sabbath walks and with Tavio. To lay claim to the city, to complete the return and the conquest by which it had been accomplished, the Jews seemed to feel a need to anchor themselves to places, and people, and events of the past.

But Salim—like Samir, the cabdriver—did not need to do this. Unlike the Jew who ran to the Western Wall and fell up against it with kisses as if reunited at last with a family member from whom he had been separated for eons, the Arab believed he had nothing to prove. No public displays of affection and connection were necessary. His bond to this city was beyond the need for public expression. It was existential. The Arabs did not need to remind themselves of their ties to this place. They just proclaimed it; they belonged here. And for them that was enough.

Perhaps, I thought, I was reading too much into Salim's simple statements. "Let me tell you what always strikes me when I speak with Arabs about Jerusalem," I began. "When I speak to the Jews, they tell me about the Jerusalem they remember. They are filled with stories that link them to a past that in some cases they can only evoke in their imagination. But when I speak to Arabs about the same thing, they take all that for granted, or at least, they don't mention it. Why?"

Yasser Barakat, a young Moslem from Shuafat whom I would meet later, would answer this same question quite simply: "We get too depressed looking at the past." In a way, Salim told me the same thing, except that he explained the nature of the depression.

"You can take useful lessons from the past," he began, "but you must not be a prisoner to it. Some of the people here can no longer distinguish between dreams, memory and reality." He sucked in and held his breath. Then, almost imperceptibly, he leaned forward and added: "I shall tell you something. In 1967, we went—a few of us, my friends—to see the house of one of them on the other side of the city where he had lived before 1948. There had been a eucalyptus tree in the front under which he had played as a boy. For him, the tree was everything. For all the years he had lived behind the barriers that separated the two sides of the city, he thought of that tree. There were others like it on our side, but for him the smooth bark and the hanging branches on which he had climbed and carved his name were irreplaceable. So now, after the war—maybe six months afterward—he went back to the house to look at the tree. But when he got there the tree was gone. Nothing left. The woman living in the house said she knew nothing of a tree there. And so we left and went home. What could we say? What could we remember? We could not any longer see things as they were.

"But as long as we are here, we are here. That is a fact. And we shall begin from that fact. We are here."

Not long after my meeting with Salim, I met Ely Gorodetzer, whose story seems now to serve as an appropriate epilogue to what I learned that afternoon. This was not my first meeting with Ely. I watched him grow up in my hometown of Brookline, Massachusetts. His father and brothers sat in the pew in front of mine at the synagogue. Then, after I had gone to college, I heard that he and his family had moved to Israel. They were living in Jerusalem. Every so often, on my trips to Israel, I would run into one of the Gorodetzers or hear news of them through the hometown grapevine. They loved Israel. But during the last twenty years, I had not seen Ely, and so—like others once known and never seen again—he dropped into my sack of unused memories. Then, at twilight one Sabbath, about two weeks after my meeting with Salim, while standing near the Western Wall waiting for the holy day of rest to fade into the night and the workweek to begin, I saw him—or more precisely, he saw me.

Except for a little blond beard on his face, he looked not too different from what I remembered: a slightly built boy with an open, sweet, almost innocent face and a soft voice. We talked for a while. He worked now in computers. But although he was a man professionally linked to the high-tech horizon of tomorrow, he lived in the Old City, bonded to the memories of yesterday. In these waning minutes of daylight, I could see his apartment, which was, he explained, not far away. He was living in the Moslem Quarter, in a house which he assured me was once owned and inhabited by Jews.

Walking out through an alley and up some steps, we passed by the Shevuvanim (the name means "those sons who have returned") Yeshiva which during the 1970s Jews established in a large building atop the souks along the Street of the Chain. "That building also once was owned by Jews," Ely assured me. "We have the papers for it. Now we've got the building back too."

Not far away, also in the Moslem Quarter, was Torat Cohenim, a small academy established by other Jews, descendants of the priestly tribe. It stood along the ancient north–south route that traced the valley. In anticipation of the Great Redemption they were certain was at hand, they had settled here, in the shadow of the Temple Mount and the golden Dome of the Rock that rested upon it, to review the laws pertaining to the ancient services and sacrifices which once their forebears carried out upon that high and holy spot and which, they believed, they, their heirs, would soon again prepare. "FREE TOURS OF THE TEMPLE MOUNT. ASK FOR ELIEZER UPSTAIRS," read the sign above the door. Their past heritage—of which they had no doubt—gave license to their present action.

I had visited them once, young boys in knit skullcaps. They prayed with eyes shut tightly, straining for a vision of a future. And when they spoke the ancient words of prayer "and to Jerusalem Your city, return in mercy, and rebuild it speedily in our days," they clenched their fists and waved their arms as if to urge on messianic dreams and hold their destiny in their hands.

"I live up here," said Ely, taking us through a low, dark, ominous-looking tunnel which opened into a small courtyard. A few Arab boys at play blocked our passage; he shooed them away, as he did the cats that foraged nearby in the garbage which lined the alley.

"Aren't you afraid to live here?" I asked as I bent through the narrow passage and shuffled over the rocky pavement. The look upon the Arabs' faces had not been one of welcome.

"Why should I be?" he said with the same old innocence I had seen in his face as a boy. "I live in a house once owned by Jews. This is my ancestral home."

"But they've lived here too," I objected.

He paused. "You remember," he continued, "how Nehemiah answered Sanballat the Horonite, Tovia the Ammonite and Geshem the Arab when they objected to his return to Jerusalem?" He quoted from the second chapter of Nehemiah: "Then I answered them, and said to them: The God of Heaven, He will bring us success and we His servants will arise and build, and to you there is no portion, nor right, nor memorial in Jerusalem." He focused his eyes on mine. "That's how it was, and that's how it is. We are back now, whether they like it or not.

"Look here."

He pointed to the side of a nearby doorway where now an empty cleft marked the place in which on sacred parchment the handwritten words "Hear, O Israel, the Lord our God, the Lord is One" had once been placed to mark the site of a Jewish home.

"They chased us away once, took our homes and ripped out the *mezuzot*; but we didn't forget where we lived. We came back. That's what Zionism is all about."

He grew up in Brookline, I was thinking, as did I, but now "we" had returned to this our home, a darkened, arched chamber behind a rise, north and west of the Temple Mount.

"Don't you think the local Arabs believe that they lived here too?" I asked again.

"That's what they *say*, but they took our homes illegally. Besides, if not for the P.L.O. they would sell these places back to us. They don't feel any of the attachments to them that we do. They're just as happy to get the money, and they'd take it if they weren't afraid that the P.L.O. would have them killed for selling.

"But look"—and he pointed to a dilapidated stone house across from us—"we paid over two hundred thousand dollars for this building. And believe me, the owner was happy to get it, to go somewhere else. Look, we're doing a lot better than the Americans did for the Indians."

"Do you really think they all want to leave?"

"*We* want to *come back*. Look, it's not what you think; I get along with my neighbors."

"Do you speak Arabic?"

"No, but they understand me."

He lived with a gun by his bed.

We walked for a bit through the neighborhood; I was in a hurry to get back to the Wall to end the Sabbath there, where light and darkness meet.

"Usually, I take a few hours to show people around here; there's so much to see and learn," Ely said, walking me back.

He knew it all, every alley, every building. The stories dripped from his lips, and the memories echoed in his consciousness.

And I thought of Salim, Samir and the others who had lived their entire lives in this city and whose stories remained enclosed within them, whose memories were a private treasury. And here was Ely, with his gun and heritage, back from Brookline. Home.

"Protect yourself from everyone traveling to Jerusalem" were the words of an old Arab saying.

The conqueror can restore the past, replant the missing trees, rebuild the destroyed houses, retell the once-forgotten stories. But let the conquered go back home and when the tree he planted there is missing or the house destroyed, he can tell no story that will bring it back to life nor share a memory of the past.

CHAPTER
·16·

JERUSALEM
DAY

Pray for the peace of Jerusalem.

PSALM 122

*T*oday is the twenty-eighth of Iyar in the year 5745. On this day, eighteen springs earlier, Jerusalem—a city divided for nineteen years until 1967—was once again reunited. From municipal buildings, lampposts and windows—especially where Jews live—blue-and-white flags, some emblazoned with the Shield of David and others with the golden Lion of Judah, symbol of the City of David, fly once again. Since last night, Israelis have been celebrating and reiterating the ties that now and always have bound Jews to Jerusalem.

Over the radio, a national sing-along and storytelling hour is carried on as folk songs and recollections of Jerusalem are shared by the masses. And on television, program after program weaves itself around the theme of Jerusalem. There are films, news clips from the past, dances and memorials for the fallen. Sharing a memory with the viewers, General Mordecai Gur recalls the moment when, standing atop the Mount of Olives, he awaited the order to take the Old City. He describes how, even before the official command was given, Rabbi Shlomo Goren, then the chief military chaplain, urged him forward toward the ancient walls and domes.

"In everyone, the secular among us as well as the religious, the anticipation and enthusiasm were so high that I was not certain we could hold ourselves back." He speaks in the monotone of a hard-boiled military man. "But at last we received the order for which we had been waiting and we moved forward."

And then, his features and tone softening, he continues: "And if you'll just permit me to add one more recollection . . ." Subtly but unmistakably, his demeanor changes, and from out of the military man emerges another voice, that of a Jew who is on his way to liberate the ancient Jewish capital. "I stopped in at my mother's house to make certain she was all right and to show her that I was."

Then he returned to his post, prepared to retake the city of his fathers. He recounts how he and his troops moved forward with the order and took the holy mountain and the remnant wall of the Temple compound. And then, appearing to forget that he is in front of the television camera, he gazes off into the distance as if he could once again see the events of that day, and recalls the moment when, ignoring the normal army precautions that required all radio communication to be in code, he passed the emotional and historic message to his superiors: "The Temple Mount is in our hands." And out of this Jewish son emerges an expression of Jewish collective memory.

He pauses, this tough soldier who went on to become chief of the general staff, a smile gradually spreading across his features, and then with what seems almost a sense of wonder, turns toward the interviewer and adds: "Imagine, after two thousand years, we Jews were able to say, 'The Temple Mount is in our hands.'"

In Nachla'ot, a working-class neighborhood not far from the city center, the sixth-grade class in the Uziel religious public school for boys has put together a play to commemorate Jerusalem Day. In the back courtyard, where everyone has assembled for the celebration, seven boys—many of whose parents or grandparents came from Morocco, Iraq, Yemen, Poland, Russia, Germany, Hungary and some more recently from South Africa, Great Britain and the United States—step forward to declaim and recite legends describing the timeless beauty of Jerusalem. Their performance ended, they walk silently off the stage.

Seven more boys—among them my oldest son, Adam—now step forward to repeat a modern *midrash*. In it the events of eighteen years ago, like those of the Exodus from Egypt and all the subsequent turning points in Jewish history, are represented as part of a divinely ordained plan revealed in an imagined dialogue in a heavenly court. *The Six Days and the Seven Gates* was written by Yitzhak Navon, the former President and current Minister of Education and Culture:

> Seven gates there were in the walls of Jerusalem, and none of them knew through which one the liberators of the Old City would enter. And thus, each gate would leap up and dance before the others and say: "Enter through me, for I am more worthy than the rest!"
>
> The Holy One, blesssed be He, sat upon His throne on high, the ministering angels at His right and His left. So He said to them: "Which gate is worthy of having the redemption come through it? For just as there cannot be two angels to carry out a single mission, so there cannot be two gates to bring about one salvation." But none of the angels had an answer.
>
> At last, the angel Michael stood and suggested: "Master of the Universe! All are pleasant and worthy. Therefore, summon each and let it make its case before You, and then You will judge among them."

So it was, each gate making a bid to be the one through which the redemption of Jerusalem would come. And as each presented its case before the heavenly court, and angels debated the merits of one's case over another's, while below on earth the war over the city raged, people died and the time was mercilessly passing.

At last, the voice of Jacob's beloved wife Rachel, who lay buried on the road between Jerusalem and Bethlehem and who for generations had awaited the end of the exile and the return of her children to this their promised land, cried out in agony: "Master of the Universe, how long will You lead my sons to slaughter? Did You not once say to me: 'Hold back your voice from crying and the tears from your eyes and your sons will return to their borders'? Were You then speaking of living or dead sons?"

Said the Holy One, blessed be He: "Rachel, my daughter, that which I promised you I shall fulfill. But see, only one gate is left to make its case. We shall listen to it and make a judgment.''

And so with only the Lions Gate left to speak, God turned to it. But it said nothing until at last in a fiery fury the Almighty demanded it make its case.

''Master of the Universe,'' began the gate, ''with each passing moment I can see from here the soldiers upon the eastern hills and upon Mount Scopus approach the walls; they fall and die. Let them therefore come from any gate at all, but let them enter *now*, so that not a single one more of them may fall!''

And because it thus mercifully humbled itself, the Lions Gate was selected, and through it the walls were breached and the Temple Mount and the holy Western Wall recaptured.

I heard the words of this story from my son, and now I am no longer sure which words are my son's and which those of the *midrash*, so completely did each assimilate the other. And I am not certain whether this boy born in Pennsylvania and raised in New York described the events as they happened in 1967 or as they were recounted in 1985, for the memory and the facts of history have become blended into a single consciousness.

''All this happened in the year 5727,'' he concludes. ''And when the fighting had ended, the Jews reached the Kotel, kissed it, and they danced around singing, 'The Kotel is in our hands, the Kotel is freed!' ''

A *shofar* was blown, and everyone present recited the words of the time-honored prayer ''*U't'ka be-shofar godol l'chayrutanu* [May the great ram's horn be blown heralding our liberation].''

''Jerusalem was united and free.''

The two-o'clock news today begins with the following item:

''We have received a message from the Soviet Union from the Prisoners of Zion there:

'' 'On this great day we here recall the ancient words of the psalm: If I forget thee, O Jerusalem, may my right hand forget its cunning.

'' 'And we remember as well the words of the time-honored prayer which we also recite today: Next year in Jerusalem.'

''They who languish in the Soviet Union will yet join us here.''

In Jerusalem, as throughout the country, kindergartens participate in the delicate task of enculturation and socialization. Housed separately from all other schools, the *gan*, as the kindergarten is called, acts as one of the bridges over which children pass on their first steps out of the world of the family on the way to "becoming an Israeli." The *gannenet*, the teacher there, is thus a cultural gatekeeper, ushering her charges on toward peoplehood. Perhaps even more than the parents, she (there are no men who play this surrogate-Jewish-mother role) shapes the earliest stirrings of collective consciousness. As part of her work, she often recounts the founding myths and the ancient narratives of national origins. Particularly in the religious kindergartens but also in the secular ones in this Jewish state, the holidays are festivals of profound importance and great moment, times when the *gannenet* must reach beyond herself and demonstrate that she deserves the public trust.

To be a *gannenet* requires the right balance between parenting and teaching. She must be nurturant but instructive, not quite a parent yet still emotionally close. Making formal demands, she does so in an informal atmosphere of toys and games, songs and play. Because the *gan* thus stands somewhere between home and school and between childhood and society, parents often work in tandem with the *gannenet* to prepare their offspring for their entrance into the civilization and culture.

Not surprisingly, many Israelis hold especially warm feelings for these women, and the bonds established between children and their *gannenet* last long after ties to other teachers have been dissolved by time and drowned in the river of oblivion. It is by no means unusual to find that after thirty or more years, the *gannenet* clearly recalls each of her pupils as they do her.

Today, the children in Gan Devorah and their parents have been invited to a special commemoration of Jerusalem Day. As the children enter the old Arab house in Talbieh that serves as their kindergarten, each one is pinned with the symbol of the city, a golden Lion of Judah. And then, all dressed in white and blue, they sit down, a living and breathing Israeli flag, in the center of the room. Around them, pressed into tiny chairs and benches, the parents have come along to tell stories and join in the singing of songs:

> To you, Jerusalem,
> between the city walls.
> For you, Jerusalem,
> a new light will shine
> in our hearts.
> In our hearts
> but one song sounds:

For you, Jerusalem,
'tween the Jordan and the Sea.

Although the children are just now learning the traditional folk songs, many of their parents know them well from their own school days, and as the singing proceeds, the deep voices join the high ones. Seeing and hearing their parents, listening to the teacher, the young children sing with greater enthusiasm. One generation's singing gives voice to the other. And thus, *shirah b'tzibbur*, choral singing, that Israeli national pastime and expression of belonging, passes into the life experience of yet another generation:

My Land of Israel,
beautiful and blossoming.
Who has planted and who has built it?
All of us together.
I have built a house,
And I have planted a tree,
And I have paved a road.
And so we have a land, a house, a tree and a road
In the Land of Israel.

The song, one of the first learned in *gan*, celebrates possession of the land. By activity—building, planting and paving—the settlers have made the land their own. On such a day of unification and liberation, when ties to place are to be celebrated, this is a lesson to be repeated. To acquire and own a land, one must labor to transform it. The silent lesson is that just being there is not enough—Arabs take notice.

Again and again, the children add verses to the song. They have gathered grains, planted vineyards, built cities, painted signs, dug holes—the possibilities are endless. And each one has contributed to the possession of the Land of Israel. "The Temple shall be rebuilt!" the children and their parents sing at last. Retaken Jerusalem will be rebuilt and then forever their own.

To augment the messages in the songs, the *gannenet* has asked some of the parents to tell the children about the Jerusalem they remember. For like the songs and the celebrations, memories too must be passed from generation to generation. These memories cannot be acquired by the solitary individual. They emerge only gradually in the company of others, in the effervescence of collective celebrations like this one. With each transmission, the memories seem to become more powerful.

And thus are formed attachments: Aviad's father speaks first. Recalling Jerusalem during the War of Independence, he describes the days of 1948 when he, about the same age as they are now, experienced the cutoff of food and water during the Arab siege of the city. "For three months," he tells them, "we drew water from our cisterns, taking care not to waste a single drop, for we knew there was no lake, no river, no other water for us to drink or use."

In quiet fascination, the children listen to a story that perhaps some of them hear now for the first time but as Jerusalemites they will hear again and again over the years.

People met at the cisterns in the courtyard, he tells them, and shared water, making certain they wasted not a drop.

"What is a cistern?" one of the little boys asks.

"Now that we have a pipe that brings us water straight from the Kinneret in the Galilee, we don't use them anymore," Aviad's father answers. "But once, when we depended on our own sources of water, we collected rainwater during the winter inside deep pits, hollowed out beneath the ground. If you go to some of the old neighborhoods—Me'ah She'arim or Nachla'ot, for example—in the center of the courtyards you will see the openings, which are now closed with cement."

"How did the water get inside?"

"It flowed off the roofs into the gutters and from there into pipes that emptied into the cisterns."

"Wasn't it dirty?"

"We cleaned the cisterns. But you're right—it was not nearly as sweet and clean as our water today. Still, we saved it because we knew that without it, we could not live.

"And do you know what we did? For showers, we sat in a tub and someone—usually our mother or father—poured a pail of water over our heads. And then we reused the water for washing floors or clothes.

"And when we took our showers, we used just enough water to get wet. And then we soaped ourselves. You know, today, I, like other Jerusalemites who lived through those days and learned even before how important it was to save water, still shower this way."

A few of the parents smile knowingly. Whether they remember the actual times of scarce water or only the story of them does not really matter; as Jerusalemites, they count the recollections their own as surely as if they had lived through them. Through these collected memories they have, after all, bound themselves to the affective community and to its past. Only thus have they the privilege of belonging to the present. Now their children must do the same.

The *gannenet* begins the singing again:

> And Uziyahu the King built towers in Jerusalem.
> And he fortified them.
> He built towers
> And hollowed out many cisterns.

The song is simple, the tune catchy. With each repetition it is sung an octave higher and faster, until at last everyone is screaming, nearly at the top of his lungs: "many cisterns, many cisterns, many cisterns!"

And then, more softly:

> And bring us to Zion, Your city, in joy,
> And to Jerusalem, Your Holy Temple,
> In everlasting happiness.

From the opposite side of the room, Roi's father now takes his turn to speak. Among the soldiers who took the Old City in 1967, he describes the experience of seeing the Kotel for the first time after nineteen years.

"When I was a little boy, I had gone to the Wall with my grandfather. In those days it had been surrounded by a tiny space, squeezed in among dirty buildings. Because the city was then ruled by the British, we needed special permission to go there and pray. They did not even allow us to put down chairs, so we sat on the ground and leaned against the Wall. And once the British took away a holy ark we had put there because the Arabs complained to them that it was too big. They would not even allow us to blow the *shofar* there on *Yom Kippur*. Then, when the British left, the Arabs took the Old City, and though they promised to let us back to pray at the Kotel, they never did."

A lawyer and military judge, Roi's father seems at first a bit ill at ease speaking to the kindergartners, not quite knowing how to modulate his voice so that he does not sound as if he were in a courtroom. But as he speaks and watches the thirty pairs of eyes following his every word, he seems to visibly relax and even begins to talk in the same singsong tones that the *gannenet* uses and that after her Aviad's father had echoed.

"But when we did come back at last, everything was different! We threw ourselves against the Wall and kissed it as we would kiss a member of our family whom we had not seen for a long time. That was how *I* felt. For the first time since the destruction of the Holy Temple two thousand years before, the Kotel was ours. *Ours!* We had come back. From now on *we* would keep the order. We cleaned the place and fixed it up. We brought chairs and holy arks—as large and as many as we wanted—and made room for all the Jews to come and pray there. We cleaned away the dirt, paved a square and planted a tree. And we allowed everyone else to pray at his own holy place in peace. At last, we liberated the city!"

"To the point," the *gannenet* says, a broad smile playing across her face. And she starts the children singing again, a slow and sweet melody this time. The words are the psalmist's, the sentiments now becoming their own:

> One thing have I asked of the Lord,
> That shall I seek.
> May I dwell in the house of the Lord
> All the days of my life,
> Beholding the graciousness of God,
> And visiting His Temple.

Throughout the city, Jews are on tour. This too is a way to celebrate reunification, as Miz'rachi tried to show Salim Khoury. On a rampart near the Jaffa Gate, a youth leader directs the attention of his B'nai Akiva group to the signs which remain of the physical borders that once divided the city.

"See here"—he points to a building nearby—"you can still see how the wall is white where the barriers were up against it." The group's members strain to see the wall they have passed countless times without noticing.

"And there"—he points to the pulverized Tannous Brothers building—"you can see where the bullet holes from the Jordanian guns struck."

The youngsters who listen to him are all under eighteen. For them, a divided Jerusalem is at best a part of collective memory and not personal reminiscence. But now, as they look at where the barricades were and the old battle lines, the acquired memories are passed on.

Around the corner, another group—this one under the auspices of the Society for the Protection of Nature—examines all that is left of a Jewish effort to breach the walls in 1948. The broken stones in the thick Turkish walls stand as a silent reminder of the impotence of the Jewish desire to reenter the city for nineteen years.

"We wanted to get in then, but we could not," the guide explains. "The wall was just too thick, our explosives too weak, our forces too thin."

"But now, with the help of God, we have gotten in," says one of the men on the tour.

And as if to affirm the truth of the observation, the guide answers: "Come, let us continue on the inside, where I will show you the heritage of our fathers." To review the past and bear witness to the present, they walk through the gate. No one appears to pay any attention to the Arabs standing at the doorways of their shops. This is the Jews' Jerusalem Day.

And what of al-Quds? How does Jerusalem Day pass among those who remain of the vanquished? In vain does one look for flags. Here, the day is a Sunday like any other. Inside his infirmary on the Via Dolorosa, Dr. Khatib sees a few of his patients, some of whom he will send on across the street to the hospital inside the former Austrian Hospice. In the souks, women shop for meat, vegetables, spices and coffee. Along el-Wad Street, on their way home from school, small groups of Moslem children in their striped school uniforms, their book bags on their backs, meander among the shoppers in the narrow alleys. In the Omariya School, housed on the grounds and atop the remains of the ancient Antonia Fortress that Herod built to overlook the Temple Mount, the caretaker is hosing down the worn stones of the courtyard. From its windows one can see the wide-open spaces of the Temple Mount. Along the rich brown soil and among the neat rows of olive trees surrounded by cypress, two old Arabs, garbed in long jallabiyehs and leaning upon walking sticks, shuffle toward the south, in the direction of the silver-domed al-Aqsa mosque. Coming in the opposite direction and less interested in such matters of the spirit, four little boys wildly chase one another under the arched colonnade along the western edge of the mountain.

Here, in this neighborhood, is all that remains of onetime Moslem rule. The Waqf, the Moslem religious authority, once unrestricted in its control, still determines who may or may not enter the area of the mosque and some of the other holy shrines of Islam, but that is all. In the al-Takkiye building, the seat in the 1870s of the city and district government, all is quiet now. Transformed into a school, this is no longer a place where decisions are made. No flags fly here. No parents and children gather in celebration.

Atop the Kotel and overlooking the golden Dome of the Rock, the Makhkameh, once the seat of the Shari'a court, where Moslem law was enforced and destinies were altered, is now a lookout post under the control of the border patrol. Where once the *qadi* ruled the city with an iron Islamic authority that strictly dominated not only the Moslems but all others—*dhimmi,* they were called and, in their inferior status, forbidden by Islamic law to wear the holy color green—green-uniformed Israeli soldiers now sip coffee or nap during their off-duty hours.

The inhabitants of al-Quds may be powerless to turn back the course of history that has brought them to their current situation, but they have nevertheless not accepted the changes without struggle. Although terror attacks have been kept to a minimum, they still occur. Last night, a bomb exploded at a bus stop outside Sha'arey Zedek Hospital, and two more such devices were discovered before going off. And of late, stabbings have become more frequent.

Resistance to the celebration of Jerusalem Day shows itself in less dramatic and destructive but no less unmistakable ways. On the corners of buildings where, after 1967, Hebrew versions of the street signs were added by the Israelis, there are instead signs of lingering hostility. The ceramic tiles on which the street names were hand-painted in Hebrew are by now mostly broken. The locals have smashed them away, leaving only pieces of orange clay atop Arabic and English letters. And what the Jews have named Sha'ar Ha-Arayot (Lions Gate) Street remains for the locals al-Mujahedeen (Those Who Have Fallen in an Islamic Holy War) Road.

Passing two boys throwing a rubber ball against the stones which are all that is left of a fifteenth-century Mameluke gate, I turned toward the Suq el-Nakhas, the copper market, not far from the Church of the Holy Sepulcher. Near the corner two young dark-haired, brown-cassocked Franciscan friars stood talking with a black-frocked Greek Orthodox monk. Having completed their respective morning services, they had each left behind the church and its religious rivalries and were sharing instead a spot of shade and a few warm words.

Around the corner was the Muristan. Built at the end of the last century as a bazaar by the Greek monk Aftimus, after whom it was now named, it had—some claimed—been the site of the forum in the days of the Romans. Later, during the Byzantine and Crusader periods, it became a place filled with hospices and hospitals (*muristan* in Persian) for pilgrims. Following a disastrous earthquake in the fifteenth century, it had disintegrated into a ruin. And in the days when all this was part of Greater Syria, it was dominated by a slaughterhouse and served as a dump for animal carcasses until the late 1860s. Then, during the late nineteenth century when European powers were each trying to outdo the others in staking claims in the Holy City by building here, the Germans and the Greeks divided the space, the former building the Protestant Church of the Redeemer and the latter a market designed by the monk Aftimus.

Yasser Barakat, a man who identified himself as a Palestinian, sat here in his antiquities shop. Whenever I visited with him, here or in his home in Shuafat, one of the northern suburbs of Jerusalem, he was always a perfect host. Upon my entering, he stood, smiled broadly, shook my hand and asked, "What will you have to drink, coffee or tea?" and then, when the boy from the tea shop next door brought our drinks on a brass tray, we sat together sipping sweet mint tea and talked.

As old as the State of Israel, Barakat came from a family whose origins were in Hebron, where Abraham, father of us both, lies buried.

"Four hundred years we have been in Jerusalem," he explained to me once, and then added with laughter, "and they still call us a Hebron family." In this part of the world, it takes a long time to establish connections to a place, and longer still to break them. To the Arabs, this meant the Israelis still did not belong. To the Jews, it meant they had never left.

The years since 1948 had not been bad ones for the Barakat family. Although until 1967 they were cut off from some of their land in the Mamilla neighborhood just outside the Jaffa Gate, much of their property was on the eastern, Jordanian side. In addition to the shop, which was leased from the Greek Orthodox Patriarchate, the Barakats owned the Ritz Hotel, land surrounding the al-Quds Theater, and several apartment buildings—to say nothing of their holdings in Jordan, Dubai and elsewhere in the Arab world. None of this had been confiscated after 1967.

At the time of the Six-Day War, Yasser had been away from home, studying in Morocco. Afterward, unable to stay in Morocco and not yet allowed to come back to Jerusalem, which was now under Israeli rule, he went to live with his sister in Illinois, eventually taking a degree in computers from Roosevelt University in Chicago. Finally, after a variety of applications and because there was nothing in his past to indicate that he would be a security risk in Israel, he was permitted to be reunited with his family and returned to Jerusalem in the early 1970s. Since then he had been teaching mathematics at St. George's College in the morning and in the afternoon worked in what had once been his father's but was now his own antiquities shop.

The shop specialized in things from Persia: hammered brass and copper trays and pots, carpets, antique samovars and ivory miniatures. Since the rise of the Ayatollah Khomeini and the decrease of exports from Iran, these items had become scarcer and therefore had grown in value.

"I need only one or two good sales a month to cover all my costs," he explained, and sipped his tea. Selling a carpet from Qom more than made up for days of fruitless waiting. Like his father before him, Yasser Barakat was a patient man.

With all the creature comforts his income allowed, Barakat was not happy with the life he led. "I do not feel as if I am in my own homeland," he explained. "Maybe one day they will come and say, 'It's finished. You must leave this country,' And then what can I say, what can I do? Since 1967, I have seen so many Arabs sent out from here."

How did he feel about Jerusalem Day? I wondered. "We have nothing from it. Look—do you see any flags here? The ones we want to hang we cannot, and those we can hang we would rather not. For us, there is nothing to celebrate."

"You know the Jews feel close to Jerusalem," I began, and then paused, wondering if he would concede me at least this point, even if only in accordance with the norms of friendly conversation, but he just stared straight at me, waiting for me to continue. So I did. "Everywhere and all the time, they tour it. Not just outsiders, but even those who have lived their entire lives here visit as much of the city as they can. They come to the parts of town they were separated from after 1948 and visit those. They go to historic sites, religious ones—anywhere and everywhere. And it seems to me that that is how they express, to others and to themselves, their attachment to all that is Jerusalem. And today, on this anniversary of the reunification of Jerusalem, people seem to be doing this more than ever." I took a sip of the sweet tea. He said nothing.

"If you and your people feel attachments that are equally powerful, why don't you express them too? Why do I never see Arabs touring, surveying their heritage, visiting their former homes in the west as Jews have visited theirs in the east?"

Barakat lifted his deep black eyebrows, looked up toward the ceiling and then out the wide opening of his shop. *"Aleikum salaam!"* he called to someone outside who had passed him a greeting. It seemed to me as if he had not taken my inquiry very seriously. I wondered if he would even bother answering. And then he turned to me and said, "Because they don't have the time, maybe." He paused. "Or maybe you're right," he said, getting to the implication he read into my question: "they don't have the same feeling for Jerusalem."

Months earlier, as we sat talking, Barakat had told me how once a Jew came into his shop and, after cursorily looking about for a while, blurted out that by all rights all the Arabs should be moved to Jordan. Recalling the episode for me, Barakat had said, "So I told him he was right, and maybe it would happen. Why should I try to convince someone who already has his mind made up?"

Hearing him tell me now that *I* was right, I couldn't help wondering if I were being treated with the same sort of answer. Was he telling me what he thought I wanted to hear? Maybe he, like Samir, the taxi driver, was not going to share his memories with me. Why should he?

I tried again.

"If you have visitors from out of town, what do you show them?"

"I bring them to my home."

"And if they ask you to show them the city, where would you go?"

"Oh, I would take them to the Inter-Continental [Hotel, on the top of the Mount of Olives] to show them the view of Jerusalem, then try to bring them to the Old City, to the Holy Sepulcher, the Dome of the Rock, the Wailing Wall, the Garden of Gethsemane. Where else could I want to take them? Maybe I take them through to Hadassah on Mount Scopus, show them now where we go to the new hospital. And I guess that would be it."

"You know," I began, "the tour you took covers only the eastern side of the city, what the Jordanians held. Starting with the Inter-Continental [I didn't mention that it was the most glamorous of the Arab-managed hotels in town] right up to Hadassah, you never went closer to the Israelis than the Wall. You never came to the other side of the city." I did not add that by calling it the "Wailing Wall" he was recalling the name that Jews used before 1967. Since then, the tears and wailing had ceased and now Israelis insisted on calling it either the Western Wall or simply the Kotel.

"I suppose that is correct." He smiled enigmatically.

"How often *do* you come to the western side of the city?"

"Very little," he replied, "because really I am not feeling that I belong there. It is very difficult. What it was before, it is still the same. Same feeling, same separations. Only the traffic has been changed, nothing else. Everything is still the same."

"But aren't you interested in contacts with us, in ending the separation?"

In the background the voice of the muezzin calling the faithful to prayer came over loudspeakers nearby. My host was not a praying man. Firmly attached to the modern world, he sat quietly in his chair, while around him other shopkeepers drew their shutters and hurried off to the mosque.

"Sure," he answered. "We should have mixed education, even intermarriage—why not? We have to teach your child and my child how to love each other. No separation. Why not? But are you really ready for that?"

He knew that that kind of integration struck directly at the sense of peoplehood that Israel was meant to protect. In time that sort of assimilation would mean the end for the Jews, since they were but a demographic drop in the surrounding sea of Arabs. The Jews had not struggled to create a state in order to lose it either through hatred and war or through love and assimilation. Solicitous of my obvious discomfort, he changed the subject.

"Look, I tell you," he said, leaning toward me, "there's another reason I don't come to your side." It was *my* side. However friendly we might be, the divisions remained. "If I am walking over there and a bomb or something happens in that area, I feel completely powerless because I know they will stop me. How many times have I come from Ramallah and they stop me, and they check my trunk and my car, ask questions and so on? But I live here, same as you, so why I should have to suffer all this humiliation?"

"Still, you choose to live here."

"Yes, of course. Since I am born here, I came back. Even when I was away, I always knew I was coming back here. But I tell you, many of the young people are leaving. They belong to this area, but they do not have the same economic possibilities here, so they go to other places."

"Was there ever a time when it was good? Did your father ever tell you about such a time?"

"Always he felt that we have a problem."

"Was the problem the Jews?"

"No, it was the English first, then the Zionists, even the Jordanians. I tell you even the Jordanians, when they have been good to Palestinians, have not allowed us to be who we are. But I tell you, I never asked my father these kinds of questions. There are some questions that need not be asked."

"Do you have a favorite place in Jerusalem?" I asked.

For a long time, he said nothing. I tried to understand his silence, wondering whether it was the silence of careful calculation or the silence that comes from being suddenly confronted with the unknown. I could not tell. There was something inscrutable about him. His uncertain English with its sometimes convoluted syntax prevented me from always penetrating beyond the surface of his expression, and his habit of sometimes looking off into space as he spoke kept me from looking through his eyes into the character I imagined must be behind them. At last, he replied:

"My home, my children, my wife."

Yasser Barakat was a smart man, careful with his words, always attuned to what his surroundings required. Not quite certain what I was after, he tried to answer all my questions without saying anything that would harm the cordial relations we had built up.

To tell me that his favorite place was his home, his children, his wife or to say that he took his visitors first to see his home was to deflect tension. This was a way of life and attachment that transcended place and politics. He and I—both of us together and each of us alone—could share this favorite place in Jerusalem. Union and autonomy. A brilliant answer.

Or, perhaps, he was not being careful after all. Maybe the collective self-consciousness and cultural devotion to history that would have made me, the Jew, tell him about my attachments to Batei Machse Square, to the prophecies of Zechariah written on the Jewish Quarter wall and the dreams of Herzl, to the Kotel and to its ancient stones were simply missing in his life. Maybe I, whose people had for generations articulated attachments to Jerusalem and the land around it, was asking questions for which answers had not yet evolved among my Palestinian cousins, whose nationalist aspirations were in the earliest stages of their existence. The fact that we shared the same land did not necessarily mean we shared the same level of consciousness and sense of history.

Perhaps the reason was closer to something another Arab, a lecturer at the Hebrew University, had told me when I asked him why his people did not tour this city to which they claimed such a deep attachment, as we the Jews did.

"Look," he said, a bit impatient with my question, "it's a matter of culture. You Jews are forever searching for your roots, trying to demonstrate that you belong here. You need to make everything visible. But we Arabs know it. We have nothing to prove, either to ourselves or to you. We don't need to tour what we feel and experience in our blood."

"During all the years that Jerusalem was divided, it could not guarantee peace," said the Prime Minister at a Jerusalem Day ceremony honoring the memory of those who fell during the battle for the city. "But since it has been reunited, there has been peace here."

In recent months, the municipality has erected large maps of the city throughout the downtown area and in the neighborhoods of some of the hotels. At the top is a verse from Psalm 122: "Pray for the peace of Jerusalem."

CHAPTER
·17·

THE BARRIER
OF
ESTRANGEMENT

*We are what we are, and live in a given
situation which has the characteristics—
physical, psychological, social, etc.—that it
has; what we think, feel, do, is conditioned by
it. . . . A world too different is (empirically)
not conceivable at all: some minds are more
imaginative than others, but all stop
somewhere.*

ISAIAH BERLIN,
The Hedgehog and the Fox

Yasser Barakat and I spent many more hours together, sitting on the rattan stools in his shop, sipping sweet tea and talking. Eventually he sold me one of his bronze pots; and finally I bought one of those carpets from Qom, a beautiful Paradise scene in silk. Barakat, as I have already explained, was a patient man. Yet in spite of our continued contact, the line dividing us that we uncovered on Jerusalem Day never really disappeared, and our relationship remained in a kind of frozen asymmetry. Although I —a Jew, like Miz'rachi—might be interested in al-Quds, no matter how much time he spent with me, Barakat (and for that matter, Salim Khoury too) was not really curious about the Jerusalem to which I and others like me remained attached. His attention was on the conditions of his life, his future and that of his family and people. And that concern seemed to allow no room for comprehending mine.

To be sure, I was an anomaly; most local Jews were not very much interested in learning about the Arabs either. The days when a President of Israel would dress up in a kaffiyeh and jallabiyeh to meet with Arab dignitaries—as had Chaim Weitzman—were long past. Few Jewish Israelis spoke Arabic, although it was taught in the schools, and fewer still had any Arab friends. And most Jewish Jerusalemites did not really know their way around al-Quds. There existed what social geographer Michael Romann, in his study ''The Inter-Relationship between the Jewish and Arab Sectors in Jerusalem,'' called ''the barrier of consciousness'' and ''the barrier of estrangement'' dividing the two populations of Jerusalem. One Jerusalem could not conceive of the other, and neither group was really aware, nor cared to be, of what went on in the other.

I knew Romann and talked with him often about these barriers. Although he, like me, was interested in exploring the other side of the city and breaking through the residual barriers, he remained pessimistic about the possibilities. Still, he was forever willing to try. And every so often, he would at my request lead me on a tour through the Arab neighborhoods, in hopes that we might at last find a clear passage from our side to theirs. One of those walks in particular—on the first Friday of Ramadan—aroused in me the same feeling of pessimism. It was the last of these tours we would take together.

The choice of the first Friday of Ramadan was not arbitrary. A time of atonement, prayer and daily fasting, Ramadan, the ninth lunar month, is perhaps the most important season of the Moslem year. According to tradition, on the twenty-seventh of the month, the *Laylat al-Qadr,* or Night of the Decree, the holy Koran was sent down by Allah ''as a guide for the people.'' To this day, the religious believe that the annual commemoration of such a moment must be awaited with the greatest intensity of feeling and spiritual preparation. And thus, from the time the new moon of Ramadan is sighted until the first sighting of the next new moon, Id al-Fitr, Islamic law demands that between dawn and dusk the faithful abstain from food, drink, smoking and sexual pleasures.

Normally, Moslems pray five times daily: before sunrise, slightly after noon, late in the afternoon, just after sunset and at bedtime. Although a believer may pray alone, among Moslems congregational prayer is preferred. For them, as indeed for the Jews who also favor group prayer, there is something about the proximity of other worshipers that intensifies and vitalizes the required stirrings of spirit. And when at each service—which entails two to four prostrations, or *rak'ah,* in the direction of Mecca—the crowds of worshipers, with each change of position, chant "*Allah akhbar* [God is great]," a person praying or even lying silently among them cannot help becoming moved and elevated.

On Friday, the holiest day of the week, all this becomes even more pronounced as huge crowds of the faithful assemble at the *jami,* the main mosque of the city. In Jerusalem, al-Aqsa, the silver dome atop what the Moslems call the Kharam-e-Sharif, is that holiest of places. Here many Moslems believe their prophet Mohammed, seated upon his miraculous horse el-Burak, arrived after his journey from Mecca. Here they believe he prayed with the angel Gabriel to all the prophets of old—Israelite and Christian—and, ascending from the rock now covered by a golden dome, he passed through the seven heavens, finally returning to the Holy City of Medina.

On Friday in the *jami,* instead of the simple noon prayers, additional congregational recitations of the Koran are offered, and the imam gives a *khutbah,* or sermon, during which he often explores politics (an extension of the religious domain) and other matters of the day—all of which are touched by the faith—through elaboration of one of the sacred text's verses. Standing in front of and above the mass of the faithful, he is often moved to deliver sermons that stir and arouse the passions of the entire assembly. And thus amid the bowing, chanting and exhortations, the fire of Islam is rekindled and stoked.

On Friday afternoons during Ramadan, religious and collective fervor reach their highest pitch. During this holiest of seasons, even those Moslems who throughout the year have been lax in their attendance at the mosque see to it that they come. And at night, before retiring and after completing the meal that makes possible the daytime fast, the faithful chant lengthy congregational prayers, or *tarawith,* with added zeal.

In al-Quds, the first *qibla,* or destination, toward which Moslems directed their devotions before they began facing Mecca, the days and nights of Ramadan can be keenly felt. During the daytime, a kind of lethargy settles over the Arab neighborhoods of the city. As the day drops slowly toward dusk, the pace of activity slows down to match the waning stamina of those fasting. Many of the shops in the souks draw their shutters, and the normally full center of the

East Jerusalem downtown on Salach-e-din Street thins visibly. The thick flow of people in both directions through the Damascus Gate slows to a trickle. Fewer day workers are to be found sitting along the wall on Nablus Road, and those who do heavy labor often walk about with a glazed look and parched lips. Even the normally teeming coffeehouses and well-attended card clubs are mostly closed and deserted. Nothing is quite the same as during the rest of the year. Perhaps, I thought, in this liminal period I might find my way past all the barriers into the al-Quds I had not yet fully discovered.

Because the Moslem lunar calendar has no provision for leap years, Ramadan falls at different times during the solar year, moving gradually backward from summer to winter. This year it arrived near the end of May, the time of the *khamsin* winds which bring the dry heat up from the desert. These were the days when daylight lasted longest, and fasting became most difficult. Huddling in the shade, often dressed in thin white shirts that hung down to their ankles and wearing a *ta'ir*, a crocheted white skullcap, atop their heads, the Arabs would wait patiently for night and the end of the fast to come. Perhaps among the waiting, I would find someone to talk with me and share some of his Jerusalem attachments.

As usual, I walked first to the Damascus Gate area. Here I could see those who filled the late daylight hours shopping, as if extended preparations for their evening meal could somehow shorten their wait for it. For the vegetable markets along the Bab e-Silsila, Ramadan can be the best time to offer the most colorful and succulent foods for sale ; nothing else so satisfies the hunger of those who fast as the promise of the meal to come.

All sorts of foods filled the alleys of the Old City. There were round farina cakes topped with roasted almonds, sesame cookies, glazed candies and sweets that when stacked looked like flying saucers from some exotic sugar-encrusted planet, toasted eggs, half a dozen varieties of pita, grape leaves, vegetables of all varieties, olives, spices and newly picked fruits. Against one wall two fellahin sat on the ground surrounded by boxes containing rabbits and chicks which they sold by the kilo. Every so often a rabbit tried to escape, and one of the women or a little boy—from among the six or seven who stood nearby—chased after it and grabbed it back by the ears or the nape of its neck.

When evening falls, many of the closed coffeehouses reopen, and life returns to the body of Moslems filling the streets. Lines of white and colored electric lights festoon the steps in front of the Damascus Gate, and temporary kiosks inside canvas huts fill the open field across the street. Awaiting the muezzin's call to the *tarawith*, many men sit inside sipping *tamar hindi,* sweet minted tea, or gritty Turkish coffee. Others do last-minute shopping for watermelons, which at this time of year have begun to be piled in little stalls from which they will be sold until early autumn.

And when Jewish and Christian Jerusalem have begun to shutter up for the night, the voice of the muezzin fills the air calling believers to enter the mosques and recite their prayers. Then, after once again professing their faith that "There is no God but Allah, and Mohammed is His prophet," and announcing that "Allah is great," the religious Moslems of al-Quds break their fast. And in the morning, just before the first rays of sunrise, they will get up, eat a last meal, pray and begin the entire cycle once again.

For a person who is not a Moslem, there is little more than such an external experience of Ramadan. Islam—or at least as it is practiced in this religiously sensitive city—allows for no visitors in the mosque during prayers. Even a visit in the evening to the coffee-house or kiosk, although technically possible, only reinforces the outsider's sense of estrangement, as I discovered upon once wandering into a café.

I had entered, sat down next to some men playing cards and ordered a coffee. I watched the card game. A few kibbitzers hovered around the players. As for the players themselves, there was an intensity about their attention to their hands which was broken only when a waiter walked over and threw four or five candy bars into the middle of the table. One of the players took one and put it in his pocket, and another threw the bars off to the side. The others laughed, but no one took his eyes off his cards.

And then I looked at the other tables and discovered piercing and hostile looks from every corner of the room. Finally, hearing someone murmur the words "Sabra" and "Shatilla," I took a last quick sip of my coffee and left.

Maybe I was walking in at the wrong time or going to the wrong places. Maybe I sat in the wrong seat, or maybe I should not have worn my *kippah.* But whatever the reason, I felt somehow certain that nothing I could have done would have made me feel more at home in this place or others like it. Still, I wanted to try again, and so I turned to Michael Romann.

"Take me on a walk," I asked.

Romann suggested that we go watch the worshipers returning from their noontime prayers at al-Aqsa. Perhaps proximity would at least give us a share in the experience. "You'll see," he said: "it's very exciting, like nothing you've seen before."

Walking through Herod's Gate, we came down the narrow alleys that led to al-Mujahedeen Road and brought us to a corner near the Omariyah School. From this place, Romann told me as we pressed ourselves unobtrusively close to the wall, we would get our closest look at the worshipers returning from the *jami*. My guide promised that the exodus would begin momentarily.

Our arrival was timed perfectly; moments after we arrived, the narrow street leading from the Kharam-e-Sharif began to flow with people. Men dressed in white jallabiyehs, many of them wearing brown or black cloaks trimmed in gold, marched toward us. They were followed by young children, many of them also dressed in white gowns and white skullcaps. Their polished dark features set against the pure white of their garments was hauntingly striking. Women too, many of them invisible to eyes such as mine throughout the week, their heads swathed in black kerchiefs and some—mostly the fellahin—with tattooed faces, walked in the parade. I saw old men, some lame and some simply bent by the years, leaning on sticks with handles and tips worn away by time beyond reckoning. There was something at once simple and regal about the endless procession. City people dressed in their finery walked next to poor villagers, and the young ran along behind the old, whose appearance exuded an enduring majesty.

Each of us who looks upon the strange and exotic can react in one of two ways. We may stand transfixed by the dissimilarity of what we witness, struck by its incomparability to anything we know or have experienced. Here is something too different to be understood. Mixed with such gazing is a quiet but abiding sense of estrangement. Or, if the distance is disturbing and intolerable and yet we remain to watch, we may look upon the foreign and try to discover in it outlines of the familiar, associating ourselves with what we know and sometimes seeing not what is but what we wish or expect should be there. Watching the hordes of worshipers passing by me, some close enough to brush my shoulders, I tried somehow to steer a course between these two perspectives: to look upon the novel without losing sight of its singularity while still discovering in the line of humanity before my eyes something that touched me and my experience.

For a while I watched in silence, awed by what seemed the limitless number of people coming out of the mosque. All of them were

Arabs, of that there was no doubt, but that did not make the wave after wave that passed by appear an undifferentiated mass. I saw fathers and sons; the former, garbed in robes, seemed steeped in the tradition, while the latter, in Western dress, looked as if they were already evaporating into modernity. Some carried their own prayer carpets—worn Orientals rubbed thin by years of prostrations. Others had pieces of contemporary acrylic that served the same end. I saw some people whose eyes seemed still to shine with the fire of their religious fervor, while others looked tired and hungry. The assorted expressions on their faces made it possible to watch for a long time without getting bored.

After a while, I tried to discover among these people something in their faces, demeanor, gait or expression with which I could identify. After all, in just two days I too would find myself among a sea of worshipers, walking to and from the Kotel on the Jewish holy day of Shevu'ot, when by tradition throngs of the faithful greeted the first light of morning at the remains of the Holy Temple. But the more I searched the scene before me, the harder it seemed to find the common thread. As I had found after my talks with Salim and Yasser, underneath apparent similarities lay real differences. The competing attachments we each had to this Holy City got in the way. Whenever the eyes of those who passed me met mine, they seemed to me to express a look shadowed with suspicion, which closed down the windows of empathy. And where I was not met by suspicion or the blank disattention that implied my nonexistence, I came up against a cold stare of hostility that seemed to say: Have you Jews, you outsiders, come to savor your conquest here too? Do you dare now encroach on our sacred space and time?

In the past, fired up by the Friday sermons of the imam, these Arabs or their predecessors, returning from the *jami*, had sometimes turned in the direction of the Jewish neighborhoods and taken out their anger on the *dhimmi*, the second-class citizens whose aspirations to settle al-Quds were anathema to the faithful. In 1920, at Passover time, Arab mobs had killed five Jews and wounded more than two hundred because of a rumor that the Jews had plans to take over and destroy the Moslem holy places. Now, in 1985, *kippah*-clad Jews from Kiryat Arba, near Hebron, were on trial for just such plans. And here I stood, my Jewishness atop my head, a symbol of the conqueror.

"Let's move on," I said, feeling suddenly like a trespasser and recalling the same anxiety I had felt before in the café.

• • •

Romann and I moved westward up the Via Dolorosa, trying to get away from the crowds, whose hostility—real or imagined—felt increasingly as if it were closing in on me. But each of the cross streets running north was clogged with people coming back from the *jami*. There was no place to turn. One direction led against the tide of the coming crowds, while the other sucked one into its flow. When we finally pressed our way westward across the crowds and reached the souks on al-Wad, we realized there was no escape. Once again, as I had at Easter time, I experienced the limits of my Jerusalem attachments.

"Let's turn here," I said, trying to speak loudly but finding my voice swallowed up by my rising anxieties.

Walking into a tiny alley and pushing against the crowd, we soon found ourselves opposite a kiosk, where we bought some cold drinks and stood watching the choked arteries slowly becoming emptied of people. Two boys played backgammon in the shadow of a doorway. Opposite us was the arcaded cotton market. Although for generations it had been filled with merchants selling cotton, these days it was lined with stands selling everything from toys made in Hong Kong to brass candlesticks imported from India. As long as we were here, Romann wanted to do some shopping. Many goods were much cheaper here than in the Jewish markets. So, since the crowds coming from the mosque had largely left this part of the market, he led me over under the arcade.

Still rattled and a bit nervous after my push through to here, I stayed close to him. We were standing near one of the stands when suddenly I felt a sharp jab on my shoulder. Was I about to be stabbed? Spinning about, I turned to see a thickly veiled woman holding an infant in her arms. She was followed by a young boy of about six years and a girl of maybe eight. With their palms out, the two were begging for money at the stands. Wordlessly, she held her left hand out to me. I dropped a coin into her tattooed fingers. Swiftly she stuffed the money into her bosom. As I turned back to find Romann, I saw her tap the children and point at me. In a flash they were standing by my side, their pudgy little fingers poking my arm. Dropping another couple of coins into their hands, I pulled on Romann's shoulder.

"Let's try to work our way through here back toward the Jewish Quarter," I suggested, drawing him into the bazaars and hoping we could find some way to get behind the throngs which continued to stream north toward the Moslem Quarter and the Damascus Gate.

But as I pushed against the tide of humanity in the narrow alleys, I again experienced the difficulty of going against the current. The more I tried, the harder it got. At some of the shops people stopped to buy something for the evening meal and thus dammed up the flow of walkers coming toward us, for a moment creating some space for us to move forward. But then, a moment later, the waiting crowd behind them would push its way past and tumble over and surround and separate us like a great wave.

Squeezing my way through all these people coming from their prayers, I thought of something I had learned from sociologist Ephraim Ya'ar, one of my colleagues at Tel Aviv University. In his study of Moslems, he had demonstrated that the more religious they were, the greater distance they felt from all non-Moslems. I knew too that there is an Islamic custom which discourages empty religious displays. Among Moslems, one should not appear to be religious if he is really not. That meant that these people around me were likely animated by some true faith. And here I was pushing against them to make my way through Jerusalem. The more I thought about what I was doing, the more I thought of the effrontery implicit in my actions. To go in the opposite direction while they came out of their mosque seemed almost a metaphor for the Jewish relationship to the Arabs in this city. We would push our way through them to get to where we wanted to go.

And then, I thought, perhaps if I did not push so hard, I might make contact with the people who were facing me. But that too, as I had already discovered time and again, was not easily done. If I didn't push in the opposite direction, I would be swept up in their flow. There seemed no alternative to what I was doing; Jews and Arabs were apparently going to continue to push past each other here.

Suddenly, as we stood waiting for a particularly thick group of people to pass, I heard, among the unintelligible Arabic all around me, someone say *"Yahud."* It was the Arabic word for ''Jew.''

It was as if someone had abruptly touched an exposed nerve. In the closeness of people about me, that one word released all my pent-up panic, and as I thought of all those bombs and stabbings which over the years had occurred in this city, of the hostilities fomented by the imams, of the Islamic *jihad*—the holy war—I began to ooze with sweat. And there was something else. Only a few days before, the government had released more than a thousand

convicted Arab terrorists in a prisoner exchange. Surely some of
them were now in this crowd, returning from their first Friday visit
to al-Aqsa. Who knew what they had been told in the mosque?
Romann and I were the only Jews around, and only I identified
myself with the *kippah* on my head. In this crowd, I could be easily
stabbed, with my anonymous assailant disappearing into the sea of
people around me. In my shoulder I still felt the jab of the veiled
beggar's finger.

"Mike, we have got to go," I said.

"I thought you wanted to see the Arabs," he replied with a smile.
"Have you had enough already?"

But I had already begun my rush through the crowd in the direction of the Jewish Quarter and the sanctuary it provided.

"Where are you running to?" Romann called as I moved far
ahead of him.

There was, of course, no real need for an answer. He and I both
knew that I had at last come face to face with the walls that divided
Jew from Arab; I had come crashing against the barrier of estrangement.

Forcing my way past the legions of Arab worshipers, at last I
reached the Street of the Jews. Although there was no formal dividing line here, there was no mistaking the border between the Moslem and Jewish quarters. The former was dirty and crumbling,
while the latter, fully rebuilt from the rubble it had become between 1948 and 1967, was white with new sandstone, open and clean.
Once a web of narrow, cluttered alleys that in the days of the
Ottoman Empire had been the tiny neighborhood in which Jews
were allowed to live, the Jewish Quarter had been transformed into
a new-old ghetto, with modern town houses built in a style meant to
simulate the ancient domed structures that had once stood here.

It was Friday, Sabbath eve, and the locals were doing some last-
minute shopping. They filled the little grocery off the square. From
a nearby window came an aroma I remembered well from my mother's kitchen, the smell of boiling gefülte fish; it wiped out the lingering odors of spices and sweets that had filled my nostrils in the
Arab souk. Ahead of me ran three young boys, their fringes flying
out of their shirts and their knapsacks half off their backs; on
Fridays, schools let out early. A young mother, a kerchief covering
her hair, pushed a stroller packed with her baby and a large bag of
groceries. All the local pedestrian traffic here moved in one direction, away from the Moslem Quarter.

From the doorway of the store, a young black-hatted Lubavitcher hasid called to his friend: "Ya'akov, wait for me. I have to pick up a *challah*." He grabbed two twisted breads, paid for them and, throwing them into a net bag, ran back out in the direction of CHaBaD Street.

The sights, smells and familiar sound of Hebrew gave me the sure realization that I was now safely among my own people. I leaned against a stone wall and looked back, to discover Romann strolling calmly behind me; on his face was a wry smile of recognition. There was no denying any longer that in spite of my interest in other parts of the city, it was to its Jewish parts that I felt most attached. Here was the Jerusalem in which I was at home. And so, after wandering about with monks but being unable to walk alone into a church, after sipping tea with or watching Arabs without achieving any true sense of rapprochement, after repeated encounters with the barriers of estrangement, I had turned back at last to my own Jerusalem. The time had come at last to reap the harvest of my own attachments and cease my straying in other fields.

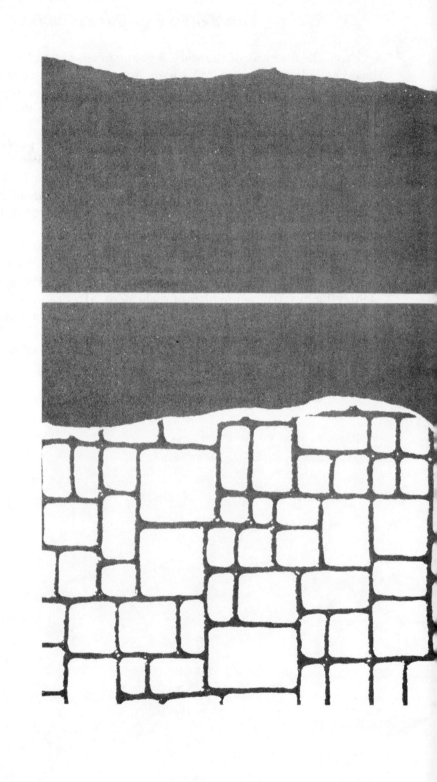

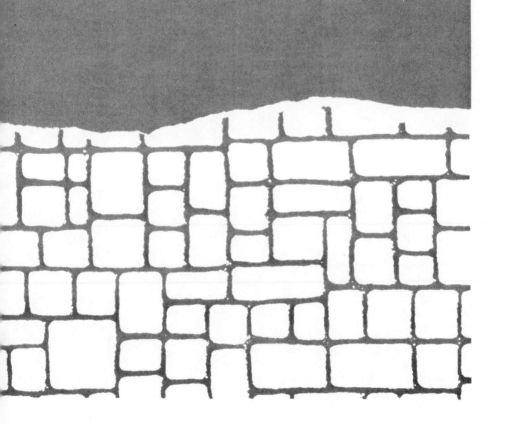

EPILOGUE

JERUSALEM IN THE END OF DAYS

I see the past, present, and future existing all at once before me.

WILLIAM BLAKE

The eternity—that is Jerusalem.

THE TALMUD: BERACHOT 58

*T*he *midrash* on the Song of Songs promises: "In the future, that it may accommodate all those who return to it, Jerusalem is destined to expand and ascend until it reaches the Throne of Glory, until it will say, in the words of Isaiah: 'The place is too narrow for me; give me place for those who would dwell within me.'"

Trying to calculate the precise moment of this great expansion, the moment when the glories of earth and Heaven meet in this holiest of places, the rabbis explained: "Jerusalem will not be rebuilt in its entirety until all the children of Israel are ingathered from their exile." Had not the psalmist proclaimed: "The Lord builds up Jerusalem; He gathers together the dispersed of Israel"? And thus the rabbis concluded: "When does God build Jersualem? When He gathers the dispersed of Israel."

But in Jerusalem, the promise of the future can get tangled in memory. Was it not the case, as the rabbis themselves recounted in the fifth chapter of Avot, that in the days of the Holy Temple, "the people stood closely pressed together and yet found enough room to prostrate themselves," and "no one ever said to his friend: 'There is no room for me to lodge overnight in Jerusalem'"? In the realm of spiritual Jerusalem, the descriptions of past and future seemed indistinguishable.

And what of the present? For nearly two thousand years, faithful Jews had waited for the morning that would bring an end to the night of their exile and allow them to pick up the threads of a past from which they had been torn. Now in the dawn of a new day, that moment seemed suddenly at hand. In the crush of reassembled Jews, Jerusalem was spreading far beyond its original borders. From the small City of David on the Ophel, it had now expanded so that its borders reached nearly to Bethlehem in the south, to Ramallah in the north, into the western hills of Judea and deep into the wilderness at Ma'aleh Adumin, on the way to Jericho. To many, everything in the present seemed to point ineluctably to the End of Days.

There were those who were convinced that this generation was witnessing *hat'chalta d'ge'ulah*—the beginning of the final Redemption, the Eschaton. The miraculous victories of the '67 war, the ingathering of exiles—even the long-lost Ethiopian Jews were back—the rebuilding of the Jewish Quarter, the new housing throughout the city so that there was room for everyone were to many of the devout evidence of a future about to join with the past, the Throne of Glory coming in touch with Jerusalem. Today a pilgrim could even ascend the steps that once led up to the Temple, and imagine more easily the glory of bygone days.

In the face of these signs, there were even some zealots who wanted to nudge the Redemption forward a bit more swiftly. At the post office in the Jewish Quarter, a new poster was being sold. On it a model of the Jewish Temple was superimposed atop Moriah, where it replaced the Dome of the Rock and al-Aqsa. And Jews who conspired to bomb the Arab shrines in preparation for that day now sat in prison; but in the hearts of many of their fellow faithful, these convicts remained heroes, agents of the prophets.

Although the millennium was always there in the air about Jerusalem, it descended on certain occasions more than others. For the Jews, Tishah B'Av, the ninth day of the Hebrew month of Av, was perhaps the most important of those occasions. Tishah B'Av, the anniversary of the Temple's destruction and the symbolic beginning of the long exile, a day which for two thousand years had been one of mourning and sadness, now nurtured the hope of new beginnings. Had not Rabbi Shimon the Just, whose words were immortalized in the Talmud, promised : "In the end of days, Tishah B'Av will become a day of joy and gladness. On that day, the Almighty will rebuild the Temple and bring back the exiles." Tears would give way to laughter.

And so it is. Although among the Orthodox, as ordained by the ancient rabbis, Tishah B'Av still remains a fast day, an occasion on which to reread the Scroll of Lamentations and ravage the soul, to others—and even to many of those who still fast and mourn in commemoration of past destructions—it has of late become a day swarming with hope. These days, Tishah B'Av is a time when thousands of Jews come to the Western Wall and—amidst the timeworn lamentations—greet one another with smiles.

It is also a civil celebration, a day to encircle Zion, count her ramparts, explore her venerated ruins while celebrating their renewal and the rebuilding of their timeless capital, Jerusalem. The television crews come to film the spectacle, and live broadcasts over the Voice of Israel allow all those tuned in to the airwaves to share in the return to the Wall.

From the first time, in 1968, when I celebrated Tishah B'Av in Jerusalem and felt the tears of two millennia evaporate, I realized that there was no other spot on earth where I could ever again commemorate this day. To be in any other place, making believe nothing had changed since the exile, to assert that the city was still, as the old prayers claimed, "mourning the loss of her children, devastated in her destruction, abased and desolate," turned mourning into an obsession and the day into a sham. Since 1979, the first full year I spent in the city, I, my wife and those of my children old enough to stay up had, like thousands of others in the city, ushered in Tishah B'Av, the anniversary of Jerusalem's past destruction and future reconstruction, with an evening tour.

Various organizations—some religious, others civilian—organize the tours. By bus and car, on bicycle and foot, people converge on the Old City in order to walk about her. But these are not peregrinations of mourning (like the Christian pilgrimages along the Via Dolorosa) ; they are walks of wonderment, exercises in the reconstruction of collective memory. For the point here is not to mourn but to recall what was lost and reaffirm what is regained.

One year the group with which we walked retraced the line of the walls as they stood in the days of Solomon's Temple, finding here and there broken stones and barely visible outlines of an earlier Jerusalem. Another time, we explored the remains of a house burned during the Roman takeover of the city, imagined the terror of that night two thousand years before while staring at the ashes and broken dishes, yet knowing all the while that we were back and that the terror was nearly over. On still another walk, we made our way to an ancient Israelite tower where archeologists had uncovered arrows left over from the battle between the troops of Nebuchadnezzar, the Babylonian invader, and the city's Jewish defenders. Here too, past losses paled before present victories. Each Tishah B'Av since 1967 and the return to the Wall, which had come to represent contact with the past as nothing else could, the pain of exile seemed to give way to triumph; perhaps that was why Israelis and other Jews—religious or not—went on these tours.

Once, the walk connected with the past by way of the future; using the words of the prophets and rabbinic texts, the group we joined traced the outlines of promised Jerusalem. Into the Valley of Ben-Hinnom we marched: two hundred or more people. The summer night was heavy with dew when at the foot of Mount Zion we stopped and, repeating the prophecies of Isaiah, Zechariah and others, visualized Jerusalem in the End of Days. Yet while the sites we sighted and the verses we recited were embedded in tradition and imagination, the topography before our eyes and under our feet brought them to life. As we gazed into the night, and past it, time easily lost meaning. Past and future were part of the same landscape, and vagary mixed with reality until at last we sat—the religious and the secular—halfway between now and forever, on the slopes of the Mount of Olives, overlooking the valley of Jehoshaphat, along the route assigned by tradition to the Messiah. There, leaning against the Tomb of Zechariah, in the silence of midnight, we listened to verses and commentaries that recounted the future as if it were a foregone conclusion. And when we had finished, we climbed back up the hill and went to the Wall to pray.

That was last year. This year the route would be different. Back from my wanderings and about to leave Jerusalem for my inescapable return to America, I was especially ready for this one last turn about the city. My wife and three of my children had already returned to the United States, and only Adam, my twelve-year-old son, and I remained. The walk was to take place around Mount Zion. We would explore newly uncovered sites and then end up at the Tomb of King David. As in years past, Yitzhak Zaks would lead us.

A travel agent, Zaks was also an amateur historian and an archeology buff (something that elsewhere might be an unusual combination but in Jerusalem made him not too different from dozens of others). We would meet him on the slopes of the mountain. For some reason—perhaps because there were more tours scheduled this year than ever before—the group assembled with Zaks this time was relatively small, no more than a hundred.

We walked first to several small caves carved into the bedrock beneath the city wall. These were burial chambers from the period of the Kings of Israel. Some of the tombs were from the eighth century B.C.E. They traced the outer edges of the city, for the dead were always buried outside the walls.

And then we set our attention on the city walls. There was something extraordinary about them. In the years since 1967, archeologists had uncovered under the eight-hundred-year-old Ottoman battlements remains of much earlier ones. There were stones there from the Hasmonean period, from the time of Herod and the Romans, from the Crusaders and from the Mamelukes. That by itself would have been impressive: after all, the Hasmoneans held the city from about 167 to 37 B.C.E.; Herod, the Jewish-Idomenean ruler set up by the Romans, dominated the city during the period of the Second Temple, and the Romans carried on until well into the Common Era, long after the final Jewish exile. The Crusaders were here between 1099 and 1187, and some regained control over the city, retaining influence until the thirteenth century, while the Mamelukes—ruling from Cairo—were in charge from the thirteenth to the sixteenth centuries. So discovering stones from so far back in time, hard evidence of other peoples and their attachment to this place, was impressive. And seeing how many had ruled over this area since David and the Jews had made it their capital gave special meaning to this Tishah B'Av. We, after all, the heirs of David, were back. All that remained of these other conquerors was stones and bones.

But there was something else even more striking. In these walls, Jerusalem had shuffled history, reordering time. Earlier and later periods of history had become mixed here. The distinctive stones of the Hasmonean period with their narrowly cut margins and very prominent, rough bulge lay atop Crusader towers and beneath the large, smooth Herodian ashlars that were framed with double margins (the external one wide and the internal narrow). Here and there one could find Roman remains, the outline of a gate in the Roman battlement. And around everything was the Ottoman wall, inside which were a variety of stones from all the other periods.

The reasons for this mixing, Zaks explained, were obvious. Conqueror after conqueror had come here and built his city on and with the remains of another. Only where there was nothing else available were new stones hewn. And so, in the endless tides of history, past had been thrown atop future. Rubble and construction, death and life, solitary stones and built-up walls coexisted here. But that, after all, was quite in keeping with this place where time lost its meaning, and there and then could easily become here and now.

Zaks led us up the steps toward Mount Zion, away from the Old City walls, past the Protestant cemetery and the Bible institute that had moved into the old Bishop Ghobat School. Both places appeared deserted at this hour. Next we passed along the side of the Greek Orthodox school and behind the Benedictine Dormition Abbey. In both, the lights were off; the monks had long since gone to sleep. Nearby, the Armenian Quarter's gates had already been locked for the night, and its church was dark as well. Although the Christians had made this mountaintop one of their holy places—in large measure because of the Cenaculum, the room of the Last Supper, located on the upper story of the building adjacent to King David's Tomb—this night Zion belonged to the Jews, and from where we stood, there were no Christians to be seen.

We passed a deep pit. There was a legend that at the bottom of it was an entrance to David's Tomb. The legend decreed that anyone daring to desecrate the royal tomb by his presence was subject to the most severe retribution. Indeed, several people had purportedly gone down into the pit and never returned, adding to the aura of mystery surrounding the place. "But finally," Zaks explained as we whizzed by the opening, "a scientific expedition descended. And they found that the pit was connected to a sewer line. At the bottom were some bones—undoubtedly those of the missing. All those who had gone down had probably been instantly suffocated by the poison gases seeping in from the sewage."

"So much for the legend of the wrath of the dead kings," said someone near the front of our group.

Zaks steered us toward the khan, an old arcaded structure that now served as a covered walkway leading into the complex of rooms that surrounded what had become the traditionally accepted Tomb of King David. In the days when caravans of traders came to Jerusalem, this had been the place where they rested their camels and sold their wares to the people of the city.

Before 1967, Zaks explained, these passages were choked with crowds that used to come here on Tishah B'Av. Tavio had told me about those days. "In the old days," Zaks was saying, "this was where we came, and after visiting the tomb, that was where we went." He pointed toward the domed roof.

A few of us climbed up a narrow stone staircase and squeezed into the slivers of flat space around the cupola. The rest lined up along the staircase. "Usually," Zaks continued from his perch on the roof, "someone would say something about the Kotel and the Old City that was just beyond the edge of our sights. So naturally a few people would bend over the side of the roof or stand on tiptoe or crane their necks to see the unseeable." He paused, and a few people craned their necks and stood on tiptoe. But there was nothing to be seen, save for the darkened alleys leading toward the Zion Gate.

"These days," Zaks concluded softly, "hardly anyone comes here anymore for Tishah B'Av; everyone goes to the Kotel." And he led us back down the stairs and through a maze of rooms that opened up onto a small courtyard.

Zaks wasn't exactly correct about hardly anyone's coming here now. In recent years, some of the rooms here had been taken over by the Diaspora Yeshiva, an institution for *ba'aley t'shuvah*—newly Orthodox Jews who had returned to the tradition after living outside it. Most of these people were young Americans. This evening, several hundred of them were gathered in one of the rooms next to the tomb. Sitting on the floor in the traditional position of Jewish mourning, they recited Lamentations and listened to their rabbi as he tried to direct their devotions. He spoke in English, peppering his talk with Yiddishisms and references to liturgy and the Scroll of Lamentations.

"The *Yidn* of those days were like butterflies," the rabbi said, his voice taking on the rising and falling cadences of Yiddish, "hovering over a beautiful flower. But that butterfly got so wrapped up in its freedom that it didn't notice that above it was a slowly descending net. So that's what our brothers and sisters who were living in *Yerushalayim* were like. They looked at their *Bais Ha-Mikdash* [the Temple], the gold, the beauty, and they were enthralled with their own power and thought they were free to do whatever they wanted, so—you know how it is; we all do—they didn't see the net that was closing in on them. They didn't believe the warnings of the *nevi'im* [prophets], and they remained blind to the dangers of their empty fascination. 'Put not your trust in princes, nor in the son of man, in whom there is no help.' They didn't realize they had nothing; it was all in God's hands. So that's what the *posuk* [verse] means when it says: 'How is the gold become dim.' ''

The moral was plain. This generation would not make the mistakes of the one that experienced the destruction and exile. These newly arrived Jews, immigrants to a place and a tradition, would not be ensnared, caught and exiled.

I poked my head in to see how these words were being received. With only a few seconds to look, it was impossible to see very much. but what I noticed most of all was the closed eyes—the same closed eyes I often saw among the pious who came to other holy places. With closed eyes, here as elsewhere, the channels to the spirit could be opened and a vision of an imagined Jerusalem perceived.

Zaks gathered his group into the open courtyard. He was near the end of his tour, after which he would take us into one of the rooms adjoining the tomb and by the light of candles recite Lamentations in the timeless and mournful melody with which it was always repeated. Now, however, he was trying to relate to the past in another way; he would tell us a little about the buildings that framed the courtyard.

He spoke softly, and so the people who still remained on the tour (some, as usual, had dropped out as the hour grew later and later) huddled around him. It gave the gathering a feeling of intimacy. ''There is some question among archeologists about the authenticity of David's Tomb. Of course, no one has found any alternative location, so it's hard to altogether dismiss this one. We do know that some people believe that this is where David brought the tabernacle when it first came to his city. Here it rested until King Solomon, his son, built the Temple.''

Zaks quoted the verses from the second book of Samuel: ''And so David and all the house of Israel brought up the ark of the Lord with shouting and the blasting of the *shofar*.''

On this evening when we were supposed to be recalling the fall of Jerusalem, a time when we Jews had left the city, he instead evoked memories of our triumphant entry. The transformation of ''mourning into celebration'' seemed to epitomize the spirit of the evening's tour.

Zaks continued: ''This place was important too for the Christians. There''—he pointed to a window of the second story—''is where they believe Jesus had His last meal.'' The room was dark now, empty. Not even a monk inhabited it. For the Christians, the story, more than the place, needed to be guarded.

''And over there,'' Zaks said, pointing to another window on an adjacent wall, ''is where the Ibn Daudi family lived. They took their name from David, and they lived here, they claimed, to watch over this holy tomb. You know, of course, that for Moslems both Jewish and Christian holy places are considered sacred. The Ibn Daudi family stayed here for generations.

''They were convinced that on the day they left, the Jews would conquer the Holy City. They are gone now; they ran away in '67. And now we are here.''

He paused, and then repeated: ''Now we are here.'' Then he stopped, and we all stood in silence. A little summer breeze suddenly blew into the courtyard, as if some spirit had dropped in.

''This is the end of our tour,'' he said at last. A few people started to leave. ''But,'' Zaks continued, ''next year, with God's help, we shall meet again—but not here.'' He paused and smiled. ''For those who want to know, for our walk next year we shall take a tour of the Temple Mount, but I shall not be the guide.'' Again he paused and smiled. ''Next year, my friends, the Messiah will lead us.''

ACKNOWLEDGMENTS

I wish to express my gratitude to a number of people who enabled me to complete this book. First, I thank my wife, Ellin, and my sons, Adam, Uriel, Avram and Jonah, whose love for Jerusalem and patience with me allowed me to spend weeks and months wandering about the city. Often, they blazed trails which I later followed. Ellin was always my most critical reader, and wherever I could, I have included her comments and criticisms in what I have written.

I wish also to thank the people about whom I have written in these pages. Without them, Jerusalem would have remained a closed book to me. Needless to say, they are not responsible for what I have written or for the way I have perceived them.

Some of the ideas embedded in what I have recorded are the products of reading. However, since I wished to free this book from the strictures of academic writing and to allow the insights to flow from the narrative and out of the mouths of the natives, I have not annotated the text. Nevertheless, there are certain works by others that deserve to be cited for their contribution to my understanding of Jerusalem. A short bibliography is therefore appended below.

As always, Arthur Samuelson, my editor, pushed me to organize my thoughts and improve my writing so that what appears on the page was the best I could do. I thank him for his efforts.

Finally, I wish to acknowledge some of my academic colleagues who at various stages in the preparation of this book, either in acquainting me with Jerusalem or in helping me sort out my thoughts about it, were of inestimable help: Victor Azarya, Robert Chazan, Menachem Friedman, Jeffery Halper, Menashe Har-El, Michael Romann, Ernest Schwarcz, the members of the Continuing Seminar on Zionist Thought and the Faculty Seminar of the Department of Sociology and Anthropology at Tel Aviv University.

BIBLIOGRAPHY

Arberry, A. J., ed. *Religion in the Middle East.* 2 vols. Cambridge, England: Cambridge University Press, 1969.

Avi-Yonah, Michael, ed. *A History of the Holy Land.* London: Weidenfeld and Nicolson, 1969.

Azarya, Victor. *The Armenian Quarter of Jerusalem.* Berkeley: University of California Press, 1984.

Ben-Arieh, Yehoshua. *Jerusalem in the Nineteenth Century: The Old City.* New York: St. Martin's Press, 1984.

———. *Yerushalayim Ha-Hadasha B'Raishitah.* Jerusalem: Yad Ben Zvi, 1979.

Betts, R. B. *Christians in the Arab East.* Athens: Lycabettus Press, 1975.

Durkheim, Emile. *The Elementary Forms of the Religious Life.* Trans. J. W. Swain. New York: Free Press, 1954.

Eliade, Mircea. *The Sacred and the Profane.* New York: Harcourt Brace, 1957.

Evans-Prichard, E. E. *Witchcraft, Oracles and Magic Among the Azande.* New York: Oxford University Press, 1937.

Gafni, Shlomo. *The Glory of Jerusalem.* Jerusalem: The Jerusalem Publishing House, 1978.

Geertz, Clifford. *The Interpretation of Cultures.* New York: Basic Books, 1973.

———. *Local Knowledge.* New York: Basic Books, 1983.

Halbwachs, Maurice. *Les Cadres Sociaux de la Mémoire.* New York: Arno Press, 1975.

Har-El, Menashe. *This Is Jerusalem.* Los Angeles: Ridgefield Publishing Co., 1981.

Kroyanker, David, with Dror Wahrman. *Jerusalem Architecture: Periods and Styles.* Jerusalem: The Jerusalem Institute for Israel Studies and the Domino Press, 1983.

Romann, Michael. *Inter-Relationship Between the Jewish and Arab Sectors in Jerusalem.* The Jerusalem Institute for Israel Studies, 1984.

365

Schiller, Ely, ed. *The Heritage of the Holy Land.* Jerusalem: Ariel Publishing House, 1982.

Silk, Denis, ed. *Retrievements: A Jerusalem Anthology.* Jerusalem: Keter, 1977.

Stephens, J. L. *Incidents of Travel in Egypt, Arabia Petraea and the Holy Land.* New York, 1837.

Turner, Victor. *Image and Pilgrimage in Christian Culture.* New York: Columbia University Press, 1978.

Wilson, C., and Warren, C. *The Recovery of Jerusalem.* New York: Appleton, 1872.

Yehoshua, Jacob. *Jerusalem in Days of Old.* 3 vols. (in Hebrew). Jerusalem: Rubin Mass, 1981.

Yehoshua, Ya'akov. *Yaldut B'Yerushalayim Ha-Yeshana.* 6 vols. (in Hebrew). Jerusalem: Rubin Mass, 1979.

Zborowski, Mark, and Herzog, Elizabeth. *Life Is with People: The Jewish Little-Town of Eastern Europe.* New York: International Universities Press, 1952.

ABOUT THE AUTHOR

nuel Heilman is a professor of sociology at Queens College of
City University of New York and is the author of *Synagogue*
, *The Gate Behind the Wall*, and *The People of the Book*. Born
ermany and raised in Brookline, Massachusetts, he now lives
his wife, Ellin, and their four sons, Adam, Uriel, Avram, and
h, in New Rochelle, New York.